AIDS TO FAITH;

A

SERIES OF THEOLOGICAL ESSAYS.

BY SEVERAL WRITERS.

BEING A

Reply to "Essays and Reviews."

EDITED BY

WILLIAM THOMSON, D.D.,

LORD BISHOP OF GLOUCESTER AND BRISTOL.

NEW YORK:

D. APPLETON AND COMPANY,

443 & 445 BROADWAY.

1863.

PREFACE.

The Essays in this volume are intended to offer aid to those whose faith may have been shaken by recent assaults. The writers do not pretend to have exhausted subjects so vast and so important, within the compass of a few pages; but they desire to set forth their reasons for believing the Bible, out of which they teach, to be the inspired Word of God, and for exhorting others still to cherish it as the only message of salvation from God to man. They hope that these Essays may be, to those whose attention they can secure, incentives to further thought and reading. They have avoided, rather than sought, direct controversy. They have excluded personality; they have not spoken with undue harshness of the views they have been forced to oppose.

For the choice of contributors and the arrangement of subjects the Editor is responsible. Most of the writers gave their names without knowing those of their coadjutors; and not one of them, but the Editor, has seen all the Essays up to the day of publication. Each has written independently, without any editorial interference, beyond a few hints to prevent omissions and repetitions, such as must arise when several writers work without concert.

On the withdrawal of one of the contributors, Dr. McCaul most kindly undertook a second paper, at a short notice. No one has a better claim to be heard on the important subjects that have been confided to him.

Professor Mansel lent much valuable aid to the Editor in an unexpected increase of labour.

This volume is humbly offered to the Great Head of the Church, as one attempt among many to keep men true to Him in a time of much doubt and trial. Under His protection, His people need not be afraid. The old difficulties and objections are revived; but they will meet in one way or another the old defeat. While the world lasts, sceptical books will be written and answered, and the books, perhaps, and the answers alike forgotten. But the Rock of Ages shall stand unchangeable; and men, worn with a sense of sin, shall still find rest "under the shadow of a great rock in a weary land."

W. G. & B.

CONTENTS.

ESSAY I.

ON MIRACLES AS EVIDENCES OF CHRISTIANITY.

CONTENTS OF ESSAY I.

ON MIRACLES

AS EVIDENCES OF CHRISTIANITY.

1. What is the exact position of Miracles among the Evidences of Christianity, is a question which may be differently answered by different believers, without prejudice to their common belief. It has pleased the Divine Author of the Christian religion to fortify His revelation with evidences of various kinds, appealing with different degrees of force to different minds, and even to the same mind at different times. The grounds of belief consisting, not in a single demonstration, but in an accumulation of many probabilities, there is room, in the evidences as in the doctrines of Christianity, for special adaptations of different portions to different minds; nor can such adaptation be regarded as matter of regret or censure, so long as the personal preference of certain portions does not involve the rejection of the remainder.

The question, however, assumes a very different character when it relates, not to the comparative importance of miracles as evidences, but to their reality as facts, and as facts of a supernatural kind. For if this is denied, the denial does not merely remove one of the supports of a faith which may yet rest securely on other grounds. On the contrary, the whole system of Christian belief with its evidences, the moral no less than the intellectual influences, the precept and example for the future no less than the history of the past—all Christianity, in short, so far as it has any title to that name, so far as it has any special relation to the person or the teaching of Christ, is overthrown at the same time.

2. For this question must be considered, not mere-

ly, as is too often done, in relation to a purely hypothetical case, to a supposition of possible means by which the Christian religion might, had it so pleased God, have been introduced into the world otherwise than it was; but in relation to the actual means by which it was introduced, to the teaching and practice of Christ and His Apostles, as they are portrayed in the only records from which we can learn anything about them. Whether the doctrinal truths of Christianity could or could not have been propagated among men by moral evidence alone, without any miraculous accompaniments, it is at least certain that such was not the manner in which they actually were propagated, according to the narrative of Scripture. If our Lord not only did works apparently surpassing human power, but likewise expressly declared that He did those works by the power of God, and in witness that the Father had sent him;—if the Apostles not only wrought works of a similar kind to those of their Master, but also expressly declared that they did so in His name, the miracles, as thus interpreted by those who wrought them, become part of the moral as well as the sensible evidences of the religion which they taught, and cannot be denied without destroying both kinds of evidence alike. "That ye may know that the Son of Man hath power upon earth to forgive sins, I say unto thee, Arise, and take up thy couch, and go unto thine house:" "If I with the finger of God cast out devils, no doubt the kingdom of God is come upon you:" "By the name of Jesus Christ of Nazareth, whom ye crucified, whom God raised from the dead, even by Him doth this man stand here before you whole:"—let us imagine for an instant such words as these to have been uttered by one who was merely employing a superior knowledge of natural laws to produce a false appearance of supernatural power; by an astronomer, for instance, who had predicted an eclipse to a crowd of savages, or by a chemist, availing himself of his science to exhibit *relative miracles* to an ignorant people—and we shall feel at once how even the most plausible of the natural explanations of miraculous phenomena deals the deathblow to the moral character of the teacher, no less than to the sensible evidence of his mission.

But there is a yet higher witness to this intimate association of the Christian Evidences one with another, in that great fact which forms at once the central point of apostolical preaching and the earnest of the future hope of all Christian men. If there is one fact recorded in Scripture which is entitled, in the fullest sense of the word, to the name of a Miracle, the RESURRECTION OF CHRIST is that fact. Here, at least, is an instance in which the entire Christian faith must stand or fall with our belief in the supernatural. "If Christ be not risen, then is our preaching vain, and your faith is also vain." Here, at least, is a test by which all the evidences of Christianity alike, internal as well as external, moral as well as intellectual, may be tried. If Christ did not truly die and truly rise from the dead, preaching is vain and faith is vain; the Apostles are false witnesses of God; nay, Christ Himself, if we may dare to say so, has witnessed falsely of Himself.

It is necessary to state the case in this manner, in order to point out the real importance of the interests at stake. Nothing can be more erroneous than the view sometimes taken, which represents the question of the possibility of miracles as one which merely affects the *external accessories* of Christianity, leaving the *essential doctrines* untouched.* Such might possibly be the case, were the argument merely confined to an inquiry into the evidence in behalf of some one miracle as an isolated fact, without impeaching the possibility of miracles in general. But such is not the question which has been raised, or can be raised, as regards the relation of miracles to the alleged discoveries

* See 'Essays and Reviews,' p. 94 (third edition). A similar view is taken by Schleiermacher, 'Der Christliche Glaube,' § 14, pp. 100, *sqq*. With far greater truth it is maintained on the other hand by Rothe ('Studien und Kritiken,' 1858, p. 23) that "Miracles and Prophecies are not adjuncts appended from without to a revelation in itself independent of them, but constitutive elements of the revelation itself."

of modern science. If the possibility of miracles be granted, the question, whether any particular miracle did or did not take place, is a question not of science, but of testimony. The scientific question relates to the possibility of supernatural occurrences *at all*; and if this be once decided in the negative, Christianity as a religion must necessarily be denied along with it. Some moral precepts may indeed remain, which may or may not have been first enunciated by Christ, but which in themselves have no essential connection with one person more than with another; but all belief in Christ as the great Example, as the Teacher sent from God, as the crucified and risen Saviour, is gone, never to return. The perfect sinlessness of His life and conduct can no longer be held before us as our type and pattern, if the works which He professed to perform by Divine power were either not performed at all or were performed by human science and skill. No mystery impenetrable by human reason, no doctrine incapable of natural proof, can be believed on His authority; for if He professed to work miracles, and wrought them not, what warrant have we for the trustworthiness of other parts of His teaching? The benefits obtained by His Cross and Passion, the promises conveyed by His Resurrection, are no longer the objects of Christian faith and hope; for if miracles are impossible, He died as other men die, and was laid unto His fathers, and saw corruption. The prayers whch we offer to Him who ascended into Heaven, and there liveth to make intercession for us, are a delusion and a mockery, if miracles are impossible; for then is Christ not ascended into Heaven.

3. In point of fact, even single miracles cannot be treated as isolated occurrences, and judged as we should judge of any similar act narrated at another time. There is a latent fallacy in the appeal which is sometimes made to the manner in which well-informed men deal with alleged marvels at the present day.* The Christian mir-

* See 'Essays and Reviews,' p. 107. A similar appeal to the practical denial of miracles is made by Kant, 'Religion innerhalb der Grenzen der

acles can only be judged in connection with the scheme of which they form a part, and by the light of all the collateral evidence which that scheme is able to furnish. The true question is, not what should we think of, or how should we endeavour to explain, a single marvellous occurrence, or even a series of such occurrences, reported as taking place at the present time? but, what should we think of one who should come now, as Christ came, supported by all the evidences which combined to bear witness to Him? If the world, with all its advance in physical science, were morally and religiously in the same state as at the time of Christ's coming; if we, like the Jews of old, had been taught by a long series of prophecies to expect a Redeemer in whom all the families of the earth should be blessed; if the events of our national history tended to show that the time was come to which those prophecies pointed as the epoch of their fulfilment; if we were in possession of a religion, itself claiming a Divine origin, yet in all its institutions bearing witness to something yet to come—a religion of type, and ceremony, and sacrifice, pointing to a further purpose and a spiritual significance beyond themselves; if one were to appear, proclaiming himself to be the promised Redeemer, appealing to our sacred writings as testifying of himself, doing works not only full of power but of goodness, full of wonder, but also full of love, and confirmed by Scriptures expressly declaring that such works should be done by him that was to come; doing them, not in secret, nor in an appointed place, nor with instruments prepared for the purpose, but openly and without effort, and upon occasions as they naturally presented themselves, in the street and in the marketplace, in the wilderness and on the sea, by the sick man's bed and the dead man's bier; and expressly declaring that he did them by the power of God and in proof that God had sent him;—with all these circumstances combined, let any unprejudiced man among

blossen Vernunft,' p. 100, ed. Rosenkranz: though Kant does not go so far as to deny the theoretical possibility of miracles.

ourselves say which would be the more reasonable view to be taken of such works performed by such a person; whether to admit his own account of them, guaranteed by all the weight of his character, or to refer them to some natural cause, which will at some future time receive its explanation by the advance of discovery. Surely those who, even in this enlightened age, chose to adopt the latter hypothesis, rather than admit the teacher's own testimony concerning himself, would be the legitimate successors of those who, under like circumstances, declared, "He casteth out devils through Beelzebub, the chief of the devils." *

4. But it is said that testimony is unable to prove a miracle as such. "No testimony, we are told on high scientific authority, can reach to the supernatural; testimony can apply only to apparent sensible facts; testimony can only prove an extraordinary and perhaps inexplicable occurrence or phenomenon: that it is due to supernatural causes is entirely dependent on the previous belief and assumptions of the parties." † Whatever may be the value of this objection as applied to a hypothetical case, in which the objector may select such occurrences and such testimonies as suit his purpose, it is singularly inapplicable to the works actually recorded as having been done by Christ and His Apostles, and to the testimony by which they are actually supported. It may, with certain exceptions, be applicable to a case in which the assertion of a supernatural cause rests solely on the testimony of the *spectator* of the fact; but it is not applicable to those in which the cause is declared by the *performer*. Let us accept, if we please, merely as a narrative of "apparent sensible facts," the history of the cure of the blind and dumb demoniac, or of the lame man at the Beautiful Gate; but we cannot place the same restriction upon the words of our Lord and of St. Peter, which expressly

* For this argument I am partly indebted to Dean Lyall, 'Preparation of Prophecy,' p. 151, ed. 1854.

† 'Essays and Reviews,' p. 107. This objection is partly borrowed from Dean Lyall, p. 23, who however uses it for a very different purpose.

assign the supernatural cause: "If I cast out devils by the Spirit of God, then the kingdom of God is come unto you:" "By the name of Jesus Christ of Nazareth doth this man stand here before you whole." * We have here, at least, a testimony reaching to the supernatural; and if that testimony be admitted in these cases, it may be extended to the whole series of wonderful works performed by the same persons. For if a given cause can be assigned as the true explanation of any single occurrence of the series, it becomes at once the most reasonable and probable explanation of the remainder. The antecedent presumption against a narrative of miraculous occurrences, whatever may be its weight, is only applicable to the narrative taken as a whole, and to the entire series of miracles which it contains. But if a single true miracle be admitted as established by sufficient evidence, the entire history to which it belongs is at once removed from the ordinary calculations of more or less probability. One miracle is enough to show that the series of events with which it is connected is one which the Almighty has seen fit to mark by exceptions to the ordinary course of His Providence; and, if this be once granted, we have no *à priori* grounds on which we can determine how many of such exceptions are to be expected. If a single miracle recorded in the Gospels be once admitted, the remainder cease to have any special antecedent improbability, and may be established by the same evidence which is sufficient for ordinary events. For the improbability, whatever it may be, reaches no further than to show that it is unlikely that God should work miracles at all; not that it is unlikely that He should work more than a certain number.

5. Hitherto we have spoken only of the miracles of Christ and His Apostles. But the miracles of the Old Testament also can only be rightly estimated through their connection with those of the New. The promise of man's redemption was coeval with his fall; and the

* St. Matt. xii. 28; Acts iv. 10.

whole intervening history, as it is told in Scripture, is a narrative of the steps by which the world was prepared for the fulfilment of that promise. The miracles of the Old Testament, as has been observed, are chiefly grouped round two great epochs in the history of the theocratic kingdom—that of its foundation under Moses and Joshua, and that of its restoration by Elijah and Elisha.* They thus have a direct relation to the establishment and preservation of the Mosaic covenant, itself a supernatural system, provided with supernatural institutions, and preparing the way for the final consummation of God's supernatural providence in the advent of His Son.† Not merely the occasional miracles of Jewish history, but some of the established and prominent features of their religion down to the time of the Captivity—the gift of Prophecy, the Shechinah, the Urim and Thummim, the Sabbatical year, and others—manifest themselves as the supernatural parts of a supernatural system, and that system one having a definite purpose and pointing to a definite end.‡ They were the adjuncts of the Law; and "the Law was our shoolmaster to bring us unto Christ."

6. The real question at issue between the believer and the unbeliever in the Scripture miracles is not whether they are established by sufficient testimony, but whether they can be established by any testimony at all. If it be once granted that testimony is admissible in the case, it is scarcely possible to conceive a stronger testimony than that which the Christian miracles can claim. It is the testimony, if ever such testimony was, not of man merely, but of God. Even as regards one who does not believe in the distinctive doctrines of Christianity, there are two witnesses to Christ which no other man, whatever may be his worth, can claim—the history of the Jewish nation before His coming, and the history both of the Jewish

* See Trench, 'Notes on the Miracles,' p. 45 (sixth edition).

† Compare Neander, 'Life of Christ,' p. 138, English translation; Twesten, 'Vorlesungen ueber die Dogmatik,' ii., p. 178; Van Mildert, 'Boyle Lectures,' Sermon xxi

‡ Compare Bp. Atterbury, 'Sermons' (1730), vol. i., p. 153.

and of the Christian world afterwards. Whether it was by natural or by supernatural means, it cannot be denied that He to whom the natural and the supernatural are alike subject has permitted the course of events in the world to bear a witness to Christ, such as has never been borne to any other person who has appeared upon earth in the likeness of a man. It cannot be denied that the prophetic writings contain descriptions which, account for the correspondence as we may, do, as a fact, agree with the person and history of Jesus of Nazareth, as they agree with no other man, or body of men; that the rites and ceremonies of the Jewish religion have a meaning as typical of Him, which no other interpretation can give to them; that the temple and its services were brought to an end after His appearance on earth, as if expressly to exclude the claims of any future Messiah; that His dominion has been spread over the civilized world to such an extent, and by such means, as no other ruler, temporal or spiritual, can claim; that superstitions have given way before His name which no other adversary had been able to shake; that doctrines have been established by His teaching which in the hands of other teachers were but plausible and transitory conjectures. However these things may be accounted for, they are sufficient at least to mark Him as the central figure of the world's history, looked forward to by all preceding generations, looked backward to by all following; they are sufficient to secure for His sayings and His acts an authority which cannot be claimed by those of any other person.

7. It is scarcely necessary to state how much this argument is strengthened when it is addressed to one who believes, no matter on what grounds, in any of the fundamental articles of the Christian Faith. I do not speak of one who believes in the narrative of the Gospels; for to such an one the miracles are not matters of question; but of one who in any sense believes in Christ as the Redeemer of mankind, though doubting some of the records of His earthly life. If God has

seen fit to redeem the world by Christ and by Christ alone, what marvel if the history of Christ and of the dispensation preparatory to Christ exhibits signs and wonders such as no other history can claim? The antecedent probability, in this case, is for the miracles, not against them. It is to be expected that an event unique in the world's history should be marked by accompaniments partaking of its own character. The miracles are not every-day events, because the redemption of mankind is not an every-day event; they belong to no cycle in the recurring phenomena of nature, because Christ has not often suffered since the foundation of the world. Round this great fact of man's redemption the accessory features of that wondrous narrative are grouped and clustered as around their proper centre; no longer the uncouth prodigies of the kingdom of Nature, but the fitting splendours of the kingdom of Grace. It was meet that He who came as the conqueror of sin and death, who had power to lay down His life, and power to take it again, should come also as the Lord of Body and the Lord of Spirit, having power over the elements of matter and over the thoughts of men's minds; foretold by predictions which no human wisdom could have suggested, testified to by works which no human power could have accomplished. Viewed as part of the scheme of Redemption, the marvels of the Scripture narrative are no longer isolated and unmeaning anomalies, but a foreordained and orderly system of powers, working above the ordinary course of nature, because their end is above the ordinary course of nature. The incongruity, the anomaly, would be if they were not there—if the salvation of the souls of men was to be brought about by no higher means than those which minister to their bodily appetites and material comforts. The daily wants of the individual, or the progressive culture of the race, may be provided for or advanced by laws which work unceasingly from day to day, and from generation to generation; but we seek no recurring law of the Scripture miracles, because we expect no recurrence of that fact to which all Scripture bears witness.

8. The above remarks, though only preliminary to the main question, are necessary in order to show what is the real point to be established, if the belief in the supernatural is to be overthrown. It is not the rarity of miracles—no one asserts them to be common: it is not their general improbability—no one asserts them to be generally probable: it is not that they need an extraordinary testimony as compared with other events—such a testimony we assert that they have. It is neither more nor less than their *impossibility*—an impossibility to be established on scientific grounds, such as no reasonable man would reject in any other case; grounds such as those on which we believe that the earth goes round the sun, or that chemical elements combine in definite proportions. In this point of view the argument is altogether of a general character, and is unaffected by any peculiarities of probability or testimony which may distinguish one miraculous narrative from another. If the progress of physical or metaphysical science has shown beyond the possibility of reasonable doubt that miracles are *impossible*—if, as seems to be the tendency of a recent argument, the assertion of a miracle is now known to be as absurd as the assertion that two and two make five*—it is idle to attempt a comparison between greater or less degrees of probability or testimony. The preceding observations will in that case only serve to show what it is that we have to surrender, and to rescue the inquiry from the particular fallacy which seeks to underrate its importance by representing it as only affecting the accidents and excrescences of Christianity. Let us, at the outset, be clearly con-

* See 'Essays and Reviews,' p. 141. It is astonishing that this acute author should not have seen the absurdity of introducing this statement in connection with testimony. No witness could possibly *see* two and two make five, or four, or any number, *in the abstract;* he must *see* it in connection with certain *visible* objects. Put the case in its only possible form:—let a man say that he had seen two balls and then two more, put together, and five balls produced from them; and, instead of an impossibility, we have but the commonest of jugglers' tricks.

vinced of the vital importance of the question, in order that we may enter on its examination prepared, if necessary, to sacrifice our most valued convictions at the demand of truth, but, at the same time, so convinced of their value as to be jealous of sacrificing them to anything but truth.

9. The inquiry concerning the possibility of miracles in general (as distinguished from that which concerns the credibility of the Scripture miracles in particular) involves two distinct questions, which must be considered separately from each other. The first of these questions relates to the position occupied by miracles with reference to experience and to the empirical laws of matter; the second relates to their position with reference to philosophical conceptions of God's nature and attributes. It is indispensable to a clear understanding of the subject that these two questions should be kept apart from each other; though it will be necessary, in discussing the first, to take for granted some conclusions which will afterwards have to be established in connection with the second. Let us then assume, for the present, that we are justified in conceiving God as a Person, and in speaking of His nature and operations in the language which we should employ in describing the analogous qualities and actions of men. We shall speak, as theists in general are accustomed to speak, of the *will*, and the *purpose*, and the *design* of God; of the contrast between His *general* and *special* providence; of His *government* of the world and *control* over its laws; reserving for a subsequent inquiry the vindication of these and similar expressions from a philosophical point of view.

10. The argument which denies the possibility of miracles, on the ground of the uniformity of nature, may be considered under two heads: first, as regards the general conception of a system of natural laws; and, secondly, as regards the special experience of the mode in which those laws are manifested. The former may be fairly stated in the words of Hume, whose reasoning has received no substantial addition from the

labours of subsequent writers on the same side: "A miracle is a violation of the laws of nature; and as a firm and unalterable experience has established these laws, the proof against a miracle, from the very nature of the fact, is as entire as any argument from experience can possibly be imagined." * The argument, as thus stated, was just as strong or just as weak at the day when it was written as at the present time: it has received no additional strength from the progress of science during the interval,—indeed it is hard to see how the evidence of "a firm and unalterable experience," if such existed at any time, is capable of being made stronger. No scientific man in the last century had any doubt that the sensible phenomena which came under his own experience and that of his contemporaries were owing to *some* natural cause acting by *some* natural law, whether the actual cause and law were known or unknown. The nature of this conviction is not altered by any subsequent increase in the number of known as compared with unknown causes: the general conception of "a firm and unalterable experience" is wide enough to contain all discoveries anticipated in the future, as well as those already made.

11. In one respect, indeed, the advance of physical science tends to strengthen rather than to weaken our conviction of the supernatural character of the Christian miracles. In whatever proportion our knowledge of physical causation is limited, and the number of unknown natural agents comparatively large, in the same proportion is the probability that some of these unknown causes, acting in some unknown manner, may have given rise to the alleged marvels. But this probability diminishes when each newly-discovered agent, as its properties become known, is shown to be inadequate to the production of the supposed effects, and as the residue of unknown causes, which might produce them, becomes smaller and smaller. We are told, indeed,

* 'Philosophical Works,' vol. iv., p. 133.

that "the inevitable progress of research must, within a longer or shorter period, unravel all that seems most marvellous;" * but we may be permitted to doubt the relevancy of this remark to the present case, until it has been shown that the advance of science has in some degree enabled men to perform the miracles performed by Christ. When the inevitable progress of research shall have enabled men of modern times to give sight to the blind with a touch, to still tempests with a word, to raise the dead to life, to die themselves, and to rise again, we may allow that the same causes might possibly have been called into operation, two thousand years earlier, by some great man in advance of his age. But until this is done, the unravelling of the marvellous in other phenomena only serves to leave these mighty works in their solitary grandeur, as wrought by the finger of God, unapproached and unapproachable by all the knowledge and all the power of man.

12. We have already observed that there is one kind of testimony which can reach to the supernatural; namely, the testimony of the person who himself performs the work; and we may now add that the fact of the work being done by human agency places it, as regards the future progress of science, in a totally different class from mere physical phenomena. The appearance of a comet, or the fall of an aërolite, may be reduced by the advance of science from a supposed supernatural to a natural occurrence; and this reduction furnishes a reasonable presumption that other phenomena *of a like character* will in time meet with a like explanation. But the reverse is the case with respect to those phenomena which are narrated as having been produced by *personal agency*. In proportion as the science of to-day surpasses that of former generations, so is the improbability that any man could have done in past times, by natural means, works which no skill of the present age is able to imitate.

* 'Essays and Reviews,' p. 109.

The two classes of phenomena rest in fact on exactly opposite foundations. In order that natural occurrences, taking place without hnman agency, may wear the appearance of prodigies, it is necessary that the cause and manner of their production should be *unknown*; and every advance of science from the unknown to the known tends to lessen the number of such prodigies by referring them to natural causes, and *increases* the probability of a similar explanation of the remainder. But on the other hand, in order that a man may perform marvellous acts by natural means, it is necessary that the cause and manner of their production should be *known* by the performer; and in this case every fresh advance of science from the unknown to the known *diminishes* the probability that what is unknown now could have been known in a former age.

13. The effect therefore of scientific progress, as regards the Scriptural miracles, is gradually to eliminate the hypothesis which refers them to unknown natural causes, and to reduce the question to the following alternative: Either the recorded acts were not performed at all (in which case it is idle to talk of the probable "honesty or veracity" of the witnesses *) or they were performed, as their authors themselves declare, by virtue of a supernatural power, consciously exercised for that very purpose. The intermediate theory, which attempts to explain them as distorted statements of events reducible to *known* natural causes, has been tried already, in the scheme of Paulus, and has failed so utterly as to preclude all expectation of its revival, even in the land of its birth. There remains only the choice between a deeper faith and a bolder unbelief; between accepting the sacred narrative as a true account of miracles actually performed, and rejecting it as wholly fictitious and incredible; whether the fiction be attributed to the gradual accretion of mythical elements, or (for a later criticism has come back again to the older and more intelligible

* See 'Essays and Reviews,' p. 106.

theory*) to the conscious fabrication of a wilful impostor.

14. The argument of Hume, which may be taken as the representative of all those which rest merely on the general conception of laws of nature, was refuted long ago by one who wrote as the advocate of his teaching in some other respects.† A miracle is *not* "a violation of the laws of nature," in any sense in which such a violation is impossible or inconceivable. It is simply the introduction of a new agent, possessing new powers, and therefore not included under the rules generalized from a previous experience. Its miraculous character, distinguishing it from mere new discoveries in nature, consists in the fact that the powers in question are supposed to be introduced for a special purpose, and to be withdrawn again when that purpose is accomplished, and thus to be excluded from the field of future observation and investigation. But the supposition of such powers need not imply any violation of the present laws observed by present natural agents. The *laws of nature*, in the only sense of the phrase which is relevant to the present argument, are simply general statements concerning the powers and properties of certain classes of objects which have come under our observation. They say nothing about the powers and properties of other objects or classes of objects which have not been observed, or which have been observed with a different result. There are laws, for instance, of one class of material agents which do not apply to another; and there are laws of matter in general which are not applicable to mind; and so there may be other orders of beings of which we have no knowledge, the laws of whose action may be different from all that we know of mind or body. A violation of the laws of nature, in this sense of the

* In this way the mythical theory of Strauss, after having overthrown the naturalistic theory of Paulus, has itself in turn been subjected to the criticism of Bruno Bauer, who rejects the hypothesis of a traditional origin of the Gospels, in favour of that which ascribes them to deliberate fabrication.

† See Brown on Cause and Effect, Note E. I have borrowed the leading idea of Brown's argument, though dissenting from some of his details, and therefore unable to adopt his exact language.

expression, would take place if, in two cases in which the cause or antecedent fact were exactly the same, the effect or consequent fact were different. But no such irregularity is asserted by the believer in miracles. He does not assert that miracles are produced by the abnormal action of natural and known causes—on the contrary, he expressly maintains that they are produced by a special interposition of Divine Power; and that such an interposition, constituting in itself a different cause, may reasonably be expected to be followed by a different effect.

15. So far then as a miracle is regarded as the operation of a special cause, producing a special effect, it offers no antagonism to that general uniformity of nature, according to which the same effects will always follow from the same causes. The opposition between science and miracle, if any exist, must be sought in another quarter; namely, in the assumption (provided that such an assumption is warranted by science) that the introduction of a special cause is itself incredible. The ground of such an assumption appears to lie in the hypothesis that the existing forces of nature are so mutually related to each other that no new power can be introduced without either disturbing the whole equilibrium of the universe, or involving a series of miracles, coextensive with the universe, to counteract such disturbance. This seems to be the meaning of the following observation by a recent writer:—"In an age of physical research like the present, all highly cultivated minds and duly advanced intellects have imbibed, more or less, the lessons of the inductive philosophy, and have at least in some measure learned to appreciate the grand foundation conception of universal law—to recognise the impossibility even of *any two material atoms* subsisting together without a determinate relation—of any action of the one or the other, whether of equilibrium or of motion, without reference to a physical cause—of any modification whatsoever in the existing conditions of material agents, unless through the invariable operation of a

series of eternally impressed consequences, following in some necessary chain of orderly connexion—however imperfectly known to us."*

This operation of a series of eternally impressed consequences could hardly be described more graphically or forcibly than in the following words of a great German philosopher:—"Let us imagine, for instance, this grain of sand lying some few feet further inland than it actually does. Then must the stormwind that drove it in from the sea-shore have been stronger than it actually was. Then must the preceding state of the atmosphere, by which this wind was occasioned and its degree of strength determined, have been different from what it actually was; and the previous changes which gave rise to this particular weather; and so on. We must suppose a different temperature from that which really existed, and a different constitution of the bodies which influenced this temperature. The fertility or barrenness of countries, the duration of the life of man, depend, unquestionably, in a great degree, on temperature. How can you know—since it is not given us to penetrate the arcana of nature, and it is therefore allowable to speak of possibilities—how can you know that in such a state of the weather as we have been supposing, in order to carry this grain of sand a few yards further, some ancestor of yours might not have perished from hunger, or cold, or heat, long before the birth of that son from whom you are descended; that thus you might never have been at all; and all that you have ever done, and all that you ever hope to do in this world, must have been hindered, in order that a grain of sand might lie in a different place?" †

* 'Essays and Reviews,' p. 133.

† Fichte, 'Die Bestimmung des Menschen,' Werke, ii., p. 178. For the translation I am indebted to an excellent American work, which deserves to be better known in this country, and to which I take this opportunity of expressing my own obligations—'The Principles of Metaphysical and Ethical Science,' by my friend Professor Bowen, of Harvard College.

Schleiermacher ('Der Christliche Glaube,' § 47, p. 260) expresses in general terms, and with express reference to miracles, the same view which Fichte has exhibited by an instance in relation to necessity in general. "A miracle," he says, "has a positive relation, by which it extends to all that is future, and a negative relation, whieh in a certain sense affects all that is past. In so far as that does not follow which would have followed according to the natural connection of the aggregate of finite causes, in so far an effect

16. Without attempting to criticise the argument as thus eloquently stated, let us make one alteration in the circumstances supposed—an alteration necessary to make it relevant to the present question. Let us suppose that the grain of sand, instead of being carried to its present position by the wind, has been placed there by a man. Is the student of physical science prepared to enumerate a similar chain of material antecedents, which must have been other than they were, before the man could have chosen to deposit the grain of sand on any other spot than that on which it is now lying? Such a conclusion has indeed been maintained in general terms, without any specification of antecedents, by the advocates of Fatalism; and it is maintained in the continuation of the passage from which the above extract is taken.* But the question is, not whether such a conclusion has been asserted, as many other absurdities have been asserted, by the advocates of a theory; † but whether it has been established on such scientific grounds as to be entitled to the assent of all duly cultivated minds, whatever their own consciousness may say to the contrary. ‡ The most rigid prevalence of law and necessary

is hindered, not by the influence of other natural counteracting causes belonging to the same series, but notwithstanding the concurrence of all effective causes to the production of the effect. Everything, therefore, which from all past time contributed to this effect is in a certain measure annihilated; and instead of the interpolation of a single supernatural agent into the course of nature, the whole conception of nature is destroyed. On the positive side, something takes place which is conceived as incapable of following from the aggregate of finite causes. But, inasmuch as this event itself now becomes an actual link in the chain of nature, every future event must be other than it would have been had this one miracle not taken place. Every miracle thus not only destroys the original order of nature for ever after; but each later miracle destroys the earlier ones, so far as these have become parts of the series of effective causes." The whole argument, as Rothe has observed, rests on the assumption of absolute determinism.

* Not however as the author's own conclusion; but as one of two conflicting doubts, to be afterwards resolved.

† "Nihil tam absurde dici potest, quod non dicatur ab aliquo philosophorum."—*Cicero, De Divinatione*, ii., 58.

‡ An attempt has recently been made to prove the non-existence of free will, by means of statistical calculations, showing an average uniformity in the recurrence of certain actions in certain periods of time. The resemblance, however, between statistical averages and natural laws fails at the very point on which the whole weight of the argument rests. A natural law is valid for a class of objects, only because and in so far as it is valid for each individual of that class: the law of gravitation, for instance, is exhibited in a single apple as much as in an orchard; and is concluded of the latter from being

sequence among purely material phenomena may be admitted without apprehension by the firmest believer in miracles, so long as that sequence is so interpreted as to leave room for a power indispensable to all moral obligations and to all religious belief—the power of Free Will in man.

Deny the existence of a free will in man; and neither the possibility of miracles, nor any other question of religion or morality, is worth contending about. Admit the existence of a free will in man; and we have the experience of a power, analogous, however inferior, to that which is supposed to operate in the production of a miracle, and forming the basis of a legitimate argument from the less to the greater.* In the Will of man we have the solitary instance of an Efficient Cause in the highest sense of the term, acting among and along with the physical causes of the material world, and producing results which would not have been brought about by any invariable sequence of physical causes left to their own action. We have evidence, also, of an *elasticity*, so to speak, in the constitution of nature, which permits the influence of human power on the phenomena of the world to be exercised or suspended at will, without affecting the stability of the whole. We have thus a precedent for allowing the possibility of a similar interference of a higher will on a grander scale, provided for by a similar elasticity of the matter subjected to its influence. Such interferences, whether produced by human or by superhuman will, are not contrary to the laws of matter; but neither are they the result of those laws. They are the work of an agent who is independent of the laws, and who, therefore, neither obeys them nor disobeys them.† If a man, of his own free will, throws a stone into the air, the motion of the stone, as soon as it has left his hand, is determined by a

observed in the former. But the uniformity represented by statistical averages is one which is observed in masses only, and not in individuals; and hence the law, if law it be, which such averages indicate, is one which offers no bar to the existence of individual freedom, exercised, as all human power must be exercised, within certain limits.

* Compare Twesten, 'Vorlesungen ueber die Dogmatik,' ii., p. 171.

† See Rothe, in 'Studien und Kritiken,' 1858, p. 33.

combination of purely material laws; partly by the attraction of the earth; partly by the resistance of the air; partly by the magnitude and direction of the force by which it was thrown. But by what *law* came it to be thrown at all? What law brought about the circumstances though which the aforesaid combination of material laws came into operation on this particular occasion and in this particular manner? The law of gravitation, no doubt, remains constant and unbroken, whether the stone is lying on the ground or moving through the air; but neither the law of gravitation, nor all the laws of matter put together, could have brought about this particular result, without the interposition of the free will of the man who throws the stone. Substitute the will of God for the will of man; and the argument, which in the above instance is limited to the narrow sphere within which man's power can be exercised, becomes applicable to the whole extent of creation, and to all the phenomena which it embraces.

17. The fundamental conception, which is indispensable to a true apprehension of the nature of a miracle, is that of the distinction of Mind from Matter, and of the power of the former, as a personal, conscious, and free agent, to influence the phenomena of the latter. We are conscious of this power in ourselves; we experience it in our everyday life; but we experience also its restriction within certain narrow limits, the principal one being that man's influence upon foreign bodies is only possible through the instrumentality of his own body.* Beyond these limits is the region of the miraculous. In at least the great majority of the miracles recorded in Scripture, the supernatural element appears, not in the relation of matter to matter, but in that of matter to mind; in the exercise of a personal power transcending the limits of man's will. They are not so much *supermaterial* as *superhuman*. Miracles, as evidences of religion, are connected with a teacher of that religion; and their evidential character consists in the witness which they bear to him as "a man approved of God

* Twesten, 'Vorlesungen ueber die Dogmatik,' i. p. 368.

by miracles and wonders and signs, which God did by him." He may make use of natural agents, acting by their own laws, or he may not: on this question various conjectures may be hazarded, more or less plausible. The miracle consists in his making use of them, so far as he does so, under circumstances which no human skill could bring about. When a sick man is healed, or a tempest stilled, by a word, the mere action of matter upon matter may possibly be similar to that which takes place when the same effects occur in a natural way: the miracle consists in the means by which that action is brought about. And those means, we are assured by the word of the Teacher himself, are nothing less than the power of God, vouchsafed for the express purpose of bearing witness that God has sent him. Is it more reasonable, taking the whole evidence into account, to believe his word; or to suppose, either that the works were not done at all, or that they were done by a scientific deception? This is the real question to be decided.

If, indeed, we include, under the term *nature*, all that is potential, as well as all that is actual, in the constitution of the world—all that can be brought about in it by divine power, as well as all that is brought about in it by physical causes,—in such an extended sense of the term, a miracle, like any other occurrence, may be included within the province of nature. We may, doubtless, believe that God from the beginning, so ordered the constitution of the world as to leave room for the exercise of those miraculous powers which He foresaw would at a certain time be exercised; just as He has left similar room for the exercise, within narrower limits, of the human will. In this sense, some of the scholastic divines maintained, with reason, that a miracle is contrary to nature only in so far as nature is regarded as an active manifestation, not in so far as it is regarded as a passive recipient of power.* If this

* This is clearly expressed in the language of Alexander ab Ales, 'Summa,' p. ii., qu. xlii., numb. v., art. 5:—" Est enim potentia activa, et est potentia susceptiva, et est potentia aptata et potentia non aptata. Et est potentia activa tam naturæ inferioris quam superioris; susceptiva autem naturæ inferioris. Et verum est quod quicquid est Deo possibile secundum potentiam

distinction is once clearly understood, the question, whether miracles may be represented as the result of *law*, or not, is a mere verbal question, which is only important from its liability to be mistaken for a real one. Properly speaking, a natural effect is not produced by a law, but by an agent acting according to a law. Every natural phenomenon has its physical cause in some antecedent natural phenomenon which it regularly follows; and the *laws of nature* are merely classifications of some of these sequences with others of a similar character;* or, as they have been aptly called, "the uniformities which exist among natural phenomena, when reduced to their simplest expression."† In this sense, miracles cannot be referred to a natural law, known or unknown; for they do not resemble any sequence of one sensible phenomenon from another; nor can any sensible phenomenon or group of phenomena be pointed out, or even supposed to exist, the occurrence of which would be invariably followed by such results. But if the term *law* be used in a different sense, to denote a method or plan conceived in the mind of an intelligent Being; and if, by referring miracles to a law, no more is meant than that they, like other events, formed part of God's purpose from the beginning, and were the result, not of sudden caprice, but of a preordained plan, by which provision was made for them, that they should be wrought at their proper time and place without disturbing the economy of the universe, —such an expression, allowing for the necessary imperfection of all human terms when applied to divine things, is perhaps the most true and reverent conception

activam, est naturæ possibile, non simpliciter, sed secundum potentiam susceptivam; et hoc est dicta possibilitas; sed non secundum activam potentiam, nec secundum aptatam." A similar view is held by Albertus Magnus, 'Summa,' p. ii., tract viii., qu. xxxi.; and by Aquinas, in 1 Sent., dist. xlii., qu. ii., art. 2. See also Neander, 'Church History,' vol. viii., p. 161, Eng. tr. ed. Bohn.

* "No further insight into why the apple falls is acquired by saying it is forced to fall, or it falls by the force of gravitation: by the latter expression we are enabled to relate it most usefully to other phenomena; but we still know no more of the particular phenomena than that under certain circumstances the apple does fall."—*Grove on the Correlation of Physical Forces*, p. 18, 3rd edition.

† Mill's 'Logic,' vol. i., p. 385.

of these events which we are capable of forming during this present life; though, like other analogies transferred from the human mind to the Divine, it is the object rather of religious belief than of philosophical speculation.

18. Our argument has hitherto proceeded on the assumption that we are justified in regarding the visible world as under the government of a personal God, and in speaking of His acts and purposes in language which implies an analogy between the Divine mind and the human. It now becomes necessary to make some remarks in vindication of the assumption itself, which has been included by recent criticism in the same condemnation with the consequences which we have endeavoured to deduce from it. Of the argument from design, "as popularly pursued," we are told that it "proceeds on the analogy of a personal agent, whose contrivances are limited by the conditions of the case and the nature of his materials, and pursued by steps corresponding to those of human plans and operations: —an argument leading only to the most unworthy and anthropomorphic conceptions.* We are told, again, that "to attempt to reason from law to volition, from order to active power, from universal reason to distinct personality, from design to self-existence, from intelligence to infinite perfection, is in reality to adopt grounds of argument and speculation entirely beyond those of strict philosophical inference."† We are told, again, that "the simple argument from the invariable order of na-

* Powell, 'Order of Nature,' p. 237. It is natural to turn to this more elaborate work, published but a short time before the 'Essays and Reviews,' as the most probable source from which to complete or explain anything which seems defective or obscure in the author's contribution to the latter volume. At the same time it is but just to call attention to some indications of a very different and a far truer view, in an earlier work by the same writer; as in the following passage, which I venture to cite, though unable to reconcile it with his latter language:—"It is by *analogy* with the exercise of intellect, and the volition, or power of moral causation, of which we are conscious within ourselves, that we speak of the *Supreme Mind*, and *Moral Cause* of the universe, of whose operation, order, arrangement, and adaptation are the external manifestations. *Order* implies what by *analogy* we call *intelligence:* subserviency to an observed end implies intelligence *foreseeing*, which, by analogy, we call *design*."—*On the Spirit of the Inductive Philosophy*, p. 166.

† Powell, 'Order of Nature,' p. 244.

ture is wholly incompetent to give us any conception whatever of the Divine Omnipotence, except as *maintaining, or acting through*, that invariable universal system of physical order and law;" and that "a theism of *Omnipotence in any sense deviating from the order of nature* must be entirely derived from other teaching."* In order to test the value of these and similar arguments, it will be necessary that we should clearly understand what this *other teaching* is, and what it teaches us; as well as the relation in which it stands to the generalizations and inductions of physical science.

In examining this question, we are not directly concerned with the higher inquiry regarding the degree and character of man's knowledge of God, as a whole and from whatever source derived, in its relation to the absolute essence of its Divine Object, and to the necessary limits of man's faculties. The difficulties connected with metaphysical theories of the Absolute and Infinite, which have driven so many speculative minds into the extravagances of Pantheism, do not affect our present argument. How any relation between the infinite and the finite can be conceived as existing;—how God can be contemplated as acting in time *at all*, whether in connection with the phenomena of the material world, or with the thoughts and feelings of men:—questions of this kind are equally applicable to every positive conception of Divine Providence which we are capable of forming, and have no direct bearing on the peculiar claims of one class of such conceptions as compared with another. The general answer to such difficulties is to be found in the confession of our ignorance as regards the mystery from which they spring and on which their solution depends; but this ignorance, arising as it does from the universal limits of human thought, has no special relation to one age or state of man's knowledge, more than to another, and is not removed by any advance in those departments which fall within his legitimate field. Pantheistic speculation has flourished with much the same result,

* Powell, 'Order of Nature,' p. 247.

or want of result, in the earliest and in the latest days of philosophy, in ancient India and in modern Germany; and if any advance is to be expected in relation to the questions with which such speculation deals, it is probably to be looked for, not in the fuller solution of the questions themselves, but in the clearer apprehension of the reasons why they are insoluble.

The question now before us is of another character. It relates to that knowledge of God which, be it more or less philosophically perfect, is that which practically determines the thoughts and feelings and actions of the majority of mankind; being connected with facts of their daily experience, and with ideas intimately associated with those facts. And the form in which it meets us at present may be expressed as follows:—Is the truest and highest conception of God to which man can practically attain with his present faculties that which is suggested by the observation of Law and Order, as existing in the material world? or is there a higher conception, derived from a different class of objects, by which the errors of an exclusively physical theology may be discovered and corrected?

19. Reduced to its simplest terms the question really stands thus:—Is Matter or Mind the truer image of God? We are told indeed, "that the study of physical causes is the sole real clue to the conception of a moral cause; and that physical order, so far from being opposed to the idea of supreme intelligence, is the very exponent of it." * We are referred to "the grand contemplation of cosmical order and unity" as furnishing "proofs of the ever-present mind and reason in nature;"† but we have yet to learn what is the exact process by which the desired conclusion is elicited from the premises.

20. In opposition to these statements I do not hesitate to repeat, with a very slight modification, the words of Sir William Hamilton, "that the class of phenomena which requires that kind of cause we denominate a Deity is exclusively given in the phenom-

* Powell, 'Order of Nature,' p. 235. † Ibid., p. 238.

ena of mind; that the phenomena of matter, taken by themselves (you will observe the qualification—taken by themselves), do not warrant any inference to the existence of a God."* The argument which would deduce the conception of God solely from physical causation bears witness, in the very words in which it is announced, to its own imperfection. The very names of *law*, and *order*, and *cause*, had a literal before they had a figurative meaning, and are borrowed, in common with the whole phraseology of causation, by the sciences of invariable succession, from those of moral action and obligation. We discern Law as Law, solely by means of the personal consciousness of *duty;* we gain the conception, not by the external observation of *what is*, but by the internal apprehension of *what ought to be.* We discern Causation, as Causation, solely in and by the productive energy of the personal will,—the one solitary fact of human experience in which is presented the *consciousness of effort*,—of *power* in action, exerting itself to the production of an effect. We discern Order, as Order, only in so far as we conceive the many as constituting the *One*,—the varied phenomena of sense as combined into a single *whole;* and the ideas of *unity* and *totality* are given only in the personal consciousness,—in the immediate perception of the one indivisible Self, and its several modes of conscious existence.† What do we mean when we speak of the *Order of Nature* as implying a presiding Mind? The language is unintelligible save as interpreted by what the personal consciousness tells us of our own mind and its control over the objects that are under its dominion. In the little world of man's thought and its objects, that Order, that System from which the Cosmos derives its name,—that Unity which binds together the diverse elements into a consistent whole,—is the factor contrib-

* 'Lectures on Metaphysics,' vol. i., p. 26.

† "Le moi est la seule *unité* qui nous soit donnée immédiatement par la nature; nous ne la rencontrons dans aucune des choses que nos facultés observent. Mais l'entendement, qui la trouve en lui, la met hors de lui par induction, et d'un certain nombre des choses coexistantes il crée des unités ratificielles."—*Royer-Collard, in Jouffroy's translation of Reid*, vol. iv., p. 350.

uted by the mind to its objects,—the product of Intelligence, comprehending, arranging, generalizing, classifying. Without this action of mind upon its objects, the little world of each man's knowledge would be, not a Cosmos, but a Chaos,—not a system of parts in mutual relation to each other, but an endless succession of isolated phantoms coming and going one by one. It is from this little world of our own consciousness, with its many objects, marshalled in their array under the rule of the one conscious Mind, that we are led to the thought of the great universe beyond,—that we conceive this also as a world of Order, and as being such by virtue of its relation to an ordering and presiding Mind. Design, Purpose, Relation of parts to a whole, of means to an end,—these conceptions borrowed from the world of mind, can alone give order and unity to the world of matter, by representing it as moulded and governed by a ruling and purposing Mind, the centre and the source of that relation which mind does not take from matter, but confers upon it. Through this alone can Chaos be conceived as Cosmos; through this alone can the Many point to the One.

21. But this is not all. The very conception of a Design in creation implies the existence of a Free Will in the Designer. If man were not conscious of a free will in himself, he could frame no designs, he could conceive no purposes of his own; and without the assumption of an analogous Divine Will, there is no meaning in his language when he speaks of the Design or Purpose of God. But in conceiving God as a free agent, we necessarily conceive Him as a Person; and this conception places Him in a totally different light from that of a mere soul of the world, or intelligence manifested in a system of material phenomena. In conceiving God as a Person, we conceive Him as standing in a direct relation to that one object in the world which is most nearly akin to Himself,—the personal soul of man, by whom He is so conceived. The personality, and, as implied in the personality, the moral nature of God, is not, as it has sometimes been represented, an isolated conception,

derived from a distinct class of facts, and superadded to another conception of a Deity derived from the order of nature :* it is the primary and fundamental idea of a God in any distinctive sense of the word,—an idea without which no religion and no theology, no feeling of a spiritual relation between God and man, and no conception of a mind superior to nature, can have any existence. To speak, in the language of modern pantheistic philosophy, of a Reason or Thought in the universe, which first becomes conscious in man, is simply to use terms without a meaning; for we have no conception of reason or thought at all, except as a consciousness. And to speak, on the side of physical philosophy, of a Supreme Mind, evinced in the laws of matter, is, in like manner, to use terms which have no meaning until we have acquired a conception of what mind is from the consciousness of the mind within ourselves. Our primary religious consciousness is that of man's relation to God as a person to a person; and, unless we begin with this and retain it in our knowledge, the very name of God is unmeaning. If this be Anthropomorphism, it is, as Jacobi has said, an Anthropomorphism identical with Theism, and without which there remains nothing but Atheism or Fetichism.†

22. The following quotation from the same eloquent and profound philosopher is probably already familiar to many readers, but is too excellent in itself and too appropriate to the present argument to be omitted.

* "At the utmost," says Professor Powell, "a physico-theology can only teach a supreme mind evinced in the laws of the world of matter, and the relations of a Deity to physical things essentially as derived from physical law. A moral or metaphysical theology (so far as it may be substantiated) can only lead us to a Deity related to mind, or to the moral order of the world."—*Order of Nature*, p. 245.

I consider this separation between two sources of theology as fundamentally erroneous. I believe that man's conception of God *as mind* is primarily derived from the personal consciousness alone; and that, however much it may be *enlarged* by the contemplation of material objects, it does not *originate* from them, and can only be legitimately applied to them in and by its primary characteristics of personality and a moral nature.

† "Wir bekennen uns demnach zu einem von der Ueberzeugung, dass der Mensch Gottes Ebenbild in sich trage—unzertrennlichen Anthropomorphismus, und behaupten, ausser diesem Anthropomorphismus, der von jeher Theismus genannt wurde. ist nur Gotteslängnung oder—*Fetichismus*."—*Von den Göttlichen Dingen*, Werke, iii., p. 422.

"*Nature conceals God;* for, through her whole domain, Nature reveals only fate, only an indissoluble chain of mere efficient causes,* without beginning and without end, excluding, with equal necessity, both providence and chance. An independent agency, a free original commencement, within her sphere and proceeding from her powers, is absolutely impossible. Working without will, she takes counsel neither of the good nor of the beautiful; creating nothing, she casts up from her dark abyss only eternal transformations of herself, unconsciously and without an end; furthering, with the same ceaseless industry, decline and increase, death and life,—never producing what alone is of God and what supposes liberty,—the virtuous, the immortal.

"*Man reveals God;* for Man, by his intelligence, rises above Nature, and, in virtue of this intelligence, is conscious of himself as a power not only independent of, but opposed to, Nature, and capable of resisting, conquering, and controlling her. As man has a living faith in this power, superior to nature, which dwells in him, so has he a belief in God, a feeling, an experience of His existence. As he does not believe in this power, so does he not believe in God; he sees, he experiences nought in existence but nature—necessity—fate."†

23. From the above principles it follows (to use the words of Sir William Hamilton) "that the universe is governed not only by physical but by moral laws;" and "that intelligence stands first in the absolute order of existence—in other words, that final preceded efficient causes."‡ But this involves, as a consequence, that the question concerning the possibility or probability of a miracle is to be judged, not merely from physical, but also, and principally, from moral grounds;

* The phrase *efficient causes* (wirkende Ursachen), here and in a subsequent quotation from the translator, must be understood in a different sense from that in which it is used by some modern writers, to denote *metaphysical* as distinguished from *physical* causes—a sense adopted above, p. 28. For the two senses of the phrase, see especially a note in Stewart's 'Philosophy of the Active and Moral Powers,' book iii., ch. ii., Collected Works, vii., p. 27.

† Werke, iii., p. 425. Translated by Sir W. Hamilton, 'Lectures on Metaphysics,' vol. i., p. 40.

‡ 'Lectures on Metaphysics,' vol. i., p. 28.

not merely from the evidence furnished by the phenomena of the material world, but also from that furnished by the religious nature of man, and by his relation to a God to whom that nature bears witness. It is altogether an erroneous view to represent the question between general law and special interposition as if it rested on mechanical considerations only—as if it could be judged by the difference between constructing a machine which, when once made, can go on continuously by its own power, and one which, at successive periods, requires new adjustments.* The miracle is not wrought for the sake of the physical universe, but for the sake of the moral beings within it; and the question to be considered is not whether a divine interposition is needed to regulate the machinery of nature, but whether it is needed or adapted to promote the religious welfare of men. If the spiritual restoration of mankind has in any degree been promoted by means of a religion professing to have been introduced by the aid of miracles, and whose whole truth is involved in the truth of that profession, we have a sufficient reason for the miraculous interposition, superior to any that can be urged for or against it from considerations derived from the material world. The very conception of a *revealed* as distinguished from a *natural* religion implies a manifestation of God different in kind from that which is exhibited by the ordinary course of nature; and the question of the probability of a miraculous interposition is simply that of the probability of a revelation being given at all. In the words of Bishop Butler, "Revelation itself is miraculous, and miracles are the proof of it."†

24. As regards the general question of the *possibility* of miracles (that of their *reality* must of course be determined by its own special evidence), Paley's criticism is, after all, the true one:—"Once believe that there is a God, and miracles are not incredible."

* This objection against miracles is urged by Voltaire, 'Dictionnaire Philosophique,' v. 'Miracles,' and is answered by Bishop Van Mildert, 'Boyle Lectures,' Sermon xxi.

† 'Analogy,' part ii., ch. ii.

For an impersonal God is no God at all; and the conception of a personal God in relation to man necessarily involves that of a divine purpose, and of the manifestation of that purpose in time. Grant this, and there is no *à priori* reason why such a manifestation may not take place at one time as well as at another; why the beginning of a spiritual system at one period may not be as credible as the beginning of a material system at another period. It would indeed be a precarious argument to attempt to reason positively from an *à priori* notion of the divine attributes to the *necessity* of creation or of revelation; but the very conditions which render such an argument doubtful only increase the force of the negative caution, which, refusing to dogmatize on either side concerning what *must be* or *must not be*, is content to seek for such evidence as is within its reach concerning *what is*.

25. With the question of the *possibility* of miracles is intimately connected that of their *value as evidences*. Both questions, indeed, must ultimately be decided on the same principle; and the influence of that principle is probably at work, though unconsciously, in the minds of some who endeavour to regard the two inquiries as wholly distinct. Sometimes, indeed, we find both united, and apparently treated as parts of the same argument on the side of denial; though it is obvious that, if the impossibility of miracles can once be shown, there is no need of any inquiry into their comparative value. Nevertheless, as if the conclusiveness of the former argument were, after all, somewhat doubtful in the eyes of its advocates, we find it coupled with an attempt to disparage the value of the miracles as evidences, even supposing their reality. It is intimated that they are not so much *evidences* as *objects* of faith, invested with sanctity and exempted from criticism by virtue of the religious mysteries with which they are connected: * and approved divines are referred to as practically making the doctrine the real test of the admissibility of the miracles, and as ac-

* See 'Essays and Reviews,' p. 143.

knowledging the right of an appeal, superior to that of all miracles, to our own moral tribunal.* The feeling which dictates this judgment is intelligible at least, if not excusable, as the result of a reaction against the opposite error of a former generation: but, when the judgment is advanced, as it often is, not merely as an expression of the personal feelings of an individual, but as a general statement of the right grounds of belief, it is at best nothing more than an attempt to cure one evil by another, introducing a remedy, on the whole, worse than the disease.

Some of the questions introduced in this connection properly belong to an earlier stage of our argument; for though they have been treated by some writers as bearing on the evidential value of miracles, supposing their reality to be admitted, they more strictly relate to the previous inquiry concerning the grounds on which we believe miracles to have been wrought at all. Thus the assertion that the Gospel miracles are *objects* of faith is undoubtedly true; but it is true in a sense which is by no means incompatible with their being also *evidences*.† To us, in these latter days, as regards the grounds on which we believe the miracles to have taken place at all, they are "objects of faith" in that proper sense of the term *faith* in which it is opposed, not to *reason*, but to *sight*.‡ We were not eye-witnesses of the miracles: we know all that we know about them from the testimony of others; and testimony of all kinds is an appeal to faith, as distinguished from sight,—*præsentia videntur, creduntur absentia*.§ But to say that miracles are in this sense objects of faith, is a very different thing from making them exempt from criticism by virtue of the religious mysteries with which they are connected. The faith which is called into exercise is only that which is re-

* 'Essays and Reviews,' pp. 121, 122.

† When it is asserted that the miracles are objects, *not evidences*, of faith, it is obvious that the word *faith* is used in two different senses. In relation to *objects*, it means an act of belief; in relation to *evidences*, it means a doctrine to be believed.

‡ 2 Cor. v. 7, "We walk by faith, not by sight."

§ St. Augustine, Epist. cxlvii., c. 2.

quired in all admission of testimony, whether connected with religious mysteries or not; which exists in all cases in which we accept, on the authority of others, statements which we are unable to verify by our own experience.

26. The often-disputed question, whether the miracles prove the doctrine, or the doctrine the miracles, is also one which properly belongs to the earlier inquiry concerning the credibility of the miracles as facts, and which, like that of *objects* and *evidences*, derives a seeming plausibility from an epigrammatic antithesis of language covering a confusion of thought. There are *certain doctrines* which must be taken into account in determining the question whether a true miracle—*i.e.* an interposition of *Divine power*—has taken place *at all*. If a teacher claiming to work miracles proclaims doctrines contradictory to previously established truths, whether to the conclusions of natural religion or to the teaching of a former revelation, such a contradiction is allowed, even by the most zealous defenders of the evidential value of miracles, to invalidate the authority of the teacher.* But the right conclusion from this admission is not that true miracles are invalid as evidences, but that the supposed miracles in this case are not true miracles at all; *i.e.* are not the effects of Divine power, but of human deception or of some other agency. And the criterion, as has been often observed, is only of a negative character; contradiction to known truth is sufficient to disprove a Divine mission; but conformity to known truth is not

* Thus Clarke ('Evidence of Natural and Revealed Religion,' Prop. xiv.) says, "If the doctrine attested by miracles be in itself impious, or manifestly tending to promote vice, then without all question the miracles, how great soever they may appear to us, are neither worked by God Himself nor by His commission, because our natural knowledge of the attributes of God, and of the necessary difference between good and evil, is greatly of more force to prove any such doctrine to be false than any miracles in the world can be to prove it true." But Clarke also shows that this admission is a very different thing from making the doctrine the proof of the miracles; that, on the contrary, the miracles are the proof of the doctrine, *provided that the doctrine be such as is capable of being proved by miracles.* See also, on the same question, Bishop Sherlock, Discourse x.; Penrose, 'On the Evidence of the Scripture Miracles,' p. 212.

sufficient to establish one.* And even the negative criterion, however valid as a general rule, is liable to error in its special applications. The certainty of the truths of natural religion does not guarantee the certainty of all the conclusions which this or that man believes to be truths of natural religion, any more than the infallibility of Scripture guarantees the infallibility of every man's interpretation of Scripture. God cannot contradict Himself, whether He teaches through nature or through revelation; but man may misinterpret God's teaching through the one as well as through the other.

27. In regarding the doctrinal criterion as properly relating to the question whether a true miracle has been wrought at all, we set aside, as unworthy of serious consideration, the supposition which has sometimes been advanced in favour of an opposite view; namely, that real miracles may possibly be performed by evil spirits in behalf of a false doctrine. This supposition, whatever may be its value as a theme for argumentative ingenuity, is not one which we are practically called upon to consider by any of the actual circumstances with which we are concerned. The objections which may justly be urged against Farmer's argument, when carried to the extent of denying the credibility of demoniacal miracles of any kind, do not apply to it when limited to such miracles as are wrought in evidence of a religion, and to the question, not of their theoretical possibility, but of their actual occurrence. It may be unsafe to reason *à priori*, from our conception of the Divine attributes, that the permission of such agency is inconceivable; but we may fairly refuse to attach any practical importance to the supposition, until some evidence is brought forward to show

* Thus Bishop Atterbury, in his Sermon on 'Miracles the most proper way of proving the Divine Authority of any Religion,' says, "Though the badness of any doctrine, and its disagreeableness to the eternal rules of right reason, be a certain sign that it did *not* come from God, yet the goodness of it can be no infallible proof that it *did*." The same argument is handled in Rogers's 'Sermons on the Necessity of Divine Revelation,' pp. 60, 109, ed. 1757. See also Warburton, 'Divine Legation,' b. ix., c. 5; Clarke, 'Evidence,' Prop. ix.

that it has actually been realized. It remains yet to be shown that in all human experience any instance can be produced of a real miracle wrought by evil spirits for purposes of deception;* and until some probable grounds can be alleged in behalf of the fact, we have not sufficient means of judging concerning the theory. Doubtless, if it is consistent with God's Providence to permit such a temptation, He will also, with the temptation, make a way for us to escape; but what that way will be, or how far the temptation is consistent with God's Providence, we cannot decide beforehand: we must wait till some actual occurrence, with all its accompanying circumstances, comes before us. The only real question at issue is not whether Christianity is a revelation from God or a delusion of Satan;—a question which no sane man at the present time would think worthy of a serious discussion; but whether it is of God or of man; and, consequently, on what grounds and to what extent it is entitled to the acceptance of mankind. What man has taught, man may revise and improve. If the doctrines of Christianity are no otherwise of divine origin than as all human wisdom is the gift of God, they have, like other products of human wisdom, no further claim to be accepted than as they may be verified by the wisdom of later generations. In that case, we may listen to the teaching of Christ and His apostles as we listen to the teaching of human philosophers, with respect and gratitude, but not necessarily with submission: we claim a right to judge and sift, and it may be to reject, as our own reason shall determine us, acknowledging no other authority than that which is due to the wise and good of every generation of mankind. But if, on the other hand, the doctrines are given to us by Divine revelation such as no human wisdom can claim, they have a right to be received by virtue of the authority on which they rest, distinct from any which they may possess through their own intrinsic reasonableness or capability of verification. Of such a Divine authority miracles are the

* See Penrose, 'On the Evidence of the Scripture Miracles,' p. 23.

natural and proper proof;—a proof which all men are disposed naturally and instinctively to admit in practice, whatever cavils may be raised against it on the ground of imaginary difficulties in theory. In the words of one of the ablest of the writers who have discussed this point, "All *natural* scepticism on the subject of miracles attaches to the question whether they were really performed, not, if performed, to the authority which they possess."* For all real purposes of controversy, the question may be stated now, as it was stated by Gamaliel of old, whether the counsel and the work be of man or of God; and the only serious inquiry that can be raised concerning the miracles of Scripture is whether they were wrought by the direct interposition of God, or were the result of human skill or other natural causes,—in other words, whether they were or were not really miracles at all.

28. The question, then, only requires to be disentangled of its confusion to be very briefly answered. If it is considered theoretically and in the abstract with reference merely to the logical character of certain doctrines in themselves, and not to the circumstances and needs of men, we may divide, as is usually done, the doctrines of religion into those which are and those which are not discoverable by human reason; regarding the former as prior to revelation, and furnishing a negative criterion which no true revelation can contradict; while the latter are posterior to revelation, and rest immediately on the authority of a divinely commissioned teacher, and mediately on the proofs of his divine mission, whatever these may be.† And it is at this stage of the inquiry that the question concerning the evidential value of miracles properly comes in. A teacher who proclaims himself to be specially sent by God, and whose teaching is to be received on the authority of that mission, must, from the nature of the case, establish his claim by proofs of another kind than those which merely evince his human wisdom or goodness. A superhuman au-

* Penrose, p. 24. † Compare Warburton, 'Divine Legation,' b. ix., c. 5.

thority needs to be substantiated by superhuman evidence; and what is superhuman is miraculous. It is not *the truth of the doctrines*, but *the authority of the teacher*, that miracles are employed to prove; and the authority being established, the truth of the doctrine follows from it. In this manner our Lord appeals to His miracles as evidences of his mission: "The works which the Father hath given me to finish, the same works that I do, bear witness of me that the Father hath sent me."* It is easy to say that we might have known Jesus Christ to be the Son of God, had He manifested Himself merely as a moral teacher, without the witness of miracles. It is easy to *say* this, because it is impossible to *prove* it. We cannot reverse the facts of history; we cannot make the earthly life of Christ other than it was. As a matter of fact He did unite miraculous powers with pure and holy doctrine; and, as a matter of fact, He did appeal to His miracles in proof of His divine authority. The miracles are a part of the portrait of Christ; they are a part of that influence which has made the history of the Christian Church what it is. It is idle to speculate on what that history might have been had that influence been different. We have to do with revelation as we have to do with nature,—as God has been pleased to make it, not as He might have made it, had His wisdom been as ours.

Such, even at its very lowest estimate, is the evidential character of miracles from the abstract and theoretical point of view. "The truths," says Bishop Atterbury, "which are necessary in this manner to be attested are those which are of positive institution; those which, if God had not pleased to reveal them, human reason could not have discovered; and those which, even now they are revealed, human reason cannot fully account for and perfectly comprehend. Such, for example, are the doctrines of Baptism and the Supper of the Lord, of the Resurrection of the same Body, of the Distinction of Persons in the Unity of the Divine Es-

* St. John v. 36.

sence, and of the Salvation of Mankind by the Blood and Intercession of Jesus. It is this kind of truths that God is properly said to reveal; truths of which, unless revealed, we should have always continued ignorant; and 'tis in order only to prove those truths to have been really revealed, that we affirm miracles to be necessary."*

29. But practically, in reference to the actual condition and needs of men, the evidence of miracles has a far wider range, and includes all those doctrines, whether natural or revealed, which have at any time been taught or revived among men by the preaching of the Christian Faith. This has been pointed out, with his usual practical wisdom, by Bishop Butler. "It is impossible," he says, "to say who would have been able to have reasoned out that whole system which we call natural religion, in its genuine simplicity, clear of superstition; but there is certainly no ground to affirm that the generality could. If they could, there is no sort of probability that they would. Admitting there were, they would highly want a standing admonition to remind them of it, and inculcate it upon them." To the same effect he continues: "It may possibly be disputed how far miracles can prove natural religion; and notable objections may be urged against this proof of it, considered as a matter of speculation; but, considered as a practical thing, there can be none. For suppose a person to teach natural religion to a nation who had lived in total ignorance or forgetfulness of it; and to declare he was commissioned by God to do so; suppose him, in proof of his commission, to foretell things future, which no human foresight could have guessed at; to divide the sea with a word; feed great multitudes with bread from heaven; cure all manner of diseases; and raise the dead, even himself, to life: would not this give additional credibility to his teaching—a credibility beyond what that of a common man would have; and be an authorita-

* 'Miracles the proper way of proving the Divine Authority of any Religion,' Sermons (1734), vol. i. p. 215. See also Bishop Sherlock, Discourse x.

tive publication of the law of nature, *i.e.* a new proof of it? It would be a practical one, of the strongest kind, perhaps, which human creatures are capable of having given them."*

In this passage, the good sense of Butler has solved the question in its practical aspect, leaving the theoretical difficulty in its proper insignificance. No doubt, if we are at liberty to suppose a totally different state of things from the actual one, we may deduce a great number of hypothetical consequences concerning what might have been the case, but is not. *If* all men possessed a perfect system of natural religion, no authoritative publication of natural truth would be needed; and no teaching which contradicted men's natural belief would have any claim to be received. And so, *if* all men were possessed of perfect bodily health, no medicine would be needed to give it them; and any medicine which tended to alter their state of health would be injurious. Unhappily, both suppositions are untrue and the conclusions practically fall to the ground with them. It may be granted that the authority of which miracles are a proof is but an accidental and relative evidence of truths of this character. Still, the accident is one which has extended over the greater part of mankind; and the relation is coextensive with it. And this consideration must serve to modify in practice the negative criterion which is allowed to be valid in theory. In whatever degree any man does not possess a perfect natural religion, in the same degree he is liable to error in judging of the truth of a revelation solely from internal evidence. And even the man who, in the present day, claims the right to exercise such a judgment, may be reminded that the knowledge on which his claim is based is in no small degree owing to that very authoritative teaching on which his judgment is to be passed:—*ἀπελάκτισε καθαπερεὶ τὰ πωλάρια γεννηθέντα τὴν μητέρα.* "The fact," says Mr. Davison, "is not to be denied; the religion of Nature *has* had the opportu-

* 'Analogy,' part ii, ch. i.

nity of rekindling her faded taper by the Gospel light, whether furtively or unconsciously taken. Let her not dissemble the obligation and the conveyance, and make a boast of the splendour, as though it were originally her own, or had always in her hands been sufficient for the illumination of the world."*

30. The whole question of the value of miracles as evidences of Christianity must, in fact, be answered by means of the same distinction on which depends the question of their credibility;—the distinction, namely, between God's general manifestations of Himself in the ordinary course of nature, and His special manifestation of Himself by supernatural signs. Those who deny the existence of any special revelation of religious truths, distinct from that general sense in which man's reason itself and all that it can discover are the gifts of Him from whom every good thing comes;—those who deny that any teaching has been made to man by special inspiration of particular teachers, in a sense different from that in which all holy desires, all good counsels, and all just works proceed from the inspiration of the Holy Spirit;—such persons are only consistent when they deny that miracles have any value as evidences of religious truth, and are still more consistent if they deny that such works have ever been wrought. If religion teaches nothing but what every man, by God's grace, may discover, or at least verify, for aimself, the distinction between natural and revealed religion ceases to exist, and with it the distinction between natural and supernatural evidences of the truth. If the ordinary witness of man's reason or conscience is sufficient for all purposes of religion, the extraordinary witness becomes superfluous if it agrees with this, and pernicious if it differs from it. But this absolute sufficiency of the natural reason is the very point which history and philosophy concur to call in question.

31. The following words of a learned and thoughtful prelate of the English Church may be cited and adopted

* 'Discourses on Prophecy,' p. 6 (4th edition).

as expressing the conclusions which I have endeavoured, however imperfectly, to establish in common with him: "It appears, then, on a review of the preceding arguments, that the Scripture miracles stand on a solid basis, which no *reasoning* can overthrow. Their *possibility* cannot be denied without denying the very nature of God as an all-powerful Being: their *probability* cannot be questioned without questioning His *moral* perfections: and their certainty, as matters of fact, can only be invalidated by destroying the very foundations of all human testimony.

"Upon these grounds we may safely leave the subject in the hands of any wise and considerate man: and we may venture to affirm that no person of such a character will, after an attentive examination of these points, ever suffer his faith in the miracles, by which the Divine authority of the Christian revelation is supported, to be shaken. Convinced that, by a fair chain of reasoning, every one who denies them must be driven to the necessity of maintaining atheistical principles, by questioning either the power, or wisdom, or goodness of the Creator, the true philosopher will yield to the force of this consideration, as well as to the overpowering evidences of the facts themselves; and will thankfully accept the dispensation which God hath thus graciously vouchsafed to reveal. He will suffer neither wit, nor ridicule, nor sophistry, to rob him of this anchor of his faith; but will turn to his Saviour with the confidence so emphatically expressed by Nicodemus: 'Rabbi, we KNOW that thou art a Teacher come from God; FOR no man can do these miracles that Thou doest, except GOD be with him.'"*

To these remarks, which are applicable to every age and race of men to whom the Christian evidences may come, it may perhaps not be inappropriate to add a further observation having a more especial reference to ourselves. The very attacks which have been made, in the supposed interests of science, upon the miracu-

* Van Mildert, 'Boyle Lectures,' Sermon xxi.

lous element of the Gospel narrative, may themselves serve, if rightly considered, to give to that very element a new significance, and to point to a moral purpose more discernible now than of old. An age of advanced physical knowledge has its especial temptations, no less than its especial privileges. Few indeed, it is trusted, will be found to repeat what one great scientific teacher of the present century has been found to assert, that the heavens declare, not the glory of God, but only the glory of the astronomer. Yet this bold and profane language is only the extreme expression of a tendency against which an age like the present has especial need to watch and pray. Against such a tendency it is no small safeguard that men of science should be trained from their earliest childhood in records which at every page tell of the personal presence of Him by whom all things were made, manifested in direct control over the delegated workings of His visible creation. It is but one form of His perpetual presence with His Church, that in founding a Faith destined to ally itself with the intellectual cultivation of all succeeding generations, He should have founded it in such a manner as to furnish, in the record of its origin, a lesson of the spirit in which that cultivation should be pursued, and a safeguard against the perils to which it is especially exposed. If there are times when the very vastness of the material system which science discloses seems to thrust the Author of all to an almost infinite distance from us;—if there are times when we feel almost tempted to echo the wish of the poet, to be "a Pagan suckled in a creed outworn," so that we might but have a clearer sight of the presence of Deity among the phenomena of nature;—if there are times when the heaven that is over our heads seems to be brass, and the earth that is under us to be iron, and we feel our hearts sink within us under the calm pressure of unyielding and unsympathizing Law, as those of the disciples of old sank within them under the stormy violence of wind and wave;—at such times we may learn our lesson and feel our consolation, as we turn to those vivid pictures which our Sacred Story portrays of the personal power of the Incarnate God visibly ruling His creation; and may hear through them the present voice of Him who spake on the waters, "Be of good cheer; it is I; be not afraid."

ESSAY II.

ON THE STUDY OF THE EVIDENCES OF CHRISTIANITY.

CONTENTS OF ESSAY II.

ON THE STUDY OF THE EVIDENCES OF CHRISTIANITY.

1. "Evidences of Christianity!" exclaims the late Mr. Coleridge in one of the most popular of his prose-works, "I am weary of the word. Make a man feel the want of it . . . . . and you may safely trust it to its own evidence."

There can be little doubt, I think, that these words express the prevailing sentiments of a very considerable number of Christians at the present day; and it cannot be denied that, for many years back, there has been a general distaste for that *apologetic* religious literature which was popular in the last century.

2. This has doubtless been greatly owing to a *Reaction* from the disproportionate attention paid to such literature by the Divines of a former age, and has taken place in virtue of that general rule which seems to ordain that *an over value of any branch of knowledge in one generation shall be attended by an unjust depreciation of it in the next.* The argumentative value of things even so important as the evidences of religion may, unquestionably, engross the public mind too much; and he who is continually occupied in contemplating and stating the proofs of its truth will fail of reaching the just standard of a Christian teacher, or a Christian man. Such a person will be like a prince who employs all his time, and strength, and resources in raising fortresses about a territory which he does not carefully govern; or like a landlord who lives but to accumulate muniments of an estate which he neglects to till. But the folly of such conduct would be no excuse for suffering our frontiers to lie open, or our title-deeds to be lost. Yet something very like such advice is

sometimes offered to us. Our forefathers, perhaps, were too apt to include all strong energy of emotion and play of fancy in their general and unsparing censures of enthusiasm; and some of us are disposed to redress the balance by appealing exclusively to the imagination and the feelings. We see that it will not do to address the head alone, and *therefore* we will not address it at all, but speak only to the heart.

Now, it is important to observe that this reaction was so far from springing from any failure of the apologists in their proper work, that it would hardly have been possible if that work had not been thoroughly done. *Their* proper work was to drive the infidel writers of their own age out of the field; and never was task more completely accomplished. No literature, of any recent date, has perished more completely than the infidel literature of the early and middle parts of the last century.

Ipsæ periêre ruinæ.

It is only some curious antiquary, loving to parade forgotten lore, who now searches the pages of such writers as Toland or Tindal, and Chubb, and Morgan, and Coward, and Collins—though some of them were really men of parts, and all conspicuous in their day. Their very names, indeed, would have passed wholly from remembrance, but that some of them were answered in works which "posterity will not easily let die;" and almost all are found by the young student of theology enumerated by Leland in his 'View of the Deistical Writers.'* They survive, like the heroes of the 'Newgate Calendar,' in the annals of that public justice which chastised their faults.

3. The long controversy with the infidels assumed, in the course of it, many forms. But these changes of position, on the part of the defenders of Christianity, were caused by the changing tactics of their assailants,

* "The best book," says Burke, "that ever has been written against these people, is that in which the author has collected in a body the whole of the infidel code, and has brought their writings into one body, to cut them all off together."—*Speech on Relief of Protestant Dissenters*, 1773.

who, when driven from one point of attack, immediately occupied a new one.

The necessity for an English apologetic * literature began to be felt even before the Restoration, and is attested by such works as Jeremy Taylor's 'Moral Demonstration,' and Hammond's remarkable little tract on the 'Evidences of Religion.' After it, still more. The press, indeed, was not yet free to the infidels (though Hobbs, by masking his attack on all religion and morality under the form of a defence of despotism, contrived to evade its restrictions); but it is plain, from incidental notices, that sceptical objections were largely circulated in MS. and in conversation. Men read, in secret, authors whose names sound strange to this generation—Averroes, Jordanes Brunus, Cardan, Pomponatius, Vanini; and their doubts, denied a free expression, festered into grotesque and monstrous forms of atheism, of which Smith, and More, and Cudworth occasionally reveal to us portentous specimens. Learning, too, was beginning to suggest literary difficulties, of which we have indications in Isaac Vossius and Sir John Marsham.

It was in this state of things that those two great works, Cudworth's 'Intellectual System,' and Stillingfleet's 'Origines Sacræ,' † were published. They were certainly very far from being popular and easy defences

* It has been supposed that our early Reformers, conscious of the weakness of external proofs, rested the authority of Scripture wholly upon its self-evidencing light. But the doctrine of the self-evidencing light had quite a different origin. The schoolmen had erected theology into a science, properly so called, which required *principles* as certain as those of natural science. They could not find *such* a certainty in moral evidence, and therefore had recourse to supernatural light. The Reformers partook in their mistake in requiring an assent out of proportion to the evidence; but substituted the infallible Scripture as its object for the infallible Church. The true distinction between *assent* and *adhesion* was drawn by Hooker in his great sermon on the 'Faith of the Elect,' and, after him, by Jackson, Works, vol. iii., Oxford, 1841.

† Let any competent person read the chapters on Ancient History in the first book of the 'Origines,' and the account of the laws against the Christians in b. ii. c. 9, and he will see that those who sneer at that great work are themselves the proper objects of pity or contempt. Stillingfleet, in his old age, and when his temper had been spoiled by flattery, and his faculties decayed by years, engaged foolishly in a controversy with Locke, in which he did not appear to advantage. Yet he singled out most of those points which later metaphysicians have deemed the weak points in Locke's harness.

of religion, but they were not intended as replies to popular attacks. They were the weapons in a war of giants.

> "Non jaculo, neque enim jaculo vitam ille dedisset,
> Sed magnum stridens contorta Falarica venit."

Those who despise them have probably never read, and certainly never understood, them.

4. The point of attack was now gradually changed. Science was every day bringing fresh aids to religion. Before the arguments of More, and Cudworth, and Green, and Ray, and Boyle, and Clarke, the position of Atheism was generally abandoned as untenable. The divines had proved to their opponents that there was such a thing as natural religion; and those opponents now adopted that system of natural religion, which had been reasoned out for them, as their own; declared its proofs to have been always so clear and convincing that nothing but the artifices of priestcraft could have obscured them; and contended that revelation should at once be set aside as a superfluous incumbrance of its perfection.* The war-cry now was, "The sufficiency of natural religion!" The points in Christianity now selected for attack were those peculiar to it as distinguished from natural religion. It was contended that miracles were incredible, or utterly insignificant; that God could not give a particular revelation; that He could not have selected a chosen people; that He could not accept a vicarious atonement; that the Gospel doctrine of eternal rewards and punishments subverted morality by making it mercenary, &c. It was such objections as these that drew forth the masterpieces of Clarke, and Butler,† and Warburton. In

* See some admirable remarks upon the latest form of the same prejudice in Dr. Salmon's 'Sermons preached in Trinity College, Dublin,' (Macmillan, 1861), pp. 160–165.

† I have seen a curious criticism upon Butler's style, in which his disuse of technical terms is accounted for by saying that he was essentially a *Stoic*, and may be compared with "Epictetus, Antoninus, and Plutarch," who moralized in the language of common life. The Stoics, I had always thought, were rather remarkable for the *use* of technical terms. "Ex omnibus Philosophis," says Cicero, "Stoici plurima novaverunt. Zeno quoque, eorum princeps, non tam rerum inventor fuit quàm novorum verborum."—*De Finibus*, lib. iii. c. 2. And most persons who have looked into Antoninus

their hands the cause of religion was safe; but, in its management by less sagacious writers, one disastrous mistake was committed, the influence of which was long felt to the injury of the Church.

In the early stage of the controversy it was the infidels who maintained (with Hobbes and Spinoza) the selfish system of morals, and the defenders of religion who asserted the nobler doctrine that virtue was an end in itself. So much, indeed, was this the case, that hardly anything excited more the general outcry against Locke's 'Essay' than the supposition that his denial of innate ideas destroyed the proper foundation of ethics. But, in time, Locke was discovered to have been a Christian; and the Platonic theory of virtue was turned by Shaftesbury (his somewhat ungenerous pupil) into a support of naturalism, and an engine for assailing Christianity. This circumstance unhappily prejudiced some of the leading divines against even what was soundest in Shaftesbury's writings. They saw an accidental gain, in proving the necessity of revelation to assure man that the practice of virtue was, under all circumstances, his dearest interest, and they caught at it too eagerly. Thus "Hamlet and Laertes changed rapiers," and some of the champions of Truth disgraced themselves by using the poisoned weapon which they had wrested from the maintainers of error.

But, though some oversights were committed in the conduct of the war, the issue of the conflict was not, on the whole, doubtful. And now, again, the position had to be altered to meet a new assault. Lord Bolingbroke gave the signal by complaining that "divines had taken much silly pains to establish mystery on metaphysics, revelation on philosophy, and matters of fact on abstract reasoning. Religion," he says truly—"such as the Christian, which appeals to facts—must be proved as all other facts that pass for authentic are proved.

will agree with his editor that, so far from taking his diction from common life, "utitur vocibus planè suis, quas raro apud alios autores invenias." As for Plutarch, one is surprised to hear that he was a Stoic. He is commonly supposed to have written some rather *smart* treatises against the Stoics.

If they are thus proved, the religion will prevail without the assistance of so much profound reasoning.*

To the proof of religion, then, as a matter of fact, the Christian divines addressed themselves: and as the points to be considered in this view were the credibility of the prime witnesses to the miraculous facts of Christianity, and the trustworthiness of the tradition by which their testimony has been delivered down to us, it was these which were the chief subjects of the apologetic literature which may be said to terminate in the works of Lardner† and Paley.

But though the defenders of Christianity had been expressly challenged to this field of argument, it was one into which their antagonists showed little serious disposition to follow them. Certainly Lord Bolingbroke's own performances, in his 'Remarks on the Canon of Scripture,' and the historical speculations which are scattered in his 'Fragments,' were not very formidable to the faith. Gradually the attack upon revealed religion fell into the hands of persons too ignorant and too manifestly unscrupulous to produce much effect upon the educated part of the public. Such writers as Burgh and Paine might do mischief among the lower classes; but they can hardly fill a place in any *literary* history.

Two really illustrious names do, indeed, close the catalogue of the infidels of the last century—Hume and Gibbon.‡ But neither appeared as an *open* assailant of Christianity, and neither owes his chief fame to those

* See Warburton's 'Doctrine of Grace.'

† "I should be ungrateful," says Mr. Westcott, "not to bear witness to the accuracy and fulness of Lardner's 'Credibility;' for, however imperfect it may be in the view which it gives of the earliest period of Christian literature, it is, unless I am mistaken, more complete and trustworthy than any work which has been written since on the same subject."—*History of the Canon*, p. 9.

‡ In reference to the supposed difficulties and discouragements under which infidels labour, it is worth observing that both Hume and Gibbon held lucrative situations under Government. At an earlier period it was Walpole's policy to patronize some of the most rabid and indecent assailants of religion; and, until the infidels had been thoroughly refuted by the weapons both of wit and argument, the most open avowal of their opinions was rather a recommendation to what was called "polite society." A strong reaction in the tone of popular literature began with Steele and Addison.

parts of his writings in which Christianity was assailed. After them infidelity in England appeared to have sheathed its sword, furled its banner, and retired from the field.

5. But what, meanwhile, was the internal condition of the Church? It was (to recur to a former comparison) too much like an estate after the decision of a long suit in Chancery to settle a litigated title. The controversy with the infidels had not been the only one of that busy century. It was an age of a thousand controversies. There was the great Nonjuring Controversy, in which political rancour was still more embittered by the gall of the *odium theologicum*. There was the great Bangorian Controversy, growing out of the former, and draining into it all the poisoned dregs of its predecessor. There was the great Convocation Controversy, which changed country parsons into clerical Hampdens, and ranged High Church divines in strange antagonism against the royal supremacy. There was the great Trinitarian Controversy, begun by Clarke and Waterland, and continued by a host of inferior writers, till the public grew weary of the very thought of Patristic literature.* These and countless minor ones distracted the attention of churchmen from observing the spiritual destitution that was spreading widely around them amidst all this polemical activity. The brilliant services of the tongue and pen in defending Christianity, or orthodoxy, or even faction, eclipsed the less showy, but not less real, and far more generally requisite, usefulness of the pastoral care, in its ordinary forms of teaching and admonition. Prelates forsook their dioceses for the nobler work of writing controversy, or asserting the political interests of their order. Discipline became relaxed; parishes were neglected; and at the end of the century the Church found itself surrounded with a swarming population, and no ade-

* Warburton made an effort, in the preface to his 'Julian,' to restore the Fathers to some credit, and to put their character in a favourable light: and, in return, he has been charged with "disdain and *ignorance* of Catholic theology."

quate machinery provided for dealing with this mass of ignorance.

It is not true, I think, that the bulk of the lower orders had been leavened with infidelity.* Their heathenism was negative, not positive; they had been suffered to grow up in gross ignorance of religion: and it was during the prevalence of such evils that the evangelical reaction—commencing with the Methodist movement—began.

6. But it would be an error, I apprehend, to suppose that it was Whitfield and the Wesleys who *originated* a Reformation. Long before them it appears manifest that a healthy reaction had set in. As the old panic dread of fanaticism abated on the one hand, and the necessities of continual controversy became less on the other, preachers insisted more and more on the peculiarities of the Christian faith as the springs and motives of Gospel obedience. Energetic efforts were made to build new churches and establish schools throughout the country: and (what is always a hopeful sign) some zeal began to be felt for foreign missions, and some sense of responsibility for the religious state of our colonies. A change for the better was going on. The case of Whitfield and the Wesleys was that of other energetic men whose names figure in history as the originators of mighty changes. They fling themselves into a great movement before it has become conspicuous to the vulgar eye: they put themselves at its head; they carry it on to extravagance, and thus accelerate and extend an impulse which they partially misdirect, and may ultimately spoil forever.

The Methodists, then, had not to convert the English population to a *belief* in Christianity; but they had to awaken a *sense* of the Christian religion in men who had been so long thinking of it as a thing to be *proved*

* Even that of the upper was greatly overrated: "The truth of the case," says Hurd, a cool observer, "is no more than this. A few fashionable men make a noise in the world; and this clamour being echoed on all sides from the shallow circles of their admirers, misleads the unwary into an opinion that the irreligious spirit is universal and uncontrollable."—See the whole passage, '*Sermons on Prophecy*,' sermon xii., *conclusion*.

that they had forgotten that it was also a thing to be *felt* and acted on; and they had to teach even the elements of that religion to vast numbers of an outlying mass beyond the range of ordinary instruction. This was the appropriate work to which the circumstances of the times really called them. But, besides the pressure of these real wants, there were other cravings of the popular mind demanding satisfaction. There was (what is to be found in every generation) the great herd of superficial minds who always require the stimulus of something new; who throw the blame of their own shallowness upon their teachers, and are always asking for something more "deep and earnest and thorough-going," or "more rational and suited to the age," than the current theology, whatever it may be. This is the common sequacious mob of "novarum rerum avidi," who are drawn, like insects, by the loudest noise and the greatest glare. This movable, and indeed restless multitude, swells the *decuman* wave of every great movement, and retires with its ebb, only to return again on the crest of its successor. Nor can it be reasonably doubted that many of those amiable but weak persons who have latterly been roving over England in the garb of Passionists and Oratorians would have been, in the days of Whitfield's popularity, preaching rank Methodism on Kennington Common, amidst a shower of mud and turnip-tops.

There was, then, in the first place, the call for something new. But there was also the call for something *fanatical*. The terrible experience of the seventeenth century had left a deep impression on the beginning of the eighteenth, of dread and bitter scorn of fanaticism. In the wild tumult of the Commonwealth the nation had been, as it were, drunk with religious enthusiasm; and, in shame and grief at the remembrance of that horrible debauch and all its crimes, they had hastily vowed a total abstinence from those feelings which Hartley describes under the odd but convenient term Theopathy. But a wild career of another kind of drunkenness had done much to efface that impression before the close of that century; and the hypocrisy of the Puritans had been thrown into the shade by the brazen profligacy of the race who succeeded them. Enthusiasm was again eagerly demanding its turn for gratification.

7. Furthermore, there was a want that has been less often remarked as one of the causes of Methodism—the want of what may be called a freer *Church-activity.* The busy, bustling democratic spirit of ultra-Protestantism had made itself so hateful in the previous generation, that, within the Church, laymen shrank from meddling. The synodical assemblies of the clergy had only spasmodic fits of action, in which they either tore themselves, or made violent assaults on others. Their time and energies were wasted in disputes between the two Houses, disputes with the Crown, disputes with obnoxious brethren;—till, at last, their action became so manifestly scandalous that the Minister was able to silence them entirely, to the general satisfaction of a public who had ceased to be entertained by their quarrels.* Thus they no longer broke the dull monotony of QUIET which it was the policy of Walpole to maintain *per fas aut nefas.*

"The Convocation gaped, but could not speak."

Outside the Church, dissent had been crushed by the rigorous laws of Charles II., and the general disgust and contempt of the nation, so effectually, that it could not recover when the Toleration came. The Dissenting teachers were generally either hard, dry, and narrow Calvinistical divines; or men of enlarged and liberal sentiments, disgusted with their own communion, and no longer retaining the old prejudices against surplices and rochettes, but kept from conformity, partly by hereditary pride, and partly by dislike to the *doctrinal* fetters of subscription to the Articles and Liturgy.†

* Like the old comedy—

"Turpiter obticuit, sublato jure nocendi."

† See the notices of negotiations for a comprehension in Doddridge's Correspondence, and compare the language of Harewood: "Our separation is not founded in vestments and surplices, in liturgies, crosses, and genuflexions, in godfathers, godmothers, and rotatory motions,—it is Athanasius who drives us from your altars."—*Five Dissertations* (1772), p. 63.

How far an ultra-liberalism had leavened the Dissenting teachers became manifest when the Arian movement carried, at one sweep, the whole body of the English Presbyterians, and a great part of the Irish, into a heresy most remote from the traditions of their forefathers.

Thus, within the Church and without, there was a demand beginning to be felt for some free and stirring ecclesiastical activity; the thought of which men had ceased to associate with any of the old organizations.

8. In such a state of predisposition, Whitfield and the Wesleys began their work by preaching the New Birth. The term had doubtless a sound and valuable meaning. But, in that sense it meant, not the production of a new *belief*, but of a new *sense* of the reality and importance of momentous truths involved in what had been already assented to.

These two things are frequently confounded by careless thinkers; but, in reality, they are quite different: and the difference is observable, not only in religious, but in ethical matters, and in the affairs of common life. In all practical matters, mere belief, or acquiescence, is one thing; and that belief, quickened into a sense of reality, and touching all the springs of action, is another: and, in all practical matters, the most mischievous consequences may result from confounding together such different things. It would be a great mistake to fancy that Faith had been produced as soon as ever the mind had been brought to recognize the connection of a conclusion with unimpeachable premisses: and it would be a great mistake, on the other hand, to suppose that all processes of reasoning might be discarded, and nothing consulted or addressed but the fancy and the emotions. "Going over the theory of virtue" may indeed, as Butler has pointed out, not only fail to make a man practically moral, but tend to deaden the *sense* of moral truths, by weakening their practical, as it shows their rational, associations. But we should not therefore listen to a hotheaded reformer like Rousseau, who would urge us to cast aside all theory and reasoning in morals, and attend to nothing but the immediate dictates of the heart.

Into such confusions and mistakes, however, the leaders of the Evangelical movement were rapidly beguiled by their own sudden and widely-spread success. They taught (and taught rightly) that we must not only believe, but feel, before we can act, as Christians. In recalling attention to the truth that the Gospel is a revelation of God's love to sinners, designed to produce corresponding affections in our hearts—that the faith of Christ is a faith that works through love, they did valuable service, which should never be dissembled or forgotten. But unhappily they went on to teach that the belief and the action were to be grounded upon the feelings, considered as the immediate and sensible operation of the Holy Spirit upon the human mind.

Now such a preposterous mistake as this could hardly have been possible for the general acquiescence of the national mind in the truth of the Christian religion. For I am persuaded that none except the very wildest fanatics (and the leaders of whom I speak were certainly not mere wild fanatics) do really thus wholly ground their faith upon an imaginary inspiration. There is, in almost all cases, a secret tacit reference in the bottom of the heart to some fixed external standard by which the extravagances of fancy and feeling are moderated and kept in check. The Methodists could assume the general truth of Christianity as a *postulatum*. They could assume that there was a Holy Spirit; they could assume the necessary coincidence of His teaching in the heart with His teaching in the Holy Scriptures; and they could try the former by the latter. In the first fervours of their preaching they plainly were tempted to appeal to the agitations which it produced in the minds and bodies of their converts as a sort of miraculous attestation of its truth; but experience soon convinced the shrewder of them that such evidence could not be relied upon, and that the true appeal must be made elsewhere. But the logical *viciousness* of the *circle* in which the mind moves in such cases can only be hidden from it when the external authority on which it falls back is thought of as something unquestioned and unquestionable. It is only in reference to heretics, who hold in common with himself the inspiration of Scripture, that the Romanist can be guilty of the absurdity of proving his Church by the Scriptures, and the Scriptures by his Church. When dealing with the infidel, he must proceed, just as other Christians proceed, by the way of moral evidence; and from the 'Summa contra Gentiles' of Aquinas down to the 'Principia' of Abbé Hooke, this is the way in which Roman Catholic as well as Protestant apologists have proceeded in the argument against infidelity. So, also, when one enthusiast meets another of opposite sentiments, but with persuasions as strong, feelings as lively, satisfaction as complete, and inward peace as perfect as his own, each is driven to "try the spirit" of his antagonist by some external test, forgetting that, upon his own principles, that standard itself was only known by the inward discernment which it is now employed to control. Where such a standard is unhesitatingly admitted by both, the fallacy may be long concealed; but as soon as its authority comes to be generally and openly questioned, the mistake becomes patent, and can only be corrected by abandoning the false principle which has produced the mischief.

One circumstance which contributed to favour the Methodistic exaggerations upon this subject was, that the doctrine of the influence of the Holy Spirit had been one comparatively *reserved* in the preaching of the preceding half-century. I do not mean that it was denied, or even wholly omitted. Such strong and wholesale charges against the teaching of the Church at that period are often made; but they are wholly without foundation. But when referred to in more than a general way, the reference was usually for the purpose of guarding against fanatical extravagance —for correcting the abuse rather than illustrating the use of that doctrine; for showing rather what was *not*, than what *was* implied in it.

It was not strange, therefore, if, in their ardour to develop fully, on its positive side, this cardinal Christian doctrine of a free and intimate communion between God in Christ and the human soul, the evangelical leaders were tempted to overstep the bounds of sobriety; and to forget that the Holy Spirit is given not to supersede, or supply the place of any of our natural faculties, but to help their infirmity, and restore them to that just balance and due subordination—that proper and healthful exercise—which have been disturbed by sin. From Him, indeed, "all holy desires, all good counsels, and all just works do proceed;" but we must first determine that our desires *are* holy, our counsels good, and our works just, before we can, without intolerable rashness, attribute them to that sacred influence; and we cannot detemine that by the mere strength of our persuasions, or the vividness of our fancies, or the depth and earnestness of our feelings, without opening a way for every wild extravagance that can support itself on strong persuasion, vivid fancy, and deep and earnest feeling.

But, in the flush and fervour of their triumph, and the general silence of the advocates of infidelity, the evangelical leaders went on securely—comparing proudly their own achievements with the performances of their predecessors—and declaring that they needed no other evidences than the manifest adaptation of their doctrine to the wants of mankind, and its living power, when received, to regenerate a sinful race.

9. The natural consequence of all this was an extensive decay of theological learning. A few leading doctrines were, for them, the essence of the Gospel, and their preaching, in too many cases, became little more than a monotonous repetition of those doctrines. For such a ministry neither deep research nor accurate thinking was at all necessary. On the contrary, it was manifest that, in order to make a great part of the Bible available for the direct teaching of the few subjects to which they confined themselves, it was needful to violate all rules of sober criticism, and confound the

Old Testament with the New by an arbitrary *spiritualising* interpretation to which reason could set no limits. The practical result of such a course was an extensive, though vague, popular impression that the test of a correct exposition of Scripture was the amount of comfort or edification that the hearer or reader sensibly derived from it. The pious feelings which a text, as he understood it, produced in his mind were unhesitatingly regarded as the consequence of the Spirit's teaching through the Word. Human agency, it was indeed acknowledged, was necessary to teach a man to read; and human agency was needful to supply the unlearned with translations of the Bible; but, beyond this, very little was allowed to any other help than prayer, for the profitable study of the Scripture.

The real tendency, it is evident, of such opinions is not to exalt the authority of the Word of God, but to destroy it. The mind of the reader in such a process of study, instead of receiving instruction from the Scripture, imports a meaning into it. We have, not an *Exegesis*, but an *Isegesis*. A certain system of doctrine is first accepted, not upon the *authority* of propounders accredited by external evidence, but for the sake of the doctrine itself: the Scripture becomes valuable only as the vehicle of this doctrine, and valuable in proportion as it can be made the vehicle of this doctrine, and the means of exciting a certain class of pious sentiments: and, as it is soon discovered that what the very elements of criticism would detect as palpable misinterpretations or mistranslations of the sacred text may be the most cherished vehicles of such doctrine, and powerful exciters of such feelings, criticism is laid aside, and the Bible becomes a kind of cipher, to be read not by reason but by fancy.

10. I am tracing here the ultimate development of false principles when left unchecked to their full operation. But, even in cases where no such extravagance was possible, we can perceive through a great part of the religious writings of the last generation a prevailing tendency to forget the aspect of *Fact*, and view only

the aspect of *Doctrine* in contemplating the truths of Christianity. Indeed, if we steadily retain in our minds the *historical* view of Christianity which is presented in the New Testament, and the primitive creeds, as a religion of Facts, it will be hard to grasp Mr. Coleridge's *dictum* as even a comprehensible utterance. It will immediately strike us as hardly intelligible to say, that the best way to convince a man that Jesus Christ was "conceived by the Holy Ghost; born of the Virgin Mary; suffered under Pontius Pilate; was crucified, dead, and buried; and the third day rose again from the dead;" is to make him sensible of a strong wish that these facts should have taken place. It would at once become plain that the religion which was to be proved by such a process must be something widely different from an historical religion.

11. While such causes as I have endeavoured to indicate were in England loosing men's hold upon the historical element in Christianity, other influences were operating at a greater distance towards the same result. The literature of Germany is eminently speculative and metaphysical. There the Governments have been accustomed to forbid, as dangerous to the public peace, the free discussion of those concrete matters relating to Church and State on which the popular mind with us is kept continually interested, and often agitated. The only scope for the activity of the human intellect in dealing with morals, religion, and politics, is in those high generalities where vulgar minds are unable to follow it. Literary men converse with, and write for, literary men, and feel no necessity to translate their thoughts into the common working-day language of ordinary life. Within the esoteric circle, one dialect is spoken; without it, another: and thus speculation is unchecked by that constant reference to the common sense of mankind which in freer countries curbs its extravagance.

These two circumstances—the encouragement of unlimited speculation within bounds remote from vulgar apprehension, and the repression of everything directly tending to agitate the mass of the people, or shake the institutions of the country—gave its peculiar character to German infidelity. The problem to be solved was, the substitution of metaphysical Pantheism for revealed religion, combined with a retaining of the structure and ordinances of the Church, together with the *language* of the Scripture and the Creeds, accommodated to the requirements of such metaphysics. The result has been truly described as a system which, "concealing scepticism under faith, using much circumlocution to reach its object, dwelling on the imagination, on poetry, on spirituality, transfigured what it threw into the shade, built up what it destroyed, and affirmed in words what in effect it denied." It was intended for a kind of EUTHANASIA of Christianity. Revelation was to die out, not amidst the insults of coarse assailants, but the compliments and tender regret of friends, and to leave behind it an honoured name and a conspicuous monument. GOD was to be merged in the Soul of the Universe: CHRIST in the Ideal of Humanity: THE INCARNATION in the union of the higher and lower principles of human nature; and THE ATONEMENT in the reconciliation of those principles through struggle and suffering. For the successful carrying out of such an enterprise, it was necessary to expel the miraculous from the documents of Christianity, without charging the authors of them with fraud or deliberate imposture: and this was attempted in two ways. The earlier project was to resolve the supposed miracles into a series of odd natural events, sometimes mistaken for supernatural by the excited fancies of the spectators. The later method proposed to turn almost the whole narrative, natural and supernatural, into a set of symbolical legends embodying the idea of the Jewish Messiah as modified by the necessity of adapting it to Jesus of Nazareth. Each of these—the naturalistic and the mythical theory—promised well at first; but each was soon found to labour under insuperable difficulties. Common sense revolted at last, even in the studies of German professors, against the clumsily elaborate explanations by which miracles were converted into natural events. A fresh hypothesis had to be made for each occurrence, and it was at last perceived that such a multitude of strange natural phenomena, crowded into the narrative of a few years, and gratuitously assumed for the mere purpose of evading the obvious meaning of the story, were really far more improbable than miracles themselves. On the other hand, the external evidence carried back the date of the sacred writings to an age when the true history of Jesus was so recent as to make it incredible that it should have been wholly smothered then by legends of a mere romantic character;* while the gravity, consistency, and perfect quietness of the style of those writings themselves made the attempt to turn them into mythical legends a task everywhere difficult in detail, and, in some cases, even ludicrously hopeless. Hence, to account for the historical phenomena of Christianity is still really an unsolved problem among German unbelievers. The plain direct account —that Jesus was the Son of God; that He died, and rose again; and sent His Holy Spirit to plant His Church in the world—is set aside by an *à priori* presumption against all miracles. But the historical evidence, the Books themselves, still remains a "stone of stumbling, and rock of offence," against which hypothesis after hypothesis is dashed to pieces.

The irreligious principles which thus, for a long time, infected the critical and philosophic and theological literature of the Continent, made it odious in England; and the policy at first acted on was to endeavour to exclude it altogether from the notice of the British public.† But such a policy was attended with greater evils than were likely to have ensued if things had been suffered to take their natural course. A great part, indeed, of the critical literature of Germany was

* Strauss, for example, is compelled to acknowledge that Luke, the author of the third Gospel and the Acts, was the companion, and most probably the disciple, of St. Paul.

† See some curious details in the Appendix to Goode's 'Life of Geddes.' The scandal occasioned by the translations of Schleiermacher, and even of Neibuhr, are matters of recent memory.

valuable in no sense whatever. Much of it was a mere succession of wild hypotheses,* springing up, like mushrooms, in the morning, and perishing at night, without leaving even a relic of their decay to manure the soil on which they had flourished. Much of it was the mere lost labour of a perverse diligence, and sinister ingenuity, like the fairy toil of the Gnomes and Kobolds in the fables of its own mines and forests. But so vast an amount of intense mental activity and unlimited research into all the recesses of learning, sacred and profane,—so free a questioning of everything; so various a combination of new ideas upon such a multitude of subjects,—could not but contain in it seeds of thought that might have usefully stimulated the natural indolence of our intellect at home. The mere love of Truth for its own sake is, in general, not sufficient to set men on work, and keep them at work. It is, to a great extent, the collision of thought, the pressure of difficulties, the agitation of doubts, that, by "troubling the waters," makes them yield their virtue. The culture of the mind is like the tillage of the soil—

"Pater ipse colendi
Haud facilem esse viam voluit, primusque per artes
Movit agros, curis acuens mortalia corda,
Nec torpere gravi passus sua regna veterno."

As it was, English scholarship seemed to have settled upon its lees; and we have scarcely ever had an age so barren of any great efforts as that of which we are now speaking.†

* "It is well known," says De Wette in the Preface to his 'Lehrbuch der historisch-kritischen Einleitung,' "that from the beginning.... the pernicious fondness for vain and arbitrary combinations and hypotheses has been brought into this department......... The burden of hypotheses under which Biblical introduction labours has been much increased in recent times." He takes credit for bringing *back* the history of the Septuagint version to the place in which *Hody* left it in 1704.

† I have purposely avoided any details of the reaction towards Church authority called the Tract Movement. It is certain that, so far from doing anything to revive the study of Christian evidences, some of the foremost leaders of that movement went even beyond the most violent ultra-Protestants in denouncing that study as dangerous; and ultimately encouraged men to "throw themselves" into a particular system, on the ground mainly of its affording scope to certain religious feelings, and gratifying certain religious tastes. This branch of the subject has been considered in the '*Cautions for the Times*.' (Parker and Son, London.)

12. But meanwhile men of leisure and curiosity, in the universities and elsewhere, disgusted with the tame and superficial monotony that prevailed around them, were repairing, as it were, in secret, to the fresh stores that had been opened on the continent of Europe. The very circumstance that this foreign literature was secluded from the vulgar gaze, and even a kind of contraband learning, gave it an additional charm. The adepts felt as if they had been initiated in some higher mysteries, and were disposed hughly to over-estimate the value of their attainments. Doubts and strange opinions which, if they had been freely expressed and ventilated in the fresh air and broad sunshine of public discussion, would have soon shrunk to their proper small dimensions, grew into giants in the shade, and over-mastered the minds that had been nursing them in secret. Then, gradually, the influence of the new opinions began to pervade the current literature of the country—not in plain and definite statements—that would have too rudely shocked the multitude, but sometimes in hints "vocal to the intelligent," sometimes in ambiguous language adapting to other purposes the religious phrases of the day, sometimes under a cloud of metaphysical jargon that bewildered the admiring reader. Thus it has come to pass that, without any open controversy, but silently, as it were, and "while men slept," the old matter-of-fact faith has died out in many minds, and religion has come to be regarded as an affair of sentiment, that should be disentangled, as soon as possible, from its historical elements.

13. It would not, I think, be very difficult to meet the patrons of such views, even on their own high philosophical ground. I think it would not be hard to prove that, even if we took the moral wants of man as the sole measure of religious truth, the Gospel which these persons preach is inadequate to meet the moral wants of man. We *require* not merely an ideal of human excellence, but to see that ideal *realized*; and to see further that the issue of that realization has been a triumph over all the ills of life, and over all the men-

aces of death. We require to be shown, *in fact*, that man can truly serve God, and that the end of that service is everlasting life. We *need* a basis of fact, an historical basis, for our religious faith; and without such a basis that faith is a mere castle in the air—a splendid vision, as practically inoperative to resist real temptation as every other ideal picture has ever proved.

But, after all, this would be only "answering a fool according to his folly;" and it is better to begin by protesting at once against the foundation of the whole theory. It is a mere delusion to fancy that man's supposed wants or his wishes are to be taken as either the major or the minor limits, or, indeed, as any measure at all, of religious truth. We cannot be justified in assuming that things exist because we seem to ourselves to want, or because we feel that we earnestly desire their existence; nor can we even be justified in disbelieving or disregarding the existence of things which seem to us superfluous, or unpleasant, or even noxious, if assured on good authority that they exist, and that it is important for us to take notice of their existence.

That man must, indeed, be a backward scholar in the school of nature who has not learned, even from his own experience, how little human wants and wishes are an evidence that the things wanted and wished for really exist. It is the common delusion of over-sanguine youth to fancy that we shall find in life exactly what we seem to require, and that circumstances will infallibly open for us those opportunities which are most suitable for the display of our talents, and the advancement of our fortunes. But how little does stern reality tally with these golden dreams of the inexperienced imagination! And shall we go on to the grave, trusting these promises of our own fancy, which every day is, with continually accumulated evidence, proving to be false?

It is not, if we are wise, to our wants and wishes that we trust, in the affairs of this world, as evidence that the means of remedying those wants, or gratifying those wishes, are in store for us; but to the proper evidence of matters of fact. And if we would find a solid basis for our *religious* faith, we must obtain for it also a similar foundation.

The truth is that we may see beforehand that the wants and wishes of a creature like man are boundless, and, in their very nature, incapable of being all gratified. All creatures are necessarily imperfect; and every imperfection is the *want* of some conceivable good; and every conceivable good is in itself *desirable;* and may, if we give the reins to our desire, become an object of our *wishes.*

> "Men would be angels, angels would be gods."

Nothing short of absolute, of infinite perfection can possibly supply all wants, and gratify all the wishes of an imperfect being, who fancies that he has only to wish strongly in order to obtain his object.

And equally vain is the notion that we may safely disregard everything that seems not suitable to our moral nature. Here, again, let us have recourse to that analogy which the great master of that argument has justly described as "the very guide of life." How ill would a child reason who should obstinately neglect every study, the use of which he could not himself discern! And, as to the things of another life, are we not all children? Shall we, who know not what an hour may bring forth,—we, whose wisest calculations and most sagacious foresight are perpetually baffled and brought to nothing in a moment by the changes and chances of even this short mortal life—shall we presume to take our own case for eternity into our own hands, and determine for ourselves what is sufficient for us to believe? The Almighty has taken us under His own care. He has promised us an inheritance of which we know little more than that it is a state of eternal holiness and happiness. He has engaged to prepare us for it here, and, for that purpose, has revealed to us those truths which He saw fitting for our discipline. Can we know so certainly how the character which He requires is to be formed, as to be able to correct the method which He has been pleased to employ? Do we know our spiritual diseases so well that we can safely reject the remedies which the Great Physician has prescribed for them? Are we, in this our state of infancy, so perfectly acquainted with all that is needful for our manhood that we can manage our own education, and determine the training by which we are to be reared for Heaven? If, indeed, the present life were the whole of each man's existence, if our only immortality were the immortality of the human race, there might be some specious ground for saying that we had now made such a survey of all our narrow domain, and gained such a knowledge of our capacities and implements, that we were at last entitled to be our own masters, and might trust to our own little skill and prudence in the management of our own little territory. But if a boundless and untried existence, beyond the limits of all our experience, really does lie before each individual hereafter, it is surely mere madness to neglect, in matters which concern that existence, the teachings of Him who alone knows the nature of that hidden world into which we are so blindly passing.

A prudent man, then, will not only inquire what it is that his heart seems to want, but also how far those wants are, in point of fact, supplied. He will not only consider what he wishes to be true, but what he has reasonable evidence for believing to be true. He will treat the truths of Religion as matters of fact, and seek for the appropriate evidence of matters of fact—that is, in other words, for historical evidence.

14. A religion disentangled entirely from all historical inquiries, and commending itself immediately to the mind by its mere intrinsic beauty and suitability to man's wants and wishes, may be a very captivating vision, and seems highly desirable on many accounts; but it is a gross abuse of words to call such a religion Christianity. Christianity is the religion which was taught by Christ and his Apostles; and it was certainly an historical religion—a religion made up of matters of fact, and propounded on the evidence of matters of

fact—which they promulgated. "That which we have heard and seen with our eyes, and our hands have handled of the Word of Life, declare we unto you," is the language of the first preachers of the Gospel; and the modern attempt to separate the ideal Christ, the type of the godlike in man, from the historical person, is not a whit less opposed to the genius of the Apostolic religion than was that teaching of the Gnostics against which the last of the Apostles raised his warning voice as the very spirit of Antichrist. The Christ of the Gnostics was an impalpable Æon; the Christ of their successors is something less substantial—an abstract idea.

Indeed, whatever may be the case with other religions, the Gospel certainly never made its way by first recommending itself to the conscious wants and wishes of mankind. It seemed, on the contrary, to contradict all man's expectations, and to outrage all their cherished feelings, and to cross all their desires. It was "to the Jews a stumblingblock, and to the Greeks foolishness." It is not until believed and acted upon that it gradually changes the temper and frame of mind into accordance with itself; it is like some of those tonic medicines which, at first, seem bitter and disagreeable, until the palate is accustomed to their taste, and the stomach braced and strengthened by their wholesome harshness.

It may, indeed, on the surface, seem strange that the Christian religion should be thus encumbered, as it were, by an apparatus of history; and that men should be required to investigate the evidence of past transactions in order to find a basis for their Faith, instead of merely consulting their hearts, and finding an *echo* there, to attest the divinity of its voice. But in this, as in other cases, we shall find, upon reflection, that what seems the foolishness of God, is wiser than men. The careful and candid investigation of the evidences on which Christianity rests—not for the satisfying a mere inquisitive curiosity, but to find truth for the regulation of our lives—is an eminently practical exercise of the understanding, and brings home the great facts of our religion *as facts* to the mind, with a feeling of their reality which the most highly raised efforts of the imagination cannot give them; and thus makes rational deliberate faith a counterpoise to the engrossing influence of sense. In the affairs of the world, we know that realities address themselves, in some shape or other, to the judgment; and that those that exclusively and immediately address the feelings and the imagination are unreal. If, then, the objects of religion entered only through this ivory gate of fancy into the mind, a steady practical faith in their reality could be hardly maintained. I say a *steady practical* faith; for, undoubtedly, if religion were a mere affair of feeling divorced from practice, or of practice divorced from motive, and reduced to the mere mechanism of custom, there might be something intelligible in discarding all investigation of evidence. Every one, even superficially acquainted with the structure of the human mind, is aware that the feelings may, as in the case of a novel or a play, be deeply interested and strongly excited, without anything but, at best, a sort of dim and transient belief in the reality of the objects which thus interest and excite them; and that, for such a purpose, scarcely anything more is necessary than that the mind should not, for the time, *attend* to their unreality. This suffices for mere feeling: but for action, a perfectly *sane* man requires more. He requires evidence as a ground of belief: and, even in an insane man,—where the fancy has become paramount, and established its throne upon the ruins of the understanding, close observers can generally detect a lurking suspicion of the deceitfulness of the mind's own visions,—an unsteady wavering flicker in the predominating persuasion, which betrays a difference of no small importance between rational and irrational belief; a secret sense of insecurity and weakness, which makes the mind of the madman, except in some high paroxysm of frenzy, succumb and quail before the calmer presence of a well-regulated intellect.

15. There is another use also served by this complication of religion with historical inquiry, which it is not unsuitable to notice. The essential connection of Christianity with the history of past ages makes a provision for the maintenance and advancement of civilization in every country in which Christianity prevails. It was this which made the preservation of learning possible when the great flood of barbarism swept over Europe, and the Church alone contained the sacred deposit of an earlier civilization—the memory of the past, and the hopes of the future. And it is this which is still a bulwark against barbarism. Barbarism is essentially that state of mind which is produced by placing it exclusively under the influences of a contracted *present* sphere of circumstances. It is, as Dr. Johnson justly said, "by making the past, the distant, and the future predominate over the present," that we are "advanced in the dignity of thinking beings." All history, more or less, renders this valuable service to the human mind; but it cannot be reasonably doubted that the history of the Church, in that view of it which the Bible presents, as one continuous body from the beginning of the world, is, of all others, the best fitted to render such a service. The idea of history, it has been truly said,* is that of the biography of a *society*. There must be, to constitute the narrative properly historical, an unity of action, interest, and purpose among the persons who are the subjects of it. Now, whether we consider the length of its duration, or the breadth of its extent,—the variety of its fortunes, or the unity of its purpose,—the diversity of its members in age, and character, and language, and manners, and habits of thought, and stages of cultivation, or the closeness of mutual relation into which all these seemingly scattered persons have been brought,—what other society can anywhere be pointed out which can form so noble and so useful a subject for the historian? It is the conception of the Church which enables the mind not only to combine, but to blend together, the pastoral simplicity of the primitive

* Arnold's Lectures on History.

times of mankind and the elaborate civilization of later ages;—to bring into one collection all the characteristics of all the climes and regions of the world;—to bring all specimens of the human family, "from the north and from the south, and from the east and from the west," and make them "sit down" before us "in the kingdom of God." Nor can I doubt that the peculiar strength, and freedom, and versatility of the modern European intellect are, to a great extent, due to the historical character of Christianity. No one can read, intelligently, so much as the prime documents of our faith, even in a vernacular translation, without feeling himself transported into a region where the modes of conception and of expression, the events and the institutions to be met with, are strikingly different from those which surround him with the associations of everyday life; without, in short, finding himself, for the time, emancipated from the mere influence of the present, and brought under that of the distant and the past. Nor could anything have secured such a potent and salutary influence to history over the human mind as the indissoluble tie by which it is connected with religion; the feeling that, in our nearest and most intimate relations, we are personally connected, as members of one body, with the remotest past and the illimitable future,—linked in one unbroken living chain, with patriarchs and prophets, and apostles and martyrs,—heirs with them of the same promise, and waiting with them for the same completion of the great mystery of God. And it is worth observing that Providence has so arranged matters, that the Eastern world—to which the language and habits of thought contained in Scripture were most familiar,—seems destined to receive back its lessons, modified by the peculiarities of Western civilization and European teaching. In those nations where the language of Christianity was, as it were, a *native* voice, it produced least influence at first as a source of permanent civilization. It was the leaven of *foreign* associations which caused a fermentation in the Western mind: and, from the blended mass which was the product of that fermentation, it seems destined to pass back to the realms from which it came, in a form fitted to produce there a similar effect.

In the same degree, then, as any system has a tendency to break the connexion between history and religion, in that same degree it tends to deprive civilization itself of one of its chief safeguards,—to withdraw from effective operation one of the most powerful causes which now stimulate research and bring the minds of the present generation into contact with those of the past. If the mind be referred immediately, for religious guidance, not to an historical document, but to a supposed infallible authority of the present Church, or to the supposed infallible authority of each man's fancy and feelings, the influences favourable to barbarism are so far restored: and I think the visible results of both experiments, so far as either has been consistently worked out, are such as to show that a retrogression towards barbarism would be their most probable consequence. To look only at the present—to live in the present—shape our habits by the present—adopt, at every change, the vogue of the day—and cast aside whatever we cannot accommodate to the taste of our own generation—this is to do our utmost to restore barbarity, and sink us below the level on which God and nature intended us to be placed. And hence we may find fresh reason for admiring the wisdom of the Divine economy which, in the case of the Jewish and of the Christian Church alike, withdrew, after a while, the living voice of inspired guides, and substituted for them, as the ultimate basis of faith, a written historical record of their teaching; thus building the Church, as a continuous body through all ages, on that foundation of the apostles and prophets, of which Jesus Christ Himself is the chief corner-stone.

16. But then it will be said,—"Is not Christianity a Gospel to be preached to the poor? and how are the mean and illiterate to judge of the historical evidences of Christianity?"

Now, undoubtedly, not in religious matters alone,

but in respect of almost every useful truth alike—moral, scientific, economical, political—the uneducated and ill-educated classes labour under peculiar disadvantages; and this, so far as it is a difficulty, is a difficulty upon every hypothesis which admits a benevolent Providence and recognises a difference between truth and falsehood.* The true lesson to be derived from the circumstance is, that we are bound, as far as we can, to raise the condition of our meaner brethren, and make them more and more capable of judging for themselves. Still, however, no doubt, great difference will continue to subsist: nor will it ever be possible to equalize all understandings, or make the opportunities and capacities of improvement the same for every mind. But each class must be contented, in this as in other cases, with such an amount of evidence as its circumstances will allow; and, if the upper classes would faithfully do their duty, this amount of evidence would not be small in any case.

Let it be observed that the form of this objection allows us to assume that Christianity is true; that it is capable of being proved true by rational evidence to well-informed persons; that, among men of literary attainments, it can hold its ground with the weapons of argument; that it needs not to fear any amount of light, or shrink from any examination however searching; and, assuming this, let us consider what the condition of the lower classes would have been, if the Church had faithfully done its duty. The Christian religion would then come before them as a religion manifestly subserving no interested temporal ends—encumbered with no artifices of priestcraft—notoriously based, from the first, upon the ground of rational evidence, and maintaining itself through all generations upon that ground alone,—open to all challengers, and ready at all times to give a reason of its hope to

* The difficulties attending the rejection of these being all the marks of design and benevolent intention in the structure of nature and the course of history.

every one demanding it;—and can it be said that this would not be good evidence to them of its truth; and evidence of the same kind as that upon which they must rely, from their circumstances, for the truth of almost everything of importance at all removed beyond the sphere of their own immediate experience?* It is the putting of Christianity upon other grounds; it is the claim of authority to silence doubt; it is the discouragement of inquiry, the contempt of reason, the depreciation of intellect in religious matters; it is the shrinking from light and correction, the suffering pure truth to be encrusted with prejudices and mistakes for fear of unsettling men's minds; it is the borrowing of the arts and language that are the common signs of imposture by the friends of truth, and leaving its own bold speech and open ways to its enemies; it is these unworthy methods that deprive the lower classes of the safeguards which, with such a religion, they might and ought to have for the security of their faith. The Providence of God has linked all classes together in mutual dependence, so that, "if one member suffer, all the members suffer with it;" and the Gospel cannot be preached to the poor, if the well-instructed scribes do not take the only measures by which it can possibly be preached with effect.

17. But, even of direct evidence, the amount is not slight that is within the reach of the humbler classes. There is much of most persuasive evidence of the truth of Christianity which not only requires no dialectical skill to make it felt, but which cannot be drawn out and stated in its full force by any amount of dialectical skill. Let any one consider with himself what the nature of the evidence is upon which he has formed his judgment of the characters of the persons with whom he converses in daily life. What a medley of slight traits, looks, gestures, chance expressions, little circumstances, each, perhaps, ambiguous in itself,

* See an interesting statement of the nature of the evidence within the reach of the lower orders, in Archbishop Whately's 'Easy Lessons' on the Evidences, pp. 23–27.

but all conspiring in one definite impression, will it appear! And all these he has gathered in and combined, not by a consciously logical process, watching for and sifting each scruple of evidence as it arose, and then deliberately putting them together, like a clever advocate to make a case; but unconsciously, and by a kind of instinct, the mind has drawn its inference from these little circumstances which he can remember, and from a thousand other evanescent phenomena which he cannot now recall. And yet all this evidence was *good* evidence, upon which he unhesitatingly relies.

Now such is the reasonable evidence which the Scriptures themselves yield to the candid and attentive reader, who is neither searching for proof nor watching for objections. It deposits, as it were, the practical persuasion of its own truthfulness and honesty by a thousand artless traits while we converse with its pages. "If we may judge," says Jackson, "of the truth of men's writings by their outward form or character, as we do of men's honesty by their looks, speech, or behaviour, what history in the world bears so perfect a resemblance to things done and acted, or yields (without further testimony than its own) so full assurance of a true narration?" [Works, vol. i. p. 27.] Men who never consciously framed a syllogism have felt, and are daily feeling, the force of such evidence. They are continually perusing the accounts of miracles so numerous and so striking that the witnesses of them could not be mistaken, and yet imbedded indissolubly* in a narrative so artless, so grave, so honest, so intelligent, as palpably to be no product of fraud or fancy; and, without any elaborate criticism or detailed process of deduction, their mind *takes* the impression which a book so circumstanced is naturally and reasonably fitted to impart. Thus many a mind that has scarcely ever felt a doubt, or heard of an infidel in

* "The miracles in the Bible," says Bolingbroke, "are not, like those in Livy, detached pieces that do not disturb the civil history, which goes on very well without them. . . . But the whole history is founded on them; it consists of little else; and if it were not a history of them, it would be a history of nothing."

Christian lands, has, in reality, based its faith upon rational evidence. Its belief has not been built amidst the noise of hammers and the ring of axes, but has grown up, "a noiseless structure," from the ground of an honest and true heart.

18. In some respects, indeed, the result of the unlimited development of critical inquiry abroad has been to diminish, rather than increase the difficulties of comparatively unlearned readers. Almost the only infidel theory which is quite intelligible to the lower orders, is that coarse one which treats the New Testament as a mere forgery throughout, or ascribes the origin of our religion to gross fraud and imposture. Now, if there be any certain result of German criticism at all, it has been to show that any such theory is utterly untenable. The Wolfenbüttel Fragments were almost the last shameful effort in that direction, and their track is a road which no one, with the smallest pretensions to literary character, would now venture to pursue. Countless other evasions of the plain force of evidence, each contradictory of the other, and each rejected with contempt by almost every one but its author, have been invented; but there is, except at Tübingen, no disposition to return to what may be called the old *orthodox* system of infidelity. To men of plain common sense, if they fully understood the whole state of the case, it would appear that all the premisses are granted which render inevitable an admission of the substantial truth of Christianity. Put, for example, Paul's undoubted Epistles, with Luke's Gospel and Acts, into the hands of a plain ordinary Englishman, and tell him, "It is no longer questioned that these letters are the genuine work of Paul; it is no longer questioned that the writer of the other Books was his companion, who compiled them while the men were still alive, who had conversed with Jesus, and seen him crucified; it is no longer doubted that Paul and Luke were sincere and honest men who had no design to impose upon their hearers; and the alternatives before you are either to admit that Christianity was really grounded upon

miracles, or to explain these documents by the methods of Paulus, or Strauss, or Weisse, or some other Naturalistic or Mythic Doctor;"—let this, I say, be the issue placed before an Englishman of ordinary common sense and information, and there can be little doubt that he would regard the first alternative as far less prodigiously incredible than the second. The case stands thus:

19. The origin of the Christian religion is not one of those events so distant as to be lost in a fabulous antiquity. Whatever gave rise to it occurred at a period of which we know a great deal, in a civilized world, and within historic times; and was something which enabled the first preachers to make more *converts* among *enemies* in five years, than our most active missionaries have made in five centuries. Within no long time after the death of Jesus we find Christian Churches diffused in the most distant places over this civilized world, continually growing in numbers and importance, under the eyes and in spite of the hostility of their powerful neighbours. The consentient tradition of all these Churches ascribes their foundation to the first Disciples of Jesus Christ, and ascribes to those Disciples the Gospel that He had been raised from the dead, and that this Resurrection, with its preceding and accompanying miracles, was the ground of their faith. Their creeds, their sacraments, their universal observance of Easter and the weekly Lord's day, all embody this tradition. These Churches are not without written historical records.* They put forward, with one consent, a body of documents, giving a detailed account of Christ's life, and death, and resurrection, and of the first preaching and fortunes of his Apostles, and embracing a collection of letters from some of those Apostles themselves. With respect to many of these writings, no literary

* "It is allowed," says Mr. Westcott, "by those who have reduced the genuine Apostolic works to the narrowest limits, that from the time of Irenæus [*i. e.* the latter part of the second century] the New Testament was composed essentially of the same books as we receive at present, and that they were regarded with the same reverence as is now shown to them."—*History of the Canon*, p. 8.

man of any character, at present, doubts their genuineness With respect to most of the rest, it is at any rate agreed that they are not mere forgeries of a late age, but books written in good faith, at a date when the true history of the times they refer to was easily to be obtained. The testimony of these documents is the same as the tradition of the Churches. They put the Christian religion upon the evidence of miraculous facts, and specially of Christ's Resurrection, as attested by the alleged witnesses of it, in the very place where He had been executed as a malefactor, and in the face of the very persons by whom He had been condemned and slain.

What we are called upon to believe is—that all the Churches were mistaken as to the grounds of their own faith; that all the documents, and the Apostles themselves, have given a wrong account of it; that the belief in the religion was not grounded on the belief in the miracles, but that the belief in the miracles was grounded on the belief in the religion; that Jesus, who (if He wrought no miracles and was the subject of no miracles) contradicted, in every circumstance of his birth, and education, and teaching, and life, and death, the best established and most cherished notions of all around Him concerning the promised Messiah, was believed, in spite of all, to be that Messiah; that miracles were ascribed to Him because the Messiah *ought* to have wrought miracles; that He was believed to have risen again because it suddenly occurred to somebody that He *ought* to have risen again; and that, by such an easy and intelligible process as this, a creed of fables was transmuted into a creed of facts, and stamped indelibly, and with one impression, upon the faith and institutions of the great Christian communities throughout the world.

This is, in plain words, the theory of the origin of Christianity corrected to the latest results of Continental criticism; and it seems to amount to this—that CHRISTIANITY HAD NO ORIGIN AT ALL. It is, indeed, not criticism that has spontaneously yielded these results; but it is the *à priori* prejudice against miracles which has forced criticism upon this strange enterprise.

20. Let any one take up (it is almost forgotten now in Germany, but may be still met with in England) Dr. Strauss's 'Life of Jesus,' and he will see at once that the author is all through merely working out a foregone conclusion. Not one of his orthodox predecessors in the seventeenth century ever set himself with more dogged resolution to fight his way through all difficulties in defence of the verbal inspiration, scientific accuracy, and textual integrity of every jot and tittle in the Hebrew Scriptures, and find a way, or make one, to the goal which he had determined to reach, than Strauss does to destroy it. And so with his successors; the very multitude and discordance of their theories is a witness to their insufficiency. They are the struggles of a strong animal in toils which he cannot break. The favourable posture for an infidel is that of an objector; when he is forced to recognise the necessity of having something positive on his own side, he finds his own difficulties greater than those over which he has been exulting in the case of his antagonists; and the end has been that, in Germany, thinking men are either returning to the faith of their fathers, or laying the detailed examination of the phenomena of Christianity aside as an insoluble problem. And in reality, the greater part of the panic which has lately spread among *us*, from the reappearance of the infidel controversy in England, has arisen from the security, the unhesitating acquiescence, of the previous generation. In the general silence of objectors, in the general recognition, which pervaded our whole literature, of the unquestionable truth of Christianity, men had ceased to reflect particularly upon the rational grounds of their faith. The authority of the Bible became a kind of axiom, and everything that was supposed to be involved in that authority was grasped with the same firmness of belief. In such a state of mind, the whole of its creed is no firmer than the weakest part; and hence, when open attacks began again to be made upon what men had

regarded from their childhood as essential portions of Christianity—when attention was called to the real difficulties which beset many passages, the undoubtedly strong objections which may be urged against many articles—when writers of learning and ability were quoted as authorities, not for, but against, the traditions of their youth—an alarm arose as if the whole of religion was giving way. This danger always attends the concentration of a whole system of belief upon a single point. It is like embarking a whole army at once, for a long and perilous voyage, in one gigantic transport. If the ship hold together, much is gained in speed and convenience; but if the vessel sink, all goes with her to the bottom.

It is thus with the Romanist, who builds all on the authority of the present Church. If one portion, however small or slight, of the complicated structure of his creed be shaken, the basis of it is shaken, and the entire edifice falls to ruin in a moment. And so, when the feelings of the reader have been made the test of the inspiration of Scripture;—when men have been accustomed to say, "We *feel*, from the echo in our bosoms, from the warm sentiments of devotion which it excites, from the sensible comfort that it gives, that this is and must be no less than the voice of God speaking with us;"—in such a case the decision of criticism against the genuineness or authenticity of a single book, or even of a single passage, becomes a thing formidable to the whole of faith. If the religious sense, on which the reader relies for distinguishing the divine from the human, have erred in any case, its assumed infallibility is gone; the test itself of inspiration is shown to be fallacious; and he is left doubtful whether the whole of his belief may not be founded on a mere delusion.

But a faith founded upon rational evidence is not liable to be thus shaken. If it be shown, for example, that a particular verse in the 1st Epistle of John, or even a long passage in his Gospel, is an interpolation, this does not subvert the proof of the genuineness of the rest of those pieces; since the evidence for the disputed parts, and the evidence for the rest of the documents, is not the same; and such a faith is grounded upon and proportioned to the evidence. And if the evidences of Christianity,—their nature and degrees,—and even the first elements of the criticism of our sacred books, were made an ordinary part of the instruction of every tolerably educated man, we should be free from those periodical panics which are a disgrace to the intelligence of a Christian nation.

As it is, when suddenly put upon searching the reasons of the faith that is in them, men hardly know at what point to begin, and in their confusion often seize first upon the weakest.

21. In dealing, either for the satisfaction of ourselves or of others, with sceptical objections, it is of vast importance to consider in what order they are to be dealt with. If we suffer ourselves to fall into the error of regarding each part of our position as equally strong in itself, the consequences may prove calamitous.

There are, for example, narratives of miraculous occurrences in the Bible, which, if we met with them separate from the rest, or connected with documents of a different character—if we found them in a life of Pythagoras or Apollonius—we should reasonably set aside as mere legendary stories, or exaggerations of purely natural events. It would be a grievous oversight to stake the truth of Christianity at once upon the separate defence of such passages as these. The reasonable course is to waive them at the outset;—to let them stand over for consideration in their due place;—and to consider, first of all, the most important and best circumstanced facts upon which the claims of Revelation rest. If these can be established, the others will either be not worth fighting about, or will follow as a matter of course. "Supposing it acknowledged," says Bishop Butler, "that our Saviour spent some years in a course of working miracles; there is no more presumption worth mentioning against His having exerted this miraculous power in a certain degree greater than in a certain degree less; in one or two more instances, than in one or two fewer; in this, than in another manner." (*Analogy*, part ii. c. 2.)

It is quite true—and should always be distinctly allowed—that nervous excitement, the strong tonic of a powerful faith and a lively imagination—perhaps also some subtle influence, such as animal magnetism—are capable of producing wonderful cures of some disorders; and that, if some of the narratives of miraculous cures in the Gospel and the Acts were all the miraculous narratives relating to the first planting of Christianity that we had, it might be reasonable to suppose the cures effected by some such agencies as these. But if other miracles remain which are incapable of any such solution, and sufficient to prove the claims of Christianity to a divine origin, then the natural explanations, even of the former, cease to be the more probable; because such natural effects as they assume, though possible, are more or less unlikely; whereas, there is no improbability in supposing that a person endowed with the power of miracles exerted it upon a particular occasion. It is improbable that any man ever lived in Greece of such strength as is attributed to Hercules; but if it were once established that such a person lived at a given time, there would be nothing improbable in any story of a particular exertion of that strength, merely on account of its surpassing the vigour of ordinary mortals.

Upon similar principles we should carefully avoid entangling the question of the general truth of Christianity with that of the nature or extent of the inspiration of the sacred writers. There are, indeed, some arguments for Christianity which tend to prove directly the inspiration, in some form or other, of those writers; as, for instance, that derived from the omission in their works of topics which men in their circumstances would *naturally* have introduced, an argument which has been pressed with great force by the Archbishop of Dublin in his first series of Essays.* But, in general, it is evident that our first concern with the sacred

* See also Bishop Hind's very valuable work on Inspiration.

writers is in their character of witnesses; and we should carefully distinguish in our minds the objections against their character as inspired persons, and objections against their character as trustworthy relators of facts. The question of the nature and extent of their inspiration legitimately comes in after the main facts have been established, which prove our Saviour's divine mission, and the promise of supernatural assistance which He made to His Apostles.

Some parts, indeed, of Scripture, such as the prophecies, claim inspiration directly, and on the face of them; and in the case of these, to disprove their inspiration is to disprove their trustworthiness.

But, meanwhile, in the interpretation of such writings, it cannot be reasonable to put out of sight the character which they claim, and insist upon expounding them as if they were not inspired at all.* This is a principle of criticism which is never forgotten, except in the case of Scripture. If the Christian revelation be really the completion of the Jewish—if Christ and His Church be really the development of the mystery of God, which was gradually wrought and prepared for in all the previous dispensations—and if the prophets of those dispensations really "spoke as they were moved by the Holy Ghost," it is no more unreasonable to give their lofty expressions a secondary reference to the coming glory than to find allusions to Augustus in the 'Æneid,' or to Elizabeth and Mary in the 'Faery Queen,' or to the Roman Republic in an ode to Horace's ship.† And, indeed, the very possi-

* See 'Charge of the Archbishop of Dublin,' 1861. Parker and Son, London.

† See Hurd on the 'Prophecies,' and Warburton's 'Divine Legation,' b. vi. "In the case of prophecies with a double sense," I have observed elsewhere, "we may be often sure of the secondary application of some parts of them, even though we may see clearly that other parts have no such application. . . . . Thus, for example, no one doubts that, in Spenser's Chronicle of Faery Kings (b. ii. c. x.), the following lines—

He left two sonnes, of which fair Elferon,
The eldest brother, did untimely die;
Whose emptie place the mighty Oberon
Doubly supplied in spousall and dominion, &c.—
He, dying, left the fairest Tanaquill
Him to succeed therein, by his last will.
Fairer and nobler liveth none this howre,
Ne like in grace, ne like in learned skill, &c.—

bility of such an interpretation—the continuity of thought, character, and plan, in a literature spread over so many ages, which makes it feasible—has ever struck thoughtful men, from Justin Martyr to Pascal, as strong evidence for the inspiration of that literature.

22. But to pursue these topics further would be only to repeat what has been a thousand times said already; and when infidelity comes to drop its reserve, and tell us plainly what the deep objections are that are now only hinted at in more or less doubtful forms of insinuation, it will most probably be seen that there is very little new matter to be produced in this great controversy, and that the Church is assailed in the nineteenth century with no stronger artillery than her walls have borne for eighteen centuries already. My earnest wish is, that those who think they can speak would speak out and let us know the worst.

ἐν δὲ φάει καὶ ὄλεσσον.

And if the literal truth of Christianity fall, it will certainly be a final and total subversion of the whole religion. Let no one suppose that its spirit can remain living and acting among us after its body has been decomposed. Its spirit will return to God who gave it. "That man," says one who was no narrow bigot, "who does not hold Christ's earthly life, with all its miracles, to be as properly and really historical as any event in history, and who does not receive all points of the Apostolic creed with the fullest conviction, I do not conceive to be a Protestant Christian. And as for that Christianity which is such according to the fashion of the modern philosophers and pantheists, without a personal God, without immortality, without an individuality of man, without historical faith, it may be a very ingenious and subtle philosophy, but it is no Christianity at all."*

No one, I say, doubts that these lines refer to Henry VIII. and Queen Elizabeth, though there is no consistent parallel between the succession of Faery kings and British monarchs."—*Note to Butler's Analogy*, p. 203.

To argue from the extravagant abuse of types and double senses against their existence, is like arguing that if we admit figures of speech in any writing, we cannot be sure that anything in it is literal.

* Niebuhr, quoted by Neander in the Preface to the 3rd edition of his 'Life of Christ.'

ESSAY III.

PROPHECY.

CONTENTS OF ESSAY III.

PROPHECY.

1. Hebrew prophecy, like the Hebrew people, stands without parallel in the history of the world. Other nations have had their oracles, diviners, augurs, soothsayers, necromancers. The Hebrews alone have possessed prophets, and a prophetic literature. It is useless, therefore, to go to the manticism of the heathen to get light as to the nature of Hebrew prophecy.* To follow the Rabbis of the twelfth and thirteenth centuries is just as vain. The only reliable sources of information on the subject are the Scriptures of the Old and New Testament. They contain documents written when the voice of prophecy still was heard, and it would be strange indeed to interpret coeval testimonies by theories devised by heathenized Rabbis,† nearly two thousand years after Hebrew prophecy had ceased. Even a novice in the study of the Bible perceives the falsehood of the Rabbinic assertions, that the prophetic gift dwells only in a man who is learned, powerful, and rich; and that no man can attain to it except by study, combined with a certain requisite mental conformation.‡ The attempt to explain prophetic inspiration by the phenomena of animal magnetism, seems to be still farther removed from sobriety of

* Vitringa, Typus doctr. prophet., in 'Observationes Sacræ,' lib. vii. p. 4; Carpzov, 'Introd. ad Libr. Bibl. V. T.,' Part iii., p. 7; Knobel, 'Prophetismus der Hebräer,' i. 21; C. I. Nitsch, 'System der Christlichen Lehre,' p. 88; Tholuck, 'Die Propheten und ihre Weissagungen,' p. 1, 73.

† Maimonides and his school, whom Smith and others follow, departed from the ancient tradition, and endeavoured to remodel Judaism according to the Greek philosophy with which they became acquainted through Arab translations. Maimonides himself is remarkable for his determined effort to eliminate the supernatural from the Old Testament, and may in truth be regarded as the father of Rationalist Theology.

‡ 'Doctor Perplexorum,' p. ii. c. 3. Buxtorf's Translation, p. 284; 'Hilchoth Yesode Hattorah,' c. vii.; Salvador, 'Institutions de Möise,' i. p. 192–197.

judgment, and Christian reverence.* From the Old Testament alone, illustrated by the New, is it possible to learn the nature of prophecy and the prophetic office. To interpret the prophetic writings with accuracy, a familiar acquaintance with the original language is necessary. But a correct idea of the prophet's work and office, and of the nature of prophecy in general, may be obtained from any ordinary translation of the Old Testament by any intelligent reader. The student of the English Bible may not be able to explain the meaning of a rare Hebrew word, or an obscure and doubtful passage, nor to perceive beauties and peculiarities, observable only in the original. He must also occasionally miss the force of particular expressions, and sometimes put up with an incorrect rendering. But he can, without any Hebrew, understand the character and history of Moses or Elijah, and know that Elijah foretold a drought, or Elisha a sudden plenty: that Micaiah was a true prophet, and the son of Chenaanah an impostor, just as easily and correctly as Gesenius, or Ewald, or Bunsen.

For this no modern criticism is necessary, and in such matters no reader of the Authorized Version ought to allow himself to be mystified or silenced by an appeal to foreign critics, much less to be disturbed in his faith, as if he could not apprehend the general teaching of the Bible without profound knowledge of the Semitic dialects, and the latest results of German criticism. All these things are good in their place, but the great and essential outlines of Divine truth, whether in reference to Deity, or piety, or morality, or prophecy, are perceptible without them; and it would be just as reasonable to assert that without these things we cannot understand the Ten Commandments, as to tell the

* "The word which we, after the LXX., translate *Prophets*, means in the Hebrew, *Inspired*. Their original designation was *Seers*, men who *saw*. Clairvoyance (the so-called magnetic sight) and prophesying in the ecstatic state were of remote antiquity amongst the Jews and their neighbours; and Joseph, a man of a waking spirit, who, as a growing youth, possessed a natural gift of second sight, was able as man to see visions in his cup, just as the Arab boy in Cairo still sees them in his bowl."—Baron Bunsen, *Gott in der Geschichte*, p. 141.

reader of the Bible in the vernacular, that he cannot grasp the scope of prophecy, or know whether it has been fulfilled, until he has spent years in the study of Hebrew and of modern commentators. The essential features of prophetic truth are too boldly drawn to be hidden by the veil of translation, and have been as plain and visible in all ages to the Greek, the Syrian, and the Arab, as to the polyglot critic of the nineteenth century. A knowledge of the Hebrew text, indeed, enables its possessor at once to reject such cavils as those lately revived,* that the Hebrew words in Ps. ii. 12 for "Kiss the Son," ought to be translated "Worship purely," or that the Hebrew word for "pierce," in Ps. xxii. 17 ought to be rendered "Like a lion," or that in Isaiah ix. 6. (Heb. 5), the words "Mighty God" ought to be "A strong and mighty one." But the English reader still sees from the context, in spite of these alterations, that the 2nd Psalm speaks of an universal King, greater than David, that the 22nd Psalm portrays one persecuted to death by man, delivered by God, after whose deliverance "All the ends of the earth remember themselves and turn unto the Lord," and that in Isaiah ix., the prophet speaks of a marvellous child, who is also "The Everlasting Father, of the increase of whose government there shall be no end, to order and establish his kingdom forever;" words amply sufficient to teach the reader that Isaiah spake of no mere man.† The Hebrew student is astonished, in the present state of Biblical learning, to see such objections resuscitated. He knows that the translation "Worship purely" was invented by Rabbinic controversialists; that the version "Kiss the Son" is defended even by such an opponent of Christianity as Aben Ezra amongst the Rabbis, and by De Wette amongst the Rationalists; and adopted by Moses Mendelssohn, Fürst, and his fellow translators, who have "Huldigt dem Sohne:"

* 'Essays and Reviews,' p. 68, 69.

† Luther, who translates "Kraft, Held," had no doubts as to the right interpretation of the passage

and that the ancient Jews interpreted this Psalm of the Messiah*—that the rendering "Mighty God" is adopted and defended by Hitzig and Knobel.† But, without depreciating the value of Hebrew learning and criticism, it may be safely asserted, that the nature and teaching of prophecy may be collected from any tolerable version: and, therefore, the Apostles, guided from above, did not perplex the Gentiles by discussing the differences between the LXX. and the Hebrew Text, but wisely used, and sanctioned the use of that Greek Version, which they found providentially prepared, already partially known amongst the heathen, and at that time regarded with reverence by the Jews. They understood how Divine Truth may be apprehended by the unlearned in a translation, and hidden from the wise and prudent with all their knowledge of the original.‡ With regard to Hebrew prophecy, there are three things equally perceptible in the original and in the versions, and at present specially requiring attention. These are:—the supernatural mission of the Prophets, their power to predict future events, and their announcements of a coming Saviour.

2. A prophet is a man specially called and sent by God to communicate a Divine revelation.§ This is apparent in the first place from the names given to those Divine messengers. They are called *Prophets*,

* This is confessed even by Rashi, in the 11th century, who says, "Our Rabbis interpreted this Psalm of the Messiah;" to which was added in the older copies of his commentary, "But in order to answer the heretics, it is better to interpret it of David," words still found in the commentary on the xxist Psalm.

† Knobel's reasons for rejecting the translation "strong and mighty one," are thus expressed:—"Because אֵל never occurs as an adjective, and if adjective, ought to be after גִּבּוֹר. The phrase אֵל גִּבּוֹר 'mighty God' occurs x. 21. Elsewhere also גִּבּוֹר is adjective to אֵל, as *e. g.* Deut. x. 17; Jer. xxxii. 18."—'Commentary on Isaiah,' p. 73.

‡ Matt. xi. 25.

§ Et huc forte respexerunt Patres ecclesiæ cum Prophetas Θεολόγους, *rerum divinarum consultos* dixere. Ita Pseudo-Dionysius, cap. 8, de Cœl. Hierarchia, p. 95. τῶν Θεολόγων εἷς, ὁ Ζαχαρίας, &c. . . . . . . in quem locum ita commentatur Pachymeres, p. 104. τοὺς ἱεροὺς προφήτας Θεολόγους φησὶν, ὡς λόγους Θεοῦ ἡμῖν ἐξαγγέλλοντας. Carpzov, 'Introd. ad Lib. Bibl. V. T., Part iii. p. 4.'

seers, *men of God*, *men of the Spirit*. The Hebrew word for *prophet* (Nabi) is, according to its etymology, supposed by some to signify "an inspired person;" by others, with more probability, "An utterer or announcer." * Its meaning, and that of the English word *prophet* as used in the Old Testament, are fully explained by a comparison of two passages, in the book of Exodus: the first, vii. 1, "See I have made thee a God to Pharaoh, and Aaron thy brother shall be thy prophet." The second, iv. 16, "And he shall speak for thee (A. V. be thy spokesman), and thou, thou shalt be to him for a God." What is *prophet* in the first is *mouth* in the second. Moses was to be as God to Aaron, Aaron as prophet, or mouth, or spokesman to Moses; Moses to communicate to Aaron, and Aaron to declare the message to Pharaoh and the people. According to this, *prophet* means the declarer or interpreter of the Divine will. He is one who does not speak *of himself* (ἀφ' ἑαυτοῦ), the workings of his own mind, but declares the mind and will of God, and speaks what he receives from without.†

3. The title "Seer"‡ refers rather to the mode of receiving the Divine communication than to its utterance to others. It is derived from Numb. xii. 6, "If there be a prophet among you, I, the LORD, will make myself known to him in a vision (sight, מראה)." The *Seer* is therefore one who receives a Divine communication in a vision. His vision is not the offspring of his own mind, but the LORD makes himself known (התורע)

* Carpzov, 'Introd. ad Lib. Bibl. V. T.,' Part iii., p. 3. See Gesenius, 'Thesaurus;' Winer's edition of 'Simonis Lexicon;' Knobel's 'Prophetismus,' i. 103; Bleek, 'Einleitung in das alte Testament,' p. 412; Tholuck, 'Die Propheten und ihre Weissagungen,' p. 24.

† Heidegger says, "נביא proprie est omnis verborum alienorum, ex alieno, non proprio nutu et voluntate pronunciator, orator, qui, ut R. D. Kimchi loquitur, Echo ad instar, nihil profert aut profatur, nisi quod prius accepit." 'Exerc. Bibl.' viii. § 27. Augustine, "Nihil aliud esse Prophetam Dei, nisi enunciatorem verborum Dei hominibus." Carpzov, ibid., p. 8. Comp. Spinoza, 'Tractat. Theolog. Polit.' c. 1, who is, with regard to prophecy, more candid than the Essayists.

‡ For this there are two Hebrew words used, but which are equivalent in sense. They are both found in Isai. xxx. 10, "which say to the Seers (ראים) see not, and to the prophets (lit. Seers, חוזים) prophesy not (see not) unto us."

to the prophet. It is something received from without. "Her prophets also find no vision *from* the LORD (מיהוה)" (Lam. ii. 9). But the word "vision" does not necessarily imply ecstasy or symbolic representation. It is often equivalent to "The word of the LORD," as, in 1 Sam. iii. 1, "The word of the LORD was precious in those days; there was no open vision (חזון)." Samuel was a *Seer*, but "the LORD revealed himself to Samuel by the word of the LORD" (1 Sam. iii. 21). So the first chapter of Isaiah, which is destitute of all symbolic imagery, is called "The vision (חזון) of Isaiah;" whilst the second chapter has as its title, "The *word* that Isaiah, the son of Amos, *saw* (חזה)."*

4. The designation "man of God," also implies intimacy, communion with God, or commission from Him, as the similar phrases, "men of David," "men of Hezekiah," meant those who were in attendance on those monarchs, whom they employed; and, in this sense, the prophets are called "the servants of Jehovah," and "the messengers of God" (2 Chron. xxxvi. 16).

5. The phrase "man of the Spirit, רוח" (Hos. ix. 7), explains the agency by which the communication came, namely, by the Spirit of God; as St. Peter says, "Prophecy came not at any time by the will of man, but holy men of God spake, being borne away (φερόμενοι) by the Holy Ghost" (2 Pet. i. 21). The Old Testament also makes this impetus of the Spirit the essence of prophecy. In Numb. xi. is related the appointment of the seventy elders to assist Moses. The Lord says, "I will take of the Spirit which is upon thee, and will put it upon them;" and, accordingly, in the 25th verse, it is said, "The Lord came down in a cloud, and spake unto him, and took of the Spirit that was upon him, and gave it to the seventy elders; and it came to pass that when the Spirit rested upon them, they prophesied and did not cease." In like manner, with regard to Eldad and Medad, "The Spirit (הרוח) rested upon them . . . and they prophesied in the camp."

* Comp. Ps. lxxxix. 20; Amos i. 1; Obad. i. 1; Hab. ii. 2, 3; Nahum, i. 1.

That which caused these two men, as well as the seventy elders, to prophesy, was the resting of the Spirit upon them, and, therefore, Moses makes this resting of the Spirit equivalent to the gift of prophecy. "Would God that all the Lord's people were prophets, and that the Lord would put his Spirit upon them." * From this passage alone we learn, 1st, That it is the resting of the Spirit of the Lord upon a man that makes that man a prophet. It was not the spirit of Moses, but the Spirit that was upon Moses, that was given to the seventy elders, that which Moses himself calls "the Spirit of the Lord." We learn, in the next place, that it is the Lord who gives the Spirit. Moses was not able to confer it, and it was given altogether independently of Moses to the two men, not present at the tabernacle. The persons upon whom it was conferred, did not choose themselves, and did not take the gift by their own will. Similar instruction is derived from the history of Saul. Samuel (1 Sam. x. 6) said to him, "The Spirit of the Lord will come upon thee, and thou shalt prophesy with them . . . . and when they came thither to the hill, behold, a company of prophets met him, and the Spirit of God came upon him, and he prophesied among them." It does not appear that he had any previous qualifications, or preparations, or training, as required by Maimonides; nor yet his servants (1 Sam. xix. 20), of whom it is said, "The Spirit of God was upon the messengers of Saul, and they also prophesied." And so, when he came himself on that occasion, certainly in no pious frame of mind, the Spirit came on him also, and he, like his messengers, prophesied involuntarily. They were *φερόμενοι,* borne away by the Holy Ghost, just as the wicked Balaam prophesied when "the Spirit of God came upon him," and Caiaphas unwittingly uttered a Divine oracle concerning the vicarious death of the Lord. "And this spake he not of himself, *ἀφ' ἑαυτοῦ,* but being High Priest that year, he prophesied" (John xi. 51).†

* Compare Joel ii. 28. In the Heb. Text, iii. 1.

† Comp. 2 Sam. xxiii. 2; 1 Kings, xxii. 24; 2 Chron. xxiv. 20; Isai. lxi. 1; Jer. i. 9; Ezek. xi. 5; Joel ii. 29; (Heb. iii. 2); Mic. iii. 8, &c., &c.

6. This view is confirmed by the Scripture contrast of the false prophet. He is described as one who is not sent by the Lord, and who has not the Spirit of God, but speaks out of his own heart his own imaginations. "They speak a vision of their own heart, and not out of the mouth of the Lord; I sent them not, nor commanded them."* "They prophesy out of their own hearts—they follow their own spirit, and have seen nothing. They have seen vanity (שוא) and lying divination, saying, The Lord saith; and the Lord hath not sent them; and they have made others to hope that they would confirm (fulfil, לְקַיֵּם) the word."† And, therefore, even the Great Prophet of the Church dwells frequently upon the fact that He is sent, and that His doctrine is not His own. "My doctrine is not mine, but His that sent me. If any man will do His will, he shall know of the doctrine, whether it be from God, ἐκ τοῦ Θεοῦ, or whether I speak of myself, ἀπ' ἐμαυτοῦ. He that speaketh of himself, ἀφ' ἑαυτοῦ, seeketh his own glory."‡ As, therefore, a true prophet is one who is sent by God, who runs not of himself, upon whom the Spirit of God rests, who speaks the word of God and not his own; and as there were pretenders, whom God did not send, whose words were not inspired by His Spirit, a test, whereby one could be distinguished from the other, was necessary both for the satisfaction of the prophet himself, and for the protection of the people from imposture. To have been trained in the schools of the prophets (for a time there were such schools §) was not enough to constitute a man a prophet. The prophetic commission could not be given by the schoolmaster, nor could the doctrines of men, or their instruction, communicate a Divine message, so as to

* Jer. xxiii. 16, 21, 32, and xiv. 14, &c.

† Ezek. xiii. 2–9.

‡ John vii. 16–18; comp. Isai. lxi.

§ "Concerning the origin, arrangements, and duration of the so-called schools of the prophets, no detailed or circumstantial information is found in the Old Testament. Schools of the prophets are mentioned only in the histories of the prophets Samuel, Elijah, and Elisha, that is from 1100–900, which period must therefore be regarded as the time of their existence." Knobel, *Prophetismus*, ii. 39, 50. What imaginative historians have written on this subject is, therefore, of little value.

make the speaker's word the word of the Lord. Neither Deborah nor Huldah had thus received the prophetic call. Indeed, it does not appear that any of the great prophets had been trained in those schools. Nothing less than an outward, clear, unmistakable call of God could satisfy the mind and conscience of the prophet himself. Neither inward persuasion, nor dream, nor ecstasy, was in itself sufficient. Moses was awake and in full possession of all his faculties when he saw a bush burning but not consumed, and heard the voice of the God of Abraham, and Isaac, and Jacob. Samuel thought that Eli called, and went twice to the aged priest, before he knew that it was the Lord's voice; and was, therefore, fully roused from slumber before he received the Divine message. Isaiah's eyes were opened to see the Lord on his throne, and his ears to hear the words "Whom shall I send, and who will go for us?" Jeremiah objected his youth, and did not accept the commission until the Lord put forth his hand and touched his mouth. Ezekiel felt that "the hand of the Lord was upon him." Amos was a herdsman, and a gatherer of sycamore fruit, and the Lord took him "as he followed the flock," and said, "Go, prophesy unto my people Israel." There was a supernatural call. A specific message, also, was delivered, and therefore the prophet was able to say, "Hear ye the word of the Lord," "Thus saith the Lord." Even after this external and supernatural call, every time the prophet uttered a new oracle, it was the result of a new communication, and a special command. He was still unable to prophesy at will. He might inquire of the Lord and ask counsel, as Moses did in the case of the Sabbath-breaker, or of Zelophehad's daughters, but had no permanent habilitation to declare the will of God. Without this supernatural call, and without this specific message, no one can, according to Scripture idiom, without great confusion of mind, or wilful and dishonest abuse of language, be said to possess anything like prophetic inspiration. The Apostles of the New Testament, called directly by the Lord Jesus Christ, moved by His Holy Spirit, and entrusted with a specific message, were and may be called prophets in the true sense of the word, for they were able to affirm that the Gospel proclaimed of them was "not of man, but by revelation of Jesus Christ;" and they communicated it "not in words, which man's wisdom teacheth, but which the Holy Ghost teacheth." But to speak of Poets, ancient or modern, or Philosophers, or Lawgivers, as being inspired, like Moses or Isaiah, is simply to confound things Divine and human, and to manifest great mistiness of apprehension, or daring profanity of spirit. It is just as contrary to Scriptural statement,* and as revolting to Christian reverence, as to identify the prophetic character and calling with that of the demagogues of Greece.† Poets and Philosophers exercise the high natural gifts bestowed by God, according to the movings of their will or the impulse of their genius; apply, and sometimes abuse them, according to the state of their hearts; but do not pretend to any external call from God, nor claim for their words the reverence due to the word of the Almighty. The Hebrew prophets announced themselves as God's messengers, claimed obedience and reverence for their message as the word of God, and therefore carried with them credentials for the satisfaction of the people. These credentials were, according to the Hebrew Scriptures, *miracle* and *prediction*.‡ To accredit Moses as His messenger to the children of Israel, He empowered him

* "At quamvis scientia naturalis divina sit, ejus tamen propagatores non possunt vocari prophetæ."—Spinoza, *Tractat. Theolog. Polit. Opera*, tom. iii. p. 16.

† Leo 'Vorlesungen,' 159, 168; Berlin, 1828; Salvador, as above, p. 197.

‡ This is admitted even by D. F. Strauss: "To accredit his Divine mission to the people, God enabled Moses to perform certain acts beyond ordinary human power; and Moses refers to this to prove that he did not come of himself but was sent by God. . . . . Hand in hand with *miracle, prediction* appears in Biblical history as a credential of Revelation. Thus in the Old Testament God gives Moses a prediction, the fulfilment of which should certify his Divine mission (Exod. iii. 12). . . . . In the case of the prophets the occurrence of wonderful events which they had predicted is the proof of their Divine commission (1 Kings xvii. 1, xviii. 41, &c.). The prophets also, not rarely, foretell the occurrence of some event, soon to happen, that its occurrence may be a sign, that what they have predicted concerning the distant future is from God (1 Sam. ii. 34, x. 7, and 1 Kings xiii. 3, 2 Kings, xix. 29; Isai. vii. 2; Jer. xliv. 29)."—*Glaubenslehre*, vol. i. p. 86–89.

to make three superhuman manifestations of power, saying, "If they will not believe thee, neither hearken to the voice of the first sign, that they will believe the voice of the latter sign." And therefore the prophet like unto Moses, also appealed to His works as greater testimony than that of John the Baptist,* and says, "If I had not done among them the works which none other man did, they had not had sin, but now have they both seen and hated both me and my Father." The Law of Moses also provided another criterion of a true or false prophet, in the fulfilment or non-fulfilment of his word, "When a prophet speaketh in the name of the Lord, if the thing follow not, nor come to pass, that is the thing which the Lord hath not spoken" (Deut. xviii. 22). To this Jeremiah alludes when he says, "The prophet which prophesieth of peace, when the word of the prophet shall come to pass, then shall the prophet be known, that the Lord hath truly sent him" (Jer. xxviii. 9).

7. To declare the will of God, and deliver His message, whether it regarded the past, the present, or the future, was the prophet's great duty. And therefore, when the Jewish lawgiver was communicating moral or ceremonial precepts, received from God, and when the Messiah, in his Sermon on the Mount, was explaining the spirituality of the Law, they were, in the strict sense of the word, *prophesying* just as much as when Moses predicted the destinies of Israel, and the Lord foretold the destruction and treading down of Jerusalem. To have received a call and message direct from God, and to deliver it, constituted the essence of prophetism. But if we are to form our idea from the Scriptures, we must admit that the Hebrew people believed that the prophets were endowed with, or could attain to, superhuman knowledge, for the benefit and advantage of His people. This belief was rooted in their conception of the Divine character. Whether we take the Hebrew Scriptures as inspired or not, it is an incontrovertible fact that the fundamental idea of the Hebrew religion

* John xv. 24; comp. Matt. xi. 1–5.

is that Jehovah is a God who reveals Himself to his creatures; that He has not left the human race to grope their way to the regions of religion or morality as they best can, but that from the beginning He has taken His children by the hand, cared for their welfare, made known to them His will, and marked out for them the way to happiness. This idea runs through all the books of the Old Testament,—Law, History, Psalms, Prophecy,—and is taken up in the New Testament, where is the fullest revelation of the love of our Heavenly Father to man. But the Hebrew believed not only in God as one who reveals Himself for the benefit of the race, but as the loving and watchful Father, who superintended all the everyday concerns of each individual, and who, though He dwelt in the high and holy place, yet had regard to the lowly, and considered nothing too small or insignificant for His care. This is evident in the prayer of Abraham's servant to be guided to Rebekah, in the increase of Jacob's cattle, in Leah's fruitfulness, in the answer to Hannah's prayer, not to mention many similar and well-known traits in the lives of God's ancient saints. As, therefore, the Hebrew people, high and low, regarded the prophet as a messenger from God, enlightened and instructed by the Holy Spirit, they ascribed to him a supernatural knowledge and the power to give information not attainable by human reasoning or sagacity —in fact the same power possessed by the High Priest of procuring from God a miraculous response by means of the Urim and Thummim: and as they believed in God as their Father, they trusted that He was interested in all their troubles and anxieties, and would not consider their temporal concerns too insignificant for His gracious consideration. Hence it is recorded that Rebekah went to inquire of the Lord respecting the subject of her anxiety. David inquired of the Lord, by means of the ephod, whether he should smite the Philistines and save Keilah; and again, whether the men of Keilah would deliver him into the hands of Saul; and received answers from the Lord. So Saul's servants thought they might go to Samuel and inquire concerning the lost asses. In like manner King Jehoshaphat wished to inquire of the Lord, by means of a prophet, before he ventured into the battle against the Assyrians. And again, when he and Jehoram were in difficulties from want of water, he asked, "Is there not a prophet of the Lord here that we may inquire of the Lord by him?" Even ungodly men like Zedekiah (Jer. xxi. 2, and xxxvii. 17), and the elders of Israel (Ezek. xiv. 1—7), or heathens like king Benhadad (2 Kings, viii. 7, 8, &c.), believed in this power, and were glad, when occasion required, to avail themselves of it. And there is not only no intimation that they erred in making such inquiries, but Joshua and the men of Israel are represented as having done wrong because they made peace with the Gibeonites, and "asked not counsel at the mouth of the Lord" (Josh. ix. 14). And when Ahaziah sent to Ekron to inquire of Baal-zebub, "the angel of the Lord said to Elijah the Tishbite, Arise, go up to meet the messengers of the King of Samaria, and say unto them, Is it not because there is not a God in Israel that ye go to inquire of Baal-zebub, the god of Ekron?" Indeed, some Christian commentators of great name, as well as some of the Rabbis, think that in the Law God has made special provision for this sort of inquiry when He forbids them to be diviners or consulters with familiar spirits, and promises them a prophet like Moses to reveal His will (Deut. xviii. 10—19). It is certain that Isaiah insists on the duty of inquiring of the Lord when he says, "And when they shall say unto you, Inquire of the familiar spirits, and of wizards who peep and mutter: Should not a people inquire of their God? For the living, should they inquire of the dead?" (viii. 19.)*

In some of the cases just mentioned inquiry is made respecting the future, and it is evident that David and

* Lowth, and after him, Knobel, translate the last clause, "Instead of the living [God] should they inquire of the dead [idols?]," but contrary to the parallelism. The prophet is remonstrating against the practice of inquiring of the spirits of departed men. אוב is the spirit of a dead man, and therefore מתים must refer to something similar.

Jehoshaphat, as well as Zedekiah, believed that through the priest or the prophet they could receive from God, respecting contingencies, answers which the Divine prescience could alone supply; that is, that through the Divine help the priest or the prophet could predict future events. This faith rested upon the doctrine of God as taught in the Law, and exemplified in the whole of their previous history. Before there were prophets God Himself predicted the future. The announcement of the flood to Noah and the limitation of the day of grace to 120 years* are predictions. Noah knew the future of the human race, and by the Divine instruction was enabled to provide against the coming calamity. The declaration, at a time when Abraham was childless, that his posterity should be afflicted in a strange land for 400 years, but that their enemies should be punished and they come forth with great wealth, was clearly a prediction. Jacob is represented as having on his death-bed predicted what should befall his posterity "in futurity of days" (באחרית הימים). Joseph's interpretation of Pharaoh's dreams was a prediction of the seven years of plenty and of famine, and came from God as well as the dreams. "What God is about to do he showeth unto Pharaoh" (Gen. xl. 28). It is recorded of most of the prophets mentioned in the historic books that they uttered predictions. Deborah foretold the fate of Sisera. The man of God announced to Eli the judgments coming upon his family, and the death of his sons in one day. Samuel confirmed this prediction and declared its certain fulfilment, and it is remarked "that the Lord let none of his words fall to the ground. And all Israel, from Dan to Beersheba, knew that Samuel was accredited (or verified נאמן) for a prophet to the Lord." Micaiah foretells the defeat of the allied armies of Judah and Israel, and rests his prophetic pretensions upon the fulfilment of what he had an-

* The words "Yet his days shall be 120 years" do not refer to a diminution of the long life of the antediluvians, nor to the subsequent measure of human life, but to the length of the day of grace, given them to repent. Such is the interpretation of the Targums, Luther, Calvin, and many of the best modern commentators. See Delitsch on Genesis, p. 237, 8.

nounced. "If thou return at all in peace, the Lord hath not spoken by me. And he said, Hearken, O people, every one of you." Elijah predicted that there should be no rain but according to his word, the death of Jezebel, the extermination of Ahab's posterity. Elisha foretold the overthrow of the Moabites, the three defeats of the Syrians. All these things, as well as the birth of Josiah, and the continuance of Jehu's posterity on the throne of Israel to the fourth generation, are related as predictions, in the ordinary sense of the word, —as supernatural communications from the Lord, and the fulfilment specially noticed.

It may indeed be said, and has been said, that these predictions and the narratives connected with them are mythical narrations, written after the events when the historic substrata had had time to be transmuted into the supernatural. But that, if true, would not alter the fact that the Hebrews believed in the power of the prophets to predict events by supernatural aid from on high; that this belief is inseparably connected with their ideas of the Divine Being, and everywhere visible in the historical books from Genesis to Nehemiah; in fact that the power of predicting future events is one of the essential features in the character of a prophet. And as it is incontrovertibly a part of the popular belief, so it is the doctrine of the prophets themselves, as recorded in their writings. It is hardly possible to open a page of any book of the prophets on which there is not a prediction. "By far the greatest portion of the prophetic discourses consists in delineations of the future, or predictions referring partly to the Jehovah people, and therefore to the kingdoms of Israel and Judah, partly to foreign nations who came in contact with the Hebrews, ... partly to individuals of the former, seldom of the latter."* Amos lays it down as an axiom that the Lord reveals to the prophets his purposes before they are realized. "Surely the Lord God will do nothing, but he revealeth his secret (סודו) to his servants the prophets." (Amos iii. 7.) Upon

* Knobel's 'Prophetismus,' i. 293.

which, Hitzig says: "The prophet predicts the coming evil, which is always an ordinance of Jehovah; for Jehovah makes him acquainted beforehand with that which He has decreed." Isaiah makes the prediction of future events a distinguishing characteristic and prerogative of Deity, and therefore a proof that the God of Israel is the true and living God. "Remember the former things of old: for I am God and there is none else: I am God, and there is none like me. Declaring futurity (אחרית) from former time, and from ancient times the things that are not yet done" (xlvi. 9, 10); upon which words Knobel thus comments: "The better view consists in the knowledge that Jehovah, and none besides, is God, that He is God and nothing like Him. To this view they can easily come by remembering the former things, that is, the prophecies formerly given, which are now being fulfilled (xlii. 9). These prove Jehovah's foreknowledge, and thereby His Godhead." In like manner Isaiah makes the want of predictions amongst idolaters a proof that their gods are no gods. "Produce your cause, bring forth your strong reasons, saith the King of Jacob. Let them bring them forth, and show us what shall happen: Let them show the former things what they be, that we may consider them and know the latter end of them; or declare for us things for to come. Show the things that are to come hereafter, that we may know that ye are gods" (xli. 21–23); where Gesenius says, "A new challenge to the idols as in verse 1, &c., again with a reference to Cyrus, but also with a reference to former predictions of the prophets, such as the heathen had none to show." Knobel's words are still stronger: "Let them bring forth their proofs, especially that one which rests upon correct prediction of the future; for the foreknowledge of the future is the peculiar attribute of God, and proves Deity, on which account it was also the credential of the true prophet. (Deut. xviii. 21. Jer. xxviii. 9.) And, on the contrary, the idols never were able, nor are they now, to announce the future. They should declare the things to come hereafter, that is, what should afterward happen, and Jehovah will see and recognise that they are gods, namely, when their prediction is accomplished." In these places, and many more, it is taught that Jehovah gives predictions to His servants the prophets, and also that He fulfils them. "He confirmeth the word of His servants, and performeth the counsel of His messengers" (Isai. xliv. 26); that by so doing He proves not only that the prophets are true prophets, but that He Himself is the true God. We have in fact the same proof of the truth of Divine Revelation that has been urged in modern times from fulfilled prophecy, and which has the highest possible sanction in the words of our Lord, "And now I have told you before it come to pass, that when it is come to pass ye might believe." (John xiv. 29: comp. xiii. 9, and xvi. 4.)

8. It is evident that the Hebrew people believed that their prophets could predict the future. The prophets themselves affirm that they have the power and utter predictions. Were they impostors, or did they deceive themselves? That they were impostors, is not believed by those Rationalists who have given most attention to this subject, as Gesenius, Ewald, and Knobel, and is disproved by their doctrine and their life. Concerning God they teach that He is One, the Lord, Creator of the heavens and the earth, Everlasting, Almighty, Omniscient, Free, All wise, Holy, a righteous Judge, a merciful Saviour, the Governor of the world, forgiving iniquity and sin.* Their notion of the religion acceptable to Him is also equally free from fanaticism and formality. They denounce those who "draw near to God with their lips, but remove their heart far from Him." They teach that to reform the life is better than external demonstrations. "To what purpose is the multitude of your sacrifices? . . . Wash you; make you clean; put away the evil of

* See Isai. xl. 28, xliv. 6; Jer. x. 10, xxiii. 23, 24; Isai. xiv. 24, 27; Jer. xxxii. 19, xvii. 10; Hab. i. 13; Mal. ii. 10; Isai. lxiv. 8; Jer. xi. 20; Joel ii. 13; Mic. vii. 18; Dan. ii. 28; Ezek. xxxi. 9; Amos iii. 6; Ezek. xviii. 4; Hos. xiii. 14, &c., &c.

your doings from before mine eyes; cease to do evil, learn to do well; seek judgment, relieve the oppressed; judge the fatherless; plead for the widow" (Isaiah i. 11—17). "I will have mercy, not sacrifice." They proclaim that honesty, mercy, and humility are the weightiest matters of the Law. "What doth the Lord require of thee, but to do justly, and to love mercy, and to walk humbly with thy God?" (Mic. vi. 8.) To preach such doctrine was their business; and boldly to reprove all who lived in opposition to it, whether kings, or priests, or people, was their practice, and this without fee or reward, for they received nothing for their prophesying, but often exposed themselves to persecution and death. They sought not wealth, or honour, or favour, or ease. They were temperate, self-denying, patient, valiant for the truth, leaning upon God as their stay, and looking to God alone for their reward. They were neither morose ascetics, nor unlettered fanatics. Married and living amongst the people, in cottages and in courts, they discharged the ordinary duties of citizens. They cultivated letters, and have left a literature unique in the history of the world; if judged according to a human standard, unsurpassed in genius, sublimity, grandeur; but in purity and morality unequalled by any nation in any age. This prophetic order beginning, if reckoned from Samuel, nearly 400 years before the birth of Rome, and closing when the bloom of Grecian genius was only appearing, is, when compared with the state of the world around them, a phenomenon as wonderful as the power of prediction which they claimed. The best days of Greece and Rome can furnish no heroes, patriots, or moral teachers to compare with this long and wonderful succession of holy, disinterested, bold reprovers of vice and preachers of virtue, unambitious examples of genuine patriotism, living for the glory of God, and the good of man; whose writings are so imbued with imperishable and universal truth, that for nearly twenty-four centuries after the death of the last of the goodly fellowship, they have continued and still continue to touch the hearts, and influence the faith, the thoughts and lives of the wisest, greatest, and most excellent of the human race. That such men could be deceivers, or that imposture could have exercised a power so enduring, is impossible. That they could have been self-deceiving enthusiasts is equally incredible. Neither their doctrine, nor their lives, nor their writings savour of enthusiasm, nor can they be accounted for as mere ebullitions of genius. Why did not the poetic inspiration and colossal intellect of Greece produce similar results? Why did not Euripides prophesy? Why did Plato never rise to moral purity?* "It is because of the theocracy," say modern diviners. Moses founded a theocracy, and prophetism was the necessary result. But this is only to remove the difficulty one step farther back. Why did not the Spartan, or Athenian, or Locrian lawgivers, or the royal disciple of Egeria found a theocracy like that of Moses? Why did not their legislations bring forth prophets? In a certain sense prophecy did arise out of the original relation established between God and Israel. The same Divine Being, who commanded the theocracy, gave also the prophets, inspired them with their doctrines, revealed to them the future, and enabled them to utter predictions far beyond the powers of human foreboding, sagacity, or conjecture, which by their fulfilment, of old and in the present time, demonstrate that they were not self-deceiving enthusiasts, but spake as they were moved by Him who knows the end from the beginning.

9. It has indeed been said by foreign writers, and lately repeated in this country, that the predictions arose out of the circumstances of the days in which the prophets lived, and do not extend beyond the horizon

* Of all the great writers of antiquity Plato is the most striking witness to the corruption of fallen human nature, and the propensity of the grandest intellect, when left to itself, to extenuate the foulest and most odious vice. In nothing does the superiority of Hebrew ethics shine out more brightly. See Wuttke, 'Handbuch der Christlichen Sittenlehre, pp. 55–67. At the same time the mercy inculcated in the prophets may be favourably contrasted with the Greek doctrine concerning slaves, incurables, cripples, exposure of children, abortion, suicide, &c.

of their times. The interpreter "cannot quote Nahum denouncing ruin against Nineveh, or Jeremiah against Tyre, without remembering that already the Babylonian power threw its shadow across Asia, and Nebuchadnezzar was mustering his armies." * Some foreign critics, though in the same spirit, take a different view of the occasion of Nahum's prophecy, ascribing it to an attempt by the Medes and their eastern allies. "This is the remarkable expedition," says Ewald, speaking of the Medes and their oriental confederates under Phraortes, "which Nahum saw with his own eyes, when, predicting the approaching end of Nineveh, he wrote his still extant oracle; he lived in Alqûsh, somewhat farther east of the Tigris, and was therefore able, in that place, to see the whole host as it advanced against Nineveh." † The latter supposition, that Nahum lived near Nineveh, is for good reasons rejected by Knobel, who affirms that he lived at Elkosh in Galilee, and, therefore, did not see the Median power advancing against the Assyrian capital. With regard to the relative strength of the Babylonian and Median powers in comparison with that of the Assyrian empire at that time, there was nothing to lead the prophet to anticipate that either the one or the other was able to take Nineveh, or overthrow the Assyrian monarchy, but the contrary. According to Knobel, who, in the eyes of Rationalists, is an unexceptionable witness, Nahum wrote this prophecy between the years 713 and 711 B.C. Nineveh was not overthrown until about 612. ‡ Just about the time when Nahum wrote, or, according to others, three or four years § later, the Medes under Deïoces revolted from the Assyrians, and set up an independent monarchy. Their power at that time could not have been very formidable, for fifty years later, when the Median empire had been consoli-

* 'Essays and Reviews,' p. 68.

† 'Geschichte Israel's,' iii. 389. See also Knobel's 'Prophetismus,' ii. 212.

‡ According to Prideaux; but according to Usher, 626. Weber ('Weltgeschichte,' i. 47) places the total destruction of Nineveh in 606.

§ According to Knobel, the Medes revolted in the years immediately preceding 710, and made Deïoces king, and he reigned from 710 on. Comp. M. von Niebuhr, 'Geschichte Assur's und Babel's,' pp. 177, 178.

dated by the long and wise government of Deïoces, it was still unable to cope with the Assyrians, by whom their army was utterly defeated, their king slain, and their capital taken. The effort of Phraortes was equally unsuccessful, and therefore Hitzig says, "The attack of Phraortes is not a sufficient ground [for the confident tone of the prophecy]. The Assyrians destroyed him and his whole host. The capital, which Ewald supposes to have been vigorously besieged, does not appear to have been approached by any danger of the kind." * The Babylonians were just as little a match for the Assyrians, for, some fifty years before, Esarhaddon had seized Babylon, and reunited it to the Assyrian monarchy. † When, then, Nahum wrote, the shadow of the Babylonian or Median power was not such as to cause much alarm for the existence of Nineveh. Notwithstanding the loss of an army of 185,000 men, the Assyrian power was still the greatest in the world; and whilst it was still the greatest, whilst the kingdom of Babylon was still so inferior as to be unable to undertake anything against it by itself, and was therefore glad to seek the alliance of Hezekiah, one hundred years before the event, Nahum predicted the siege and utter destruction of Nineveh. "And it shall come to pass, that all they that look upon thee shall flee from thee, and say, Nineveh is laid waste . . . The gates of thy land shall be set wide open unto thine enemies; the fire shall devour thy bars. Draw the waters for the siege, fortify thy strong holds; go into clay, and tread the mortar, make strong the brickkiln. There shall the fire devour thee: the sword shall cut thee off, it shall eat thee up like the cankerworm!" ‡ Can any of those men who now assert that this prophecy was a mere conjecture, tell us what will be the fate of Paris or London one hundred years hence? They deny the miracle of supernatural foreknowledge, and believe what is more incredible far; that unassisted human

* Hitzig's 'Minor Prophets,' p. 225. Comp. von Niebuhr, pp. 188, 189.

† According to Niebuhr, Sennacherib seized Babylon, and made Esarhaddon viceroy, pp. 177, 8.

‡ Nahum iii. 7, 14, 15.

knowledge can lift the veil from futurity, and presage the destinies of empires. Nahum is, however, not the only prophet who uttered predictions concerning the Assyrians. "Assur had not yet passed the Euphrates as a conqueror, and the victorious Jeroboam still reigned in the kingdom of Israel, when the prophetic voice of Hosea and Amos already threatened their countrymen with the scourge of Assyria. (Amos vi. 14, vii. 17; Hos. x. 7, 8, xiv. 1.) Some years before the fall of Samaria, Micah uttered these words:—"What is the guilt of Jacob, is it not Samaria? And what are the idol-high places of Judah, are they not Jerusalem? Therefore I will make Samaria as an heap of the field, and as plantings of a vineyard: and I will pour down the stones thereof into the valley, and I will discover the foundations thereof." But for three years the Assyrian was obliged to lie before the well-fortified city before it fell. Concerning Judah also Micah uttered the oracle:—'Evil came down from the Lord to the gate of Jerusalem,'* and thereupon begins the announcement of the desolation of particular country towns of Judea. But at that time Shalmaneser passed by the kingdom of Judah in peace, and Hezekiah continued to pay his tribute. It was not until the throne had got a new occupant in Sennacherib that he ceased to do so, and thus brought the Assyrian host before the gates of Jerusalem, and caused the fulfilment of the prophecy. But long before this, when the unbelieving Ahaz called upon Tiglath Pileser for help against Syria and Israel, Isaiah, with prophetic eye, looking far beyond the then present, announced to him that through the King of Assyria danger should come upon him, and his father's house, and his people, such as had not been since the division of the kingdoms. (Isai. vii. 17, 18.) Ahaz himself sank into a state of disgraceful Assyrian vassalage, and, perhaps, even experienced the horrors of war in his own land. (2 Chron. xxviii. 20.) But in

* He might have added, "O thou inhabitant of Lachish, bind the chariot to the swift beast; she is the beginning of the sin to the daughter of Zion; for the transgressions of Israel were found in thee."

the days of Hezekiah the word of the prophet was fulfilled in full measure by Sennacherib."*

But the accuracy of Micah's language and of Isaiah's prophetic foreknowledge are worthy of attention. Micah foretells utter destruction to Samaria; to Judah only chastisement, which should reach to the gate of Jerusalem, but no farther. "For it is incurable, every one of her blows—it (the blow) is come to Judah. He hath reached (נגע touched, or smitten) as far as the gate of my people, to Jerusalem . . . . . . For the inhabitant of Maroth waited carefully for good; but evil came down from the Lord to the gate of Jerusalem. O thou inhabitant of Lachish, bind the chariot to the swift beast." From the history it appears that the word of Micah was exactly fulfilled. "In the fourteenth year of King Hezekiah, Sennacherib King of Assyria came up against all the defenced cities and took them [Lachish among the number]. And the King of Assyria sent Rabshakeh from Lachish to Jerusalem with a great army." (Isaiah xxxvi. 1, &c.) The land of Judah was overrun; the evil reached even to the gate of Jerusalem, for the city was invested; but, in conformity with Micah's words, it never entered the city—the Assyrian power was broken, and the king returned by the way he came, as Isaiah had foretold. There is no doubt about the predictions, or the fact that they were uttered before the event, nor yet about the fulfilment. In the time of Ahaz, Isaiah, who had also foretold the chastisement to be inflicted on Judah by the Assyrians, expressly announced a miraculous destruction of the Assyrian host. "Therefore shall the Lord, the Lord of Hosts, send among his fat ones leanness; and under his glory He shall kindle a burning like the burning of a fire. And the light of Israel shall be for a fire, and his Holy One for a flame: and it shall burn and devour his briers in one day; and shall consume the glory of his forest and of his fruitful field both soul and body, and they shall be like the pining away of a sick man," &c. (Isai. x. 16–19.) And, again,

* Tholuck, 'Die Propheten und ihre Weissagungen,' pp. 83, 84.

xxx. 27–32, Isaiah also predicts that the Assyrian shall be broken in his land at least thirty years before the event. That the Assyrian power should be broken was then improbable; that it should be broken on the mountains of Judah more improbable still, beyond human conjecture, and yet it was accomplished. The prediction is found Isai. xiv. 24—27. "The Lord of Hosts hath sworn, saying, Surely as I have thought, so shall it come to pass; and as I have purposed so shall it stand: that I will break the Assyrian in my land, and upon my mountains tread him under foot: then shall his yoke depart from off them, and his burden depart from off their shoulders. This is the purpose that is purposed upon the whole earth; and this is the hand that is stretched out upon all nations, for the Lord of Hosts hath purposed, and who shall disannul it? And his hand is stretched out, and who shall turn it back?" Modern, even sceptical, criticism assigns this fragment to Isaiah, and considers it as a part of the prophecy beginning at x. 5, and going on to the end of chapter xii. The wording is remarkable. It implies miracle, and by miracle the Assyrian host was destroyed: the fulfilment is not only narrated in the history, but recorded in several Psalms, and von Niebuhr shows how, notwithstanding the continuance of Sennacherib's empire, and its prosperity under Esarhaddon, the Assyrian power was then really "broken."

With regard to Assyria's successor, Babylon, there are predictions equally sure. That one hundred and fifty years before the event, the Babylonian captivity was foretold in the most unequivocal and remarkable language by Isaiah, is as certain as any fact in history. In the xxxixth chapter of that prophet we read that on Hezekiah's recovery Merodach Baladan, King of Babylon, sent to congratulate him. Hezekiah vaingloriously exhibited to him all his wealth. Isaiah was soon at hand to rebuke his vanity, and announced the Lord's purpose concerning Hezekiah's posterity. "Hear the word of the Lord of Hosts: Behold the days come, that all that is in thine house, and that which thy fathers have laid up in store until this day, shall be carried to Babylon: nothing shall be left, saith the Lord. And of thy sons that shall issue from thee, which thou shalt beget, shall they take away: and they shall be eunuchs in the palace of the King of Babylon." It is certain that Nabonassar had shaken off the Assyrian yoke, and made Babylon an independent kingdom, and that some twelve years after his death reigned Merodach Baladan.* The genuineness of the chapter in Isaiah has never been doubted. The circumstances of Babylon were not then such as to raise any conjecture respecting its future greatness. It was independent, but not superior to Assyria; on the contrary, as we have already said, Babylon was soon after reduced again to Assyrian obedience.

Micah also predicted the captivity and the deliverance from Babylon. Ch. ii. 10, he says, "Arise ye and depart: for this is not your rest: Because it is polluted it shall destroy you even with a sore destruction;" iii. 12, he announces that Jerusalem shall be ploughed as a field, Jerusalem become heaps, and the temple and its place be desolate; iv. 10, he says, "Thou shalt go forth out of the city, thou shalt dwell in the field, and thou shalt go even to Babylon: there shalt thou be delivered: there the Lord shall redeem thee from the hand of thine enemies." This prediction is the more remarkable, because, as we have seen, he predicts the overrunning of the land of Judah by the Assyrians, declares that the evil should only come to the gate of Jerusalem; and v. 5, 6, foretells the deliverance in the land of Israel. "This one זה [the Messiah, the Son of God] shall be the peace, when the Assyrian shall come into our land," and announces the wasting of the land of Assyria.† He could not, therefore, have expected that Assyria was to bring them to Babylon; and still less that at Babylon they should be delivered. Micah prophesied before the destruction of Samaria, i.e. before 724, that is, about a hundred and forty years before the destruction by Nebuchadnezzar, and con-

* Niebuhr, pp. 46, 47, and 169. † Mic. i. 9, ii. 4, 5, 10, vii. 13.

sequently about two hundred before the deliverance from Babylon. *

10. The mention of Babylon reminds us of another remarkable and indubitable prediction as remarkably fulfilled, and the fulfilment of which shows the groundlessness of recent insinuations. One of these was noticed above. "He cannot quote . . . . . . Jeremiah [denouncing ruin against Tyre] without remembering that already the Babylonian power threw its shade across Asia, and Nebuchadnezzar was mustering his armies." But surely the writer of these words could not have forgotten that the ruin of Tyre by the Chaldeans had been predicted long before the days of Jeremiah. In the twenty-third chapter of Isaiah is found the burden of Tyre. The siege, the interruption of her commerce, the flight of her citizens, and the lamentations of her mariners and her colonies, are all graphically foretold here—and even the authors of the ruin are named. In the thirteenth verse, A.V., we read, "Behold the land of the Chaldeans. This people was not till the Assyrian founded it for them that dwell in the wilderness: they set up the towers thereof, they raised up the palaces thereof; and he brought it to ruin." There are various translations of this verse, † but that the Chaldeans are predicted as the destroyers of Tyre is admitted by some of the highest modern authorities. Knobel says, "*Behold, the land of the Chaldeans.* With the word 'Behold' the author introduces something new to which he directs special attention. That something is the destroyers of Tyre whom he is about to name. Gesenius has "The sense of verse 13 is—Behold, this people of the Chaldees, a little while ago

* Tholuck remarks well, that as the Babylonish captivity is foretold both by Isaiah and Micah, and yet their writings admitted to be genuine, the main objection against the genuineness of Isai. xiii, xiv. and xl.–lxvi. is removed.

† Hitzig has

Behold, the land of the Chaldeans,
The people there, that was no people.
Assur created it for the inhabitants of the desert.
They erect their castles,
Destroy her palaces,
Make her a heap of ruin.

inhabitants of the deserts, to whom the Assyrians first assigned settled habitations and made it a people: this hitherto insignificant people, scarcely deserving mention, shall be the instrument of the destruction of the ancient world-wide famous city of Tyre." If this be the sense, as is generally agreed, then we have a prediction far surpassing the powers of human foresight, and not suggested by existing circumstances. The deniers of prediction feel this, and therefore use the most violent means to get rid of it, not scrupling to alter the text and change the meaning of the Hebrew words. Even the great Ewald is not above this violence. Without a shadow of critical support he would for "Chaldeans" substitute "Canaanites," and interpret "Behold, the land of the Canaanites (the Phœnicians), this people is no more, Assur has made it a desolation; they (the Phœnicians) erected their country villas, they built their palaces, he made it a ruin." I. Olshausen is guilty of still greater violence: he would strike out of the verse a number of words at the beginning, including, of course, "Chaldeans." Meier proposes to substitute "Kittiim" for "Chaldeans," and to strike out the latter part of the verse: all which criticism Knobel unceremoniously calls "bodenlose Willkühr." Others would get rid of the whole as ungenuine, not written by Isaiah, but by some one in the time of Jeremiah and Ezekiel.* Knobel and Gesenius get rid of the difficulty by finding the event alluded to in Shalmaneser's attempt on Tyre, when he subdued the whole of continental Phœnicia, but was unable to take New Tyre on the island, and established a blockade for five years. The Chaldeans, they say, served, and were some of the best troops, in the Assyrian army. But this is also to do violence to the text. The prophet does not say that the Assyrians should destroy the city, but explicitly and emphatically points out the Chaldeans as the ruiners of Tyre. "Behold, the land of the Chaldeans. This is the people—it was not [a people], Assur founded it

* Gesenius, 'Commentary,' p. 716.

[the land] for the dwellers in steppes. They erected their watch-towers; they roused up her palaces; they made her a ruin." Knobel and Gesenius, in the passages quoted from their commentaries, plainly admit this. But the only siege of Tyre by the Chaldeans was the thirteen years' siege by Nebuchadnezzar, and every unprejudiced mind must admit that it alone answers to the prophet's words, and therefore receive the prophecy as a prediction. Sooner than do this, Knobel, who believes and proves the prophecy to be genuine, says we must reject it as ungenuine, and ascribe it to Jeremiah. "To assert the genuineness of this portion, and yet to refer it to the siege of Tyre by Nebuchadnezzar the King of the Chaldeans, an event which happened a hundred years later, Ezek. xxvi.–xxviii. (as Jerome, Vitringa, I. D. Michaelis, Drechsler, Hengstenberg), is impossible, because in the time of Isaiah there could not be a foreboding, much less a certain and definite announcement of anything of the kind." Such is the honesty and trustworthiness of "the higher criticism." Better to reject a prophetic passage, which it proves to be genuine, than admit a prediction. Here is a plain proof that the criticism proceeds from previous rejection of prediction, not that the unbelief proceeds from the criticism. The critical De Wette says the same in his Introduction to the O. T. "The prophecy concerning Tyre, c. xxiii., has been denied to be Isaiah's on account of the mention of the Chaldeans, and because it has been supposed that its fulfilment must be found in history; also because of the supposed Chaldaising language (verses 3, 11). But these objections can be some of them entirely confuted, and others shown to be weak."* The preceding statement is a remarkable exhibition of the untrustworthiness of Rationalist criticism on account of the previous dogmatic prejudices of the authors against inspiration and prediction. It is also a specimen, one out of thousands, of how much reliance is to be placed on Professor Jowett's statement, "that the

* This has been done by both Gesenius and Knobel in their commentaries.

diversity amongst German writers on prophecy is far less than among English ones. That is a new phenomenon which has to be acknowledged."* Any one who would take the trouble could show that the contrary is the fact; that there is such a love of novelty, and such unrestrained efforts after originality, that the diversities of opinion on any one subject, easy or difficult, are much greater than in England.

But to return; Professor Jowett says that this is one of the passages which have not been fulfilled. "For a like reason the failure of a prophecy is never admitted, in spite of Scripture and of history (Jer. xxxvi. 30; Isai. xxiii.; Amos vii. 10–17)."† What he considers unfulfilled in this prediction he does not say; but there are two points to which he probably alludes. The first is, that there is no historic account of Tyre having been taken by assault by Nebuchadnezzar. But no such event is predicted in this chapter. The prophet foretells a siege by the Chaldeans, great calamities, Tyre reduced to a ruin—this is all matter of history. Tyre was besieged for thirteen years.‡ In so long a siege the city must have suffered severely. Nebuchadnezzar overran all Syria and Phœnicia: § he must, therefore, have taken Old Tyre on the continent; and modern critics now admit that if New Tyre on the island was not taken by assault, it submitted to the Chaldeans by capitulation, and that the Tyrian royal family was carried to Babylon. So Gesenius says, "The siege probably ended with a peaceable agreement and alliance, as we see that subsequently the Tyrians sent to Babylon to fetch Merbal, one of their later kings (Joseph. contra Apion. i. § 21)." And Tholuck (p. 133), "That which, after the searching investigations of Hengstenberg and Hävernik, should never have been questioned, has now, since the farther researches in Movers (ii. 1, p. 461), found pretty general reception (also in Duncker, i. 172; Niebuhr, p. 216); that certainly, if not a con-

* 'Essays and Reviews,' p. 340.
† 'Essays,' p. 343.
‡ Josephus, Antiq. lib. x., c. 11. Contra Ap. i. 21.
§ Contra Apion. lib. i. c. 20.

quest, yet a capitulation of the Tyrians must have taken place, in consequence of which they again became vassals of the Chaldeans, and were obliged to submit to the removal of the royal family to Babylon. The plainest proof of this is seen in the fact, that about a year later they were attacked as Chaldean vassals and subdued by Hophra, who had been formerly their ally. That this conquest could have been effected by the Egyptian king by a surprise, shows in what a low state their fortifications and their power must have been."* It is therefore historically certain that Tyre was besieged, and reduced to a state of ruin by the Chaldeans, just as Isaiah had foretold about a hundred and thirty years before, when the Chaldeans were as yet mere mercenary troops in the armies of Assyria. It is equally certain that after the fall of Babylon, Tyre became independent, rich, and prosperous again, as the prophet foretold. "It shall come to pass in that day, that Tyre shall be forgotten seventy years, according to the days of one king: after the end of seventy years shall Tyre sing as a harlot." The discord amongst critics about the meaning of the seventy years and the days of one king, is just as great as that already noticed. Two opinions meet most favour: one, that of the Rationalists, that seventy is a round number, and that seventy years mean a long time; the other, that *king* here means *dynasty* or *kingdom* of the Chaldeans, as Dan. vii. 17, viii. 20, which is the view of Aben Ezra, Vitringa, Lowth, Döderlein, Rosenmüller, &c. If either be true, the objector cannot fairly say that the prediction has not been fulfilled.

With regard to the concluding verse, in which the prophet foretells that after Tyre's recovery from Babylonian vassalage, "Her merchandize and her hire should be holiness to the Lord," the most that can be objected is, that we have no record of its fulfilment. But from this it does not follow that this part of the prediction

* That is, to what a state of ruin they had been reduced by the previous thirteen years' siege.—See also von Niebuhr's 'Geschichte Assur's und Babel's,' p. 216.

was not accomplished. The fulfilment could only have taken place after the restoration from Babylon, and before the destruction by Alexander. The records of events in Scripture from the return of Zerubbabel to the close of the Canon are too brief too afford us any light as to the relations between Tyre and Jerusalem. In the days of Solomon we know that they were friendly, Hiram contributed to the building of the temple, and the friendship must have continued unusually intimate, as Amos denounces punishment upon Tyre for "not having remembered the brotherly covenant." (Amos i. 9.) There is, therefore, nothing improbable in the supposition that, after Tyre's recovery from almost ruin, friendly relations were re-established, and rich offerings made in the temple at Jerusalem. The marvellous fulfilment of the former portion respecting the Chaldeans is a guarantee for the Divine origin and accomplishment of the latter. Hitherto objectors have only asserted, not attempted to prove, the non-fulfilment.

There are other fulfilled predictions to which the reader's attention might satisfactorily have been turned, but the charge of non-fulfilment made in 'Essays and Reviews' constrains us to consider a passage in Jeremiah, and another in Amos there referred to, in support of the allegation. The former, Jer. xxxvi. 10, is thus given in the Authorized Version:—"Therefore thus saith the Lord of Jehoiakim, King of Judah, he shall have *none to sit* [literally, 'none sitting' *] upon the throne of David; and his body shall be cast out in the day to the heat, and in the night to the frost." † To this Hitzig in his commentary objects, that Jehoiakim had a son, Jehoiachin, who did sit upon his throne, and that in 2 Kings xxiv. 6 (Heb. 5), we read, "So Jehoiakim slept with his fathers, and Jehoiachin his

* The present participle יושב is used to denote continuance. See Ewald, Gramm. § 350.

The verb ישב signifies *to abide, continue, endure*, as well as to sit. Gen. xxiv. 55: Ps. ix. 8; Jer. xxx. 18.

† Compare xxii. 19: "He shall be buried with the burial of an ass, drawn and cast forth beyond the gates of Jerusalem."

son reigned in his stead." If Jeremiah had, after uttering the prophecy, committed it to writing, and then died before Jehoiakim, this objection might have some weight; but when it is remembered that Jeremiah lived many years after the death of Jehoiakim, and, if his words had been falsified by events, might have altered them, and yet did not, but left them as originally uttered, the objection ceases to have any force at all. The prophet must have been satisfied after the event, that his words expressed what had happened. Jehoiakim had in fact no son "sitting," or continuing on the throne of David, for three months after Jehoiachin's elevation, he was deposed and carried away. The words, "He slept with his fathers," signify simply that he died, affirming nothing about his burial. Here Ewald is much more thoughtful and more candid than the English Essayist or his German forerunner. In the 'Geschichte des Volkes Israel,' iii. p. 400, Ewald gives an account of the death of Jehoiakim and of the treatment of his corpse in agreement with Jeremiah's words, and, in a note, adds, "The particular circumstances of the death of Jehoiakim are very obscure. The formula, 'He slept with his fathers,' 2 Kings xxiv. 5, means nothing more than his death; that he was taken prisoner is mentioned, 2 Chron. xxxvi. 6; but what actually occurred may be inferred with tolerable probability from the words selected by Jeremiah xxii. 18, &c., and xxxvi. 30. For, though the prophet had certainly predicted the king's unhappy end long before, he wrote down the words after the event." Ewald, therefore, saw the impossibility of these words containing an unfulfilled prediction. The English objector might have saved his criticism from appearing as the dictate of passion rather than the conclusion of judgment, had he taken time to consider the prophet's words impartially.

Another example of this unhappy hastiness in taking up objections is found in the reference to Amos vii. 10–17. In our English Bible the passage reads thus:—"Then Amaziah the priest of Bethel sent to Jeroboam

King of Israel, saying, Amos hath conspired against thee in the midst of the house of Israel: the land is not able to bear all his words. For thus Amos saith, Jeroboam shall die by the sword, and Israel shall surely be led away captive out of their own land. And Amaziah said unto Amos, O thou seer, go flee thee away into the land of Judah, and there eat bread, and prophesy there: But prophesy not again any more at Bethel; for it is the king's chapel and the king's court." Amos asserts his Divine call, and utters this prediction against Amaziah:—"Therefore, thus saith the Lord; thy wife shall be an harlot in the city, and thy sons and thy daughters shall fall by the sword, and thy land shall be divided by line; and thou shalt die in a polluted land; and Israel shall surely go into captivity forth of his land." As the Essayist does not specify the particulars which he supposes unfulfilled, we can only state the objection according to Hitzig. First, then, he may suppose that the prediction is not fulfilled because Jeroboam II. did not die by the sword; but if the objector will look at verse 9, he will see that Amos did not predict anything of the kind—the prophet's threat is not against Jeroboam, but his house. "I will rise against the house of Jeroboam with the sword," which threat was fulfilled when Shallum conspired against Jeroboam's son and successor, and slew him and reigned in his stead. (2 Kings xv. 10.) The words, "Jeroboam shall die by the sword," were a malicious addition of Amaziah's to induce Jeroboam to drive Amos from Bethel. Hitzig's attempt to prove that "house of Jeroboam" included Jeroboam himself by referring to Isai. vii. 13, where "house of David" includes Ahaz and his family, is a miserable failure. To make the cases parallel, Isaiah must have said, "Hear ye now, O house of Ahaz."

The next portion of the assaulted prediction foretells that Israel should go into captivity. Taking Knobel's dates, Amos uttered his prophecies between 790–784 B. C., i. e. before the death of Jeroboam. The final car-

6*

rying away of Israel by Shalmaneser occurred about sixty years after: so that here is an undoubted prediction undoubtedly fulfilled.

There remains only the denunciation against Amaziah, his wife and children, the fulfilment of which is not recorded. But surely this is not surprising, when the excessive brevity of the accounts of the kings and revolutions that followed, is taken into consideration. There is nothing impossible or improbable in the fate predicted. Within thirty years from the date of the prophecy, the Assyrians began their incursions into the land of Israel. Although, then, the fulfilment of this particular is not related, it is not improbable. The fulfilment of the other two particulars is a guarantee that this also was accomplished. This objection, however, like others of the kind, has this value: it shows that the objector believes that the Hebrew prophets did lay claim to the power of predicting future events.

11. Here our attention has been directed to one of many wondrous predictions concerning the destinies of Israel, which have excited the astonishment of readers in all ages. Moses foretold the dispersion of the disobedient people, and their preservation in the midst of the nations. The theme has been taken up by all the later prophets. The fulfilment is before our eyes. Israel has been scattered to the four winds, but is still preserved. Of the nations by whom and amongst whom they were first dispersed the Lord has made a full end. He has chastened Israel in measure, but has not permitted them to disappear.* The Assyrians, the Babylonians, the Romans have utterly perished. The Ten Tribes are "wanderers among the nations." The people of the Jews, rich, powerful, intelligent, survive all the revolutions of Empires, ancient, medieval, modern, and await the consummation of the Lord's oracles.† But as this is matter of notoriety, is not disputed or explained by Rationalists or Essayists, it is enough to refer to this proof of revelation, as wonderful as the answer to Elijah's prayer (1 Kings, xviii.).

* Jer. xxx. 11, xxxi. 35–37; Isai. vi. 11–13; Amos ix. 9.
† See Butler's 'Analogy,' Part ii. c. 7.

12. But that which gives to Hebrew prophecy its peculiar charm, and its paramount importance, is that it contains predictions respecting Redemption and the Redeemer. That there are Messianic prophecies has been the belief of Jews and Christians for more than two thousand years, and is fully admitted by the New School of Theology. But, much beyond this, the agreement between the old and new interpreters does not extend. For some of the prophecies applied in the New Testament to the Messiah, the modern school has new interpretations. Of others, and those most important, it denies the genuineness; and one of the vital questions now brought before the English mind is, whether we are to follow the New Testament, or the new German critics. The innovators in England do not pretend to offer anything original of their own. They repeat in English what they have derived from one class of German writers. And, as German learning stands deservedly in high repute, there is a danger of the unwary receiving without question, what appears to come on authority so respectable. Hence the present necessity of such frequent references to the sources from which they draw, and also of recalling attention to the real question at issue, namely, whether the New Testament or German critics are to be our guides in interpreting prophecy. Now, placing for a moment the New Testament writers on the lowest level, regarding them merely as included amongst the ancient Jews, their opinion must be of some value. Theirs were the prophetic books. For their fathers and for themselves they were written. They were orientals. They inherited the traditional interpretation of their people. Their interpretation has been accepted by the intelligent of other nations. The Christian Church, composed of a great variety of races, abounding in minds of all possible types, in different stages of culture, approved and adhered to the old Jewish interpretation for many centuries. True, that only two or three of the Fathers understood Hebrew, and that the early Church was dependent upon the Greek and Syriac, and

the medieval Church on the Vulgate, versions. But, as was said above, and at the present time ought to be kept in remembrance, however many of the beauties and peculiarities of the writer may be lost in a version, the grand substance, the purpose and intent of the whole, which is, after all, the real meaning of any book that has a meaning, may be grasped in any tolerable translation by any intelligent reader. And that which suggests itself to the common sense of mankind, as the meaning, whether derived from version or original, is undoubtedly the true meaning. And so it is with prophecy. To readers of ancient or modern versions, or of the original, the general scope and intent has ever appeared the same. And, therefore, at the revival of letters, and at the Reformation, when the original language of the prophets came to be studied, the general sense, handed down from the New Testament writers by the Fathers and medieval divines, still commended itself to students as acute in intellect, and to scholars as familiar with the Hebrew language, as any who have lived in the last hundred years. Indeed it may be doubted whether Hebrew has been so nearly a mother-tongue with any recent critics, as it was with the Buxtorfs, Wagenseil, Edzard, and others of old; and whether any modern commentators have been naturally more competent to grasp the general sense than the Reformers, and those who followed them. And yet, from the Reformation down to the last quarter of the eighteenth century, the old interpretation prevailed. Romanists and Protestants were still of one mind as to the general outline of prophetic truth. Wonderful if ancient Jews, Fathers and Medievalists, Protestants and Romanists, were all mistaken, and the true sense hidden until about fifty years ago.

13. If the New School were all of one mind; if all modern critics were unanimous in their judgments, and uniform in their interpretations, and their conclusions had been arrived at by unbiassed investigation, such unanimity of opinion, and conclusions so deduced, would naturally have great weight. But the variety

and diversity of opinion in the German Rationalist School is unbounded. They agree only in that negative view, which necessarily arises from the common origin and the common principles of their theology. The origin of their theology is undoubtedly Deistic infidelity;* its fundamental principles, that there is no supernatural revelation of Deity, and therefore no Divine prediction,† consequently that there can be no real predictions concerning Jesus of Nazareth, or anybody else.‡ Criticism derived from such a source, and guided by such principles, must be eminently untrustworthy. The conclusions forerun the investigation. If there can be no prediction at all, then there can be none relating to our Lord; and therefore from their general principle, before any investigation is made, it follows that neither the xxiind Psalm, nor Isai. vii. 14, nor any other Psalm or prophecy, can be interpreted of the Saviour, and therefore investigation can only be made in order to show that the foregone conclusion is true. The investigators may be learned, profound, acute, diligent, honest, but their principles hinder them from acknowledging that any prediction ever was or can be fulfilled, and compel them to conclude that it is not; and therefore their criticism and conclusions in such matters must be regarded not only with suspicion, but as probably untrue, the result of their dogmatic prejudices, and therefore utterly insufficient to outweigh the common judgment of Jews and Gentiles for more than two thousand years.

14. Such would be the opinion of the student who had never heard of Evangelists, Apostles, or Rationalists in his life, but considered the subject, apart from all religious interests, merely in a scientific point of view.

* See 'Letters on Rationalism,' passim.

† At vero quibus miraculorum auctoritas implicita est scrupulis, iisdem vel gravioribus etiam decreta de vaticiniis proposita premuntur. *Primum* enim quævis predictio divinitus patefacta, qua fatum inevitabile hominis aut populi cujusdam, quod ex re quadam ab ipsis perpetranda pendet, diserte nunciatur, ideæ Dei sanctissimi et benignissimi repugnat, *fatalismum* fovet et libertatem hominum moralem tollit.—Wegscheider, *Institutiones*, p. 217.

‡ "So muss wohl zugegeben werden, dass ein Erweis Christi als Erlösers aus den Weissagungen unmöglich ist."—Schleiermacher, *Der Christliche Glaube*, i. 2, a. 105.

But in the question between the New Testament and modern criticism the Christian sees something more than an alternative between ancient Judaism and modern heathenism—he sees that it is an alternative between Christ and unbelief. The interpretations of the New Testament are the interpretations of Christ and of those to whom, "beginning at Moses, and all the prophets, he expounded in all the Scriptures the things concerning himself" (Luke xxiv. 27), "whose understandings He opened that they might understand the Scriptures" (Luke xxiv. 45); to whom He sent His Holy Spirit to "bring all things to their remembrance whatsoever He had said unto them," and to "guide them into all truth." (John xiv. 26, xvi. 13.) He cannot depart from their interpretations, and adopt the new and contradictory criticism, without admitting either that Christ knowingly accommodated Himself to the errors of the times, or that He was mistaken, or that His discourses have been incorrectly reported; any one of which admissions is equivalent to a renunciation of Christianity. The first is the supposition of some of the elder Rationalists, the second of some of the later, and the third apparently of many modern critics. To admit the first is to deny our Lord's integrity, to concede the second is to make him a mere fallible man, and to receive the third is to take away the main ground of our faith in Christ. The lowest theory of inspiration, at all comdatible with faith, is that "it protects the doctrine." Our Lord's doctrine is contained in His discourses, and part of those discourses is His interpretation of prophecy, and the promise of the Holy Spirit to guide His disciples. If in those discourses, or those of His disciples, the prophecies are falsely interpreted, the doctrine is not protected, the promise of the Spirit cannot have been fulfilled, and we are brought to the horrid and blasphemous conclusion that Christ, "The Way, the Truth, and the Life," was fallible, and that His word is not to be depended upon. From these consistent and necessary conclusions the Essayists do not shrink any more than their German masters. They reject the New Testament interpretation of prophecy, and then consistently deny the authority of the New Testament itself. He who would sweep away all predictive prophecy insinuates that the Gospel portrait of our Lord is dimmed "by the haze of mingled imagination and remembrance, with which his awful figure could scarcely fail to be at length invested by affection."* Another says that "The New Testament writings leave us in uncertainty as to the descent of Jesus Christ according to the flesh, whether by His mother He were of the tribe of Judah, or of the tribe of Levi;"† implies that His birth at Bethlehem and the announcement of it by the Angels are doubtful; and that the three first Gospels, though more trustworthy than the fourth, contain only "more exact traditions of what he actually said." A third, who, following Reimarus,‡ doubts whether any one passage from the Psalms or Prophets quoted in the Epistles is rightly interpreted,§ insinuates that our Lord's prediction concerning the day of judgment has failed because it is inseparable from that of the destruction of Jerusalem, and in another work expressly teaches that in this matter our Lord was mistaken.‖ Thus the example of foreign critics and their followers at home warns us that if we give up the prophetic interpretations of Christ and the Apostles, we must prepare also to part with our Christianity, and begin a painful and not very profitable search for those crumbs of Divine truth, which these kind critics still suppose to be scattered about in the Prophets and Evangelists, and which can only be recognized by the verifying faculty of the critic. But if we believe in Christ, and those whom He taught by His Spirit, we must take their principle of interpretation as ours, and rest assured that the interpretations which they have given exhibit the true mind of that Spirit who spake by the prophets. The wise men, and the scribes, and the disputers of the day may decry

* 'Essays and Reviews,' p. 80. † Ibid., pp. 180, 203.
‡ Wolfenbüttel, 'Fragments,' § 34–45. § Page 406.
‖ See Professor Jowett's 'Commentary to the First Epistle to the Thessalonians,' p. 108–111.

this principle as unscientific, and protest that it is better not to read the Bible at all, than to read with such restrictions; but Christians may be content with the wisdom that came down from above, and with the liberty wherewith Christ has made them free. Where our Lord or an inspired Apostle has spoken, we abide by the interpretation.

15. Here, however, it is necessary to guard against mistake. Where passages of the prophecies are cited or applied, attention must be paid to the mind and intention of the speaker or writer, as sometimes Old Testament language is used without any intention of intimating a fulfilment of prophecy either direct or typical. The words were suitable to express the feelings or thoughts of the writer, and they were adopted. Thus when St. Paul says, "I say, have they not heard? Yes, verily, their sound went into all the earth, and their words unto the end of the world," there is no reason for supposing that the Apostle looked upon Ps. xix. 4 as a prophecy fulfilled in the preaching of the Gospel. The Psalm speaks of the heavens and the firmament. But the words aptly and beautifully expressed what the disciples of Christ had already done, and Paul was guided to adopt them, the rather because in the Psalm itself the parallel is drawn between the book of nature and the book of revelation, the harmonious testimony of the works and word of God. Another instance occurs 1 Cor. xv. 32: "If the dead rise not, let us eat and drink, for to-morrow we die." Here is a quotation from Isai. xxii. 13. The words of the prophet forcibly depicted the character of those of whom the Apostle was speaking, and they are adopted accordingly. This principle is demonstrated by 2 Tim. ii. 19: "The foundation of God standeth sure, having this seal, The Lord knoweth them that are his." The latter words are a quotation from Numb. xvi. 5, referring to the rebellion of Korah and his company, but adopted by the Apostle, just as the later prophets, especially Jeremiah, express their message occasionally in citations from their predecessors or from the Pentateuch.

In the next place, it is to be observed that Old Testament passages are sometimes cited simply to confirm a doctrine, or to form the foundation of an argument; as when the Apostle says (Rom. ix. 7), "Neither because they are seed of Abraham, are they all children: but in Isaac shall thy seed be called." The latter words are cited to prove that mere fleshly descent does not constitute a right to the inheritance or God's favour. Ishmael was according to the flesh the child of Abraham, but it was to Isaac and his posterity that the inheritance of the promises was given. In like manner our Lord (Matt. xiii. 14) applies Isai. vi. 9, 10 to the Jews whom He addressed, and St. Paul applies the same words (Acts xxviii. 26) to the Jews at Rome. They contain a general principle of God's dealings with men, applicable at all times. So St. Paul (Rom. x. 12) employs the words of Joel, "Whosoever shall call upon the name of the Lord shall be saved," to prove that there is no difference between the Jew and the Gentile. The stress is upon the words *πᾶς γὰρ ὅς* [כל אשר] "every one." Not to the Jews only, but to every one who calls upon the name of the Lord, God promises salvation, therefore there is no difference, &c. The object for which the quotation is made must be kept in view, else the conclusiveness of the argument will be missed, and a wrong interpretation given to the prophecy. As for example (Acts xv. 15—17), where James proves the right of the Gentiles to be received into the Church without circumcision, he says, "Simeon hath declared how God at the first did visit the Gentiles to take out of them a people for His name. And to this agree the words of the prophets; as it is written, After this I will return, and will build again the tabernacle of David, which is fallen down . . . that the residue of men* might seek after the Lord, and all the Gentiles on whom my name is called, saith the Lord." Some readers and interpreters fix their eye upon the tabernacle of David, and seeing that that was not literally fulfilled, take it figuratively of the Christian Church, and thereby do

* Amos, ix. 11, 12.

violence to the words of the prophecy, and at the same time miss St. James's argument. The question was, whether the Gentiles, i.e. without circumcision and obedience to the Mosaic Law, could be received into the Christian Church. The majority of Jewish Christians thought that they could not. St. Peter proved that these persons were wrong by an appeal to fact. St. James shows the same by a reference to prophecy. His object was not to quote and show a fulfilment of one prediction, but the general tenour of all respecting the call of the Gentiles as such, and therefore he says in the plural, "To this agree the words of the prophets." At the same time he selects one, in which the Gentiles [גוים, ἔθνη] are mentioned by name with the addition "all," "all nations," and where it is said that the name of the Lord is called upon them. The stress of the argument rests upon the word "Gentiles," and upon the fact that God's name is called upon them; as if he would say, "Here in Amos men upon whom the Lord's name is called are still spoken of as Gentiles; they cannot therefore be persons circumcised and keeping the Law, and therefore the name of the Lord may now also be called upon Gentiles as such, and therefore there is no necessity for circumcising them. To enter the Church of Christ it is not necessary that they should cease to be Gentiles, or become proselytes by circumcision." *

16. In the next place words are quoted from the prophets, which contain no prediction at all, and are yet spoken of as being fulfilled, because the event to which they allude was a type of that to which they are applied. Our Lord and, after Him, the Apostles, lay down the principle that past history may represent that which is to happen hereafter. Thus the Saviour refers to the brazen serpent, and to Jonah as prefiguring His resurrection, and even the time of it on the third day. St. Paul teaches that Hagar and Sarah are

* The account of this dispute is a strong testimony to the credibility, knowledge, and good faith of the writer. The Pharisees believed that proselytes of the gate, i.e. proselytes without circumcision, could only be received when all the twelve tribes were in the land.

typical of the covenants; the Paschal lamb of Christ's atoning death; the passage of the Red Sea of baptism; the smitten rock of Christ. The author of the Epistle to the Hebrews, St. Peter in his allusion to the deluge, and St. John in his mystical application of the names Sodom, Egypt, and Babylon, confirm the principle, which helps us to interpret passages of the Old Testament, such as those where the Messiah is called David, and to understand passages of the New Testament, where what was spoken of David is applied to our Lord. The principle also solves the apparent difficulty of two passages strongly insisted upon by the enemies of Christianity. Concerning our Lord's early sojourn in Egypt, St. Matthew says, that it happened "that it might be fulfilled which was spoken of the Lord by the prophet, saying, Out of Egypt have I called my Son," —and respecting the slaughter of the children at Bethlehem, "Then was fulfilled that which was spoken by Jeremy the prophet, saying, In Rama was a voice heard." In neither case does St. Matthew quote predictions, but Hosea's and Jeremiah's references to past history. When Hosea said, "Out of Egypt have I called my son," or when Jeremiah spoke of Rachel weeping for her children, neither was uttering a prediction of the future, but alluding to facts long past. Hosea was alluding to the Exodus eight centuries before, and Jeremiah to the carrying away of the Ten Tribes one hundred years before he wrote. St. Matthew therefore speaks of them as fulfilled in the only way in which facts can be fulfilled, in events the antitypes of those referred to.

17. But after making allowance for these and numerous other similar applications of prophecy, there remain many which the Lord and the Apostles interpret as specially spoken in reference to Christ and Christianity. It has ever been the belief of all orthodox writers that Christ claimed to be the Messiah foretold by the prophets. It is also acknowledged by Rationalist divines. Thus Von Cölln says that the sick who had been healed, the common people, his own imme-

diate adherents, acknowledged Him as the Messiah, and adds, "That Jesus approved, and even called forth this view of Himself, is evident from His words and His conduct. 1st. From His answer to Peter (Matt. xvi. 17); His approval of the acclamations of the people (Luke xix. 34, 40; Matt. xxi. 15, 16). 2nd. From His assuming the names belonging to the Messiah, especially the titles Son of God and Son of Man from Dan. vii. 13, 14. 3rd. From His claiming the privileges attributed to the Messiah, as the full unfolding and explanation of the Law (Matt. v. 17); the assertion that He was Lord of the Sabbath (Matt. xii. 8); His reformation of the temple service (John ii. 13, 20); His dispensation of His disciples from the usual fasts (Matt. ix. 14); and His claiming the right to forgive sins. 4th. From His express declaration that He was the Messiah (John iv. 25, 26; xvii. 3; Matt. xxvi. 63, 64, &c).—This his assertion that He was sent from God, as the founder of a new theocracy, Jesus proved to be true—1, From the Holy Scriptures of His people, which bare witness of His person and His works. According to the general convictions, the Law and the Prophets spake of an ideal theocracy. There was an unanimity of opinion as to the passages which treated of the ideal King, and also as to the particular features of his character as drawn [by the prophets]. Whosoever, therefore, gave himself out for the Messiah, was under the necessity of proving that these features were found in him. Jesus, therefore, often employed the declarations of the Law and the Prophets to convince the Jews that He was the Messiah. . . . The application of the prophetic passages to Himself cannot be explained as *accommodation*, as Jesus in the circle of His confidential disciples, and after Him the Apostles in their discourses and Epistles, adhere to this application." * The same author teaches elsewhere (p. 89) that our Lord received the Law and the Prophets as

* Von Cölln, 'Biblische Theologie,' ii. p. 116–18, and 89; comp. Wegscheider, 'Institutiones,' § 119, especially *Note C.;* Knobel, 'Prophetism,' i. 338; De Wette, 'Biblische Dogmatik,' § 189.

the inspired word of God, and "employed the prophetic oracles in these writings as testimonies to His own appearance and works (John v. 39, 46; Luke iv. 21). He pointed out especially and often that His sufferings must happen according to the announcements of these Holy Books, and were therefore inevitable ordinances of God: Matt. xxvi. 24; Mark ix. 12, xiv. 49; Luke xviii. 31–33, xxii. 37, xxiv. 26, 27."

18. Now the two prophets to whose writings our Lord and the Apostles most emphatically refer are Daniel and Isaiah; and by their references they not only interpret particular passages, but establish the genuineness of the books. Our Lord not only cites the prophet Daniel by name, when speaking of "the abomination of desolation" (Matt. xxiv. 15), but has been pleased to adopt from that book the designation of His kingdom, and the title which He appropriates to Himself. The expressions "Kingdom of Heaven," and "Son of Man," are confessedly taken from the second and seventh chapters of Daniel. The latter expression is particularly important. Meyer says—"Its simple meaning is, *The Messiah.* It is derived from the awful and striking representation in the prophetic vision (Dan. vii. 13) so well known to the Jews, and occurring also in the pre-Christian book of Enoch, in which the Messiah appears in the clouds of heaven, as 'The Son of Man' (ὡς υἱὸς ἀνθρώπου), surrounded by the angels of the Divine throne of judgment (see Ewald, 'Gesch. Chr.,' p. 79), that is, in a form nothing different from that of an ordinary man. Jesus, inasmuch as in Him the Messiah was come, was, in the realisation, that Son of Man whose form was seen in Daniel's vision. As often, therefore, as Jesus in His discourses says 'The Son of Man,' he means 'The Son of Man of that vision of Daniel,' that is, The Messiah."* It is

* H. A. W. Meyer's 'Comm. on Matt. viii. 20.' Fleck also says: 'Denotatur enim *is, quem omnes norunt,* qui *omnium ore fertur* (sensu eximio ita vocatus) *filius hominis Danieliticus*=Messias." 'De Regno Divino,' p. 121. The italics are Fleck's. He also refers to the Rabbis, Wetstein, Grotius, Lampe, Stahl, Kuinoel, Lücke, Tholuck. See also the references given above to Von Cölln, Wegscheider, De Wette, Knobel.

needless to say how often this expression occurs in all the Gospels in our Lord's discourses, especially on the most solemn occasions, as when He describes His second advent (Matt. xiii. 41, xxiv. 27, 30, 44, xxv. 31); when He speaks of His passion (John iii. 13, 14) on the very eve of its accomplishment (Matt. xxvi. 24); and when, after formal adjuration, He declares Himself the Christ, the Son of God, "Hereafter shall ye see the Son of Man sitting on the right hand of power, and coming in the clouds of heaven;" so that it is impossible to separate the essential elements of Christ's teaching from the book of Daniel, and equally impossible to suppose that He who came into the world to bear witness to the truth would ground His claims and His most solemn doctrine on a forgery. The question of the genuineness and authenticity of Daniel cannot, therefore, be separated from that respecting the fallibility or infallibility of the Saviour. By asserting that the book of Daniel is ungenuine—a forged and false prophecy—men charge our Lord with the uncritical ignorance of His times, or a deliberate application of a document which He knew to be false. But the student need not be alarmed at the greatness of the issue. He must remember that the original assault on Daniel was made by the heathen Porphyry, an able but bitter enemy of Christianity in the third century, and is continued, partly in the original form of objection, by those who deny all supernatural revelation, make our Lord himself a mere man, and are as opposed to the doctrine of Christ's proper Deity as Porphyry himself. It must never be forgotten by those who read Rationalist books, that even when, like Schleiermacher and his school, they use the expression "Son of God," they use it in a non-natural sense, rejecting the accounts of His supernatural birth, and regarding Him as the Son of Joseph and Mary.* They are interested, therefore, not only in getting rid of the predictions in Daniel, especially such an one as the seventy weeks, but also

* Compare 'Essays and Reviews,' pp. 82, 88, 89, 202, 203, 351, 352, 354, 355; and Schleiermacher's 'Glaubenslehre,' 3rd edit., pp. 64–69.

in setting aside a remarkable testimony to the Old Testament doctrine of the Deity of Messiah. The two main Rationalist arguments against the book of Daniel are—first, that in their opinion it contains accurate predictions concerning Antiochus Epiphanes, which they borrow from Porphyry; and secondly, that it relates miracles, and therefore according to their own system cannot be true. This is strongly urged by Knobel. "The history of Daniel," he says, "has a legendary, almost a fairy-tale complexion, and represents the events in a manner in which they could not possibly have happened. They could have assumed this form only after a long oral transmission. For in Hebrew history, where numerous myths and legends occur, as, for example, in that of the patriarchs, of Moses, Balaam, Samson, Elijah, Elisha, the narratives were committed to writing a considerable time after the events; when, on the contrary, events have a natural appearance, as in the books of Ezra, Nehemiah, the first of Maccabees, there they were generally committed to writing at the time, or very soon after the events. This is an historic canon, of the validity of which there can be no doubt."*

To men holding such axioms of criticism, the book of Daniel must, as a matter of course, be as ungenuine as the narrative of our Lord's miracles. Criticisms, therefore, founded on such principles must always appear questionable to a thoughtful inquirer, even if he is not able to show their weakness or falsehood. The believer in the Gospels will feel assured that they are not unanswerable, and a little inquiry will satisfy him that they have been answered again and again, by scholars trained in the schools of modern German philology and criticism, and every way equal to the task. Within the last thirty years, Hengstenberg, Sack, Hävernik, Reichel, Schulze, Herbst, Vaihinger, Delitsch, Oeler, Auberlen, Zündel, have stood forward as successful vindicators of the genuineness of Daniel's prophecies. Kurz, Keil, v. Hoffmann, Drechsel, Baum-

* 'Prophetismus,' ii. 401.

garten have also confessed their adhesion to the ancient faith.* A defender of the accuracy of Daniel's chronological statements has appeared in Marcus von Niebuhr, in his History of Assyria and Babylon. These writers show, one or other of them, that those interpreters who would make the seventy weeks end with Antiochus Epiphanes contradict and confute one another; that that period must begin at the going forth of the decree to rebuild Jerusalem, and must extend to the times of our Lord; that from the necessary and proved relations between chapters ix. and xi., the latter looks far beyond the days of Antiochus. They have answered the objections from the length of Daniel's life, from supposed contradictions, from history, from dates. They have proved that some of the supposed Græcisms are not Græcisms at all; that others were naturalised in the time of Daniel, the Greeks having had relations long before with the Assyrians; and, above all, that the Canon of the Old Testament was closed within one hundred years of the restoration of the Jewish State, and the book of Daniel, if not written before, could not have been admitted into it; that therefore the book of Daniel is both genuine and authentic.†

19. The other prophecy, whose genuineness Rationalist criticism has specially delighted to dispute, is that which is also specially vouched for by the New Testament, namely, that contained in the latter part of Isaiah (chapters xl.—lxvi.) and which seems really the connecting link between Old and New Testament revelation. It is a singular coincidence that those portions of the Old Testament which are most essential to New Testament theology—as the Pentateuch, the book of Daniel, and the latter part of Isaiah—are just those parts which Rationalist criticism has selected as the favourite fields on which to display its skill. Those Messianic predictions, which it can explain with plausibility as expressing Jewish hopes of earthly grandeur and prosperity, and incompatible with the teaching of

* Compare Auberlen's 'Der Prophet Daniel,' pp. 164–177.
† Compare what Bishop Butler has said: 'Analogy,' p. ii. c. vii. 3.

Christ, it pronounces to be genuine. The prophecies which represent the Son of Man as a heavenly judge, coming in the clouds of heaven (Dan. vii.); the Messiah as cut off (Dan. ix.); Sion's King as meek and lowly, and riding upon an ass (Zech. ix.); the good shepherd, sold for thirty pieces of silver (Zech. xi.); pierced by the inhabitants of Jerusalem (Zech. xii. 10, xiii.); despised and rejected of men, cut off out of the land of the living, one upon whom the Lord hath laid the iniquities of us all (Isaiah liii.)—are just the predictions which it proves to be ungenuine. The book of Daniel, the latter half of Zechariah, and the conclusion of Isaiah, which, if genuine, are fatal to Rationalist theology, are by Rationalist criticism condemned as ungenuine, in direct opposition to the teaching of the New Testament. The quotations from Zechariah are well known, the determination of our Lord to fulfil the ninth chapter of that prophecy obvious in the Gospels. The condemned portion of Isaiah is also emphatically honoured by the Lord and His Apostles. From the beginning to the end it is quoted as the work of Isaiah, and as fulfilled in our Lord. John the Baptist begins the interpretation with the opening prediction (Isaiah xl.) by declaring, "I am the voice of one crying in the wilderness, make straight the way of the Lord, as said the prophet Esaias" (John i. 23). Matthew xii. 17—21 explains Isaiah xlii. 1—3 of our Lord, and as the prophecy of Isaiah. The corresponding passage (xlix. 6) respecting the Lord's righteous servant is interpreted by St. Paul of the call of the Gentiles (Acts xiii. 47). The fifty-third chapter is appropriated by our Lord Himself (Luke xxii. 37); and, after Him, explained by Philip (Acts viii.); by St. Peter (1 Epist. ii. 24, 25); and in the Epistle to the Hebrews (ix. 28) of the sacrifice of Christ. Chapter lxi. 1 is also interpreted by our Lord of Himself (Luke iv. 17—21); and the end of the prophecy (lxv. 1) is in the Epistle to the Romans (x. 20, 21) expounded of the conversion of the Gentiles, and the unbelief of the Jewish people. Thus the whole of the prophecy, from the beginning to the end, is in the

New Testament ascribed to Isaiah as the writer, and cited as being fulfilled in our Lord, His sufferings, and His salvation. Both statements are denied by Rationalist writers, so that we cannot follow the latter without rejecting the teaching of the Lord and His Apostles, and the common belief of the Christian Church and the Jewish nation for nearly 1800 years. With regard to the authorship of this portion of Isaiah, there was during that long period only one opinion. One solitary rabbi in the twelfth century suggested a doubt on the subject, but, with the exception of Spinoza, was not followed by either Jews or Christians. It was not until men had ceased to believe in Christ that they began to question the latter prophecy of Isaiah. The Buxtorfs, the Carpzovs, Glassius, Gussetius, Cocceius, Venema, Vitringa, Schultens, Danz, the Michaelis, acquiesced in the judgment of antiquity. Even Paulus says that the diction is as pure as in the other parts of Isaiah. Eichhorn adduced no instances of later language. Bertholdt confesses that there are no traces of later usage. The first, and the great objection still, is that Cyrus is mentioned by name. When men came to teach either that God could not know beforehand the name of one of His creatures, or if He could, could not or would not communicate it before the existence of that creature, they necessarily thought that the prediction concerning the conqueror of Babylon must have been written after his appearance. The denial of the genuineness came first, the criticism came after, similar to that famous course of law which first condemned and executed, and afterwards proceeded to trial. Yet the process has led to beneficial results. The Rationalist dogmatic criticism has been subjected to a thorough examination by Hengstenberg, Hävernik, Kleinert, Drechsler, Keil, and others. The objections have been fairly met, and the claims of Isaiah to the latter chapters vindicated on various grounds, as, for example, the plain references to those chapters in the books of Nahum, Habakkuk, Zephaniah, Jeremiah; the circumstances of the times described, so exactly agreeing to the days of Isaiah, not to the close of the exile; the historical relations; the similarity of style and manner—the peculiarities of diction; the entire tone and colouring, not to mention other evidences external and internal. Indeed, Ewald and Bleek have made a fatal rent in the adverse criticism by confessing that the passage lvi. 9—lvii. 11, was written before the exile. "This passage," they say, "may be received with the highest probability as a prophetic oracle, uttered before the exile, perhaps by Isaiah himself; more probably not long before the exile, certainly at a time when the Jewish State still existed, as it is only on this supposition that the contents and composition can be understood." *

20. Even that chapter which invests the controversy with its chief interest (liii. 1—12) is supposed by Ewald to be the work of a prophet *anterior to the author of the other chapters;* and, referring to the strong traits of personal individuality, not personification, especially in verse 8, he says—"*The belief of after times, that the historic Messiah is here to be found, lay certainly very near at hand.*"† Indeed the prophetic picture of the sufferings of Jesus of Nazareth is so lifelike, that when it has been for the first time brought before Jews ignorant of the passage, they have affirmed that the chapter has been inserted in the Christian editions of the Hebrew Bible; whilst others, not a few, have been brought by it to faith in Christ. It is not, therefore, to be wondered at that for more than seventeen centuries the Christian Church received the prophecy as genuine; and that the Fathers, the medieval writers, the Reformers, Protestants and Romanists after the Reformation, with the one exception of Grotius, interpreted it of our Lord, until Deistic infidelity found its way into the hearts and minds of so-called Christian divines, and the necessities of the new theology imperatively demanded a new interpretation. First Neology and then Ration-

* Bleek, 'Einleitung,' p. 456; Ewald, 'Propheten des alten Bundes,' pp. 407, 8.

† Ibid. in the note.

alism set to work, and the result is a curious specimen of the alleged agreement of modern German expositors of prophecy. Here is one of the most striking and extended prophecies to be found in the Bible; not an obscure verse, where agreement is impossible, but an oracle running through twenty-seven chapters; and yet German commentators have not yet decided as to the fundamental principle of interpretation, whether the subject is an individual or a personified aggregate. Neither do the two parties formed by this difference agree among themselves. Of the first class, some interpret it of King Uzziah, others of Josiah, others of the prophet Isaiah himself, others of an unknown prophet persecuted and killed in the exile;* Bunsen alone, after Grotius, of the prophet Jeremiah. In the second class, the greatest names of Germany stand arrayed against each other. Eichhorn, Hendewerck, Köster, Hitzig, Ewald, Beck, interpret the prophecy of the Jewish people, actual or ideal. Paulus, Thenius, Maurer, von Cölln, Knobel, say that "The servant of the Lord" means the better portion of the exiles. Rosenmüller, Gesenius, De Wette, assert that he is a personification of the collective prophetic order.† For several of these interpretations, these distinguished writers are indebted to Jewish polemics. The application to Josiah was invented by Abarbanel in the sixteenth century; that to Jeremiah by Saadiah Gaon, in the ninth century; that to the whole Jewish people was known to the Jews with whom Origen disputed, and is most generally accepted by modern Jews; that to the pious or better portion of the people is found in Rashi, in the eleventh century. The ancient Jewish interpretation was that which referred the prophecy to the Messiah. From the LXX. it can be inferred with certainty that they distinguished between the servant of the Lord and the people of Israel. This is evident from their translation of xlii. 6 and xlix. 6, where they

* See Hengstenberg, 'Christologie,' i. p. 306; Gesenius's 'Commentary,' iii. pp. 164–172.

† See Knobel, 'Commentary,' pp. 382–390.

plainly make the Lord's servant "The raiser up of Jacob," and "The restorer of the dispersion of Israel," and "a covenant of the people," which words cause such difficulties to Rationalist interpreters as to make them violate the commonest proprieties of Hebrew idiom. When, therefore, the LXX. inserted the words "Jacob" and "Israel" in xlii. 1, "*Jacob* is my servant, and I will help him: *Israel* is mine elect, my soul hath accepted him,"—they did not mean to apply those words to the people, but to give to the servant of the Lord that title which he has in the Hebrew text in xlix. 3. "And He said to me, Thou art my servant: Israel art thou, in whom I will be glorified,"* where Gesenius, and before him J. D. Michaelis, in order to get rid of the plain meaning, propose to set critical authority at defiance, and oust the word "Israel" from the text. The LXX. have it here all right, where they plainly distinguish between the Lord's servant and the people, and thereby prove that they thought the words "Jacob" and "Israel" titles of this servant, and not the name of the people. And, therefore, in xlii. 19, "Who is blind but my servant? or deaf as my messenger that I sent? who is blind as he that is perfect, and blind as the Lord's servant?" which they interpret of the people, and not of the servant; they turn the singulars into plurals to prevent mistake—*καὶ τίς τυφλὸς ἀλλ' ἢ οἱ παῖδές μου, καὶ κωφοὶ ἀλλ' ἢ οἱ κυριεύοντες αὐτῶν; καὶ ἐτυφλώθησαν οἱ δοῦλοι τοῦ Θεοῦ.*

The early traditions of the Hebraist Jews are clear and unequivocal, and are identical with the New Testament interpretation, as is admitted even by the modern Rabbis,† who, for polemical reasons, interpret differently. Aben Esra, in the twelfth century, says, "Many have interpreted this chapter of Messiah because our ancients of blessed memory have said that

* This is the translation given by Gesenius of the text as it stands.

† By modern Rabbis are meant those who lived from the 11th century on, when, partly owing to the hostility excited by the Crusaders in the Jewish mind, and partly from their intercourse with the Mahometans, Jewish interpretation and Jewish theology underwent a great change, and diverged widely from ancient Judaism as well as from Christianity.

Messiah was born the same day that the Temple was destroyed, and that he is bound in chains." Rabbi Alshech, who flourished in Palestine in the middle of the sixteenth century, makes a similar confession—"Behold our Rabbis have with one mouth confirmed, and received by tradition that King Messiah is here spoken of . . . . . . He beareth the iniquities of the children of Israel, and behold His reward is with Him." The truth of these confessions may be seen by consulting the ancient books of authority. In Isai. xlii. 1, and lii. 13, Jonathan, about the time of our Lord, adds *Messiah* after the word "servant;" "Behold, my servant, the Messiah." The book of Zohar, regarded with the utmost reverence by all pious Jews, and parts of which are certainly from the first century of Christianity, also says plainly that Messiah bears the sins of the people, and that "If he had not removed them from Israel and taken them upon himself, no man could bear the chastisement of Israel on account of the punishment pronounced in the Law. This is what is written—*Surely He hath borne our sicknesses.* The Talmud (Sanhedrin, vol. 98, col. 2), the Psikṭa, and Yalkut Shimoni, all have the same interpretation. "Behold my servant shall deal very prudently—this is the King Messiah. He shall be exalted, and extolled, and be very high. He shall be *exalted* more than Abraham. . . . He shall be *extolled* more than Moses. . . . He shall be higher than the ministering angels. 'But He was wounded for our transgressions, He was bruised for our iniquities: the chastisement of our peace was upon Him, and with His stripes we are healed.' Rabbi Huna, in the name of Rabbi Acha says, the chastisements were divided into three parts:—one to David and the fathers; one to the rebellious generation; and one to King Messiah." Indeed, such possession had this interpretation of the Jewish mind, that it found its way into the prayers of the Synagogue, and there it remains until this day. In the Liturgy for the Day of Atonement is found the following remarkable passage, which is given from

David Levi's edition of the Synagogue service books, and in his translation. "Before he created anything, He established His dwelling (the temple) and *Yinnon.** Our righteous anointed is departed from us: horror hath seized us and we have none to justify. He hath borne the yoke of our iniquities, and of our transgression, and is wounded because of our transgression. He beareth our sins on His shoulder that He may first pardon for our iniquities. We shall be healed by His wound at the time that the Eternal will create Him (the Messiah) as a new creature. O bring Him up from the circle of the earth, raise Him up from Seir, to assemble us the second time on Lebanon by the hand of *Yinnon.*" † The Jewish editor, David Levi, endeavours to break the force of this passage by a note, explaining "our righteous anointed" of Josiah. But as he confesses that the whole passage refers to the Messiah, with whose name it begins and ends, and as the Hebrew words for "our righteous anointed One," literally, "Messiah our righteousness," are a common Rabbinic designation of the Messiah, taken from Jer. xiii. 6, this interpretation can only be regarded as a polemic evasion to avert the Jewish mind from the Christian interpretation of Isai. liii. Even in Levi's translation the passage speaks for itself, and as found in the service for the most solemn day in the whole Jewish year, proves that the Messianic interpretation was not only the ancient, but the national reception of the chapter. ‡ The Rabbinic tradition of two Messiahs, one to suffer and the other to reign, seems also to be a witness or a homage to the ancient interpretation of this chapter, and to the deep national conviction of the need of an

* *Yinnon* is the Hebrew word translated in the A. V. "shall be continued," Ps. lxxii. 17. But according to Jewish tradition, it is a name of the Messiah. "*Yinnon* was His name before the sun," i.e. before the creation of the world. As it comes from the verb נון, *to propagate*, they seem to have taken it in the same sense as צמח, חטר, נצר, and to have understood by it the Sonship of Messiah.

† "The name of the Messiah, as alluding to Psalm lxxii. 17." (Levi's Note.)

‡ Compare also the Prayers for the Feast of Passover, p. 72, where is another quotation of Isaiah liii. 13, which David Levi himself says means the true Messiah.

atonement. That this national persuasion ought to have some weight, even if not supported by the New Testament, will be admitted by candid readers. It acquires double weight from the fact that this interpretation is contrary to the worldly hopes of a conquering Messiah, so ardently entertained in the days of Roman domination in Palestine, and to which Rabbinic polemics still return in order to prove that Jesus cannot be the Messiah. With such hopes and prejudices, the idea of a suffering and despised Messiah could never have arisen, nor have been entertained, if it had not previously existed, and been received as true and genuine. The idea of pardon and salvation through the sufferings of another was equally contrary to the self-righteous doctrine of the Pharisees. The existence and continuance of such an interpretation, is, therefore, strong proof of its antiquity, and of its original source. The national interpretation of one of their own records, under such considerations, ought to have at least as much weight as the discordant and controverted opinions of critics living, according to their own showing, 2300 years after the record was written, and filled with antecedent prejudices against a true exegesis.

He must indeed be a man "that leans to his own understanding," who can lightly esteem the judgment of the ancient Jewish Church, and the common consent of all Christian scholars for nearly 1800 years,* and believe that he has found what such a goodly company have failed to perceive. But the Christian bows to still higher authority than the common judgment of this mighty host of the great, the good, the wise, and the learned, in so many ages and nations: he learns from Him whose Spirit spake in the Prophets, and guided His disciples and Apostles into all truth. Christ and His Apostles have interpreted this chapter of His sufferings, death, and resurrection-glory; and the providence of God has verified the interpretation.

* The one exception of Grotius makes the universal agreement the more striking.

Not to speak of the past, our eyes still see the fulfilment of this prediction. The most improbable prophecy in the world was this which predicted that a Jew, despised by his people, numbered amongst transgressors, cut off out of the land of the living, should, nevertheless, prolong his days, be the light of the Gentiles, and God's salvation to the ends of the earth. And yet this is what has been accomplished, and is accomplishing itself before our eyes. In spite of all the pride, prejudice, and power of Greeks and Romans, the ignorance. and fury of barbarian invaders, the self-sufficiency of human knowledge, the vices of civilisation, Jesus of Nazareth has triumphed, and triumphs, and is still the light of the world. The Christian humbly and thankfully accepts the teaching of the Lord, and the testimony of God's providence. The wondrous outline stands vividly marked on the page of prophecy; the fulfilment as unmistakably inscribed on the prominent pages of the world's history. The one answers to the other, as the mirror to the human face, and he cannot be mistaken. No microscopic investigations of criticism can make the agreement doubtful. He does not despise or disregard the labours of even hostile critics. On the contrary, he carefully considers their every suggestion, thankfully receives the light which they have thrown on words and phrases, acknowledges their diligence, their genius, their learning, and their honesty so far as their dogmatic prejudices allow them to be impartial. But Christ has spoken, and by Christ's words he abides. He, therefore, believes that the prophets spake as they were moved by the Holy Ghost; that they uttered predictions; that many of the most seemingly improbable have been fulfilled, and are pledges that the remainder shall also be accomplished. He cannot join in the unbelieving cry, "Where is the promise of His coming?" He does not believe that "since the fathers fell asleep all things continue as they were from the beginning of the creation," but that Christ "in His majesty rides prosperously on in the cause of truth, and meekness, and righteousness;" and "though the vision tarry," he waits for it, assured that it is "for an appointed time," and that "at the end it shall speak and not lie—it will surely come, it will not tarry."

ESSAY IV.

IDEOLOGY AND SUBSCRIPTION.

CONTENTS OF ESSAY IV.

IDEOLOGY AND SUBSCRIPTION.

1. The term Ideology is strange, and certainly not welcome to English ears; nor is it, perhaps, much to be feared that the system which bears the name will find many adherents, or exercise any direct influence upon the current of religious thought. A summary rejection may, therefore, at first sight, appear to be an effectual and satisfactory mode of disposing of its claims. Such, indeed, might be the case if we considered merely the abstract speculations with which Ideology is connected: but in its applications and bearings it assumes a very practical form. It touches the most important questions of morality, the most vital truths of religion. It affects the veracity or trustworthiness of the witnesses of revelation, the genuineness and integrity of its documents, their origin and interpretation, and by a strictly logical, though not perhaps a very obvious consequence, the relations between the Church, her people, and ministers. Such points must be scrutinized; the true character of the system, the principles on which it rests, and its inevitable results ought to be distinctly ascertained. Should it prove, as in all former controversies has been the case, that some great truths, not generally recognized in their fulness, find in the system, false and pernicious as it may be, a partial and inadequate expression; and that the very objections of ideologists enable us to comprehend, somewhat more clearly than heretofore, some essential characteristics of the Christian revelation, that result, at least, will be welcome to those who watch with interest, though not without perplexity and apprehension the progress of a religious speculation in

an age remarkable for fearlessness, and, it may be hoped, for sincerity, in the pursuit of truth.

2. The object of Ideology, as it is described in the writings of Strauss, who first presented it in a complete and systematic form, was to reconcile belief in the spiritual truths which he recognized as the ideal basis of Christianity, with rejection of all the miraculous events, and by far the largest portion of the narrative, with which those truths are connected. The rejection rests upon an assumption of the utter incredibility of miracles, as irreconcilable with philosophical principles, and as contrary to experience; and it is supported, as we shall see presently, by an unscrupulous use of arguments supplied by various schools of infidelity. But the chief peculiarity of the system is that, subject to this assumption, it professes to account for the existence of a belief in the facts, and for the form in which the facts are represented, and to explain the real significance of narratives involving supernatural elements. The ideologist, or idealist, asserts that such narratives are myths, which it would be absurd to regard as true in the letter, but which may yet be treated with respect, and even with reverence, as symbols and representations of ideas which are of permanent interest and importance to mankind. The facts did not, and could not, occur in the manner or under the circumstances described in Scripture, but they may yet be substantially, that is, ideally true, as products of human consciousness, as expressing at least the aspirations or presentiments of a nature akin to the divine. Many writers of this school (and Strauss himself in several passages) adopt, at times, a far more offensive tone, and do not hesitate to attribute the origin of large portions of the Gospel narrative to the prepossessions of the writers, to their ignorance, credulity, and fanaticism, or to selfish and interested motives. We do not propose to discuss those speculations. The only form in which the theory of ideologists is calculated to produce any effect upon generous and elevated minds, is that which accepts the ideal principles as true, while it de-

nies the historical character of the relations in which they are bodied forth.

3. One point strikes us *primâ facie* in considering this theory: and that is the very remarkable contrast which it exhibits to the position of those who formerly, either in England or on the continent, denied the objective facts of revelation. The strongest attacks have proceeded hitherto, not only from a distinct, but a diametrically opposite point of view. Sceptics and infidels used to argue that the doctrinal statements in the Bible are opposed to reason, and more especially to the moral consciousness of man; and they rejected the historical relations chiefly because they involved miraculous attestations to those statements. That position was at least consistent and intelligible; the issue one about which there could be no mistake. The Christian advocate had, of course, to prove that the history was sustained by evidence sufficient to satisfy impartial inquirers; but his great duty was to vindicate the Scriptural representations of the Divine attributes, and the principles on which God is described as conducting the moral government of the world. In the new system, on the contrary, the very adaptation of the doctrines of Scripture to our spiritual nature is taken as a proof, or presumption, that the forms in which they are presented must have been invented or remoulded by the plastic imagination of man. It is assumed not merely that the existence of certain feelings, opinions, or aspirations accounts for belief in the facts narrated by the evangelists, but that, taken as a whole, the objective system of revelation sprang out of the belief—was spontaneously evolved from the half-conscious operations of the human mind. Thus the need of a reconciliation with God was repudiated as a superstition by the old sceptic; according to the idealist, it was the feeling of such a need which invested the death of an innocent man with the attributes of a sacrificial atonement. The longing for communion with God, derided as mysticism by the former, according to the latter, originated the idea of the incarnation; while all that

appeared necessary to substantiate the doctrine, in the way of miraculous attestation or divine endowment, was supplied by the credulity or imagination of the followers of one who, at a critical period in the world's history, concentrated in himself the reverence and admiration of zealous converts. Clustering around one gracious form, one wise, and loving, and truly sublime being, human yearnings, human tendernesses, sought and found in him a visible representation of the Deity.* In short, according to ideologists, the circumstances of our Lord's nativity and baptism, His conflict with Satan, His manifestations of superhuman powers, and predictions of the immediate or remote future, His resurrection and ascension,—indeed, all the cardinal facts of religion,—are so far from being, as older sceptics affirmed, opposed to our moral consciousness, that they are all but adequate representations of the ideal, which, if it could be realized, would satisfy the very deepest and most universal aspirations of mankind.

4. Certainly no greater contrast could be imagined between two classes of men who concur in rejecting the facts, and employ nearly the same processes in their attempts to discredit the sacred narrative, so far as it involves what they are pleased to call violations † of universal laws. It may be that the two systems are not merely contrasted to each other, but that each contains a principle, which, if disentangled from the errors in which it is enveloped, may suffice for the exposure and overthrow of the opposite fallacy. Destroying each other mutually as systems, each may leave a residuum of truth available for the defence of the position which they both assail.

On the one side we have the fact that inquirers, whom none would hold to be influenced by doctrinal prejudices and prepossessions, recognize the adaptation

* Strauss in his answer to Steudel makes the whole impulsive force of Christianity centre in the personality of Jesus. In the concluding chapter of the 'Leben Jesu,' he acknowledges the peculiar and unique grandeur of our Lord's person.

† See Butler's remarks on the objections to miracles, 'Analogy,' part ii. c. iv. His theory, that miracles may be referred to some universal, though unknown, law has been strangely misrepresented.

of Christian principles * to the wants and instincts of humanity. This fact not only contradicts, but it utterly subverts, the position of those who assert that the doctrines are so repugnant to those instincts as to make the transactions incredible by which they are attested. The old dry scepticism cannot stand when confronted with such a recognition of the intrinsic excellence and spirituality of Christian truth, as is at present actually professed by the majority, or at any rate by the most intellectual and influential, among those whom freethinkers regard as the leaders and representatives of modern thought.† That form of disbelief has the ground cut away from under its feet. It must be regarded as a mere subjective impression, or an indication of disorder in a man's moral nature. The minds which reject such truths cannot be in what mere philosophers, looking on the whole matter from without, would admit to be a healthy and normal state.

Still the old sceptic has some stubborn facts on his side which are wholly inexplicable on the opposite system. There is the fact that, since the first promulgation of Christianity, multitudes have rejected, myriads misunderstood, or are utterly unable to realize its distinctive doctrines,—those, for instance, which the most thoughtful idealists regard with admiration. This is surely incompatible with the theory that the human mind could of itself have originated or developed the doctrines, or that it should, consciously or unconsciously, have distorted historical events so as to represent them in a concrete form. Those doctrines jar too harshly with the mind in its natural state, excite man's fears too painfully, to admit the supposition that they could be the spontaneous product of human consciousness. Under certain conditions, it is true that they

* That was the opinion of all the followers of Hegel until they were broken into opposite parties by the publication of Strauss's book. Of late years the denial of such adaptation marked a man's place on the extreme left, or destructive side.

† In fact the overthrow of the older Rationalism in Germany, which exactly corresponded with English Deism, is claimed as the great work of the system in which Ideology originated. See Schwartz, Zur Geschichte der neuesten Theologie, p. 95.

find an echo in the conscience, and give an intelligible solution to many dark problems of the universe: but the very first of those conditions is a subjective change of which neither sceptic nor ideologist can give any probable account. The religion which involves those doctrines, which speaks of a futurity of retribution, which contradicts the most widely spread prejudices, and sets up an exemplar utterly unlike the heroes and deities of all nations, is one which certainly could not have been devised or anticipated by man. Thus scepticism by the very fact of its prevalence overthrows the position of the ideologist: while the objections and contradictions of both find at once their explanation and their refutation in that position which we hold, not only as a matter of faith, but of experience. Christian truth, and the facts of revelation by which it is represented, are in accordance with the fundamental principles of human reason and conscience; yet they are only accepted by man when those principles are themselves distinctly recognized,—that is, when both reason and conscience are raised out of the state of corruption and degradation into which they had unquestionably sunk when Christianity was first promulgated. The accordance removes all *à priori* moral objections to the consideration of the evidence by which those truths and facts are attested, while the actual repugnance of so large a portion of mankind to admit the doctrine is absolutely fatal to the theory of its origination in human consciousness, apart from an external supernatural impulse.

5. This argument is not to be set aside as a mere logomachy, an attempt to neutralize conflicting opinions. It is but one instance among many, of the way in which truth is elicited by the collision of opposite errors. Our object, however, is not so much to confute as to convince, certainly not to exasperate, conscientious opponents; and this object may perhaps be better attained by an inquiry how the contemplation of Christianity, being a perfect realization of a perfect ideal, could have suggested to any one such a theory as that which is presented to us by ideologists.

6. In some sense all philosophers admit that the outward world is the result and representation of the invisible. According to materialists all phænomena are the products and exhibition of self-sustaining and self-evolving powers which pervade all nature—that is, of invisible forces known only by their effects. According to Theists the whole universe is the product and manifestation of a creating, preserving, and ruling will. The events of history are in a special sense manifestations of the law which that will imposes upon the development of the human race. The law itself is discoverable to a certain extent by reflection upon those events; Christians believe that it is revealed fully in the sacred writings. All facts indeed are in some sense the concrete results and expression of some absolute principle, some unseen power, some general law.* There is in reality no such thing as a dead matter of fact, no chance, no casual occurrence, in the history of the world. Joined one to the other in an unbroken series of cause and effect, every fact, every event finds its necessary place in the universal order; each is a link in that chain, which according to materialists had no beginning and will have no end, which according to Theists is fastened by each extremity to the throne of God. Christians accept the statement that all existences are the result of universal law, but they hold that law to be the expression of a supreme intellect and infinite love: deriving its force solely from the will of God.

7. Here we stand on a platform on which, whether agreed or not, we can at least understand our relative positions. We may advance a stage further, and that brings us to the real issue. It may be true, that in a general survey of history, principles of law and order are discernible; but it is certain that the difficulty is great, if not insuperable, when we seek to ascertain

* This truth is recognized quite as distinctly by Butler and all other great champions of Revelation as by its strongest opponents. "All reasonable men know certainly that there cannot be any such thing as chance; and conclude that the things which have this appearance are the results of general laws, and may be reduced into them." Analogy, ii. c. iv. § 3.

the operations of those principles in individual cases,* when we would apply them to account for events recorded by secular historians. When thought sweeps over a wide expanse, it is confused by the multiplicity of apparently abnormal and contradictory phænomena—

"It is most hard, with an untroubled ear,
Those dark inwoven harmonies to hear."

Certain personages stand forth from time to time, in grand critical epochs of the world's development, as representative men, but seldom, if ever, are they adequate representatives of high, never of the highest principles.† Striking indications are given of an unseen presence by which all processes are guided, and of ends which all subordinate occurrences subserve. But over the whole there is a mist, sometimes broken, sometimes seeming to transmit light from a higher sphere, but for the most part dense and impenetrable. Aberrations and inconsistencies, contradictions and divergencies, confound the philosophic reader of history, in the attempt to arrive at a distinct perception of the general principles, the universal laws, which underlie and govern the complicated series of external events.

One unquestionable result of this fact requires special attention. The discrepancy between events as they occur in secular history, and the absolute ideas or principles which all events rightly understood exemplify and represent, is in point of fact so far recognized by the human mind, that whenever we read a narrative in which the ideal and real are presented in perfect accordance, we are all but irresistibly impressed with the conviction that it must be fictitious. Fiction, as Aristotle long since taught, is more catholic than

* Thus Butler, l. c.: "It is but an exceeding little way, and in but few respects, that we can trace up the natural course of things before us to general laws." Mr. Jowett has said, in an essay of most melancholy tendency, "In the study of ethnology, or geology, in the records of our own or past times, a curtain drops over the Divine presence."—On the Epistles of St. Paul, vol. ii., p. 483, 2nd edition.

† This position and its bearings upon Ideologists were discussed with great ability and persuasiveness by Ullmann in the 'Studien und Kritiken,' 1836, No. 3. This treatise, which was afterwards reprinted with the title 'Historisch oder Mythisch,' induced Strauss himself to modify the conclusion of his 'Leben Jesu.'

reality; that is, it is a more obvious and perfect exemplification of general principles. A perfectly good, and entirely consistent man, a life in which all events should be so ordered as to harmonize with our ideas of fitness and justice, a series of events in which the moral government of the Supreme Being should be outwardly and demonstrably exemplified, would seem to us from a purely secular point of view a sheer impossibility. The Hegelian is right, so far as ordinary men and ordinary events are concerned, in his theory that the ideal is ever striving for realization, but that it never is realized. That is an old truth which our own Hooker has stated in terms at once more simple and accurate—"All things besides, God excepted, are somewhat in possibility which as yet they are not in act." * The map of a country drawn in outlines of geometrical symmetry, a narrative in which all events are the development of some great principle and conduce to some one intelligible result, alike produce the impression of unreality. We do not see such things. They are contrary to experience. Scarcely any amount of external evidence would satisfy us of their truth.

It is just at this point that the controversy between the Christian and the Ideologist arises. The question is simply this: are the same principles applicable to secular history and to the records of a scheme which is professedly one of divine interpositions? † We see perfectly well that if they were applicable, the conclusions of the ideologist could scarcely be controverted. To one who does not view the sacred narrative as a thing apart, not merely in certain details, but in its entire construction, resting altogether upon different principles from those which he is accustomed to apply in historical investigations, its facts, whether or not what is commonly called miraculous, have *primâ facie* this characteristic of fiction. The long series of events recorded in the Bible, connected for ages with one family, but involving in its consequences all the destinies of mankind, unquestionably exemplifies certain

* E. P. i. 5. † See, for instance, Strauss's 'Leben Jesu,' Einleitung, § 8.

ideal principles, and that throughout and completely, in its organic structure and in its several parts. In the opinion of one who dismisses, without argument, all notions of supernatural intervention, such a fact is unaccountable, excepting upon the supposition that the history has been invented or essentially changed in character by the writers who have transmitted the traditional records in their actual state. Whether he attribute this to design, to the influence of high or low feelings, to superstition, ignorance, prejudice, or, on the other hand, to noble and generous aspirations, may be admitted to be a matter of considerable import so far as regards his own spiritual state; * but the result is alike destructive so far as regards the bearings of the argument upon the substantial verity of the Scriptures. The more solemn and majestic the events, the more completely in the ideologist's mind do they bear the essential character of a myth. In no portion of Holy Writ is such criticism more destructive than in that which presents to us the Life of our Lord—that perfect embodiment of an ideal, in itself without a parallel, in its realization transcending all conceptions of the human mind.†

9. We thus account for the position of the ideologist, and in accounting for it, we seem to gain a singularly distinct perception of what is surely the most positive and peculiar characteristic of Christianity. The attributes, the very nature of God, are manifested in the government of the world, viewed by the light of Scripture, but most specially and completely in the Person and works of the Son. Just in this point consists the real contrast between sacred and profane history. Profane history may not, and indeed it cannot contradict, but it certainly does not distinctly teach,

* All these influences are adopted by Strauss, as acting in co-ordination with the philosophical mythus, that which clothes in the garb of historical narrative a simple thought, a precept or idea of the time. L. J., Einleitung, § 8.

† Thus even Grotz, quoted in the 'Westminster Review,' July 1861. Strauss speaks scarcely less strongly of the marvellous and unrivalled beauty of the conception. See his answer to Ullmann, 'Vergängliches und Bleiben.' 1839.

some of the most momentous and necessary truths—such as the unity of God, the unity of the human race, the unity of human history, the universal principles of morality, or the systematic development of the purposes of an almighty and loving will. Historians, excepting so far as they have drawn light from other sources, do not in point of fact distinctly set forth all or any of these truths. Sacred history teaches them all, and teaches them not by mere abstractions, but by the representation of events in which our conceptions of what is right, reasonable, and desirable, find a perfect satisfaction. Our only postulate is one which cannot be denied on rational grounds by any but atheists* —that God has the will and the power of making Himself known to His creatures. That granted, the reasonableness and therefore the probability of such a manifestation of Himself can scarcely be denied. The intellect, freed from the shackles of sin and knowledge falsely so called, fastens with joy upon the one clue to the labyrinthine mazes of speculation. Holding it *à priori* to be possible that the Divine love may choose thus to deliver us from dark and dreary bewilderment, we gladly accept the proofs that such has been His gracious will. We believe that in another state the ideal will be thoroughly and universally realized, that each act and each existence, in its place and its degree, will be then a perfect exemplification of some eternal reality; and of this we are equally convinced that a foretaste and anticipation of that future harmony has been vouchsafed in the Scriptural narrative, most especially in the life and person of Jesus Christ.

10. It is a strange and instructive contrast which is thus presented between the effects of the Scriptural narrative upon the ideologist and upon the simple-hearted Christian. The traces of harmonious accord-

* Including all schools of Pantheism which deny the consciousness of God, and moreover those Deists who maintain the absolute necessity of all manifestations of the Divine nature in the world—who make the world, so to speak, the complete manifestation and body of the Deity. Such are J. H. Fichte, and C. H. Weisse, Schwartz, &c., in Germany; F. Newman (if, indeed, he recognizes at present any personal consciousness in God), and many others, in England.

ance impress the former with the conviction that he is listening to the record of a dream—beautiful it may be, and significant,—the dream of a poet, or a saint, of a spirit full of divine yearnings and sympathies, but still a dream—an empty, unsubstantial dream. The Christian sees in that accordance the evidence of a divine power; of all effects upon his mind the very last would be a doubt as to the reality of the objective facts which show how that power has been exerted for the regeneration of man.

11. This is a strong position to occupy, a secure resting-place for the spirit. We may profitably dwell somewhat in detail upon the thoughts which it suggests. Every fact in the life of our Master is in accordance with a spiritual principle which it actually and completely represents. Man, conscious of inherent weakness, longs for union with God. In the incarnation, God and man become one.

Man feels himself exposed to a strange fascination which attracts him towards evil and draws him away from God. In Christ he meets, baffles, and overcomes, the personal agent of all temptation. Man feels that he is a slave to nature, over which a sure instinct tells him that he is destined to rule. In Christ he exercises that dominion, making all physical forces subservient to his will. Man fears disease, affliction, and bereavement. In Christ all sorrows become medicinal, and conduce to the perfection of our renewed nature. Man has two great foes—sin, and death the penalty of sin. Christ crushes sin, and expels it from His dominions; death He converts into the last best friend, the opener of the portals of eternal life. Moved by the Spirit of God, the mind of man from age to age has uttered aspirations, more or less imperfectly comprehended, for a Saviour, a righteous Lord, a manifestation of God in a living human Person. One by one the characteristics of such a Person were traced by the spirit of prophecy: all the conditions of that manifestation, the object of His coming, the time, the circumstances, the various signs by which He might be recognized, were clearly predicted; those predictions were graven upon the hearts of the Israelites, and were even partially known to the Gentiles.* In Jesus, by a combination of circumstances which seems fortuitous, and, so far as human agents were concerned, beyond all question were undesigned, those predictions were fulfilled, apparent contradictions were reconciled; and, in a higher sense than the most gifted seers had imagined, those characteristics were exemplified. We see in Jesus perfect man, the one normal, ideal man, the one representative of the type which was in the thought of God when He moulded the frame of Adam, and breathed into his nostrils the breath of life.† In personal union with that perfect man we are taught to discern the living Word, the Son of God. If the whole structure of our religion be not a baseless vision, if all our hopes be not a miserable delusion, it is true, simply and absolutely true, that in that Person the perfect ideal is perfectly real. We expect, therefore, to find—in fact we should be confounded if we did not find—in the history of the God-man‡ just that harmony, unity, and complete interpenetration of all that is good and beautiful in abstract principles, that perfect representation of inward spiritual truths, of which genius has dreamed, but which it has vainly striven to realize. We feel that such a history must be sacramental. And thus, in the very facts which create distrust in the ideologist, we find the strongest confirmation of our faith. We are entitled to say to him —You cannot surely be so unreasonable as to call upon

* Strauss adopts the view that the whole life of Jesus, all that He should or would do, had an ideal existence in the Jewish mind long before His birth. Einleitung, § 11.

† This thought, as might be expected, is worked out very thoroughly by the best divines of modern Germany; but it belongs to the old schools of Hebrew exegesis, or, to speak more correctly, underlies all the Biblical intimation of the future Messiah's person and work. (See the account of the Adam Cadmon in Dorner's 'Einleitung to his Christology.') It is not surprising, when we consider the immense importance of the principle, that the followers of opposite and conflicting systems of philosophy should have claimed it for their own leaders. The Hegelians were especially anxious to prove that in its philosophic form the truth was recognized and taught by Hegel. See Göschel, Von Gott, dem Menschen und dem Gottmenschen.

‡ θεάνθρωπος, a most pregnant term, used very frequently by the Greek Fathers.

us to give up any part of what you must admit to be a consistent and complete realization of that which you profess to recognize as good and beautiful simply on the ground that it is too good, too beautiful, to be true.* We have, as you must confess, full access to the ideal sphere in which the soul may expatiate with delight. You cannot wish us to pass over to you, with nothing to gain, with so much to lose, even in your opinion, in our own not less than all. You offer us, in fact, nothing but the substitution of moral and intellectual speculations of the most bewildering character, in place of difficulties which a simple faith enables a sound reason practically to overcome. We, on the contrary, have every motive to call on you to pass over to our side: what you have to sacrifice is a mere notion, a novel one even in the schools of philosophy, as to the incredibility of an external and perfect manifestation of the divine. What you have to gain is the realization of the dearest and deepest hopes of humanity—hopes which nothing short of such a realization can satisfy and fulfil.

12. It would be a good thing if our countrymen, and especially our younger countrymen, would distinctly contemplate the alternative which they must in consistency adopt when the claims of the Scriptural narrative are confronted with ideologists. We may owe something even to the fearless speculators who, obscure and perplexing as their writings are in other respects, have at least brought this question to a definite issue. For young men of active and liberal spirits (indeed, for all who venture into the region of speculative inquiry, for those more especially who hang about its outskirts) the chief danger is that they may adopt opinions which are intrinsically antagonistic to truth, without any suspicion of their tendencies and necessary results. It is well that such tendencies are at any rate brought out distinctly. Some few may possibly accept the conclusions to which the speculations lead:

* Strauss, speaking of the theory in the very imperfect form which was given to it by Schleiermacher, calls it a beautiful effort of thought.

but even for them it may be better that they should arrive rapidly at the end, and find by experience its barrenness and emptiness. The recoil from the dreary void of sceptical negation has been to some, and those no ignoble spirits, the first movement towards the recovery of truth. But the great majority of Englishmen are extremely unlikely, even for a season, to find any resting-place in a system which makes the deepest and most practical convictions dependent upon metaphysical abstractions, depriving them of the foundation of positive objective facts.* Once assured that ideology simply means denial of the veracity of the writers who bear witness to miraculous facts—of the truth of the whole, or of any considerable portion of the book, in which it nevertheless recognizes utterances of a divine spirit, they will turn aside in contempt from what must seem to them a suicidal inconsistency. One great characteristic of Englishmen—the characteristic, in fact, on which they may justly rest their claims to a foremost (indeed *the* foremost) position among the representative races of humanity—is the belief in, and the love of, positive objective truth. Once convinced of the untruthfulness of a writer, no ingenuity of reasoning, no fascination of style, no adaptation of his statements to their feelings or prejudices, will induce them to listen to his words. They may be slow to discern the symptoms of untruthfulness, may be deceived and misled, but they will have but one short word to designate what they are once convinced has no founda-

* Such, too, was the state of feeling in Germany. A writer, whose bias is utterly opposed to orthodoxy, declares truly that the orthodox reaction originated among men connected with public life—leaders of the patriotic outburst—that the religious systems of the Berlin schools were too spiritualistic, too thin and fine drawn, too sentimental and indefinite to produce practical results. What men wanted was a right, massive, sturdy, popular Christianity, such as Luther preached. "In truth there was a deep chasm between the new intellectual character (Geistesbildung) presented by the leaders in philosophy and poetry, and the wants of the people. See Schwartz, 'Zur Geschichte der neuesten Theologie,' p. 67. The whole chapter is instructive, as showing the utter unfitness of Rationalism in any of its forms, Idealism included, to act on the moral and spiritual life of the people—that is, to do the special and peculiar work of Christianity. A form of religion which admits that incapacity stands self-condemned. The arguments of Origen against Celsus are particularly worthy of consideration in their bearings upon this question. See lib. vi. 2, and vii. 59, 60.

tion in fact. The very last position which they will admit as possible, or tolerate as defensible, is, that truths of infinite import should have been transmitted from the divine to the human intelligence by unveracious witnesses, or through the medium of events distorted by enthusiasts. The Englishman may be narrow-minded or prejudiced, unapt to deal with abstract speculations; but he has at least had his training,—he has been accustomed to weigh evidence, to seek for matter of fact truth in the first place, and to satisfy himself as to the good faith and correct information of those from whom he expects to receive knowledge or instruction. One thing with him is fixed and certain; whatever else may be doubtful, this at least is sure—a narrative purporting to be one of positive facts, which is wholly or in any essential or considerable portion untrue, can have no connection with the Divine, and cannot have any beneficial influence upon mankind. As for the doctrines which are based upon it, or inseparably bound up with it, they must have their origin in another region than that of light. He will not allow himself to be entangled in the mazes of speculation. Without troubling himself as to the direction in which they may lead him, he will stop at the threshold: he will say—Before I go one step further, let me know what you say to our Lord's miracles—to the miracle of miracles, the Resurrection. Is it a fact or not? As for the doctrine, which, as you say, it may represent, we may inquire about that hereafter; but let us first know on what we stand—on the shifting quicksands of opinion, or on the solid ground of positive objective fact.

13. It may be said that it is unfair to press a man, and by urging the consequences of his opinions, to drive him from a position in which even for a time he may find refuge from utter unbelief. This consideration would undoubtedly have great weight if the question regarded only the speculative inquirer. Charity cannot be carried too far in judging any man's motives, in bearing with his perplexities, and putting the most

favourable construction upon his words: but when a man propounds his opinions publicly, works them up into an elaborate system, and commends them by all the graces and artifices of rhetoric, his object is evidently not so much to satisfy his own mind, as to influence the minds of others; and for their sake it is necessary to ascertain his meaning, and to show clearly the principles upon which his system rests, and the consequences which it involves. Above all, is this our duty when those principles are introduced rather by insinuation than by direct assertion, and are directly connected with the recommendation of disingenuous acts, by which the safeguards of religion are undermined. We consider it a fortunate circumstance that, on the first appearance of ideology, so much of its true character has been disclosed. In order, however, thoroughly to comprehend its bearings, and to prove its internal and necessary connection with the ultimate principles of unbelief, it will be expedient to give some account of its origination and development in Germany. Some of the facts which follow are unknown to the generality of English readers; they certainly ought to be known by all who feel interested in the progress and tendencies of Rationalism in its most ingenious and subtle form.

14. It has been already stated that ideology was first presented as a distinct and complete system in the writings of Strauss. His Life of Jesus is universally recognized as the beginning of a new epoch in theological speculations. The writer himself has lately asserted, with characteristic arrogance, that no work of any importance has since been written upon any portion of the evangelical narrative without reference to his book. The vaunt, as we shall see, is not an empty one. That work did concentrate and systematize all that infidelity had previously advanced or suggested against the credibility of the Gospels and the whole system of Christianity as an objective revelation. The destructive criticism of rationalists, and the mysticism of Hegel, were brought together; that to discredit the

facts of revelation, this to supply a new foundation for the speculations which Strauss proposes as the substitute for historical Christianity.

15. By education and circumstances, and also, it must be admitted, by some rare and eminent gifts, Strauss was qualified for the position he assumed. He was brought up at Tübingen, an university which, in in its retention of ancient forms of discipline, still bears more resemblance to Oxford than to any institution in Germany; and, when he was a student, it was justly regarded as the stronghold of Lutheran orthodoxy. Among others less widely known, but sound in the faith,—such as Storr, Flatt, and Steudel,—Tübingen boasts of the great name of Bengel. In that school Strauss learned somewhat of the nature of the principles which he was to attack. Under F. C. Baur, since known as the most subtle and learned of neologians, but whose tendencies were then scarcely suspected, he acquired the habit of sceptical investigation, and imbibed a rooted antipathy to what the Germans call "supernaturalism"—that is, the recognition of a miraculous element in religion. Free from any taint of sensuality, he bore a high character, to which his influence among the students and professors may in part be attributed. On the other hand, utterly indifferent to the tendencies or results of his inquiries, singularly devoid of geniality or sympathy, he evinced on all occasions a supercilious disregard for feelings which he might wound, combined with a total absence of reverence for the divine. His intellect was keen and clear; his natural aptitude for dialectical subtilties was developed by intense application: he had also a power, not common in any country, and extremely rare in his own, that of presenting the results of his labours in an intelligible and interesting form, with the advantages of artistic arrangement and a perspicuous style.

16. In the year 1831, Strauss, until then a Repetent or assistant tutor at Tübingen, went to Berlin, at that time the centre of all speculative movements in theology and philosophy. Schleiermacher stood at the

head. Few men have exercised a wider or more powerful influence. His vast learning and vigorous intellect; his lively and persuasive eloquence; above all, his peculiar mode of inculcating religious principles, attracted many of the noblest and most powerful minds. The characteristic of his system was the prominence which he gave to religious feeling—subjective feeling was to him and the most influential of his followers the one test both of the importance and reality of spiritual truths: and to his teaching may be traced that aversion to what is called dogmatism, which distinguishes many of our own writers who, without adopting all his views, have passed through his school. His influence over Strauss, however, depended upon other qualities. Schleiermacher combined with a peculiarly genial and winning sweetness of character, and with a dreamy but graceful and attractive sentimentalism, a no less remarkable talent for sarcastic and reckless criticism. No man was more acute in detecting flaws, none more unscrupulous in exposing what he deemed to be inconsistencies. None had hitherto gone so far in discrediting large portions of the Scriptural narrative, or in assailing the authenticity of canonical books.* When Strauss came to Berlin, Schleiermacher

* This statement may seem too harsh. Schwartz, however, a critic who has the greatest admiration and even reverence for Schleiermacher, observes that the critical processes by which Strauss attempted to overthrow the sacred history were learned in the school of Schleiermacher. "Originating with Semler and Eichhorn, they had been developed in rationalistic circles, and *reached their highest point* in the labours of De Wette, Schleiermacher, and Gieseler." Zur Geschichte der neuesten Theologie, p. 33. A most important statement for the young student of German theology. Gieseler himself gives the following account of that great man's principles:—"Schleiermacher went very far in his concessions to modern opinion. He admitted that the piety of a Pantheist might be identical with that of a Monotheist, and reconcilable even with Christianity. That piety, moreover, could coexist with the theory which, denying the continuance of personal existence, regards the common spirit of humanity as the source of individual souls, the true living unity, of which alone eternity and immortality can be predicated; individual souls being its transitory actions, or manifestations. For the Christian as such there is no guarantee for personal duration, save that which is found in the belief of the eternal union of the Divine Essence with the human nature in Christ. The historical connection of Christianity with Judaism is external, precisely the same as with heathenism—hence he assigns to the Old Testament no normal authority. Angels are creatures of the imagination—in the idea of the devil he finds an internal contradiction—but he *consents to retain angels and devils for liturgical use.* The resurrection of

had been giving a course of lectures on the life of Jesus, which are characterized by a friendly critic as full of acute combinations and destructive scepticism. Those lectures were, indeed, the chief attraction which drew him thither.* They gave the strongest impulse to his own work of demolition.

17. It was not, however, in the system of Schleiermacher that Strauss found the true key to his own position. He was abundantly supplied with weapons for attack. Rationalists and sentimentalists had undermined the outworks of revelation: but he saw plainly that something more and something different was needed to account for the origin of Christianity; and it was perfectly clear to him that the battered and disfigured fabric of what he regarded as mere superstition could not be demolished and swept away, unless it were displaced by a system better calculated to meet the requirements of the human mind.

It seems strange that he should have fixed upon Hegelianism for that purpose; for Hegel, then in the full noontide of his influence, was regarded as the bulwark of orthodox conservatism both in church and state. The fundamental doctrines of religion, the dogmatic forms of the church, even the most abstruse and difficult speculations of theologians and schoolmen, were at that very time maintained by professors of the school of Hegel, who were recognized by him as faithful and intelligent expositors of his views. It was believed that he had effected a real and permanent reconciliation between philosophy and religion. Faith and knowledge henceforth were to work together in perfect harmony; all apparent contradictions were to be absorbed; all perplexing problems to find a solution in the higher sphere of metaphysical abstraction. A new

the body and the last judgment are to be understood not as positive truths, but as the outward representations of general truths. Eternal damnation is rejected as inconceivable."—Kirchengeschichte der neuesten Zeit, p. 240.

* See Schwartz, l. c. Strauss himself says that he procured the MS. of the lectures which had been given before his arrival. He points out the difference between his own views and those of Schleiermacher, who wished to retain, by help of naturalistic interpretations, the substance of the Gospel narration. His statement is quite compatible with that of Schwartz.

system of optimism was founded, which acknowledged the State not merely as a necessary organization, but as the highest realization of the ideal of society, and rejected all factious and democratic tendencies as pernicious errors; while, in their ecclesiastical tendencies, Hegel's principles seemed rather to verge towards Romanism than towards the dissolution of all formal authority, which appeared imminent as a development of infidelity under the thin disguise of rational Protestantism. He was, in fact, by taste, habits, and disposition a conservative, both as regarded the outward framework of church and state, and the dogmatic representation of religious truths. It may seem strange; but it was a proof of the clear insight and vigorous intellect of Strauss, that in the fundamental principles of that philosopher's system, he discerned the motive power which he required to overthrow all which it appeared to accept so unreservedly and to defend with unprecedented success.

We can scarcely hope, and will not attempt, to state those principles in a clear or even intelligible form; but some of the results, as Strauss apprehended and applied them, are practical enough. His exposition, moreover, has been justified both by the adhesion of a considerable number of those who were once the stanchest maintainers of their master's orthodoxy, and by the ultimate overthrow of the system itself, which is now, in the form which Hegel gave it, altogether a thing of the past.* Under the abstruse and cloudy statements of that philosopher,† Strauss saw clearly

* M. Scherer says—"Il a fait faillite, et c'est le positivisme qui a pris la suite de ses affaires." And elsewhere—"Ce bulle de savon a crevé depuis longtemps."

† Hegel taught that the universe is but a continuous evolution of an infinite potentiality; that the absolute is not found either in the ideal substratum, which *is not* a positive existence, or in matter of fact phenomena, which have no permanent reality, but in a perpetual process of self-development. Whatever exists has a necessary but a merely transitory existence. The ideal is ever tending to realization, but is never perfectly, and cannot be permanently, realized. It was a question among his followers whether he regarded Christianity, in the Person of its Founder, as an exception from these sweeping conclusions—whether his system was compatible with Theism. It seems to me scarcely possible to reconcile many statements in his first considerable work (the 'Phänomenologie des Geistes') with belief in a per-

involved the positive denial of the personality of the Godhead, the assertion of the phenomenal and evanescent, the incomplete and inadequate character of all existences, the absorption of individuality; in short, a complete system of pantheism, more idealistic than any previous development, and at the same time more capable of explaining the events of history both profane and sacred.

18. Strauss took some time to prepare a work in which he applied these principles to the overthrow of Christianity. The 'Life of Jesus' was published in 1835. It appeared at a period of outward calm; there was a singular cessation just then of controversy, a general feeling of security. Hegel had been dead four years. He had departed, so to speak, in the odour of orthodoxy. Marheineke, Daub, and Göschel were recognized as true expositors of his system, and as sound defenders of the faith. Schleiermacher, too, was gone. His followers claimed for him the merit of having destroyed the older forms of rationalism, which had sunk into utter contempt. Neander at Berlin, Tholuck at Halle, Steudel at Tübingen, and a host of theologians of various shades of opinion, ranging from orthodoxy to neology, but animated for the most part by deep Christian sympathies, occupied the professorial chairs; while a strong and united band of men, sound in the old Bible orthodoxy, wrought more directly upon the popular mind through the pulpit. The effect of the publication of Strauss's book is indescribable. Friends and enemies cannot find words strong enough to express the consternation, the horror and indignation of all who

sonal God. It is certain that no Christian theologians now accept the applications of his general principles to Christian dogmas. Chalybæus admits the "comfortless results" of the whole system. On the attempts of Marheineke and Goschel, some valuable remarks may be read in Gieseler's 'Kirchengeschichte d. n. Z.,' p. 242. Strauss also gives a clear account of the disputes between the scholars of Hegel in his 'Glaubenslehre,' p. 520 ff. It is, however, certain that Hegel wished to maintain religion—that he regarded the establishment of Theism as the highest problem and work of philosophy, and utterly detested all sceptical and destructive criticism, especially that of Schleiermacher—an aversion extending even to purely secular writers, as Niebuhr. His last work, on the Philosophy of Religion, is full of beautiful and devout aspirations: whether they are consistent with his philosophy or not, is another question.

retained a vestige of reverence for religion. An electric shock running through all bosoms, a trumpet sounding the signal for a conflict for life and death, an earthquake shaking the foundations of all human hopes ; such are the terms which historians use in speaking of the shock.* Our own time has lately had an example of the effect which is produced when men known only as able, industrious scholars, of unspotted character, and exemplary in all personal relations, come forward as the opponents of truths which they are bound to uphold. The excitement and panic, if panic it can be called which brought hosts of combatants to the front of the battle, had then a further justification in the talents, unity of purpose, straightforward audacity of the author—in his thorough mastery of all the weapons of attack, in the coherence of his philosophical principles—principles, as we have shown already, accepted by multitudes of thoughtful men—above all in the state of the public mind, shaken by rationalism, distrustful of its guides, unable to comprehend the position of the recognized defenders of religion, and tossed to and fro by conflicting systems of doctrine and interpretation. Strauss was at least a brave and open foe, showed his true colours, and nailed them to the mast, and met every attack manfully,—open as he certainly was to the imputation of making a dishonest use of a position entrusted to him for the defence of Christianity.

19. In that work Strauss had two distinct objects. The first was to set aside all supernatural events, to prove that the Divine did not manifest itself in the manner related, and that the actual occurrences were not divine.† The other was to set up a system in which all that Christianity attempts to accomplish should be disentangled from its imperfect form, and developed, by

* Compare Schwartz, Zur Geschichte der neuesten Theologie, and M. E. Scherer, Revue des Deux Mondes, Feb. 1861; and Gieseler. Strauss himself speaks with great exultation of the shrieks of believers. See the introduction to his second edition.

† Introduction, § 1. See also his Streitschriften, part iii., p. 59. He gives a full account of the original plan of his work (showing that the second part was that to which he attached most importance) in the treatise 'Verhältniss der Hegel'schen Philosophie zur Kritik.'

a philosophical process, from universal and permanent truths.

20. In the first part of the work Strauss collected all the objections which a remorseless criticism had raised against the historical veracity of the sacred writers: he completed them, gave them a sharper point and keener edge, combined them in a systematic form, and reduced them to a fundamental thought.* De Wette had already laid down the position, that all men of cultivated minds rejected the miraculous narratives of the Bible, and that the only question was how to account for their origin.† Strauss addressed himself to that question. First laying down far more broadly the general position, that miracles are *à priori* incredible, on the ground that the workings of the Divine in the world proceed in accordance with fixed, unvarying, and universal laws, which utterly exclude the possibility of miracles, ‡ he refers all accounts of supernatural interventions to one origin—that of *Myths.* Here again he adopts what sceptics or infidels had previously suggested. Semler had applied to the account of Samson and Esther the saying of Heyne, that all the history and philosophy of primitive antiquity originated in myths. Vater, and still more decidedly De Wette, had advocated the mythical interpretation of a large portion of the Old Testament§ history. But, as Strauss complains, that system had been applied inconsistently and timidly even to the Old Testament, and had stood side by side with naturalistic interpretations, while few had ventured to bring it to bear upon any portion of the Gospel narrative. Yet even here the way had been prepared. Schleiermacher had not hesitated to call the history of the Temptation a myth. Gabler, and others

* Schwartz, 'Zur Geschichte der neuesten Theologie,' p. 104.

† That position was taken in the work which in Germany, some thirty years ago, was put into my hands as an introduction to the study of the Hebrew Scriptures.

‡ Strauss uses precisely the same language as Baden Powell. See his Introduction, vol. i. p. 71 of the English translation. In p. 87, § 16, he gives the marks by which the unhistorical character of a narrative may be *à priori* demonstrated—the principal is the impossibility of any arbitrary act of interposition by the absolute cause.

§ Kritik der Mosaischen Geschichte, quoted by Strauss. Introduction, § 8.

of his school, held that all portions of the narrative which involved angelic appearances had the essential characteristics of myth. Some theologians had gone so far as to bring the details, first of the Nativity, and then of the Resurrection, under the same category. The barriers had been thrown down, and all that remained for Strauss to do was to carry out the principle consistently into the whole structure of the New Testament. To use his own words: "Others had driven through the grand portal of myths into the evangelical history, and had passed out again by the same; but as for all the intermediate portions, they were contented to pursue the crooked and laborious paths of natural interpretation." He left himself no portion of our Lord's life untouched. He saw too clearly the internal coherence of all its parts; he discerned the unity of the principles which underlie all its phenomena: all or nothing must be admitted. Rejecting with disdain the subterfuges of rationalist and semi-rationalist, he would not, as he says, set up the authority of one Evangelist against another. The testimony of one is worth as much, or to speak more correctly, is worth as little as the others.* A *bellum omnium contra omnes* is waged; from beginning to end he finds no single spot of firm historical ground, scarcely any mixture of ascertainable fact, amid the legendary and mythical representations.†

Strauss enters, of course, fully into the investigation of myths,‡ which had already been classified under three heads; the historical, which confound the natural and supernatural; the philosophical, which clothe in

* Schwartz, Zur Geschichte, p. 110.

† To allow time for such a transmutation of history, which, as all historians agree, is only possible in times when letters are unknown or unused, when events are transmitted by ignorance and superstition, Strauss was driven to the theory, that all the Gospel narratives were the product of the second century, a theory which is admitted universally, even by unchristian critics, to be irreconcilable with facts: with the failure of that theory the whole mythical system collapses. Dr. Arnold, who had not read the book, judging of it merely from a review, saw, of course, this point. "The idea of men writing mythic histories between the time of Livy and Tacitus, and St. Paul mistaking such for realities!" Life, ii. p. 58.

‡ L. J., Introduction, p. 26.

the garb of historical narrative some thought or idea of the time; and the poetical, in which the original idea is almost obscured by the veil which the fancy of the poet has woven around it. All these he holds to be blended in various proportions in the Gospel narrative—the great source of all the mythical embellishments being the prepossessions of the countrymen and followers of our Lord touching the person and works of the expected Messiah: the next source being that peculiar impression which was left by the personal character, actions, and fate of Jesus, and which served to modify the Messianic idea in the minds of the people.

21. The residuum from this system is thus stated by one* who is far from an unfriendly critic. The myth has eaten into the very heart of the narrative. There remains but a scanty framework of the life of Jesus. That He was brought up in Nazareth, was baptized by John; that He formed disciples, and taught in various districts of Palestine; that He opposed everywhere the outwardness of pharisaism, and proclaimed the Messianic kingdom; that at last he succumbed to the hatred and envy of the pharisaic faction† and died upon the Cross—such, according to Strauss, is the sum total of facts, which the ideas and aspirations of early Christendom enveloped in a tissue of significant legends and devout imaginings. Of the discourses of our Lord, a small solid kernel, as he thinks, can be discerned with certainty. Such, for instance, is the Sermon on the Mount. The sayings of Jesus, according to him, were so pregnant and forcible, had so strong a hold upon men's minds in their condensed gnomic form, that they were preserved in great part even in the flood of oral tradition. Even this seems, upon second thoughts, too much for him to admit. Wrenched from their natural connection, dislodged from their original site, they remain like boulders, objects of vague wonder or super-

* Schwartz. See also Scherer, Revue des Deux Mondes.

† Even this is a distortion of history. Caiaphas and his party were Sadducees; a fact which later writers of the Tübingen school have found impossible to reconcile with their theory of the origin of the Gospels.

stitious legends, until their true origin and meaning are ascertained by philosophic ingenuity and research.

22. And yet Strauss professes, and may be assumed actually to believe, that he retains the essential truths of Christianity. The last portion of his book, which he certainly regarded as the most important, is intended to draw out the eternal ideas which underlie this strange tissue of legend and myth. The supernatural nativity of Christ, His miracles, His resurrection and ascension, remain ideal truths—utterly separated as they are from objective facts. Christ, indeed, in His concrete personality, disappears from the system of the great teacher of Ideology. No individual does or can adequately represent, much less embody, absolute realities. But the Church was guided by a true instinct when, in the Person of Jesus, she found an expression of those realities. In Him was manifested more perfectly than in any individual that which is the ultimate and substantial principle of all religion, the unity of God and man. It is actually startling to find how the versatile and imaginative intellect of Strauss* can discern the blessedness and sublimity, the encouragement and consolation of the thoughts which the early Church derived from the orthodox view of Christ. Standing from without, he sees far more clearly than many who profess to believe the Gospel, the internal coherence of its highest doctrines. Only, as Strauss teaches, the true meaning of those doctrines remained to be discovered in the light of the philosophy of the Absolute.† That alone supplies the key to the whole system of Christology. Instead of an individual we have an idea. In an individual the properties and functions which the Church attributes to Christ contradict themselves: in the idea of the race they perfectly agree. Humanity is the union of the two natures—God become man; it is the worker of miracles, the sinless existence; for sin belongs to the individual, not to the race. It is Humanity that dies,

* See the concluding Dissertation, § 145.

† Concluding Dissertation, § 151, p. 437, vol. iii. English translation.

rises, ascends into Heaven. By faith in this Christ, that is, in his own human nature, man is justified before God.

23. Is this the last word of the system? It seems to go far enough. Yet Strauss had more to say. In a later work,* he boldly clears away all remaining prejudices. The world is not merely one with God—an ever changing, ever progressing manifestation of the Divine, but God has Himself no personality, no conscious Being. Man had taken the throne of Christ. He seats himself ultimately in the throne of the Absolute, which first attains to consciousness, to personal existence, in humanity.† The individual is nothing—a mere phenomenal and transitional evolution; the absolute is nothing—a mere potentiality never realized or realizable. Empty abstraction swallows up all idea and fact, the Divine and human, in one universal void.

24. Such is Ideology in the mind of its ablest, its most honest and consistent exponent. The storm produced by such a work may be conceived. All the leaders of German thought were in a tumult of excitement; the first object of those, between whose systems and that of Strauss there appeared to be a logical connection, was to shake off the responsibility. Schleiermacher's friends first rushed to the rescue, and pointed out the absolute antagonism between the genial and loving spirit of their chief, and the reckless audacity, the irreverence, and bitterness of the intruder. Hegelians were, of course, vehement in disavowing the principles and the consequences. Yet, as we have seen, Strauss did but use the weapons which had been forged for him. He scarcely went further than De Wette, on the one hand, in historical scepticism, or differed from him only in the consistency and completeness of his application of the same critical principles. Strauss might even claim Schleiermacher's own authority for

* The 'Dogmatik,' or 'Die Christliche Glaubenslehre,' published 1840, 1841.

† "Gott is nicht Person, Er wird es in der unendlichen Reihe der menschlichen Subjecte." See Schwartz, p. 218; and Strauss, Glaubenslehre, pp. 502–524.

the denial of the possibility of miracles, although, by a glorious inconsistency, that great man accepted as a Christian truth what he could find no place for in his philosophical system. On the other hand, so far as his application of the Hegelian theory was concerned, daringly blasphemous as he may seem, he was soon outstripped by even more reckless infidels. In fact, other symptoms soon removed all doubt as to the tendency of Hegelian forms of thought. Frederic Richter, a bookseller of Breslau, had already published in 1833—two years before the appearance of Strauss's 'Life of Jesus'—a work in which he proclaimed a new Gospel, as he styled it, that of eternal death.* His argument, in the opinion of very competent judges, was a legitimate deduction from Hegel's theory of individuality, though the book and the author were overwhelmed in a general outburst of indignation. Later and more consistent professors of that school did not hesitate to call the condemnation of Richter, coming as it did from Hegelians, a literary assassination. Again, one of the most thoroughgoing adherents of Hegel, Bruno Bauer, a writer who had made himself conspicuous by his heady arrogance in the cause of orthodoxy, now turning round with a sudden revulsion, poured forth a stream of writings, in which the facts and doctrines of Christianity were treated with a blasphemous insolence scarcely paralleled in modern days. The writings of Bauer and Richter, however, were easily disavowed; even the opponents of Hegel hesitated to make the calm conservative philosopher responsible for such results.

25. Two years after the appearance of Strauss's work another application of Hegel's principles was developed, which, though far less startling and urged in a far different spirit, produced a deeper and more durable sensation on the Continent. R. Rothe,† sub-director of

* Die Lehre von den letzten Dingen. Gieseler says that many Hegelians blamed Richter not for the doctrine, but for its publication, "*for discovering a secret of the school.*" 'Kirchengeschichte der n. Z.,' p. 245.

† Now Professor at Heidelberg. His book is entitled 'Die Anfänge der Christlichen Kirche, und ihrer Verfassung.'

the theological college at Wittenberg, published, in 1837, his treatise on the origin and constitution of the Christian Church. Rothe is in all respects a most remarkable man; in originality and independence of thought he stands almost alone among German theologians; his personal piety and hearty acceptance of the living truths of religion are undoubted.* Few of our own later writers have gone so far—none have gone farther, in defending, both by *à priori* arguments and historical evidence, the apostolical origin of Episcopacy, the unity and authority of the primitive Church. It seemed as though the conservation of Hegel had found a perfect exponent. Yet, strange as it may appear, the conclusion at which he arrives, following out, as the keenest critics † admit, the principles of his master, is that the Christian Church is but a temporary institution destined to be absorbed by the State; ‡ in which, like all true Hegelians, § he sees no mere system of mutual defence, or institution in which the energies of individuals may be freely developed, but the highest product of reason, the supreme development of humanity,—in a word, the moral world realized and organized. The views of Rothe are altogether too subtle, and indeed too elevated, to reach the general mind in the form which he gave them: his State is an ideal one; his hope of the realization of his theory depends upon his belief in a future personal manifestation of the Saviour; but the necessary results of his reasoning were clearly discerned by thinking men, and practical inferences were readily drawn. He recognizes himself with calm satisfaction what he believes to be early and progressive symptoms of decline and disintegration in the Church, the steady progress of

* A very strong testimony is borne to his piety by Rudolf Stier in the introduction to his new edition of the 'Reden der Apostel,' 1861, p. viii. He says of him—"Dessen innerstes Glaubensleben ich wohl kenne." In some points Rothe shows a strong tendency to Romanism, and speaks of Mühler's 'Symbolik' in terms of almost unqualified eulogy.

† For instance, E. Scherer in the 'Revue des Deux Mondes,' p. 849, Feb. 1861; and Schwartz, 'Zur Geschichte der neuesten Theologie.'

‡ "Der vollendete Staat schliesst die Kirche schlechthin aus."—'Anfänge,' p. 47.

§ See his note, p. 13, where he collects Hegel's definitions of the State.

encroachments on the part of the State; and, in connection with outward changes, an internal modification of opinions, feelings, and principles, tending towards a final identification of the secular and religious, the natural and the Divine. He does not hesitate to assert that the religious life itself must find its true and satisfactory realization, not in the Church but in the State.* Though resting on far other grounds, there is a remarkable resemblance between his theory as well as the arguments by which it is maintained, and that of our own Arnold.† The supremacy of the State in all matters, both of discipline and doctrine, is the rightful and legitimate development of Christianity; it decides what shall be taught, and how it shall be taught; and in the mean time it treats, and has a right to treat, the national Church, as no less properly an organ of the national life than a magistracy or a legislative estate.

26. The philosophy of ideology, thus consistently carried out by writers of very different feelings and principles, leaves man without a church, without a Saviour, without a living soul. There remained, however, still a sort of profession of religion, a religion of vague, dreary abstractions, but still, such as it was, an element in which philosophers might find some materials for the religious sentiment, while the common herd might be guided by the retention of the old doctrinal forms. That delusion was soon dissipated. Feuerbach took up the argument where Strauss left it,

* P. 51.

† Dr. Arnold, of course, did not derive his opinions directly from Rothe, whose work he read in 1838. In a letter written that year to Chevalier Bunsen, he expresses his entire agreement with Rothe in his theory as to the identity of Church and State; but, as might be expected, rejects as entirely his conclusions touching the apostolical origin of episcopacy. See 'Life,' &c., ii. p. 105. It will be remembered that the Chevalier Bunsen, with whom Arnold says distinctly that he agrees more thoroughly than any of his friends, was deeply imbued with Hegel's principles, and more especially with their application to the relations between the Church and the State. There can be little doubt that he gave the first impulse to Arnold's mind upon this subject, or at least confirmed it in the direction which it took after the reaction from what he somewhere calls his Oxford Toryism. The numerous and peculiar coincidences between Arnold and his German prototypes can otherwise scarcely be accounted for. He learned German somewhat late in life.

and drew from it the inevitable conclusion, that man himself is the only proper object for the reverence and the worship which had hitherto been directed to the idea of a God. Theology was thus converted to anthropology. Instead of loving God, men are to love one another. Sacraments will disappear, but then the eucharist will be found in wholesome meals; baptism, in the healthy use of cold baths! Natural science will take the place of religious, moral, and metaphysical speculation. Atheism thus stood out in its bareness and barrenness—yet not even then in its utter hatefulness. It remained for a numerous school of philosophical radicals to get rid of the last vestiges of superstition. Feuerbach recognized the virtues of unselfishness, courage, truth; * he was an admirer of the higher developments of genius, in science, literature, and art. He speaks of humanity as a real being. A whole host of writers soon sprang up who rejected all such delusions with utter contempt; they saw clearly that they had no meaning disjoined from the religious element, and heaped upon himself the contumelious epithets which he had unsparingly applied to his predecessors. The dogmas of socialism and communism were preached with the wildest fanaticism; † poets, politicians, socialists, and natural philosophers came forward to demand the extirpation of all faith, to denounce the belief in the invisible as the root of all human weakness and misery, to proclaim the sacred law of egotism—the religion of the flesh; and for a time they seemed to have succeeded. They appealed to man's strongest passions; they appealed also to some deep principles. It was felt that the religion preached

* This is too favourable a view. In his poems, which, like the 'Thalia' of Arius, are intended to popularize his tenets, his cynicism is revolting. In his axioms he lays down the principle—Thy first duty is to do good to thyself.

† See Schwartz, 'Zur Geschichte der neuesten Theologie,' pp. 227, 240, 242. It must be noted that Schwartz and Scherer (who takes precisely the same view—see 'Revue des Deux Mondes,' Feb. 1861, p. 851) are ultra liberals. Schwartz names Herwegh, Ruge, Marr, Voght, &c., as leaders in this new crusade. Gaspard Schmidt, better known by the assumed name of Stirner, was, perhaps, the most influential writer. Gieseler, l. c., pp. 30 and 275, may be consulted.

by the professors of all schools tainted by rationalism or by ideology was a farce, a delusion, a fraud; the materialists carried the day, took the lead in the revolutionary movement of 1848, and suddenly, to their own amazement, found themselves triumphant amidst the ruins of Church and State.

27. A long and powerful reaction followed. Utterly worn out, unmasked, and confounded, ideology, together with the metaphysical speculations with which it was connected, sank into obscurity and contempt. The very last thing to be expected was that it should have been transplanted into a soil of all apparently the most uncongenial—that it should be offered to Englishmen as a useful help in the interpretation of the Scriptures. A very brief summary of points distinctly advanced, or undeniably suggested, by some of the latest advocates of the system in England will show the fundamental identity of principles between them and the German ideologists; although we gladly admit that, whether withheld by reverence, or by fear of offending men of all shades of religious opinion, not to speak of legal penalties and disqualifications, few among us have ventured to present the most offensive insinuations; none have dared to apply the principles to the whole substance of the Scriptural narrative.

28. The doctrine of personal annihilation, of the absorption of the individual consciousness in the infinite Spirit—a doctrine, be it noted, which is distinctly proclaimed among ourselves by Freethinkers, and directly based upon Pantheism, or a spurious Theism—is not of course preached, nor is it likely to be preached, by any one who cares to obtain or retain a hold upon the attention of English Christians; but it finds an echo, a partial expression, what sounds like a preparation. Divested of what is most repulsive in form, the principle is insinuated, the way paved for its reception. Every attempt to get rid of the idea of individual responsibility, to exempt any considerable portion of mankind from the universal law of retribution, is a step, and a very decided step, towards the denial of the continuity of

personal consciousness. A nearer approximation to the scepticism of the Ideologists could perhaps hardly be made than that which we find in the suggestion, that, after some possible state of new probation for rudimentary spirits, for germinal souls—after the completion of the sublunary office of the Christian Church—all, both small and great, may find a refuge in the bosom of the universal Parent TO REPOSE, or to be quickened into higher life.*

29. We have seen how nearly the theories of the Church coincide. As a function of the State, destined to be absorbed (and if such its destiny, surely the sooner the better) in that institution, it ought, of course, to concern itself exclusively with the ethical development of its members.† Rothe, indeed, looked for such absorption only when the State should be thoroughly penetrated with Christian doctrine, transformed and glorified by Christian principles—when its ideal should be realized under the government of its head. Taking lower, more matter of fact and practical grounds—free, as it would almost seem, from the religious prepossessions which biassed the German thinker, English writers are found to advocate the immediate completion of the process. "Speculative doctrines"—that is, all dogmatic teaching—"should be left to philosophical schools." "The ministry of the Church is to be regarded simply as a function of the national life." Divested of its special doctrines, its creeds, and articles, and all peculiar manifestations of a divine life, the Church could of course be little or nothing more than an instrument for developing the moral character of the nation.‡ We are distinctly told concerning "the doctrines of an isolated salvation, the reward, the grace bestowed on

* See E. and R., p. 206; and compare Jowett on Romans, vol. ii. p. 489.

† There is a radical difference between this theory and that of our Reformers, as stated by Hooker. The latter proceeded on the assumption that the State accepts the doctrines taught by the Church. "How should the Church remain by personal subsistence divided from the Commonweal, when the whole Commonweal doth believe?" "The truth is that the Church and the Commonweal are names which import things really different; but those things are accidents, and such accidents as may, and always should, lovingly dwell together in one subject."—'Ecclesiastical Polity,' Book viii.

‡ E. and R., p. 196.

one's own labours, the undisturbed repose, the crown of glory, in which so many have no share, the finality of the sentence on both sides—that reflections on such expectations as these make stubborn martyrs, or sour professors, but *not good citizens*." * If so, these doctrines, which, invidiously as they are here stated, are, rightly understood, the very life of Christianity, must be discountenanced ; even if for a time tolerated of the State, they must be discarded altogether, when it is once fully awakened to the consciousness of its true relations to the Church.

30. Still clearer, less capable of being explained away or denied, is the agreement of the English ideologists with the fundamental principles of their German teachers. Ideology proceeds from the *à priori* assumption that all miraculous interventions are impossible, since the Divine, whether conscious or unconscious, personal or impersonal, does not and cannot, without self-contradiction, violate its own laws. All the school in England more or less distinctly concur in the elimination of the supernatural element from Scripture. The least advanced represent it as a serious hindrance to the reception of Christian truth by men of cultivated intelligence. The German master adopted and gave a new and keener point to all detailed objections to narratives involving that element: the same course is pursued in numerous passages of the "Essays and Reviews." †

With regard to myths, the special characteristic of ideology, one writer at least cannot be open to Strauss's charge of inconsistency. He has not merely entered into the fields of Scriptural history through the portal of the myth and passed out again leaving the main facts untouched. ‡ The incarnation of our Lord, His descent from David, the circumstances of His nativity, His temptation, transfiguration, His most remarkable miracles, including those attested by all the Evangelists,

* Here we seem to hear Rothe, p. 54.
† E. and R., pp. 179, 180. See Archdeacon Sinclair's Charge, 1861.
‡ E. and R., p. 202.

—nearly all, if not all, the grounds for an "historical faith" are referred substantially to "an ideal origin." As for the Old Testament, we are told that "previous to the time of the divided kingdom, Jewish history contains little that is thoroughly reliable." Its miraculous events may be taken as parable, poetry, legend, or allegory—that is, simply as myths. The German saw plainly enough that, in order to find time and place for the development of myths, the authenticity and genuineness of the historical records must be denied. He scarcely went farther than a writer who speaks coolly of "links deficient in the traditional records of events" which are related by St. Matthew and all the Evangelists.

A crucial test of a man's feelings towards the Person of Christ Himself is undoubtedly supplied by his reception or denial of the Gospel of St. John. The early rationalists rejected it on the ground that it is inconsistent with the simpler, more accurate representations of Christ in the other Gospels. The modern neologians hold that it is the product of the higher development of the Christian consciousness in the post-Apostolic age. According to the school of pantheistic rationalism, aptly and truly designated the modern gnosticism, the representation of the Saviour in that Gospel is too true, that is, too perfect an embodiment of the ideal, to be historical. But of all hypotheses, the most offensive, the least supported by any shadow of evidence, is that which connects the origin of the Gospel with the gnostic heresy,* and brings down its date to the year 140. That hypothesis is noticed without an expression of indignation by one writer, who in his own name expressly asserts that there is no proof that St. John gives his voucher as an eye and ear witness of all that is related in his Gospel. Strauss demanded no more than this. Here is a πoῦ στῶ for the subversion of all positive evidence of historical Chris-

* Thus Hilgenfeld. See a brief summary of opinions in Lange's Bibelwerk, iv. p. 20, an excellent work, which will meet the requirements of many students.

tianity. The mythical process has free play; and it is only a question of time, of discretion in meddling with stubborn prejudices, how soon and how far the objective facts of an external positive revelation may be rejected, how the doctrines themselves may be remoulded, under the supreme and ultimate authority of the natural conscience, into accordance with the requirements of an enlightened age.

31. The question of course arises—how is it possible that men of honour holding such opinions can retain, or endure, their position as ministers and teachers of a Church, which, liberal as it undoubtedly is in dealing with all questions about which believers in a positive revelation may conscientiously differ, has no less certainly pronounced a clear and decisive sentence upon each and all the points controverted or denied by Ideologists? That the difficulty is felt is sufficiently obvious. The principal object of the only treatise in which the leading principles of this form of neology have been distinctly commended by a minister of the Church of England, is to justify the conduct of himself and those who maintain the same views. In this part of his undertaking he has been supplied with weapons from the same foreign armoury. In the writings of all schools of rationalism and neology, a prominent place is assigned to the vindication of absolute liberty of sceptical speculation, not merely for students, but for professors of theology. We need not, however, trace the connection.* That is of little moment. The arguments in this case have at least the merit of being intelligible and practical. Whether the Church has at present, and has had from the beginning, safeguards to preserve her doctrines from corruption—whether she has a right, and has exercised the right, to exact from all her ministers a pledge that so long as they retain her commission they will deliver those doctrines in

* The history of the struggle of Rationalists, more especially the Lichtfreunde, partisans or followers of Strauss, to get rid of all doctrinal tests, the Creeds included, is given by Gieseler, who, though differing from them in important points, sympathizes with them to some extent in that desire. See 'Kirchengeschichte d. n. Z.,' pp. 250 and 263.

their integrity to the people—whether the act of subscription by which the ministers give such pledge involves a moral, or a mere legal obligation—such questions stand upon independent grounds, and may be discussed without any reference to the sources from which the arguments we have to consider may, or may not, be derived.

32. In this controversy the first point must needs be to ascertain the practice of the Apostles as recorded or intimated in the New Testament, and in the next place the practice of the Church in various periods of its development; the most important, in a general point of view, being that critical epoch which terminated the first struggle with heathenism. Scarcely secondary is the position taken by our own Church, when it thoroughly investigated all points of principle and organization at the time of the Reformation—a position retained without any substantial modification at the present day.

33. With regard to the first point, the ingenuity and disingenuousness of those who deny the propriety of doctrinal limitations are equally conspicuous. The subject is introduced, so to speak, casually, and disposed of with little intimation of its surpassing importance. If the Apostles* enforced a rule of faith, and made the teaching of sound doctrine an absolute and universal condition of holding office in the Church, the principle is of course decided, whatever difficulty may be felt at any time about its practical application. Now, the first impression made upon every thoughtful reader of the New Testament is undoubtedly, that the whole system of Christian morals, most especially as concerns those characteristic peculiarities which distinguish the Christian from the heathen moralist, is not merely interwoven with the external facts and positive doctrines of Christianity, but is altogether based upon them, and derives from them its sanctions, its power, its life. The manifestation of the Divine life in man is a reflexion and efflux from the manifestation of God in

* See, e. g., 2 Timothy i. 13, 14; ii. 2, iii. 10, 14.

Christ. The understanding and heart, the spiritual and the moral nature of man, are equally under the dominion and control of truths, which man has indeed a natural and inherent capacity for apprehending when set before him, but which, in the actual state of his faculties, he is certainly unable to discover. Those truths are given in revelation in the two-fold form of facts and doctrines, equally positive, equally indispensable to the development of the spiritual man. The denial or perversion of either excludes a man from the benefits of the revelation—a result which follows of necessity from the very notion of a revelation, for why should truth be revealed but to be accepted? We are not at present concerned with the question how far such result is reconcileable with the Divine attributes, or we might observe that the denial of what God has revealed must needs involve some penalty in beings responsible for the use of their faculties; nor do we touch the case of those to whom the revelation has not been given; Charity feels no need of speculations concerning those whom she leaves in faith and hope to the mercy of their Maker. We are not confining the effects of the atonement, which may, and doubtless do, extend far beyond the sphere of our contemplation; but simply indicate the limits within which its full effects are experienced—limits undoubtedly coextensive with its reception by the intellect and heart. Christ made confession of faith in Himself, and in the truths which He proclaimed, the condition of salvation. The Apostles, guided by His Spirit, exacted a declaration of belief in those truths as a preliminary condition of admission to the Church, full in every case in proportion to the capacities of their hearers and their opportunities of knowing the truth, fullest and most explicit in the case of those whom they appointed to the work of the ministry. If so, the conclusion is obvious, that the Church would cease to be a Church if she commissioned any to teach in her own and in her Master's name, when they are at direct issue with herself upon points which from the beginning have been held by those who denied, as well as by those who accepted them, to pertain to the very foundations of the faith.

34. That position, however, clear as are the principles on which it rests, is now for the first time assailed; not indeed directly, but by implication. We are told generally, that whereas the Apostles enjoin the infliction of the last penalty, that of excommunication, for moral turpitude, they deal with speculative questions, even those which touch fundamental doctrines, simply by the way of controversy. The case selected is that of the fornicator at Corinth, which is contrasted with that of heretics who denied a corporeal resurrection. With regard to the former there is no question. The proceeding of St. Paul in that case is, of course, of the highest importance as a proof of the existence and enforcement of disciplinarian powers in the Apostles, and in the Church, whose rulers were reproved for not having exercised them without St. Paul's intervention. It might be pointed out that the offence then punished consisted most probably in the infringement of a positive precept, which, though recognized by the moral instincts of heathendom, was first distinctly promulgated by the Apostolic council at Jerusalem;* and with reference to other controverted matters, that the circumstances under which the sentence was pronounced would lead to the conclusion that the powers deposited in the Church, and more especially in the Apostles as representatives of the Head of the Church, are in their essence independent of the State. With regard to the other point, which concerns the Apostle's mode of dealing with heretical opinions in fundamental matters, we wholly repudiate the inference drawn from a partial statement of his proceeding. It is said that St. Paul does not call for the expulsion of those among the Christian converts who had no belief in a corporeal

* It is Hooker's opinion, in which the latest and some of the acutest critics, as Ritschl, 'Die Entstehung der altkatholischen Kirche,' p. 129, and Wieseler, concur, that πορνεία, in Acts xv. 20, means illicit marriages. Ritschl proves that St. Paul enforced the decree—a point of considerable importance in the controversy with the Tübingen school.

resurrection. That may be: weakness of faith, errors in points of faith on the part of *converts*, *hearers*, and *learners*, were dealt with tenderly, by the way of controversy. The very objects of the Christian Church would otherwise be defeated. But the question is, whether St. Paul held that the opinions ought to be tolerated? Whether they could be professed or retained without forfeiture of the distinctive privileges of Christians? What does he say of those who held them? What but that, if those opinions were maintained, their faith was vain, they were yet in their sins; Christ had died in vain? If such a declaration be not tantamount to excommunication, to cutting off those who obstinately persisted in such errors from Christian privileges, words have no meaning. Self-condemned, they became aliens, relapsed into the state of unconversion, by the very fact of their denying, not indeed a speculative opinion, but what (as even ideologists admit, strangely inconsistent as such admission is with the system they * advocate) St. Paul always represents as the corner stone of the Christian belief. Of course the Apostle proceeds in the first instance by the way of controversy, or, to speak more correctly, of demonstration. Of course his one great desire is to persuade, to convince, to win to the truth, those who were weak or unsound in the faith; to clear up obscurities, and to remove difficulties from their way. Nor does he fail to show the inward harmony between the ordinary course of nature and the miraculous intervention of that Power by which the laws that regulate the course of nature were ordained. That, however, is no more than he does in the case of offenders against the moral law. He exhausts all the resources of persuasion, expostulation, and warning; he appeals to the reason, the conscience, the heart, before he hints at any measure of a judicial character, even in the case of those who "defile the temple of the Holy Ghost."

* There is no point on which Ideologists, even those who partially adopt the system, are more generally agreed than the necessity of explaining away the fact of the Resurrection.

But, as in this latter case, when all such preliminary endeavours proved to be ineffectual, he resorted ultimately to the exercise of the awful powers entrusted to the Apostles as governors of Christ's Church, as assessors with Him on the throne of judgment; so also, beyond all doubt, he was prepared to act, even as he had acted in the case of Elymas at the very beginning of his ministry, in the case of all stubborn impugners of fundamental truths.

In fact, the expressions which he uses in reference to those who attacked tenets which would undoubtedly be regarded by many as purely speculative and dogmatic, sound even harsh, and would be indefensible as they are painful, did they not proceed from a principle of infinite importance to the integrity of the Christian faith. "I would that they were cut off that trouble you;" "Let him be accursed who preaches to you another Gospel;" these and similar* expressions had no reference to evil livers, as such, but to teachers and maintainers of evil doctrines, with which all corruptions of our moral nature are connected, but which have their origin in that higher element of our spiritual and intellectual being, for the regulation and conscientious use of which our responsibility is grave, even in proportion to its excellence and the incomparable majesty of the objects with which it is concerned.

We must further remark, that in order to bring the argument, such as it is, to bear upon the question of subscription as a condition of exercising the functions of the Christian ministry, it should have been shown that St. Paul admitted any man to preach publicly, in the capacity of an appointed teacher, against the Resurrection, or any other doctrine which had been plainly declared, or that he and his fellow Apostles failed to exercise the right of deposition, when admonition and warning were found ineffectual to secure the cause of truth. Such is not the conclusion which we draw from the case of Hymenæus and Alexander, whom the

* Galatians v. 12; 1 Timothy iv. 1, 2; 2 Timothy iii. 8, 9; Titus i. 11, iii. 10. Compare 2 John 10, 11; 2 Peter iii. 17; Acts xx. 28–30.

Apostle "delivered to Satan (the same sentence as that pronounced in the case of the Corinthian fornicator—one which, whatever might be its effect, undoubtedly amounts to excommunication), that they might learn not to blaspheme;" nor from that of Hymenæus and Philetus, which is even more immediately to the point, "who erred concerning the truth, saying that the resurrection is already past"—unless, indeed, we presume that St. Paul allowed their word to "eat as doth a canker," and to "overthrow the faith" of his converts, without using the power "given to him by the Lord" for the protection of the weak brethren, "for whom Christ died."

35. The practice of the early Church is too clearly established by a multitude of public acts to be open to a similar course of argument. The determination of the general body and the recognized representatives of the Christian community to exclude all teaching contrary to its fundamental principles, to guard its doctrinal deposit by strict, definite, and unmistakable declarations, is the most prominent fact which meets every student of ecclesiastical history, which, indeed, is recognized most distinctly by those who feel a rooted antipathy to every shade of what they are pleased to call dogmatic intolerance. A different, and not unplausible line of argument, is therefore adopted. The statement is hazarded that the State, rather than the Church, is responsible for this exclusiveness.* We are told † that, together with the inauguration of multitudinism, Constantine inaugurated a principle essentially at variance with it—that of doctrinal limitation; and we are informed that historians, who are cer-

* It is a singular instance of the influence which has been exercised, directly or indirectly, by the writings of one of the most subtle and ingenious of modern controversialists, that even this argument is derived, though used for very different purposes from Newman's theory about the Thirty-nine Articles. 'See Romanism and Popular Protestantism,' Lecture ix. p. 278. "Their imposition in its first origin was much more a political than an ecclesiastical act; it was a provision of the State rather than of the Church, though the Church co-operated—the *outward form* into which our religion was cast has depended in no slight measure on the personal opinions and wishes of laymen and foreigners."

† E. and R., p. 160.

tainly all but unanimous upon the point, are wrong in supposing that the increasing strictness of definitions in the Christian creed must be attributed to the rise of successive heresies. Such assertions can, of course, only be refuted completely by a searching inquiry into the records of Christian antiquity; but they may be met by some decisive facts; and we have no hesitation in asserting that the part thus assigned to the first Christian emperor is diametrically in opposition to historical facts. So far from inaugurating the principle of doctrinal limitation, Constantine from first to last had one paramount object, and that was to get rid of doctrinal discussions, and to bring about a compromise between conflicting parties—in fact, to do exactly what we are told would have been so desirable, viz., to enforce forbearance between the great antagonistic parties, and to insist on the maxim that neither had a right to limit the common Christianity to the exclusion of the other. Constantine looked upon the controversy between Catholics and Arians, as the representatives of the secular authority are generally disposed to do, altogether from without; and the special points under discussion were to him matters of utter indifference.* The course which he had pursued in the first instance was the very wisest that could be devised; nor, considering the unparalleled importance of the crisis and the results of his decision, do we see how Christians can doubt that it was brought about by the great Head of the Church. He called together from all quarters of his empire the governors of the whole Christian community, and referred the questions under discussion to their arbitration. The result was absolutely decisive. The Nicene Creed was drawn up as a declaration of what was included in that common Christianity. It defined the true limits beyond which no teacher† could go without infringing the fundamental principles of the faith. With the exception of one word, that Creed con-

* See his epistle to Alexander and Arius. Euseb. V. C., ii. 69, 70.

† It must be remembered that subscription was exacted at once of the clergy, as being teachers, but not of the laity. Anathemas, however, were pronounced against all who openly denied the doctrines of the Creed.

tained no single statement in which, both as regarded substance and form, all Churches had not previously coincided. That word represented not "the hardening of fluid and unsettled notions," but the existence of one fixed universal conviction, that the centre and life of Christianity is found in the recognition of the absolute and perfect Godhead of its Founder and Head. The word was chosen, not by Constantine, but by those divines who clearly perceived the vital character of the question at issue. They chose it because nothing short of an exact definition would deliver Christendom from the corruption with which it was menaced. The word was open to cavil, and, if left unexplained, to fair objection;* but with such explanation as was at once given and accepted, it expressed the mind of the universal Church. It must not be supposed that the object was to express the personal opinions of the Bishops present; even the arguments by which they might defend those opinions were matters, comparatively speaking, of indifference. In selecting that word they were actuated but by one wish—that of expressing clearly and unmistakably the conviction of the entire body in whose name they spoke. The most unlearned, the least conversant with technical terms or philosophical discussions among them, were rejoiced to have that word, feeling that they could not show their faces to their own congregations if they returned without having recorded such a decision as might exclude for ever the incongruous and hostile element from the sphere of Christian communion. Constantine did but give effect to the universal will. They inaugurated the doctrinal limitation; he gave it for the time legal validity. Nor must it be lost sight of, that all the special pleading, all the philosophical speculations and technical innovations began, as indeed has always been the case, not with the

* See Athanasius, 'De Syn. Nic.,' § 20–24, and Basil, Ep. 52, with Garnier's note. It is well known that all the great divines of that age were quite satisfied with an honest acceptance of the doctrine expressed by Ὁμοούσιος, even in the case of those who for a time were unwilling to receive that word. Few writers of late have dealt with the question so fairly as the Benedictine editors, or as Tillemont, 'Mémoires H. E.,' tom. iv. p. 125.

maintainers, but with the opponents of the old Catholic doctrine. "That there was a time when God the Word was not; that He was alien in essential substance from the absolute God;" these and similar forms of what the Church then rejected—and so long as she exists will ever reject as blasphemy—had their origin in the catechetical schools tainted most deeply by neoplatonism. The necessity of a new, a more searching and comprehensive, and at the same time a more exclusive term, was entirely owing to those metaphysical speculations. The Church acknowledged the truth of the conclusion drawn by its most clearsighted champions, that the introduction of an intermediate Being, neither truly God nor truly man, was a subtle but unquestionable form of polytheism,* subversive of all the principles on which the redemption of humanity depends. The decision was, undoubtedly, exclusive. It excluded It ejected as a poison, a gangrene, a treasonable lie—the doctrine which is too often regarded as a mere verbal error, or one depending upon the inherent imperfection of a finite intellect; but for that exclusiveness the Church, and the Church alone is responsible. So far indeed was the State from taking upon itself the responsibility of this "doctrinal limitation," that within a very short time its whole power was brought to bear upon the Church, in order to compel it to reverse its decision and to eliminate that one word from its creed. During the reigns of two most able and powerful sovereigns no means of fraud, intimidation, or violence were spared to produce the result which is now represented to be so desirable—that of sweeping away the limitary definition which shut out the only influential dissentients from office and communion in the Church. It was assuredly a providential dispensation to test the sincerity of the Church's faith, and to demonstrate its independence of the State. An age of terrible struggles intervened before the final triumph; but during that time the principle took such root that no storms have

* This is the great, the palmary argument of Athanasius, adopted by Basil, Gregory, and all the great divines who have written against Arianism.

since shaken it. One point requires especial notice; it is often overlooked: neither Constantine nor his successors attempted to introduce the terms of the Arian heresy in the formularies which they recommended,* freely as they allowed the doctrines of Arianism to be preached; they merely wished to exclude from the Creed the one word of doctrinal limitation; and in that attempt they failed. The early Church knew that it was a matter of life or death; and in the position where that Church left us we stand, with a Creed definitely stating, not explaining or discussing, but simply declaring, those doctrinal facts † without which our common Christianity would be a mere name.

36. That the actual position of our own Church is definite and unmistakable is recognized both by those who maintain, and not less distinctly by those who assail it, as is shown by the direction of their attacks. It is in principle precisely that of the Apostolic Church, in fact of all portions of the Church, in the best and purest ages. The first object of our Church is to determine the grounds on which all its doctrine is based. That she does by enumerating the canonical books of Holy Writ, to which alone she appeals for authoritative confirmation of her teaching. Belief in the Scriptures, in their genuineness, authenticity, and divine orgin—belief in them not merely as fundamental, but as the *foundation of all fundamentals*,‡ the sole and sufficient warrant for the Creeds § themselves, is the first condition of communion, a condition not stated simply because it is assumed as a point about which no question could be raised by Christians. The Bible is to our

* Hence not only Constantine, but even Constantius is spoken of in terms of respect by stanch but candid upholders of the orthodox doctrine, as Hilary, Ambrose, Theodoret, and Gregory Nazianzen. See the preface to G. N. Or. iv. p. 76, ed. Ben.

† I use the expression advisedly—the doctrines of the Church are facts, and the facts are doctrines.

‡ The term first used, if I mistake not, by Newman. See 'Romanism and Popular Protestantism,' p. 287. It coincides with Chillingworth's well-known saying, and with Hegel's "Dabei," i. e., with the Creeds, "galt in der protestantischen Kirche die Bestimmung, dass die Bibel die wesentliche Grundlage der Lehre sey."—'Philosophie der Religion,' p. 29.

§ Article viii.

Church* as it was to the early Church, as it was most distinctly and emphatically to the Churches of the Reformation, the Word of God. The three Creeds are accepted and set forth as the condensed declaration of the articles of faith which she holds, on the ground of their scripturality, to be true, and on that of their importance to be fundamental. In the Thirty-nine Articles of Religion she exhibits the whole body of her theology as contradistinguished from that of churches which had corrupted, mutilated, or added to, the truth. The general objects of those Articles are to repudiate the errors of the Papal system, and to maintain what is called the Catholic doctrine,—that is, the whole system of doctrines recognized by the Church of Christ as opposed to early heresies.† So far her position is clear. With regard to the acts of adhesion required of her members, we find the same substantial identity of principle with the early Church. As to hearers of the word, to attendants upon her services, we readily admit that no formal act of adherence beyond what is given in baptism, and is afterwards implied by their acceptance of her ministrations, ought to be required. Nor does our Church require it.‡ As we believe to have been the practice in the Apostolic age, she admits all applicants to free participation in any ordinances from which, judging for themselves, they expect to derive benefit; nor does she retain even so much of the discipline of the post-Apos-

* See Articles xvii. (the last words), xx. xxii. xxxiv. There cannot be any reasonable doubt that the "word of God" in these Articles means the Bible. In other passages it might possibly be explained away, but the expressions "Holy Scripture" and "word of God" were most certainly synonymous in the mind of the compilers of the Articles, as they are now in the mind of the imposers of subscription. The results of denying that the word of God is co-extensive with Holy Scripture are drawn out clearly enough in E. and R., pp. 176, 177.

† See Dr. Arnold's 'Life and Correspondence,' ii. p. 136. The passage is quoted further on. Compare Waterland, vol. ii. p. 302.

‡ This does not touch the case of the Universities. Of course, any collegiate or corporate institution has the right to impose its own conditions for admission to its privileges or benefices. There is great force in the arguments of the pamphlet, written, I believe, by Mr. Maurice, 'Subscription no Bondage,' 1835—"In all schools and universities there is a contract expressed or implied between the teacher and the learner, as to the principles on which the one agrees to teach and the other to learn—and to state the terms of this contract is at once the most honest method, and the most serviceable to education."

tolic Church as might be held desirable in order to protect the most solemn rites from profanation. Even that risk is incurred in preference to the possible exclusion of timid and scrupulous believers. Our Church, to use a somewhat pedantic but not inexpressive term, is multitudinous, in the sense that it does not inquire minutely and jealously into the qualifications and opinions of its members, but opens wide its gates day and night, and offers freely to all the leaves that were given for the healing of the nations. But that is quite a different question from the terms of admission to the functions of the ministry.* Our Church has learned from St. Paul, from his fellow Apostles, and from his Master, that an imperfect knowledge, much more denial of the truth when it extends to fundamental principles, when it touches the "Divine personalities," and the authority of God's word, is an insuperable disqualification for the ministerial office.

37. It is disingenuous to represent this difference between a lay and clerical member of the Church as implying that one is free to inquire, the other bound to profess what, be it true or be it false, may not be true to him. The layman is simply treated, so far and so long as he chooses to be so treated, as one whose opinions are in process of formation; whereas the other, by the mere fact of his assuming the functions of a teacher, declares that upon all essential points his mind is already made up. A school of theology may, within certain limits, be a fair arena for speculative conflicts; but the chair of the professor, and *à fortiori* the pulpit of the minister, should be occupied by one who is in possession of the truth. It has been stated, that whenever laymen are put in positions where their influence may

* Thus Waterland—"Subscription is not a term of lay communion, but of ministerial conformity, on acceptance of trusts and privileges," vol. ii. p. 362. Again, "This writer cannot distinguish between ejecting and not admitting, nor between Church-communion and Church-trusts. I said not a word about ejecting any man out of communion," ib. p. 392. Bishop Bull takes precisely the same view, 'Vindication of the Church of England,' vol. ii. p. 211, ed. Burton. So also does Bishop Jeremy Taylor, 'Ductor dubitantium,' iii. c. 4. In accordance with this principle, Athanasius admitted the Semi-Arians to communion, although they would not accept the term Homousion; but he would not allow them to hold office in the Church.

affect the religious principles of members of the Church, the same guarantees are exacted as in the case of ministers. Though incorrect in point of fact, that statement bears witness to the reasonableness of the condition, that professed teachers of the Church's doctrines ought, in some form or other, to give an assurance that they know what these doctrines are, and that they receive them and intend to teach them without any essential modification. There are several conceivable ways in which the Church may satisfy herself upon this point; but surely the easiest and most natural—the least open to the charge of unfairness—is to state clearly, broadly, and completely, the principles, and doctrines, which she holds to be fundamental, and to require of those who are candidates for the most important of all offices, a declaration deliberately made and attested by the simple act of subscription, that they are one in mind and in convictions with herself. The Church can do no less than demand such a pledge, that at the time when a man accepts the office, he allows,* that is, he honestly and unreservedly approves and assents to her code of faith.

38. This, it is said, is equivalent to a *promise* that a man will believe, and that is a promise which it is not in his power to fulfil. But so far as regards *belief*, subscription is not a promise, but a declaration.† Whatever promise is implied concerns not our convictions, but our acts. We pledge ourselves simply to this, that, so long as we hold an office of trust, we will not

* It is strange that any scholar should raise a question as to the meaning of this word. It occurs frequently in our early formularies, and always in the sense of approving and accepting. See also Luke xi. 48; 1 Thess. ii. 4. As to its meaning in Subscription, Jeremy Taylor writes thus (l. c.) :—"Lubens et ex animo subscripsi, that's our form in the Church of England. Consentiens subscripsi: so it was in the ancient Church, as St. Austin reports. I consent to the thing, my mind goes with it."

† Thus Jeremy Taylor, l. c., c. xxiii. "Ecclesiastical subscription only gives witness of *our present consent*, but according to its design and purpose for the future it binds us only to the conservation of peace and unity." His view of the act of subscription is of great importance. "It implies that he who subscribes does actually approve the articles overwritten—does, *at the time*, believe them to be such as it is said they are; true, if they only say they are true; useful, if they pretend to usefulness; necessary, if it is affirmed they are necessary. For if the subscriber believe not this, he by hypocrisy serves the ends of public peace, and his own preferment."

contravene the purposes for which it was instituted. The objects of our faith are, indeed, immutable truths; but, knowing the changeableness of the subjective faculties which apprehend them, and the manifold disturbances to which spiritual development is liable, we make no promise that we will retain those convictions; although, from the very nature of convictions touching the highest interests of our being, we entertain a hope, a trust, a something in all honest men approaching to, and in single-hearted believers identified with, a confident assurance that we shall retain them to the end. The promise, however, as to acts is binding, on the plainest grounds of moral obligation, and that without any reference to the possible contingency of legal penalties and disqualifications in case of its violation.

39. This point is of primary importance. It concerns our conscience more nearly than any considerations bearing upon our ministerial position. It has been lately asserted, as I believe for the first time, that the moral obligation of the act of subscription is commensurate and identical with the legal obligation. Now the effect of this doctrine, were it generally adopted, would be the practical annihilation of all obligation, in the great majority of cases where any question could arise. It is but too obvious that a man may, if not directly, yet by insinuation and unmistakable inference, attack even the fundamental doctrines of the Church without incurring the danger of legal conviction. In fact, so far as the mere legal obligation is concerned, there could be no object whatever in requiring subscription. That act does not render a man liable to legal consequences in a higher or different degree than would the acceptance of an office to which certain conditions are attached by the legislature. It is perfectly competent to the supreme authority to inflict deprivation for any infringement of those conditions, without reference to the previous concurrence of ministers in the definition of their duties. The act of subscription would be superfluous, if it did not superadd to the legal a perfectly distinct and incomparably higher obligation,

—even one which binds the conscience of an honest man.*

40. The existence of the moral obligation does not, however, determine its exact nature and extent. The question still remains, how far the act of subscription implies conformity between a man's inmost convictions and the doctrinal formularies of the Church.† That the conformity does not necessarily extend to an absolute and entire acceptation of any human formularies, as exhaustive or perfect representations of Divine truth, may readily be conceded. Such a demand would, in fact, be tantamount to an assumption of verbal and plenary inspiration, which the compilers of the documents and the imposers of subscription would be the first to disclaim. The conformity must, however, amount to as much as this. Taking the articles of religion in their natural and obvious meaning,‡ as upon the whole with singular unanimity, and in the most essential points with absolute unanimity, they have been understood and interpreted by our great divines, the subscriber recognizes in them a faithful exhibition of Christian doctrine, the rule of his public teaching, the authoritative expression of the faith once delivered to the saints. On two points especially, an explicit and unhesitating act of adhesion is demanded—the canon of Holy Scripture, and the Creeds which present its fundamental doctrines in a concentrated form.§ Short of this con-

* See the touching and unanswerable statement of Mr. Whiston, quoted by Waterland, vol. ii. p. 400.

† This is the declaration of the four Oxford Tutors in 1841:—"We readily admit the necessity of allowing that liberty in interpreting the formularies of our Church which has been advocated by many of our most learned bishops and eminent divines; but this tract puts forth new and startling views as to the extent to which that liberty may be carried. For if we are right in our apprehension of the author's meaning, we are at a loss to see what security would remain, were his principles generally recognized, that the most plainly erroneous doctrines and practices of the Church of Rome might not be inculcated in the lecture-rooms of the university and from the pulpits of our churches."

‡ See Dr. Waterland on 'Arian Subscription,' vol. ii. p. 335. Bishops Bull, vol. ii. p. 211, and J. Taylor, quoted above.

§ To these should be added the doctrine of the Sacraments. The statute of Elizabeth 13, which requires subscription to all the Articles, specifies in the first place such only as concern the confession of the Christian faith and the doctrine of the Holy Sacraments. See Collier, 'Ecclesiastical History,' vol. vi. pp. 485 and 489.

formity, it is certain that a minister cannot sympathize with the spirit, or give effect to the purposes, of the Church. Common sense, in this case fully in accord with the highest reason, is a sufficient guide to the most cautious and scrupulous inquirer. Nor can I forbear from quoting the words of one whom no man will suspect of any tendency to dogmatic intolerance, any disregard of even exaggerated sensitiveness. In a letter to one who had felt much perplexity about subscription, after alluding to difficulties formerly experienced by himself, Dr. Arnold* writes thus :—"The real honesty of subscription appears to me to consist in a sympathy with the system to which you subscribe, in a preference of it, not negatively merely as better than others, but positively, as in itself good and true in its most characteristic points. Now, the most characteristic points of the English Church are two; that it maintains what is called the Catholic Faith as opposed to the early heresies, and is also decidedly a Reformed Church as opposed to the priestly and Papal system." Such must have been the feelings of the Oxford tutor† who some twenty years since bore this testimony to our Church, with especial reference to its safeguard of subscription—"I know not where free scope may be found for the feelings of awe, mystery, tenderness, and devotedness, when they struggle for utterance in the breast of the spiritual man, more freely than in our own communion: where our sons are taught, *without adding thereto, or diminishing aught from it*, the great mystery of godliness: God manifest in the flesh, justified in the Spirit, seen of angels, preached unto the Gentiles, believed on in the world, received up into glory." No one holding those principles could feel any difficulty in subscription. Such a man is satisfied, not because he is safe from legal consequences, but because he feels himself in harmony with the spirit of his Church, because he knows that he is offering an honest act of fealty, and is willing, without subterfuge or equivocation, to carry

* 'Life and Correspondence,' vol. ii. p. 177.
† 'Letter to Rev. T. T. Churton by Rev. H. B. Wilson,' 1841.

out her intentions to the best of his ability. Should it, indeed, unhappily be the case, that in after years his mind should be so affected as to reject not merely a word here and there, the meaning or application of expressions about which the most learned and candid writers have differed, or even positive determinations upon questions of subordinate importance, but the great truths, the objective facts, the fundamental doctrines set forth plainly and unmistakably in those formularies, then surely the moral obligation is positive. It leaves but one alternative. He cannot do the work which he has undertaken, cannot preach the doctrines, cannot proclaim the facts which are the very foundation of the Church: how can he retain the trust? If people did not understand this to be our feeling as ministers, they would speedily seek for some other guarantee. If it were generally believed that, when called upon to clear himself from "odious imputations," a minister might put a stop to all further inquiry by simply renewing his subscription, with a clear understanding that thereby he means no more than that he recognizes a legal obligation, retaining the right of explaining away, or even denying privately and publicly, the very statements to which he puts his hand, the whole body of the laity would scout the very notion of subscription, would reject it as illusory, as a mere sham.* The only light in which they look upon subscription is, that it is a means of ascertaining what truths a man holds, and what he holds himself bound to teach,—not surely upon what terms he may consider himself justified in retaining office or emoluments in the Church. They will be

* These words express with equal force and accuracy the general feelings of the laity. "If the Church of England really possesses that element of vitality which her sons proudly believe to be inherent in her, she will never flinch from vindicating the integrity of her Articles and the uniformity of her belief; but if she should be ill-advised enough to allow her tests to be broken down and rendered void by strained and licentious expositions, if she place her only hope of safety and unity in allowing her sons to profess one creed and believe another, let her prepare for that well-merited downfall to which deceit and double dealing never fail to conduct." A tract bearing the title, 'The Articles Construed by Themselves,' Oxford, 1841, attributed, as I believe, to R. Lowe, Esq., formerly of Magdalen College, now Vice-President of the Committee of Council on Education.

prepared to allow time for consideration to any man harassed by perplexing doubts: no man would be regarded with more entire sympathy and tenderness than one whose spirit might be overwrought in its struggles with storms which haunt the higher regions of intellectual life: but so long as he works, prays, preaches, administers the sacraments of the Church, or discharges the kindred and no less responsible duty of forming the character of youth under the sanction of the ministerial office, laymen presume, and would be scandalized to hear it doubted, that he holds substantially the convictions which he professed, when formally, publicly, deliberately, at a most critical moment of his life, he signed his name in token of unfeigned assent to the Articles of his Church.

41. One reason assigned for the removal of all doctrinal tests may require special consideration.* It is stated that there is a wide-spread and increasing alienation from the Church; that the minds of thoughtful men reject the views of Christian doctrine commonly advanced in our churches and chapels — that is, in other words, by the teachers of nearly all religious denominations: and it is distinctly implied, that this alienation is to be attributed to the growing sense of incompatibility between the tenets generally regarded as essential to Christianity, and the conclusions of reason from the progress of science, and more especially "from the advance of general knowledge concerning the inhabitancy of the world. We might question the fact of an increasing alienation. We might argue that, compared with the state of the church in the last century, her existing condition is one of wider and far more effectual influence; that every test upon which reliance can be placed indicates a strengthening of religious convictions; that the number of communicants is multiplied at least tenfold; that the very face of the country is changed by the

* Mr. Wilson can hardly hope to disprove his own forcible statement. "Schemes of comprehension of necessity defeat their own design: if weak brethren are included on the one hand, weak brethren are excluded on the other."—Letter to Rev. T. T. Churton.

multitude of churches built, enlarged, or restored; and that, for the first time since the Reformation, our Church has grappled with the real difficulties of her position, sends forth missionaries to all quarters of the earth, and has organized the colonial episcopate. We might point to many of the greatest names in art, science, literature, and politics, which within the same period have recognized in our Church a true manifestation of the Divine life. Nor, again, can it be denied that the alleged facts of the census of 1851, in themselves most questionable, have been most unfairly applied. Certainly, of all inferences, the least reasonable is, that the absence of some 45 per cent. of the population from public service was in any way attributable to conscientious objections to the doctrine taught in our churches, or to a conviction that heathenism, after all, is no very lamentable condition of two-thirds of the human race. We should have thought that ignorance, vice, and indifference, on the one hand, on the other, the want of sufficient and proper accommodation, were generally recognized as the main causes of what certainly was a most painful result of an inquiry into the actual number of worshippers. Upon these points we need not dilate; but this we maintain without hesitation,—the alienation, to whatever extent it may really exist, is not owing to the doctrines set forth in the Creeds of our Church, and embodied in her liturgical formularies. The surest way of emptying any church or chapel is to substitute for earnest preaching of those very doctrines which are specially selected for attack or suspicion, a vague, cold, rationalistic system of so-called Christian ethics.* Let the people suspect that their ethical development is the single object of all the instrumentality of the Church, they would simply throw it off as cumbrous and superfluous; and they would be right. The experiment has been tried here and abroad. It has had one unvarying result. In

* Not but that our strictest dogmatical writers are most careful to assign its right place to morality. Waterland says, with reference to this very question of subscription, "Every heresy in morality is of more pernicious consequence than heresies in point of positive religion."

Germany, where for a time it had free play, it alienated the great body of the nation from the communion of the Church. In England sufficient proof has been given that a "prudential system of ethics" not only fails "as a restraining force upon society," but that, disjoined from the vital doctrines of Christianity, it leads rapidly to the decay, and ends in the dissolution, of any denomination by which it is adopted. This is the case even in independent communities where the principal parts of the service are adjusted by the minister and his congregation—where prayer and psalmody may be kept in harmony with preaching, however rationalistic. But in a church where the doctrines taught in the Creeds find an expression in every prayer, the contradiction between the sermon of a rationalist and the words which he is constrained to utter in his ministerial functions, will always be, and ought always to be, fatal to his influence. If the congregation have good reason to suspect that, in reciting the Creeds, the minister looks upon himself as subjected to the hard bondage of uttering what he inwardly disavows, or regards as an "unhappy" form; that in the petitions of the Litany he uses expressions touching the "Divine personalities" which are to him little more than metaphysical abstractions, or speculative conclusions of the schools; if they believe that, from the opening prayer to the final blessing, there has been a constant struggle, a series of inward protests, jesuitical reservations or interpretations, going on within the mind of the reader; whatever else may be the effect upon their hearts, one effect is sure, their moral sense will be shocked, they will recoil in indignation from such hypocrisy. Even supposing he should have communicated to them his own unhappy doubts and repugnances, they will feel that it is a bad and evil thing for them to share in acts of such glaring and flagrant inconsistency. They will soon desert the church altogether, or testify their contempt for the ordinances or the minister, by their demeanour when he preaches, or by their expressive silence in the acts of common worship. One thing must be looked in the face. The abolition of subscription to those doctrines which find expression in our Liturgy * would be utterly futile unless that Liturgy itself were entirely reconstructed. No partial reform, not the widest reform which has ever been suggested, or would be tolerated by the most indifferent and sceptical congregation in this land, would free from intellectual bondage the conscience of those who are now calling for the relaxation of subscription. It is not a mere phrase here and there which would change their position; it is the very spirit of Christianity, full of the recognition of its most special and characteristic truths, which drives the minister to the alternative of speaking as a believer in each and all essential doctrines, or of standing self-convicted and self-condemned in the presence of Him whom he mocks by the utterance of prayers which he inwardly disavows.

What we desire is this,—to bring into the fold of Christ's Church all who are estranged from its communion; but it must be a complete and an honest work. Our commission is to give and teach the truth, the whole truth, and nothing but the truth. The Christian faith is a perfect and indissoluble whole. We cannot consent to mutilate or disfigure it. We cannot entrust it to the care of any ministers who are not prepared to give full and satisfactory pledges that they accept it as a whole. We have no fear of any consequences, so long as men can rely upon the trustworthiness of the agents through whom the Church acts. The one thing of which all need to be assured is, that their ministers hold fast the form of sound words; the truth once delivered to the saints; the canon of Holy Scriptures, which are able to make wise unto salvation; the knowledge of the Father and the Son, which is eternal life; in a word, faith in the Incarnation and the Atonement, without any subtlety of interpretation, in the plain sense accepted by all the Churches of Christendom. Upon subordinate, or purely specula-

* This was distinctly felt by the leaders in the Arian controversy in the last century. See Dr. Waterland's tract on 'Arian Subscription,' vol. ii.

tive questions, considerable latitude of interpretation is conceded — the wider and freer the better for the cause of truth. But this liberty is conceded because men doubt not that they who use it accept those fundamental truths. Abuse of the concession—attempts to strain the liberty so as to unsettle the doctrines nearest to the hearts of Christians, would speedily bring about results the very opposite to those contemplated by many who struggle against existing limitations. It must be borne in mind, that if changes were made, they would probably be made in a different direction from that pointed out by latitudinarians. To increase, not to diminish our securities,—to exclude, not to admit incongruous and adverse elements—such would be the great object of all earnest Christian men; of those who would undoubtedly take the lead should the national ark be unloosed from its moorings, should the storms of angry and unscrupulous controversy once more thoroughly rouse the national spirit. We are far from wishing for any increase of stringency. So far as regards the terms of admission to the ministry, we are satisfied with existing safeguards, provided always that men do not palter with us in a double meaning, that we are safe from special pleading and equivocation, that declarations are made in the sense in which those who hear them are well known to receive them,—that, in a word, we have precisely the same kind of confidence which is felt by all honourable men who are parties to compacts involving the recognition of weighty duties distinctly set forth and understood.

We need not fear the issue of the controversy. It may justify watchfulness, but not alarm. It is true that some questions have been raised, which are not likely to be finally settled in this generation. The elements which have thrown the mind of Europe into a state of disturbance, have undoubtedly penetrated very deeply into England. Our young-men will have to pass through a fiery trial. It is not an age for rest, for unreasoning acquiescence in past traditions. The progress of religious knowledge will in future be more beset by speculative and intellectual difficulties than has been the case in former years. Candidates for the ministry must not be contented with meagre introductions to Holy Scripture, or a superficial analysis of its contents. It will be their duty — a duty more strongly felt than ever—to ascertain the grounds on which the Canon of Scripture has been received by the Church, and the proofs of the genuineness and authenticity of its contents; they will test more closely and severely the evidences of all the doctrinal statements, to which after careful examination they will have to declare their assent. But in all this work they have abundant help. The close, microscopic examination of the Book of Life is daily bringing its secret beauties into clearer light. The progress of historical research opens new fields of discovery in which the Scriptural exegetist finds valuable materials. The deep spiritual meaning of many an obscure passage or neglected fact is discerned more distinctly by those who, candidly but warily, scrutinize the objections of antagonists to the faith. The current of religious thought flows in broader and deeper channels than heretofore, and the vessels of those who sail under the sure guidance of the Spirit of God will reach the haven freighted with treasures of great price. Antagonisms may indeed become stronger, secessions perhaps be more frequent; superstition and infidelity may claim each its share in the spoil of troubled and faithless spirits; but the revelation of Christ will not lose its hold upon the heart of the humble, nor upon the intellect of the truthful inquirer. Our branch of the Church will not be disinherited of its privileges or stripped of its safeguards; it will eject rationalism in every form, more especially in the most un-English and Jesuitical of all forms, that of Ideology. It will continue to do its own proper work, preparing its members not for a dreamy state of repose in the bosom of the universal Parent, but for a full, perfect, and conscious life in the presence of the living God.

ESSAY V.

THE MOSAIC RECORD OF CREATION.

10

CONTENTS OF ESSAY V.

THE MOSAIC RECORD OF CREATION.

1. Almost all ancient nations have traditions respecting the origin of the universe. These traditions differ in detail and representation according to the genius of the people by whom they have been preserved, but they retain a family likeness, and certain points of contact with each other and the Mosaic cosmogony, with which some exhibit a striking resemblance. Thus the Etruscans relate that God created the world in six thousand years. In the first thousand He created the heaven and the earth; in the second the firmament; in the third the sea and the other waters of the earth; in the fourth sun, moon, and stars; in the fifth the animals belonging to air, water, and land; in the sixth man alone.* The Persian tradition also recognizes the six periods of creation, assigning to the first the heavens; to the second the waters; to the third the earth; to the fourth trees and plants; to the fifth animals; to the sixth man.† Others mention the darkness, the chaotic mass of waters, the Spirit of God; so that even in the judgment of modern critics, there must have been "a primitive, cosmogonical myth, universally pervading antiquity."‡ How and when that universal myth arose, modern criticism does not say; and yet it is a striking fact that there should be such a tradition, and that amidst the variety of modifications the original identity should still be perceptible. Christian apologists have found in the resemblances a presumption of its being derived from the original revelation, and in the consent of the various human families, com-

* Suidas in voc. Τυῤῥηνία.

† Zend Avesta, Kleuker. p. 19; Anquetil du Perron, tom. ii. 348; Burnouf, Yaçna, tom. i. p. 297.

‡ Knobel on Genesis, p. 6.

bined with the manifest superiority and historic character of the account in Genesis, a proof of the Divine origin of the Mosaic Record, and of the unity of the human race.* Modern theology, on the contrary, teaches that the Mosaic cosmogony is only the Hebrew form of the original myth, bearing the palm indeed on account "of its simplicity, dignity, and sublimity," but still unhistoric in its relation, and inconsistent with the results of modern criticism and science.

To discuss all the details of criticism would require volumes. But one alleged result, often stated in an offhand, popular way, asserted with unhesitating confidence, and repeated as absolutely certain, requires notice. It is said that in the Book of Genesis there are some portions in which God is spoken of exclusively as Elohim—in others exclusively as Jehovah [the LORD in the Authorized Version]. This exclusive use of the one Divine name in some portions, and of the other in other portions, it is said, characterizes two different authors, living at different times, and consequently Genesis is composed of two different documents, the one Elohistic, the other Jehovistic, which moreover differ in statement, and consequently that this book was not written by Moses, and is neither inspired nor trustworthy. Now, not to notice the defectiveness of this statement as to the names of God, who in Genesis is also called El, El Elyon, Most High God; El Shaddai, God Almighty; Adonai, Lord; nor the fact that in other books, as Jonah and the Psalms, the same exclusiveness is found; let us look at this statement as a supposed result of criticism. It is generally urged as if on this point critics were all of one mind, agreed in the portions which are Elohistic or Jehovistic—unanimous as to the characteristic differences of style in the separate portions, in fact as if the theory came with the authority of universal consent. Were this the case, it would necessarily carry with it great weight. For, though the conclusions of criticism dif-

* Grotius 'de Veritate,' who has given an ample collection of ancient testimonies, lib. i. § xvi. Faber, 'Horæ Mosaicæ, vol. i. pp. 17–40.

fer from the demonstrations of pure science and the inferences of induction, yet, when unanimously adopted by those competent to judge, they deservedly influence the minds of all reasonable persons. But this is not the case in the present theory. The popular statement given above does not represent the true state of the case. The fact is, that there is here the greatest variety of opinion, and the modifications of the above apparently simple theory are so widely divergent, as either to shake the value of the criticism, or throw a dark shade of doubt on the competence of the critics. In the first place, there is a difference as to the extent to which the theory is to be applied. Some confine it to the Book of Genesis; others include Exodus to chapter vi.; others, as Knobel, Bleek, and Ewald, assert that the Jehovistic and Elohistic differences can be recognized through the whole Pentateuch to the end of Joshua. Some, as J. D. Michaelis, Jahn, Vater, Hartmann, regard Genesis as a loose and unsystematic stringing together of disjointed fragments. 2. But passing these by, let us look at the state of the Elohistic and Jehovistic theory, as stated by Bleek in his Introduction.

i. In the year 1753, Astruc, a French physician, taught that the Book of Genesis is made up of twelve memoirs or documents, of which the two principal are the Elohistic and the Jehovistic. From these Moses composed the book, which he wrote in twelve columns. Copyists mixed these together, and hence the present form of Genesis.

ii. Eichhorn asserted that the present Book of Genesis is based upon two pre-Mosaic documents, distinguished by Elohim and Jehovah, and that the author, in relating any event, selected that document in which the fullest account was contained. Sometimes the accounts are mixed together. Some other documents were consulted.

iii. Ilgen supposes seventeen documents, but only three authors, one Jehovist, two Elohists, and is so acute in his scent as sometimes to divide even single verses between the three, and give to each his own.

iv. De Wette's theory, in the first edition of his Introduction, is, that a continuous Elohistic document pervades and forms the basis of the whole book, and extends to Exod. vi. In this the author inserted what he found in one, or, probably, in several Jehovistic documents.

v. Von Bohlen believes in the same Elohistic basis, but denies the existence of Jehovistic documents. The author of the book in its present state is the Jehovist, so that only two persons are concerned.

vi. Gramberg makes three authors—the Elohist, the Jehovist, and the compiler, who does not scruple sometimes to substitute one Divine name for the other.

vii. Ewald exhibits a variety of opinions: first, he began by holding the unity of Genesis, and proving it against both the document and the fragment hypothesis. His arguments have not yet been refuted, either by himself or others. Secondly, about ten years afterwards he taught that the basis of the Book of Genesis is an ancient writing, of which considerable remains are found in the whole Pentateuch, and which is distinguished by peculiarity of language, especially by the use of Elohim up to Exod. vi. 2. This author had incorporated into his book more ancient documents, as the Decalogue and Exod. xxi.–xxiii. At a subsequent period arose another work on the ancient history, which ascribed the use of *Jehovah* to patriarchal times. From this later work portions were inserted into the former by the author of the present Book of Genesis, so that here there are at the least four writers concerned. Thirdly, Ewald extended and modified this theory by supposing more than two treatments of the ancient history forming the contents of the Pentateuch, and the Book of Joshua. He ascribes Genesis in its present form to that writer, whom in his first edition he calls the fourth narrator, and in his second edition the fifth narrator of the primitive histories, who lived in the time of Jotham. This work had several predecessors; according to the first edition, three; according to the second, six. Three of these are Elohistic.

viii. Hüpfeldt takes as the basis of our Genesis three independent historic works; two Elohistic, one Jehovistic, and makes in addition a compiler.

ix. Knobel believes in two documents: first, the Elohistic, forming the basis of the Pentateuch and of Joshua; second, the Jehovistic, which again has two previous sources. There are, besides, free Jehovistic developments, in which the compiler sometimes followed hints in the two documents, sometimes popular tradition, and sometimes his own conceptions.

3. This enumeration is far from exhausting the varieties, but is sufficient to show the want of unity. The reader will perceive that some assert one Elohistic document—others, two—others, three. In like manner some make one Jehovist; some more. Some make the Jehovist identical with the compiler; others make him a different person. Some make two, others three, others four, Ewald seven documents by different authors the materials of Genesis. Now every one can understand that there is a great difference whether the Elohistic and Jehovistic portions be assigned to one or be divided amongst two, three, or more persons. He who says that there is only one Elohist must believe that in the whole Elohistic portion there is unity of style, tone, spirit, language. If there be two Elohists, then the former is mistaken as to the unity, and there must be two diversities of style; but if there be three Elohists, then both first and second critics are mistaken, and there must be three different styles. The portions assigned to each must also be smaller. Let the three Elohists be A, B, C. The first critic says that the whole belongs to A. The second critic says, No; part belongs to B. The third critic says part belongs to A, part to B, and part to C. And thus the most celebrated critics convict each other of false criticism. Hüpfeldt condemns Knobel; Ewald condemns Hüpfeldt and Knobel; Knobel condemns Ewald and Hüpfeldt. If Knobel's criticism is correct, Hüpfeldt's is worthless. If Ewald be right, the others must be deficient in critical acumen. They may all be wrong, but only one of the three can be right.

But take into account all the other differences enumerated above, one supposing that the documents are pre-Mosaic, another that they were written in the times of Joshua or the Judges, another in the time of David, another some centuries later; and how uncertain must the principles of their criticism appear,—how valueless their conclusions! With such facts can any sane person talk of the results of modern criticism as regards the Book of Genesis? or be willing to give up the belief of centuries for such criticism as this?

It is self-evident that criticism leading to such inconsistent conclusions must be in a high degree imaginative: a little examination shows that it is also unreasonably arbitrary. In order to make out the theory that there are two authors, one of whom is known by the exclusive use of Elohim, and the other by the exclusive use of Jehovah, and that the former is more ancient than the latter, it is necessary to point out paragraphs in which those Divine names are exclusively used, and also to prove that the Elohist does not refer to the Jehovistic document; for if the Elohist plainly refers to what the Jehovist has related, the latter cannot be posterior to the former, and the theory fails. Now, unhappily for the theory, the word Jehovah does occur in the Elohistic passages, and the Elohist does refer to the Jehovistic narrative. Thus in Genesis ii. 4, the two names occur together. "These are the generations of the heavens and the earth when they were created, in the day when Jehovah Elohim made the earth and the heavens." Now if this verse belongs to what precedes, then the following narrative, which has also the unusual union of the two names, was written by the Elohist, and the first three chapters are by one author. If it be written by the Jehovist, how comes it to have Elohim as well, and why does it differ both from Elohist and Jehovist documents by the union of the names? Here is a difficulty which has divided all Germany, and arrayed Rationalist against Rationalist, and Orthodox against Orthodox, and for which there seems no hope of solution, unless violence be offered to the text, and men be persuaded, against the evidence of manuscripts and ancient versions, that the words "These are the generations of the heavens and the earth" stood originally as the heading before the first verse of the first chapter, and that the word Elohim in ii. 4 is an interpolation of the Jehovist. Take another example:—Genesis v. is said to be Elohistic, and it is certain that *Elohim*, God, occurs five times; but in verse 29 appears the word *Jehovah* to disturb the theorist; and not only is this word there, but the verse refers to the Jehovistic chapter iii. 17. What is to be done? The verse stands in all the manuscripts and ancient versions. But, if the Elohistic theory is to stand, it must be got rid of somehow. It is an interpolation, says the theorist; it was put in by the compiler. In like manner the theorists cut off chapter vii. 9—24 from its context, and say, It is Elohistic. But lo! in verse 16 stands "Jehovah." The same canon of the old Socinian criticism is again applied; the unwelcome word is an interpolation. One instance more. The xlixth chapter is said to belong to a long Elohistic portion. But in the 18th verse occur those words of Jacob, "I have waited for thy salvation, O Jehovah." Again the same violence is repeated. The disturbing verse is an interpolation. Is this criticism? Is it a fair and legitimate proceeding to alter the text, and that not once, but frequently, in order to make it suit one's theory? To discard the consent of manuscripts, ancient versions, all printed editions, and cry out, Interpolation, interpolation, without any authority at all? There is no more certain sign of helpless prejudice or critical incompetence, than to have frequent recourse to violent and unauthorized alteration of the text; and yet without this the theory of the Elohistic and Jehovistic documents, even if it were unanimously received by modern critics, could not be made out. Arbitrary separations of what evidently belongs together, and unwarranted assertions of interpolation, prove its unsoundness. The variety of its modifications, one neutralizing the other, as has been shown above, demonstrates the uncertainty and untrustworthiness of the results.

4. But the theory rests upon an assumption totally false, that the names Elohim and Jehovah are synonymous, and that they can be used indifferently, one for the other. The names are not synonymous, and cannot be so used. There is the same difference between Elohim and Jehovah, as between *Deus* and *Jupiter*, or *homo* and *Petrus*. The one expresses the genus, the other stands for the individual, and is a proper name. Elohim answers to our own word *God* or *Deity*, and is, therefore, used of false Gods as well as of the true. *Jehovah* stands for the personal, living, self-revealing Being, and is explained in those two passages, Exod. iii. 14, "I am that I am;" and xxxiv. 6, when, the Lord having said, "I will proclaim my name before thee," proclaimed "Jehovah, Jehovah, God [El] merciful and gracious, long-suffering and abundant in goodness and truth;" and can therefore be applied to none but the one true and eternal God, as is said, "I am Jehovah; that is my name, and my glory will I not give to another." This distinction is strongly marked in the words of Elijah, "If Jehovah be Elohim, follow Him; if Baal, then follow him." Here it would be impossible to interchange Elohim and Jehovah, or to say, "if Baal be Jehovah." There is an essential difference in signification, and, though Jehovah is the true God, and the true God Jehovah, and therefore sometimes either might be used, yet, in consequence of the essential difference, there are cases where there is a peculiar propriety in using one rather than the other; and there are other cases in which one must be used, and the other cannot. As *Jehovah* is the proper name of God, it does not take a genitive case or a suffix. It is, therefore, impossible to say in Hebrew, "the Jehovah of Abraham, Isaac, and Jacob," or "My, thy, our Jehovah." In such cases, *Elohim* must be used, as "The *Elohim*, God of Abraham," &c. "My Elohim, my God, our Elohim, our God," &c. Again, as Jehovah signifies the self-revealing, that word can-

not occur in the mouth of those to whom He has not revealed himself, nor, ordinarily, in the mouth of Hebrews speaking to such; and, therefore, when Moses and Aaron use it to Pharaoh, they add "the God of Israel" to make it intelligible. But still Pharaoh asks, "Who is Jehovah? I know not Jehovah;" and they explain, "The Elohim, God of the Hebrews hath met with us." There is no room here to go through and illustrate all the peculiarities of these Divine names. But what has been said is sufficient to show that the exclusive use of Elohim cannot be received as a characteristic mark to distinguish one author from the other, inasmuch as, in the cases above enumerated and others, the use of Elohim is compulsory; and neither Moses, nor Samuel, nor Isaiah, could in these cases leave out Elohim, and substitute Jehovah. Thus, in Gen. xl. 8, the word Elohim occurs once, when Joseph says to the Egyptian prisoners, "Do not interpretations belong to God, *Elohim?*" Here *Jehovah* could not be used. Again, in xli., the word *Elohim* occurs eight times. In six of them the use was compulsory. In xliii. 23 it occurs twice with suffixes or genitive, and no other word could be used, and so in other instances.* And, therefore, the use of the word cannot be the characteristic peculiarity of one author. In the first chapter of Genesis, Moses might have used either Elohim or Jehovah, except in the 27th verse, where *Elohim* was compulsory. But in the opening of the Divine teaching, it was necessary to make clear that God is Creator, that the world was not eternal, nor independent; and also that Jehovah is not one among many—not the national God of the Hebrews—but that Jehovah the Self-revealer, and Elohim the Almighty Creator, are one. Therefore, in the first chapter, *Elohim* is used throughout. The Deity is the Creator. But in approaching that part of the narrative where the personal God enters into relations with man, and where *Jehovah*

* Ewald in his 'Composition der Genesis,' and Hengstenberg in his 'Authentie des Pentateuchs,' vol. i. pp. 306–391, have examined all the instances where the names occur, and explained the propriety or the necessity.

was necessary, Moses unites the names, and says, "Jehovah Elohim, the Lord God." Had he suddenly used *Jehovah* alone, there might have been a doubt as to whether *Jehovah* was not different from Elohim. The union of the two names proves identity, and this being proved, from the fourth chapter on, Moses drops this union and sometimes employs *Jehovah*, sometimes *Elohim*, as occasion, propriety, and the laws of the Hebrew language require. The use of these names, therefore, can prove nothing against the unity of the narrative.

5. But, in truth, independently of all philological criticism, the unity of the first two chapters of Genesis may be proved by comparing one with the other. They do not contain two distinct accounts of "the Creation."

The second chapter does not narrate the creation of heaven or earth, or light, firmament, sun, moon, or stars, sea, or dry land, fish, or creeping things. The second chapter, therefore, is so far from being a cosmogony, that it is not even a geogony, and, therefore, the fourth verse of the second chapter, "These are the generations of the heavens and the earth when they were created, in the day that the Lord God (Jehovah Elohim) made the earth and the heavens," cannot be the title or summary of what follows, but are an exact recapitulation of what is narrated in the first chapter. They mention first the creation of "the heavens and the earth;" second, the making of "the earth and heavens" in the very order in which the process of creation is related in that chapter, but of which not one word is said in what follows. The second chapter is obviously not an account "of the creation," but of the particulars of the formation of man, and his early history. Ewald said long ago, "The aim of the first connected narrative (ch. i. 1—ii. 3) is to exhibit God as the Creator of the universe. . . The author then passes over from the perfected picture of the created universe, to that which must have been to him, as to all writers of history, the most worthy of note, to the history of man. Yet he closes the first picture with the words (ii. 4), 'These are the generations of the heavens and of the earth.'" * The second chapter is, therefore, an integral part of a relation contained in the three first chapters, connected with the chapter by verse four, and preparing for the account of the Fall by telling us beforehand of Paradise, of the tree of knowledge, the prohibition to eat of it, and of the formation of the woman. Indeed, most recent writers admit, that whether there be different sources or not, the author has formed them into one narrative; there cannot, therefore, be contradiction. There are differences to be explained by the different objects which the author had in view. In the first, his object was to give an outline of the history of the universe; in the second, to relate the origin and primitive history of man, so far as it was necessary, as a preparation for the history of the Fall. In the former, therefore, all the steps of creation are treated in chronological order. In the latter, only so much is alluded to as is necessary for the author's purpose, and in the order which that purpose required.

6. So much for modern criticism. But the new theology also asserts that the Mosaic cosmogony is contradicted by the discoveries and progress of science, and that, therefore, Moses could not have been inspired. This is a straightforward objection, deserves a fair and full consideration, and ought not to be met with what objectors can only regard as evasions. Such are the assertions, that the first chapter of Genesis is poetry, or a series of seven prophetic visions, † or the mere clothing of a theological truth. To urge such suppositions is not to defend the ark of God, but to abandon it to the enemy. If the first chapter of Genesis be poetry, or vision, or parable, it is not historic truth, which is just what objectors assert. There are in this chapter none of the peculiarities of Hebrew poetry. The style is full of dignity, but it is that of prose narrative. There is no mention of prophetic vision, no prophetic formula employed. It is not said, "The vision which Moses

* 'Composition der Genesis,' pp. 192, 193. To this division Ewald adheres, as appears from his Essays on the subject in his 'Jahrbuch' for 1848, p. 77, and 1849, p. 132.

† So Kurz, and after him, Hugh Miller.

saw," nor "I lifted up my eyes, and behold." The prophet or historian is kept entirely out of sight, and the narrative begins at once without any preface, "In the beginning God created the heavens and the earth," and then goes to the account of Paradise, the birth of Cain and Abel, &c., without any break or note of transition from vision to history. The Book of Genesis is history. It is the historical introduction to the four following books of the Pentateuch, or rather, to all following revelation, and the first chapter, as the inseparable beginning of the whole, must be historical also. When the Lord recapitulates its contents in the Fourth Commandment, and makes it the basis of the ordinance of the Sabbath, He stamps it as real history. To suppose a moral, or even a ceremonial command, based upon a poetic picture, or a vision, or an ideal narrative, would be absurd. The Lord also treats "the first chapters of Genesis" as real and authoritative history, when He makes Gen. i. 27, and ii. 23, 24, the foundation of His doctrine concerning marriage and divorce. As history, therefore, they must be received, whatever difficulties that reception may involve. Some, indeed, hold that in reading the Bible, a distinction is to be made between statements relating to religion, and those relating to physics, that the former are to be received, and the latter disregarded, as "The purpose of revelation is to teach man what he cannot find out by his unassisted reason, but not physical truths, for the discovery of which he has faculties." But, what are we to do when a truth is both religious and physical, such as "God created the heavens and the earth"? And how are we to distinguish between what can be and what cannot be discovered by man's natural faculties? On the one hand, the leading intellects of Germany are still disputing about the eternity of the universe, and the relation of the finite to the absolute; and on the other, Deists and Theists, and Rationalists, teach that all religious and moral truth can be discovered, and has been discovered, by man's natural powers—can be known in no other way, and that, therefore, revelation is unnecessary. Besides, if the first chapter of Genesis be not given to teach us the facts and order of creation, why is it there at all in all its circumstantiality? Are we to believe that Divine revelation begins with an unscientific misstatement of physical truth? If the first chapter be the offspring of human error, where does Divine truth begin? This principle raises many new difficulties, and removes none. We, therefore, adhere to the plain grammatical statement, as a Divine revelation of the origin of the universe, not yet superseded by the theories of the speculative philosophy, nor antiquated by the discoveries of modern science.

7. The first supposed difficulty in the Mosaic statement is the age of the world. According to the teachings of Geology and Astronomy, the existence of the heavens and the earth is to be reckoned by myriads of thousands of years. According to Moses, it is alleged, they are of yesterday. To know whether this difficulty is real, it is first necessary to know what Moses has actually said. And here it is not intended to propose anything new, but to revert to the ancient exposition of the phrase, "In the beginning," for upon this the question really turns. The first proposition is "In the beginning God created the heavens and the earth," and here it is necessary to observe that *Reshith*, the Hebrew word for "beginning," is in the original without the definite article. Moses says, "In Reshith [not in the *Reshith*], Elohim created the heavens and the earth." The antiquity and correctness of this reading are proved by the Septuagint, Chaldee, and Syriac versions.

LXX. *Ἐν ἀρχῇ*, Chaldee בקדמין, Syriac ܒܪܫܝܬ, and so it is also found in the Evangelist's allusion, John i. 1. The uniformity of the reading, and the care with which it had been preserved for centuries—notwithstanding the natural temptation to supply the article—testify that there was an uniform traditional meaning attached to it, different from that possible, if the word had the article. What this meaning is, is plainly seen in the first verse of St. John's Gospel. Now that Socinian exegesis is a thing of the past, all divines, English and foreign, agree that St. John here makes a pointed reference to Gen. i. 1, and that in the words ἐν ἀρχῇ, "In the beginning," he expresses *Duration* or *Time*, previous to Creation. So Dean Alford, "Ἐν ἀρχῇ = πρὸ τοῦ τὸν κόσμον εἶναι." "In the beginning" is equivalent to "Before the world was." Tholuck says that the phrase expresses "Eternity *à parte ante.*" Meyer also takes it of duration before time, and translates it *Vorzeitlichkeit* (pre-temporality), and says that it is equivalent to the Septuagint version of Prov. viii. 23, "In the beginning, before he made the earth;" and to the words of our Lord "Before the world was;" and of St. Paul "Before the foundation of the world" (Ephes. i. 4). De Wette has nearly the same words and the same references. Lücke also says that the phrase "In the beginning" includes the idea of pre-mundane existence (*des Vorweltlichen*), and answers to "Before the world was" (John xvii. 5). All are agreed that "Beginning" refers to *duration* or *time*, not to *order*, and that it is indefinite in its signification, and may mean previous eternity, or previous time, according to the subject spoken of.* They who believe that St. John was inspired will receive his interpretation of the first words of Genesis as infallibly correct, and therefore interpret them there as in the Gospel. But even if St. John be regarded as an ordinary writer asserting an important truth, his adoption of the interpretation proves that it was known to the Jews of his time, and this is further proved by the nearly contemporary testimony of the Targum.

Its author Onkelos gives the same meaning, and proves that it was then the received interpretation. For the Hebrew *B'reshith* he gives *B'kadmin* (בקדמין) *in antiquities*, or *former times.* The word *K'dam*, equivalent to the Hebrew *Kédem*, signifies, as Buxtorf says, "*ante, antiquitas, prioritas, principium.*" In the plural number, as Onkelos here has it, it signifies, not

* Similar is the meaning of the words in the Doxology, "As it was in the beginning, is now, and ever shall be."

order, but time, "*ancient times, former times, eternity.*" For example (Gen. xxviii. 19), "Luz was the name of the city מלקדמין, *from antiquities*, or *former times.*" Again (Ps. lxviii. 33), "To him that rideth upon the heavens of heavens of antiquity," the Chaldee has דמלקדמין, "that were from *antiquities*, or *former times*," which our translators followed, and have rendered, "the heavens of heavens which were *of old.*" Again (Deut. xxxiii. 27), "The Eternal God (literally, the God of *antiquity* or *priority*);" Onkelos has, "The God who is from *antiquities*, דמלקדמין." Here the word is applied to eternity.* When, therefore, Onkelos translates the first word of Gen. i. 1, by *B'kadmin* in the plural, and without the article, he meant, *in antiquities*, in *former times* or *duration*, *of old.*

The LXX. use *ἐν ἀρχῇ* in the same way, and thereby prove that this interpretation was far more ancient than Onkelos. Thus, in Ezek. xxxvi. 11, they employ *ἀρχῇ* to render *Kadmah* (*former state*), and give as the parallel *ἔμπροσθεν* for *Rishah*, nearly related to *Reshith*. *Κατοικιῶ ὑμᾶς ὡς τὸ ἐν ἀρχῇ ὑμῶν, καὶ εὖ ποιήσω ὑμᾶς ὥσπερ τὰ ἔμπροσθεν ὑμῶν.*

Again, in Prov. viii. 23, they apply it to express *duration* antecedent to creation. *Πρὸ τοῦ αἰῶνος ἐθεμελίωσέ με· ἐν ἀρχῇ πρὸ τοῦ τὴν γῆν ποιῆσαι.*

In Deut. xxxiii. 15, it signifies *antiquity*. For "ancient mountains," literally "mountains of antiquity," the LXX. have *ἀπὸ κορυφῆς ὀρέων ἀρχῆς*, parallel to *βουνῶν ἀενάων*. According, then, to the LXX., "in the beginning" means "*in former duration, of old.*"

This is also the meaning of the Hebrew. The word *Reshith* having, according to its form, an abstract meaning, and coming from *Rosh* or *Resh*, head, signifies first of all, as Gesenius says, "the being head;" and, therefore, applied to rank or quality, would express "*superiority*"—to order, "*priority*," like its synonym קדם, whose first meaning is *priority*—to time, "*anteriority*." To "former time," "state at a former time," it refers in Job xlii. 12, "The Lord blessed the

* Compare Jonathan on Micah v. 2.

latter end of Job more than his beginning," where the LXX. translate more exactly, ὁ δὲ κύριος εὐλόγησε τὰ ἔσχατα Ἰὼβ ἢ τὰ ἔμπροσθεν, and so Hirzel has "אחרית, die spätere, ראשית, die frühere Lebenszeit." So in Jer. xxviii. 1, "in the beginning (*Reshith*) of the reign of Zedekiah," *beginning* does not mean the first day, nor the first year, but the former part of his reign, as the prophet immediately adds, "in the fourth year." This is also the meaning in Isai. xlvi. 10, "declaring the end from the beginning," properly, "declaring futurity from former time," as is explained by the following clause—"and from ancient times the things which are not done." According then, to the Hebrew, the meaning of the first verse of Genesis is, "In *Reshith* (anteriority), i.e., in former times, of old, God created the heavens and the earth;" and the article is omitted to exclude the application of the word to the *order* of creation. This is also the sense given in other words by the Psalmist (cii. 26). "Of old (לפנים * formerly) hast thou laid the foundation of the earth."

The sum, then, of all that has been said is, that the words, "In the beginning," refer to "time or duration," not to *order*—and thus, therefore, the first verse does not mean, "At first God created the heavens and the earth," nor, "In the beginning of creation he created the heavens and the earth," but "Of old, in former duration, God created the heavens and the earth." How long ago is not said. The Hebrew word is indefinite, and can include millions or milliards of years just as easily as thousands. The statement of Moses is, therefore, not contrary to the discoveries of geology, which alleges the earth to have existed for myriads of years before the creation of man. Moses's words are big enough to take in times indefinite, exceeding the powers of human comprehension. They also answer the more ancient objectors, who found it absurd that God created nothing in previous eternity, and had remained inactive until a few thousand years ago.† The words

* Compare Isa. xli. 26, where מלפנים is parallel to מראש.

† See Augustine 'de Civit. Dei,' Lib. xi. 4, 5; 'Confess.' xi. 10. Com-

of Moses, rightly understood, say just the contrary. They leave "the when" of creation undefined.

8. But though thus comprehensive as to the time, they are precise as to the fact of creation. Moses says "God created," and *Bara*, the word here used, is peculiar. There are three words employed in the old Testament in reference to the production of the world —*Bará*, he created; *Yatzár*, he formed; *Asáh*, he made—between which there is this difference, that the two last may be, and are, used of men. The first word *Bará* is never predicated of any created being, angel or man, but exclusively appropriated to God, and God alone is called Boré בֹּרֵא Creator. Creation is therefore, according to the Hebrew, a Divine act—something that can be performed by God alone. In the next place, though, according to its etymology, it does not necessarily imply a creation out of nothing, it does signify the Divine production of something *new*, something that did not exist before. See Numb. xvi. 30; Jer. xxxi. 22. And therefore Gesenius says, in his 'Thesaurus,' "In that common disputation of interpreters and theologians concerning the creation out of nothing, some appeal to this word [Bará] as if it could be inferred from its etymology, or proper signification, that in the first chapter of Genesis, not a creation out of nothing, but a conformation of eternal matter is taught. But, from what has been said, it will be abundantly plain, that the use of this verb in Kal is altogether different from its primary signification, and that it is more used of new production (see Gen. ii. 3) than of the conformation and elaboration of matter. But that in the first verse of Genesis the first creation of the world out of nothing, and in a rude and unformed state, and in the remainder of the first chapter the elaboration and disposition of the recently created mass is set forth, is proved by the connection of things in this whole chapter. Thus, also, the Rabbis (as may be seen in Aben Esra to Gen. i. 1) say that 'creation is a production of something from

pare also 'Origen de Principiis,' iii. 5, and 'Calvin's Commentaries on Genesis.'

nothing.'" This is also the explanation given in the Psalms. In Ps. cxlviii. 5 we read, "For He, He commanded, and they were created." The parallel passage (Ps. xxxiii. 9) says, "For He, He said, and it existed (ויהי). He, He commanded, and it stood." It is true that the *how* of creation, the link between the Divine will and the realisation, is not made known. Perhaps to finite minds it is incomprehensible. But, notwithstanding, the word *creation* is more than a name for our ignorance of the mode of production. It teaches that neither the world, nor the matter of which it is composed, is eternal or self-existent—that the universe is not a pantheistic emanation, but a work of the Divine will and power; and this Mosaic doctrine, in accordance with all sound reason, has not been shaken by any discoveries or theories of science. Even though the nebulous theory were demonstrably certain; though all the starry hosts were mere agglomerations of elementary matter, which was once diffused like "an universal fire-mist" throughout all space, and impressed with fixed laws, or endowed with self-evolving powers, yet there must be a maker of that fire-mist and its fifty-five elementary substances—there must be a law-giver, who imposed those laws, or communicated those powers, and who produced that change of temperature, without which agglomeration would have been impossible—that is, there must have been a Creator, and therefore the words of Moses would still be true, "God created the heavens and the earth." "Sic philosophi debuerunt, si forte eos primus aspectus mundi conturbaverat, postea cum vidissent motus ejus finitos et æquabiles, omniaque ratis ordinibus moderata, immutabilique constantia, intelligere inesse aliquem non solum habitatorem in hac celesti ac divina domo, sed etiam Rectorem et Moderatorem, et tanquam Architectum tanti operis tantique muneris." *

9. In order to understand the Mosaic narrative, the next thing to be considered is the meaning of the phrase "The heavens and the earth," and the purpose of the whole verse. Some take it as a title or summary

* 'De Nat. Deorum,' Lib. ii. c. 35.

of the contents of the chapter. But this view is forbidden by the conjunction "and," with which the second verse begins. "In the beginning God created the heavens and the earth. 2. *And* the earth was without form, and void." This "and" makes the second verse a continuation of the narrative begun in the first. The proposition, "And the earth was without form, and void," implies that the earth was in existence, and that something had been said of it with which the "and" is the connecting link. Besides, if the first verse be not a part of the narrative, but only a heading, the creation of the earth is not mentioned at all in the narrative itself. The first verse is, therefore, not a summary, but a part of the history of creation.

Others suppose that the first verse describes the creation of the materials out of which heaven and earth were afterwards formed. But this is simply to put into the verse what is not there. "Heaven and earth" never mean materials, and if they did, that meaning would not agree with the context. The connecting "and" of the second verse shows that the earth of the second verse is that earth spoken of in the first verse, not the materials. Moses is very precise and clear in his statements, and as he names "the heavens and the earth," no expositor can legitimately give that phrase a meaning which it has not in any other place in the Old Testament. The first question then, here, is, what Moses intended by "the heavens," for the word is plural, and has no singular in Hebrew. That something different from the firmament is intended is plain from the order of the narrative. It is not said, God made the earth and the heavens, but of old, in former duration, God made the heavens and the earth. Then it is related that the earth was without form, and void; darkness was upon the face of the deep; the Spirit of God moved upon the face of the waters; God said, Let there be light. Then, on the second day, God made the firmament, and called it heavens. The heavens of the first verse were made in former duration, before the moving of the Spirit, before the appearance of light.

The heavens of the seventh and eighth verses, were made on the second day, after the earth and after light. The difference of time proves a difference of subjects, just as there is a difference between the earth of the first verse, which means the whole terraqueous globe, and the earth of the tenth verse, which is only the dry land. And this difference between the heavens of the first verse and the firmament is strongly marked in the fourth verse of the second chapter—"These are the generations of the heavens and the earth, when they were created, in the day that the Lord God made the earth and the heavens." In the first half reference is made to the primitive creation, and therefore the order of the first verse is preserved. In the latter half reference is made to the creation of the earth in its empty state, and the subsequent making of the firmament; and, therefore, earth is put first, before heavens, an inversion that must be intentional, as the phrase "heaven and earth" is in Scripture a standing formula, but the inversion "earth and heaven" occurs only once more in the Bible (Ps. cxlviii. 13). The first expression, "the heavens and the earth," comprehends all created things, the universe; the second, "earth and heavens," takes in only the earth and that portion of the universe immediately connected with it. The object of the historian is first to assert that God is the Creator of all created things, invisible as well as visible; then to narrate the manner in which this earth was prepared for the abode of man by the same Almighty Being, so as to leave no room for the eternity of matter, nor yet for two Creators, one of whom made the high and holy spiritual world, the other, this lower and material world. The Jews knew that there were other heavens, as those where angels dwell, mentioned xxviii. 12–17, whither, perhaps, Elijah was carried (2 Kings ii. 1), and the heavens where is the throne of God (Ps. xi. 4; ciii. 19), called also *the heavens of heavens*. That these heavens and the angels were made before the earth and the firmament appears from Job xxxviii. 7, "When the morning stars sang together, and all the sons of God shouted for joy." They are, therefore, included in the statement of the first verse, "Of old God made the heavens and the earth," as they certainly are in the first verse of the second chapter, where Moses, summing up the entire work of creation of the universe, the primitive creation and the six days' work, says, "Thus the heavens and the earth were finished, and all the host of them." The expression "host of heaven" sometimes means the heavenly bodies, sometimes angels: thus, in Deut. xix. 4, it evidently refers to the former; in 1 Kings xxii. 19, Isa. xxiv 21, Ps. cxlviii. 2, it as plainly refers to the latter, who are called "Jehovah's host" (Josh. v. 14, 15), and "God's host" (Gen. xxxii), where the corresponding word מחנה is used. Therefore, in this summing up of creation, "all the host of them" is mentioned to include angels, often referred to in this Book of Genesis, and to teach that they were not independent beings, but creatures of God. According to the Bible, then, this earth is not the centre of the universe. Long before it was fashioned for man there were heavens, and morning stars, and angels; regions more glorious than the earth, heavens more ancient than the firmament, heavenly inhabitants who excel in strength, and who looked on in wonder and adoration when they beheld the earth fashioned by the Creator. The ken of Moses and the Hebrews was not limited to this earth, nor their idea of duration to the time that man has existed. They knew that the earth in its present condition was later than the heavens and their host, and the human race young when compared with the angels of God.

10. Verse 2.—The next statement made by Moses is so far from being in opposition to the discoveries of science that it is an extraordinary anticipation of what geology teaches. It presents to us the earth before its habitation by man, covered with water, and utterly devoid of inhabitants or life. "The earth was [or, as others translate, *had become**] desolation and emptiness, and darkness upon the face of the raging deep,

* Dathius. Post hæc vero terra facta erat vasta et edserta.

and the Spirit of God brooding upon the face of the waters." Very similar are the statements of geologists, who, though believing that the earth was first in a state of igneous fusion, suppose that before the various formations and deposits began, it was first entirely covered with water. So Pfaff says, "We soon perceive not only that by far the greatest part of our earth was under water, but that to water it owes its origin, and that under water the entire gradual formation of these mighty masses took place." And again, "The earth was at first a molten fiery sphere, over which existed a thick atmosphere, containing all the water of the earth. In consequence of cooling a firm crust was formed, which was everywhere uniformly covered by water, condensed in like manner by the same cooling process."* The conflicts between the waters and the fiery heat, as the crust of the earth was broken, fell in, or was upheaved, are vividly described by M. d'Orbigny, and his account answers well to the words of Moses, "The earth was desolation and emptiness, and darkness upon the face of the raging deep." It is not necessary to accept this theory of "a molten fiery sphere," as the Neptunists describe a somewhat similar state, produced by water only, and a sober though able author speaks of it only as a guess. "Geology . . . may guess at conditions of original igneous fluidity or aqueous plasticity in the mass, and may hint at some great law of secular contraction; but it must be confessed that on these and similar points science is yet unable to offer anything like the certainty of demonstration."† But the great facts of the submersion of the earth, and its desolation and emptiness, were stated by Moses more than 3000 years ago, and his statements have not only not been disproved, but have been confirmed, by the deductions of modern scientific research. But how this state of "igneous fluidity or aqueous plasticity," and consequent desolation and emptiness, arose; whether God created the

* Pfaff's 'Schöpfungsgeschichte,' pp. 3 and 615. See also D'Orbigny, 'Cours élémentaire,' tom. ii., Fascic. i. 261; Lardner's 'Pre-Adamite Earth,' § 187; 'Essays and Reviews,' pp. 213, 14.

† Page's 'Advanced Text-book of Geology,' p 25.

earth desolate and empty, or whether it became so in consequence of some mighty catastrophe, neither Neptunists nor Vulcanists can tell us, nor has Moses expressly declared, though the latter appears to some to be implied in his words. There seems to be a contrast between the state of the heavens and that of the earth. "Of old God created the heavens and the earth. And the earth was desolation and emptiness," not so the heavens. If Dathius's translation, "The earth had become desolation and emptiness,"* be correct, it would follow this was not the earth's original state. How the change from the chaotic, the desolate and the empty, was effected, science cannot tell. Moses informs us that it was by the action of the Divine Spirit. "The Spirit of God *brooding* on the face of the waters," not "the wind of God," as the verb *rachaph* [to brood] is never used of wind. "The Spirit streamed forth from God upon the chaos, communicated to it life-power, and made it capable of development at God's bidding, and of bringing forth plants and animals. For, according to the Old Testament, the Spirit of God is the quickening principle of the world, and all life is an outgoing from God; according to Psalm civ. 30, even the life of the vegetable kingdom."†

11. VERSES 3, and 14–19.—The next Mosaic statement is found in verses 3–5, "And God said, Let there be light, and there was light. And God saw the light, that it was good, and God separated between the light and between the darkness. And God called the light day, and the darkness He called night. And evening happened, and morning happened, one day,"‡ and has

* This translation is supported by the fact that the verb היה is, in some twenty places in this chapter, correctly translated by γίνομαι and *fio*, and not by εἰμί or *sum*, and has elsewhere, without a following ל, the same signification, e.g. Isai. lxiv. 5, 9, where see Ewald, Zunz, and Rosenmüller. That the earth was not originally desolate also seems to be implied in Isai. xlv. 18. "He created not the earth a desolation" [Tohu].

† Knobel in loc. Comp. Gesenius, 'Thesaurus,' in Rad. רחף. "De Spiritu Dei, qui rudi creationis moli *incubabat fovens* et vivificans."

‡ The exact force of the Hebrew words, especially of the verb היה *fio*, is more apparent in the LXX. than in our Authorized Version. Καὶ εἶπεν ὁ θεός Γενηθήτω φῶς, καὶ ἐγένετο φῶς. Καὶ εἶδεν ὁ θεὸς τὸ φῶς ὅτι καλόν, καὶ διεχώρισεν ὁ θεὸς ἀνὰ μέσον τοῦ φωτὸς καὶ ἀνὰ μέσον τοῦ σκότους· καὶ

given occasion to many objections. Celsus found it strange that Moses should speak of days before the existence of the sun.* "How did God create the light before the sun?" asked Voltaire. "How did He make the day before the sun was made?"† "Modern astronomy," says D. F. Strauss, "found it contrary to order, that the earth should not only have been created before the sun, but should also, besides day and night, have distinction of the elements and vegetation before the sun."‡ "Light and the measurement of time are represented as existing before the manifestation of the sun, and this idea, although repugnant to our modern knowledge, has not in former times appeared absurd," is the objection of 'Essays and Reviews;'§ and, as is evident, is not the result of modern science, having been broached already by Celsus. As, however, recent writers give modern science the credit of it, it becomes necessary to ask, what does modern science teach with regard to the relative ages of the earth and the sun? The answer is, Nothing, absolutely nothing as a scientific certainty. Whether sun and earth were created simultaneously, and in their present relations—or, whether the earth, already created, wandered within the range of solar attraction, or whether, after the sun existed, the earth was called forth within that range, science does not know. It has, however, without any reference to the Book of Genesis, proposed a theory, which has been accepted by some of the most scientific men of these days as highly probable.‖ Had it been devised for the express purpose of removing the supposed difficuties of the Mosaic account, it could hardly have been more to the purpose. It supposes that the

ἐκάλεσεν ὁ θεὸς τὸ φῶς ἡμέραν καὶ τὸ σκότος ἐκάλεσε νύκτα, καὶ ἐγένετο ἑσπέρα καὶ ἐγένετο πρωΐ, ἡμέρα μία.

* Origen 'contra Celsum,' vi. 60, tom. i. 678.

† Voltaire's Works, vol. xxxiii. 403.

‡ 'Glaubenslehre,' vol. i. p. 622.

§ P. 219.

‖ Of the theory in its present form La Place is the author. Perhaps the first suggestion came from Sir W. Herschel. It has been adopted by the great German astronomer, Mädler, and extended to comets. It has been defended by Pfaff, and its truth has been taken for granted by Humboldt, 'Cosmos,' i. 85, 90, iv. 163. It is also advocated by the author of 'Vestiges of the Natural History of Creation.'

whole solar system was originally one mass of vapoury or nebulous matter, which, according to the laws of gravitation, assumed the form of an immense sphere. This sphere received (from without) an impulse which caused it to revolve on its axis from west to east. In consequence of this revolving motion, it became flattened at the poles and swollen in the equatorial region, and in consequence of the greatness of the centrifugal force at the equator, and the contemporaneous condensation and contraction of the nebulous mass, a free revolving ring, similar to that of Saturn, detached itself in the region of the equator. This ring not being of uniform density, and in consequence of contraction, broke in one or more places, and these fragments, in obedience to the laws of gravitation, became a sphere or spheres, that is, a planet, or planets, all necessarily revolving from west to east, round the parent mass. Another ring was formed in like manner, and another planet came into existence, and so on until the whole solar system was complete. A similar process took place with regard to some of the planets, and thus they got their moons.*

Now, according to this theory, not only the earth, but all the planets of our system, existed before the sun in its present condition. As these planets are now not self-illuminating, it may be supposed that the rings, when detached from the original nebulous mass, were dark also, and therefore that the equatorial matter of the parent nebulous sphere of which they were com-

* La Place, 'Exposition du Système du Monde,' 6ème édition, note vii. pp. 465 and sqq.; Pfaff's 'Schöpfungsgeschichte,' Kap. xiii.; Humboldt's 'Cosmos,' as above. This theory is also applied by La Place and others to account for the zodiacal light. M. Plateau has furnished an ingenious experimental verification. He mixed alcohol and water until the mixture was of the same specific gravity as oil. The mixture was then put into a glass box, and a certain quantity of oil introduced, which immediately took the form of a globe. He now applied an axis, which passed through the axis of the oil globe, and caused the box to rotate rapidly. In consequence of the rotation the oil globe flattened at the poles and swelled out at the equator. A more rapid motion disengaged a ring of oil, revolving in the same direction as the oil globe. This ring broke, and the fragments formed globes or planets rotating on their axes, and revolving round the parent globe. See Pfaff, p. 318; also 'Vestiges of the Natural History of Creation,' reprint of sixth edition, pp. 11–14.

posed was also devoid of light—that therefore the sun did not receive its luminous atmosphere until all the planets had been detached. But, until this luminous atmosphere existed, they could not derive their light from the sun. If, on the other hand, it be supposed that these detached rings were luminous, and that the planets formed from them were luminous also, then the planets had a light of their own, independent of the sun. But however that be, so much follows from this theory, that the earth existed before the residuary parent globe could be called the sun, or could perform its office of luminary to the system. If the earth therefore had light during this period, it must have been derived from some other source. That this is possible cannot now be denied. The discoveries with regard to heat, combustion, electricity, galvanism, show that there may be light independent of the sun. It is also now generally received that the sun itself is an opaque body, and that solar light proceeds from a luminous atmosphere by which it is surrounded.* The progress of science has, therefore, neutralized the objection that light could not exist before the sun. Indeed it has done more—it has proved the accuracy of the Mosaic language. Moses does not call the sun "*Or*, light," but "*Maór*, a place or instrument of light," a luminary, or candlestick,† just what modern science has discovered it to be. Thus, so far is the Mosaic doctrine of light from being opposed to recent discoveries, that if Moses had wished to describe the modern doctrine concerning light, he could not have expressed himself more happily. "Scripture does not say that God created the light, or made it, but said, 'Let it be, and it was!'

* Arago's 'Astronomy,' pp. 56, 57; Pfaff, p. 621; Humboldt's 'Cosmos,' iii. 271, etc.; Walker's 'Physical Constitution of the Sun,' p. 6. The wonderful discoveries of Kirchoff and others in solar chemistry are supposed by some to confirm La Place's theory, and to prove that the earth was before the sun, and had a light of its own.

† Knobel, in his Commentary, has "Lichtorte." For the meaning of nouns formed by prefixing מ, see Ewald's 'Grammar,' §§ 337 and 339:—"מ may signify, first, that wherein anything happens, the place of action (the so-called מ loci); .... secondly, the instrument of action; thirdly, the what of the action." Compare also Simonis 'Arcanum Formarum,' pp. 447–504; Gesenius's 'Lehrgeb,' p. 494, § 14.

If, then, light be not a separate and definite body, but only vibrations or undulations of ether, somehow set in motion, the sacred writer could not have expressed its appearance in words more beautiful or more agreeable to truth." *

Now, this theory of La Place may or may not be true,† but it is an offspring of modern science, and implies, just like the Mosaic account, the pre-existence of the earth before the sun became the luminary of the system. It does, indeed, also imply the pre-existence of the great parent nebulous globe, but this is not contrary to the Mosaic account. Moses does not say that the body of the sun or moon and stars were created on the fourth day, but according to the Hebrew, "God said, Let there be light-holders in the firmament of the heaven, ... and let them be for light-holders in the firmament of the heaven to give light upon the earth, and God made the two great light-holders . . . . . and God gave ויתן, them in the firmament of heaven to give light upon the earth, and the stars." The Hebrew word, Asah, make, may signify "make ready, prepare, dress" (see Gesenius's 'Lexicon,' in verb.). The creation of the sun or parent globe may be included in verse 1, and the work of the fourth day consisted in furnishing it with its luminous atmosphere. When this took place, and the sun began to shed its light, then the moon, and the earth's fellow planets, "the stars," of verse 16, became luminaries also. The stars of this sixteenth verse are certainly different from those morning stars of which Job speaks, which were in existence long before, and, as connected with the sun and moon, seem naturally to mean those belonging to the solar system, and which received their light on the fourth day, when the sun became luminous. Having

* 'Cosmogony of Moses,' by M. Marcel de Serres, Professor of Mineralogy and Geology at Montpellier, German edition, p. 45. Compare the language of St. Paul, 2 Cor. iv. 6. It is a curious fact that the Hebrew verb נהר, which signifies "to flow," also signifies "to shine, give light." נְהָרָה, light. Job iii. 4.

† Compare Whewell's 'Indications of the Creator,' pp. 54, 162, and his 'Philosophy of Discovery,' pp. 304, 305; 'Plurality of Worlds,' p. 199.

thus seen how modern science proves that the earth and light might exist, and, according to scientific theory, probably did exist before the sun, it is no longer difficult to conceive, how there might also be a measure of time. What that measure was, the length of that "one day," of which Moses speaks, it is now necessary to inquire.

12. The question, then, naturally arises, How are we to understand the word "day"? Is it a period of twenty-four hours, or is it an indefinite portion of time? It is quite certain that the Almighty could not only arrange the earth in six ordinary days, but that He could create the whole universe by a momentary exertion of His power. The shortness of the time, therefore, is no valid objection. The contrary objection that six ordinary days are too long, and that instantaneous creation is more worthy of Omnipotence, is just as strong. But nature and Scripture both teach us that it has pleased God to work gradually. His purpose was to fill the earth with inhabitants, and yet only a single pair was created. He announced the Redeemer in Paradise, but 4000 years passed away before the fulness of the time was come. It is His will that the whole earth shall be filled with the knowledge of Himself; but the diffusion of that knowledge has been left to gradual preaching and human instrumentality. So in nature, trees, animals, and men have small beginnings, and require time to attain to perfection. This twofold course of the Divine procedure, in grace and in nature, guards us against the necessity of supposing that the arrangement of the earth was of necessity sudden, or a series of instantaneous exhibitions of Omnipotence. The facts of creation, however, must be gathered from the Mosaic statement. Moses undoubtedly reckons six days. But it is an old and true observation, that in the Bible the word "day" often signifies undefined periods of time, as "the day of the Lord," "the day of vengeance," "that day," "the night is far spent, the day is at hand." In this narrative (ii. 4) the word takes in the whole time of the

creative work. The first three days were certainly not measured by the interval between sunset and sunset, for as yet the sun was not perfect, and had no light. The first day consisted of an alternation of light and darkness. But how long the light lasted, and how long the darkness until the next dawn, is not said. That there was an alternation of light and darkness, is related in the words, "And God divided between the light and between the darkness. And God called the light Day, and the darkness He called Night." First there had been universal darkness. "Darkness was upon the face of the deep." Out of this darkness God caused the light to shine. "God said, Let there be light, and there was light." It might, then, be supposed that this light being as universal as the darkness had been, there was now only continued, uninterrupted light in the world, and no darkness more until the new order of things commenced in the fourth day. The sacred historian guards against this supposition by relating that God divided between the light and the darkness, and that, in consequence of this division, evening happened, and morning happened, so that one stage of creation was divided from the other by an interval of darkness. The time of light in which the Divine work proceeded, He called Day, and the time of darkness He called Night.* It was not a day measured by the presence of the sun's light, nor a night measured by the absence of that light. There was light and there was darkness, and God called the light Day, and the darkness He called Night. The union of these two periods of light and darkness He calls "one day," "a second day," "a third day," to mark the distinctive breaks in the progress of the development of the world. In the fifth verse "day" is taken in two senses,—first, of the duration of the light; and secondly, of the whole time of light and darkness together. But how long the light continued before it was evening, or how long the darkness continued before it was morning, or

* Compare the words of our Lord, "I must work the works of Him that sent me, while it is day; the night cometh when no man can work."

what was the duration of the two together, we are not told; and so far there is nothing to cause us to conclude that the whole was equal to twenty-four hours. It is true that David Strauss* urges the mention of "evening and morning," and thence concludes that they must be common days; and there is a general persuasion that Moses here reckons according to the usual custom of the Hebrews, from evening to evening, supposing that the original darkness is the first evening, and that the space of time occupied by it and by the light which succeeded, is described as the first day. But this mistake arises from confining the attention to the English translation, which says "And the evening and the morning were the first day."† But the Hebrew and the ancient versions have "And evening happened, and morning happened, one day." Now if the first day begins with the original darkness, then the first day consists of the original darkness, the light, and the evening that followed, ending with the morning, and thus the first day would have an evening at the beginning and an evening at the end. The mention of *morning*, "evening happened and morning happened," ought to have guarded against this mistake. Evening and morning do not together make a day, but only a part of a day. The whole day is not complete until the following evening. But that Moses does not here reckon from evening to evening is proved from the account of the first day. The evocation of light is the prominent object of the first day's work, but it is after this evocation of light that it is said "And there was evening, and there was morning, one day." If, therefore, the day began with the evening, light was created before that first day began, and there would be no account at all of what was done the first day. The first day must, therefore, be reckoned as beginning at the appearance of light, and continuing through the evening to the dawn. The appearance of light, with

* 'Glaubenslehre,' p. 624.

† This is plainly the source of error in 'Essays and Reviews,' where it is said, "The space of time occupied by the original darkness and the light which succeeded, is described as the first day." P. 219.

the darkness that followed the evening until the next dawn, is the first day. With that dawn the second day begins. This mode of reckoning, unique in the Bible, and peculiar to this first chapter of Genesis, suggests that the days are peculiar too. To know the length of the first day, it would be necessary to know how long the night continued after its first appearance until the evening came, and then how long from evening until the first dawn. But this is not told us. The ordinance concerning the reckoning of time, "Let them be for signs, and for seasons, and for days and for years," was not given until the fourth day, and could have no application until after the creation of Adam. Not by the sun, then, were the days measured, but by light and darkness, which God called Day and Night, of the length of which we are not informed; and, consequently, there is nothing in the text to compel us to restrict the days to the time of the earth's diurnal motion. If the length of the days is to be measured by that of the seventh, the day of God's rest, those days must be indefinite periods, for the day of rest still continues. It is said, chap. ii. 2, "And he rested on the seventh day from all the work which He had made," without any mention of evening and morning. The day of rest, therefore, still continues, and this is plainly expressed and argued in the Epistle to the Hebrews, "Let us therefore fear, lest a promise being left us of entering into His rest, any of you should seem to come short of it," or, as some moderns translate, "Let us then be careful, lest as a promise to enter into His [God's] rest still remains, any of you appear remaining behind." On which words Stuart says, "In chapter iv. 1, he brings forward the assertion that the promise of entering into the rest of God still remains, addressed to the Hebrew Christians as it was to the Israelites of old. . . . But what is the rest in question? Is it quiet possession of the land of Canaan? No, says the Apostle. Believers *now* enter into the rest (verse 3), i.e. (adds he) the same kind of rest as was anciently proffered. Moreover, God calls it *κατάπαυσίν μου,* My rest, i.e. (adds he) such rest as God enjoyed, after He completed the creation of the world, consequently spiritual, heavenly rest. This is plain (as he goes on in verse 4) from what the Scripture says, Gen. ii. 2, concerning the rest of God." According, then, to this declaration that God's rest or Sabbath still continues, the seventh day of creation is an indefinite period and the other days may be also. The six days are days of the Lord, God's days, as the first Sabbath was God's rest, and, therefore, as God rested on His seventh day, man is commanded to rest on his seventh day, and God blessed and sanctified it.

13. But though the Mosaic language implies that the six days of which he speaks are six periods of time, it does not follow that they are to be identified with the six periods commonly received in geology. Indeed, to those who have no theory to establish, it is apparent that they do not agree, neither is it necessary that they should. That the Mosaic account is not contradicted by modern discovery is quite sufficient. The impossibility of identifying these periods is evident from the fact that of the work of two days in the Mosaic account geology knows nothing, and astronomy nothing certain; namely, that of the first on which the light was called forth; and of the fourth day, when the sun and the planetary system were perfected. Moses gives an outline of the history of creation, such as would be intelligible to those for whom he wrote, and suitable as an introduction to Divine revelation, and on both accounts necessarily limited in the matter and brief in the narration. He, therefore, notices only those things necessary to a true religious system, or perceptible by men. After the original creation of heaven and earth, and the condition of earth, he mentions the evocation of light and the creation of the ether, in which the heavenly bodies move, as effected in the first two days. Whether anything else was created in those two days, he neither affirms nor denies. So far therefore as the Mosaic record is concerned, these two days may include the whole of the primary, secondary, and tertiary

formations, with all their products, their flora and their fauna. The products of those periods, buried in the earth, were, so far as we know, utterly unknown to the Israelites and their contemporaries, and to mankind for many ages after. Even to ourselves the knowledge is recent. For Moses to mention them, was not only unnecessary, but would have been altogether out of place. Such details would have encumbered the outline, and turned away the attention from God the Creator to things at that time invisible and unintelligible. The object of the Mosaic narrative is to explain the origin of the universe and of its parts, as they were known or visible to men of that day. So soon, therefore, as he has mentioned the light and the ether, he advances at once to the preparation of the earth for man; and thus the third day presents the dry land in its present state, with its flora differing from the preceding geological stages. Of this state of things, Page says: "At the close of the Pleistocene period the present distribution of sea and land seems to have been established; the land presenting the same surface of configuration, and the sea the same coast line, with the exception of such modifications as have since been produced by the atmospheric, aqueous, and other causes, described in chap. iii. At the close of that period, the earth also appears to have been peopled by its present flora and fauna, with the exception of some local removals of certain animals, and the general extinction of a few species." * According to the Mosaic account the growth of grass, herb and fruit trees, begun on the third day, must have gone on through the fourth. Then on the fifth day the marine, and on the sixth the land animals of the present period were called into existence. The words of Moses, "Let the dry land appear," are in exact accordance with what geology relates. The rise of the ocean had buried the tertiary world in its waters. "The disruption of the earth's crust, extending W. 16° S., and E. 16° N., through which the chain of the great Alps was forced up to its pres-

* 'Advanced Text-book,' p. 300.

ent elevation, which, according to M. d'Orbigny, was simultaneous with that which forced up the Chilian Andes, a chain which extends over a length of 3000 miles of the western continent, terminated the tertiary age, and preceded immediately the creation of the human race and its concomitant tribes. The waters of the seas and oceans, lifted up from their beds by this immense perturbation, swept over the continents with irresistible force, destroying instantaneously the entire flora and fauna of the last tertiary period, and burying its ruins in the sedimentary deposits which ensued. . . . When the seas had settled into their new beds, and the outlines of the land were permanently defined, the latest and greatest act of creation was accomplished by clothing the earth with the vegetation which now covers it, peopling the land and the water with the animal tribes which now exist, and calling into being the human race. . . . The most conspicuous condition which distinguishes the present from all past periods is the existence of the human race among its fauna, the attributes of which are so peculiar as to place it out of all analogy with the other classes of animals. Another striking physical difference between the present and all former periods consists in the different divisions of the earth's surface into climatological zones, each zone having its peculiar fauna and flora. In all former ages and periods, including those which immediately preceded the present, no traces of climatic difference have been found."* In all this there is nothing inconsistent with the Mosaic statement. There is one most striking and extraordinary coincidence: Moses represents the earth as existing for a long period before the sun became its source of light and heat. During that period there could have been no climatic difference, as this depends upon the position of the earth with reference to the sun. Now this exactly agrees with the conclusions of geology, which asserts, as we have seen, that before the human period there was no difference of climate, that the earth was not dependent on the sun

* Lardner's 'Popular Geology,' §§ 553, 555, 561.

for its temperature, that there was apparently one uniform high temperature over the whole earth, and consequently that the flora and fauna of warm climates are found, in the prehuman period, in latitudes where they could not now exist. Here then is an instance of the extraordinary scientific accuracy of the Mosaic account.

14. Another objection to Scriptural cosmogony is, that the Bible asserts that the earth is immovable. "The Hebrew records, the basis of religious truth, manifestly countenanced the opinion of the earth's immobility." * The proofs of this proposition are not taken from Moses, who says nothing on the subject, but from such pages as Ps. xciii. 1,—"The world also is established that it cannot be moved;" and Ps. civ. 5, —"Who laid the foundations of the earth, that it should not be moved forever." See also Ps. cxix. 90, 91. According to this mode of interpretation, it can also be proved that the Hebrews also held that a pious man was an immovable fixture; for it is said, Prov. x. 30, "The righteous shall never be moved," the same word in Hebrew. But this objection rests on simple ignorance of the Hebrew word translated "moved." This word, Mót (מוֹט), signifies, as Gesenius says, "to waver, to shake, to totter," and, therefore, it is applied to the feet of one in motion in Ps. xvii. 5,—"Hold up my goings in thy paths, that my footsteps slip not;" or, as the margin has it, "be not moved." Can any one be found so silly as to suppose that David prayed that his feet might be immovably fixed? The whole prayer implies motion, walking in the Lord's ways; and the latter part of the petition is that his feet might not "totter," that he might not stumble. So far, therefore, are the above passages from declaring that the earth is immovable, that they necessarily imply its motion. "The world is established that it cannot totter," not even in that velocity of motion with which it compasses the sun. A totter, a slip, would be of dreadful conse-

* 'Essays and Reviews,' p. 208. See also Hitchcock's 'Religion of Geology,' pp. 25 and 43.

quence to its inhabitants; but the Lord has so arranged and steadied its motions, that no *totter* is possible. The wonderful mode of its suspension in space, as well as that of the heavenly bodies, as necessarily implied in the Scriptural doctrine of an ethereal expanse, is also beautifully expressed in Job xxvi. 7. "He stretcheth out the north over the empty place; he hangeth the earth upon nothing." To infer that Scripture teaches the immobility of the earth because it speaks of sunrise and sunset, or because Joshua said, "Sun, stand thou still," is just as fair as to attribute the same error to the compilers of almanacks and astronomical tables, or to scientific men in their common *parlance.* There are certain popular phrases which no universality of science will ever banish from general use. The great historian of the Inductive Sciences, like all other people of common sense, uses the popular language. "The motions of the sun, the succession of the places of his rising and setting at different times of the year, the greatest height which he reaches . . . . would all exhibit several cycles. . . . The *turning back* of the sun, when he had reached his greatest distance to the south or the north, as shown either by his rising or his height at noon, would perhaps be the most observable of such circumstances." * If Copernicus himself had been in a similar position with that of Joshua, he would have used just the same language. To the end of time the most scientific of men will continue to speak of sunrise and sunset—the sun passing the meridian, or sinking below the horizon; and he who would try to substitute a more exact phraseology would be regarded as more of a pedant than a philosopher.

15. VERSES 6–8.—*The Mosaic firmament not a solid vault.*—In close connection with this objection is that directed against the Mosaic account of "the firmament." It was already urged by Voltaire, and in recent times oft triumphantly repeated, to show the supposed ignorance and gross conceptions of the Hebrew people. Gesenius, Winer, Knobel, &c., have

* Vol. i. p. 127.

patronized it; their statements have been transferred wholesale into popular English works, and lately repeated in "Essays and Reviews" (pp. 219, 220):—"The work of the second day of creation is to erect the vault of heaven (Heb., *rakia;* Gr. *στερέωμα;* Lat., firmamentum), which is represented as supporting an ocean of water above it. The waters are said to be divided, so that some are below, some above the vault. That the Hebrews understood the sky, firmament, or heaven, to be a permanent solid vault, as it appears to the ordinary observer, is evident enough from various expressions made use of concerning it. It is said to have pillars (Job xxvi. 11), foundations (2 Sam. xxii. 8), doors (Ps. lxxviii. 23), and windows (Gen. vii. 11). No quibbling about the derivation of the word *rakia*, which is literally 'something beaten out,' can affect the explicit description of the Mosaic writer, contained in the words, 'The waters that are above the firmament,' or avail to show that he was aware that the sky is but transparent.

"*Note.*—The root is generally applied to express the hammering or beating out of metal plates; hence something beaten or spread out. It has been pretended that the word *rakia* may be translated *expanse*, so as merely to mean empty space. The context sufficiently rebuts this."

This objection, if well founded, would be conclusive proof of the opposition between astronomic science and the Mosaic cosmogony. But, happily, it is the weakest of all the objections, and the most easily refuted by Scripture statement, and by the history of interpretation. "The Hebrews," says Mr. Goodwin, "understood the sky, firmament, or heaven to be a permanent solid vault." Here are two assertions: First, that the Hebrews understood the firmament or heaven to be a vault. Secondly, that they regarded that vault as solid. The first assertion, a repetition of Gesenius's *hemisphærii instar*, is totally without foundation. The word *rakia* signifies not *vault*, but, as all allow, *an expanse*, *something spread out*, whether solid or unsolid.

and therefore incompatible with the idea of vault or arch. But the main part of the objection is that the firmament, or heavens, are solid or firm. Now, according to Scripture, the firmament, or heaven, is that space or place where birds fly. They could not fly in a solid vault; therefore the firmament cannot be a solid vault. This is proved by the following references. In Gen. i. 28, birds are called "the fowl of the heavens" (not "air," as the Authorized Version has it)—a description utterly inapplicable if the heavens be a permanent solid vault, in which the heavenly bodies were fixed. "The fowl of the solid vault" would be nonsense. If the heavens be the expanse, beginning at the earth, extending to the stars, and including the air, the description is appropriate; and so convinced were our translators that *the heavens* have this meaning, that they have here and elsewhere translated "fowl of the air," not "fowl of the heavens." The reason why Moses calls birds fowls of the heavens is because they fly in the heavens, as we read, Deut. iv. 12, "any winged fowl that flieth in the heavens." And again, Prov. xxx. 19, "The way of an eagle in the heavens." And again, Jer. viii. 7, "The stork in the heavens knoweth his appointed time." In all these passages, "heavens" means the place where birds fly.* In Psalm lxxviii. 36, the word means the place where winds blow—"He causeth a wind to blow in the heavens;" in both cases the region of the atmosphere. The Biblical writers must, therefore, have considered the heavens or firmament as something analogous to the air, an expanse, or ether, not a hard solid vault.

The idea of expanse, independent, or even exclusive of solidity, is also to be inferred, from the manner in which other verbs † simply signifying *to extend or spread out*, are applied to the heavens: as, for instance, Isaiah xlviii. 13, "My right hand hath spread out (tippechah) the heavens." Isaiah xl. 22, "That stretcheth

* These passages also give the true meaning of the words in Genesis i. 30, where the Authorized Version has, "In the open firmament of heaven," literally, "upon the face of the firmament of heaven."

† The verbs נטה Natah, מתח Mathach, and טפח Taphach.

out (noteh) the heavens like a curtain (literally, like fineness), and spreadeth them out (*vaiyimtach*) as a tent to dwell in." The comparison to a tent does not suggest solidity—the comparison with a fine curtain excludes it. The Hebrew word (Dok) here used for curtain, is cognate with *Dak*, "fine dust," and signifies, as Gesenius says, "*Fineness*—hence *fine cloth*, a garment, a curtain." The same idea of something unsolid, unpermanent, and movable, is conveyed in the similar figure, Ps. civ. 2, "Who stretchest out the heavens like a curtain [Yerihah]." The Hebrew word here used for *curtain* means "something tremulous," and, as Gesenius gives it, "*a curtain, hanging*, so called from its tremulous motion"—a simile most unsuitable for a solid vault, most appropriate for an ethereal expanse or fluid.

But besides *Rakia* and *Shamaim*, there is another word, *Shechakim*, said to be used sometimes for heavens, which also excludes the idea of solidity. Gesenius thus gives the meaning: "שַׁחַק. 1. *Dust*, fine dust. Isai. xl. 15; 2. *A cloud*, Arab. *thin cloud*, pp., as it would seem, *cloud of dust*, or the like. Mostly in plural, *clouds*. Metonym. for the *firmament*, the *heavens*, the *sky*, i. q. שָׁמַיִם and רָקִיעַ, comp. in English *the clouds*. Job xxxvii. 18, '*Hast thou like him spread out the sky* (שְׁחָקִים), *which is firm like a molten looking-glass?*'" A cloud of dust is nothing solid, and, therefore, when the word *Shachak*, signifying *cloud* of dust, is transferred to the clouds of heaven, it implies that, in the mind of him that transferred it, the clouds of heaven are also devoid of solidity. But here it will be replied, In the passage of Job, just referred to by Gesenius, "the sky" is compared to a molten metallic mirror—it must, therefore, be firm, like a metal plate. Now, granting for a moment that "sky" is here a possible translation, the conclusion drawn does not follow. If the sky be solid and firm, and able to bear up a whole heavenly ocean of water, is it not rather a descent from the poetic, indeed a very considerable bathos, to compare its strength to that of a woman's metal mirror?

The beauty of the simile is lost. Luther's poetic mind and shrewd common sense saw this, and, therefore, when there was no dispute about the matter, showed that here there is a contrast rather than a comparison. The expanse, he says, is rarer and finer than the atmosphere in which we live, and yet, through the power of the Divine word, strong as if it were metal.*

Take into account the exact meaning of *Shechakim*, *clouds*, or *substances unsolid as a cloud of dust*, and the beauty and force of the figure come out still more strongly. When, therefore, it is remembered that "the Hebrews" regarded the heavens or firmament as including the place where birds fly—that they liken it to fineness or fine cloth, that they regard it as tremulous, like a tremulous curtain, and thought that it was of the nature of the clouds, שחקים, and that the clouds were of the nature of a cloud of fine dust, and might be called by the same word, it will be seen that they did not consider the heavens as a solid vault, but as an ether similar to the atmosphere.

That the word *Rakia* signifies *expanse* is also proved by Jewish tradition. It is that sense which appears when the Jews began to write lexicons and grammars, and is preserved to this day. David Kimchi, in his *Book of Roots*, explains the word *Rakah* first by *Paras*, to spread out, and he is followed by both Spanish and German Jews, who translate *Rakia* expanse.

The Jewish-Spanish version has "Espandidura;" the Jewish-German "Ausspreitung;" the Pentateuch by Zunz, Arnheim, and Sachs gives "Ausdehnung." The 'Jewish School and Family Bible,' by Dr. Benisch, has "expanse." At the revival of letters Christians learned Hebrew from the Jews, and received the old Jewish interpretation "expanse." So Vatablus and Peter Martyr have "Sit expansio in medio aquarum." Calvin has both *extensio* and *expansio*—"Sit extensio in medio aquarum . . . . et fecit Deus expansionem;" and so Sebastian Munster, Mercerus, the Geneva French Bible of 1588, Luke Osiander, 1597, and Cypriano de

* See the passage quoted below, p. 259.

Valera, 1602, who has "Sea un estendimiento en medio de las aguas." And Luther, though he retained the word "Veste," answering to "firmament," explains it as a fine and subtile expanse. In his Commentary to verse 6, he says, "God takes this thick and shapeless lump of vapour, *nebel* (nebula), created the first day out of nothing, and commands it to spread itself out . . . . . for the word *Rakia* signifies among the Hebrews something extended and spread out, and comes from *Raka*, to spread out . . . . when, therefore, Job says, xxxvii. 18, 'The heavens are made firm as with iron,' he has respect not to the material, but to the Word, which can make the softest thing in nature into the strongest and the firmest. . . . . for we know how subtile the air is in which we live. . . . But the heaven is naturally still more subtile and thin." * Vatablus gives a similar explanation. Having remarked that heaven is by the Hebrews sometimes called *Shamaim*, sometimes *Rakia*, he says, "It is distinguished into two parts, the upper part, which is called ether, which is fire, and the lower part, which is called air." Calvin (*in loc.*) gives a similar interpretation. "Moreover, the word *Rakia* comprehends not only the whole region of the air, but whatever is open above us, as the word *heaven* is sometimes understood by the Latins." Now, it is to be remarked that these interpretations were given when the old system of astronomy was still in fashion, and received by those who give these interpretations, as the Jewish Rabbis and the Reformers. They cannot therefore be accused of quibbling, or of advocating a new interpretation to help them out of difficulties arising from the discoveries of Copernicus and Galileo. This sense continued to be received by Hebrew scholars until the infection of Deistic infidelity fully influenced the minds of men to make out a case of ignorance against Moses and the Hebrews. It is found in Mariana, 1624; Hottinger, 1659; Seb. Schmidt, 1697; Baumgarten and Rom. Teller, 1749; J. C. F. Schultz, 1783; Dathius, 1791; Ilgen, 1798. Even in the first edition of Gesen-

* Luther's 'Werke.' Walch. vol. i.

ius's 'Lexicon,' 1810–13, though he says that the Hebrews looked upon heaven as solid, he explains *rakia*, not as a solid expanse, but "Etwas ausgebreitetes." In later editions he wavers, sometimes inserting, sometimes omitting, the word "solid" or "firm." *

But, it may be asked, if such be the Jewish tradition, how the LXX. and Vulgate came to render *Rakia* by *στερέωμα*, *firmamentum*. The answer is, that by *στερέωμα* the LXX. also understood a fine and subtile ether which held the heavenly bodies in their places. *Stereoma* was chosen not to express something itself solid, but something that strengthened or made firm the heavenly bodies. They took the word in the transitive sense, like *βεβαίωμα*, *δήλωμα*, *πλήρωμα*, &c.; and this is proved by the Vulgate having *firmamentum*, which form of word signifies something that makes firm, like *ornamentum*, *complementum*, *alimentum*, *monumentum*, &c. In this sense stereoma is elsewhere used by the LXX., as Ezek. iv. 16: "I will break the staff of bread, *στερέωμα ἄρτου*;" and Esther ix. 29: "And the confirmation of the letter, *τό τε στερέωμα τῆς ἐπιστολῆς*." And again Ps. xviii. 3: "The Lord is my rock, *στερέωμά μου*," where the Vulgate has firmamentum meum. That Jerome took firmamentum in the same sense appears from his Commentary on Isa. xxvi. 1, where for חֵל, *bulwark*, Symmachus has *στερέωμα*; and Jerome remarks: "Pro eo quod nos vertimus *antemurale*, Symmachus *firmamentum* interpretatus est." And again on Ezek. iv. 16, on the words "staff of bread:" "Verbum Hebraicum *Matteh* prima Aquilæ editio *baculum*, secunda et Symmachus Theodotioque *στερέωμα*, id

* In the 'German Manual' of 1823, in the verb רקע we find—"(1) Stampfen mit den Füssen.... (2) Stampfen, breitschlagen, daher.... (3) Ausbreiten, aber nur von festen Körpern. . . . Im Syr. befestigen, gründen." In the Latin edition of 1833 it is not found. In Robinson's translation, the word "solid" is found in the substantive, but not in the verb. The reference to the Syriac shows that the idea "firm" is not included: Syr. ܪܩܥ—firmavit, stabilivit, Aph. fundavit, pertundendo et constipando firmavit, ut facere solent, qui fundamenta, ædium jaciunt." According to this, and Gesenius is right, the Syriac word does not mean to beat out or ram something that is solid or firm, but by ramming or beating to make firm that which was not firm before.

est *firmamentum* interpretati sunt." The Septuagint adopted the word, as Le Clerc has shown in his Commentary, from the Oriental or Chaldaic philosophy: "Hinc cœlos רקיעין *Rekihin*, et ut loquuntur Græci eorum interpretes, *στερέωμα*, quod inferiora *comprimerent* ac *firmarent*, deosque præsides uniuscujusque cœli *'Ανοχεῖς* et *Συνοχεῖς*, *sustentatores* et *coactores* appellabant." He refers in proof to a passage in Thomas Stanley's 'History of Philosophy,' in which, though that writer calls *stereoma* a solid orb, yet he shows that this *stereoma* was of a nature of an ethereal fluid:* "The first of the corporeal worlds is the empyreal (by Empyræum the Chaldæans understood not, as the Christian theologists, the seat of God and the blessed spirits, which is rather analogous to the supreme light of the Chaldæans, but the outward sphere of the corporeal world). It is round in figure, according to the oracle, 'enclosing heaven in a round figure.' It is also a solid orb, or firmament; for the same oracles call it *στερέωμα*. It consists of fire, whence named the Empyreal, or as the oracles, *the fiery world*, which fire, being immediately next the incorporeal supramundane light, is the rarest and subtilest of bodies, and, by reason of this subtilty, penetrates into the æther, which is the next world below it, and, by mediation of the æther, through all the material world.

"Chap. xiv.—The æther is a fire (as its name implies) less subtile than the empyræum; for the empyræum penetrates through the æther; yet is the æther itself so subtile that it penetrates through the material world. The second æthereal world is the sphere of fixed stars. . . . The third æthereal world is that of the planetary orb, which contains the sun, moon, and planets."

According, then, to this meaning of *stereoma* the word gives no countenance to the idea that the firmament is a solid vault, capable of sustaining an ocean of water above it. On the contrary, it conveys the idea

* 'History of Philosophy,' by Thomas Stanley. Chaldaick Philosophy, chap. xiii.

of a fine, subtile fluid pervading space, and agrees, therefore, with the Biblical usage, which makes it an expanse extending from the earth to the heavenly bodies, including the airy space in which birds fly.

Having thus shown, from the usage of the Biblical writers, the uniformity of the Jewish tradition and the LXX., that the meaning of *Rakia* is an expanse, not a solid vault, the fiction of "an ocean of water above it" falls of itself. That rests upon the supposition of a "permanent solid vault," and is altogether incompatible with the true meaning of an ethereal expanse. But independently of this incompatibility, the theory of "an ocean" above the firmament is a mere fiction. There is not one word about it in the Bible. The sacred text says that the firmament was to separate the waters which were under the firmament from the waters which were above the firmament. It also relates the gathering together of the waters under the firmament and the formation of the ocean, but it says not one word about the gathering together of the waters above the firmament into an ocean or reservoir; that is pure invention of those who wish to burden upon "the Hebrews" what they are entirely innocent of. Indeed it is admitted by Gesenius and others, though not noticed by the Essayist, that the Hebrews knew better, and were acquainted with the true origin of rain. Gesenius says that the Hebrew poets describe a firmament, "Super quo oceanus cœlestis existat, apertis firmamenti cancellis pluviam demittens in terram (Gen. i. 7, vii. 11; Ps. civ. 3; cxlviii. 4) vulgarem nimirum intuitionem secuti, licet vera rerum ratio iis minimè incognita sit." (Vide Gen. ii. 6; Job xxxvi. 27, 28.) He does not ascribe the fiction of an ocean to the Hebrews generally, but only to the poets following popular notions. It is therefore unfair to charge it upon "a Hebrew Descartes," who must have been up to the science of the day.

But it is said that the Hebrews believed that heaven had pillars and foundations, that there were windows and doors in heaven, on the opening of which the rain descended. With equal reason might these wise interpreters say that the Hebrews believed that there were bottles in heaven, and that the celestial ocean, or part of it, was first bottled off before the earth could be supplied with rain, or that "the waters are bound up in a garment" (Prov. xxx. 4), or that the ocean has bars and doors (Job xxxviii. 10, 17), or that the shadow of death and the womb have doors (Job iii. 10), for all these are spoken of. If these are figurative, so are the windows and doors of heaven. As in Job xxxviii. 37, "Who can number the clouds in wisdom? or who can stay the bottles of heaven?" bottles are parallel to and explained by "clouds;" so in Ps. lxxviii. 23, there is a similar explanatory parallelism—"Though He had commanded the clouds from above, and opened the doors of heaven;" and few children in a Sunday or National school would take bottles or doors literally. The common people are not so dull as Gesenius and some other intellectual wonders of the day think. Who ever met a rustic, accustomed to look at the heavens, who thought it was a solid vault, and that the stars were fixed in like nails? The common people are not so silly: they judge by what they see. They do not see a solid vault, but they see the lark and the eagle soaring aloft in the air, and they think that all beyond is just alike. They never dream of a solid obstacle in the way. That solid vault savours much more of the fancy of the poet adding a trait of grandeur to a description, or of the school of the philosopher inventing a theory to account for the motions of the heavenly bodies, than of the practical common sense of the common people. The most uneducated know very well the connexion between clouds and rain, and in this the Hebrews were not behind other people. The two passages pointed out by Gesenius—Gen. ii. 6, and Job. xxxvi. 27, 28—prove that the Hebrews knew the connexion between evaporation and rain, especially the latter. "For he maketh small the drops of water; they pour down rain according to the vapour thereof, which the clouds do drop and distil upon man abundantly." The Hebrew language has various words for "cloud" or "clouds"; they are all found in connexion with rain. Thus, Gen. ix.: "When I bring a cloud, ענן, over the earth, my bow shall be seen in the cloud." The clouds might excite apprehension of another deluge; the bow dispels it. Deborah was able to tell how, when the Lord went out of Seir, "the earth trembled, and the heavens dropped (distilled); the clouds, עבים, also dropped water." (Judges v. 4.) In 1 Kings xviii. 44, 45, the little cloud, עב, rising from the sea, was recognized by Elijah as a sign of coming rain; and when the heavens were black with clouds and wind, "a great rain" followed. Solomon says (Prov. iii. 20), "By his knowledge the depths are broken up, and the clouds, שחקים, drop down dew," which reads very like a commentary upon Gen. vii. 11, "the fountains of the great deep were broken up, and the windows of heaven were opened." These are only a few specimens of the many passages that bear upon the subject; but sufficient to show that "the Hebrews" knew very well that rain did not come from a celestial ocean, through windows and doors, nor yet from bottles in the heavens, but from the clouds. Indeed, the connexion between the two furnished materials for the proverb, "Clouds, נשיאים, and wind, and no rain; such is the man whose promise of a gift is a lie." (Prov. xxv. 14.)

But though there be no ocean above the firmament, may there not have been, may there not still be, waters above the firmament? Such was the opinion of the learned F. Von Meyer, adopted by Kurtz in his first edition of 'Bible and Astronomy,' and lately advocated by Delitsch. That such a supposition is not unscientific, appears from Dr. Whewell's 'Theory of the Solar System':—"The planets exterior to Mars, Jupiter and Saturn especially, as the best known of them, appear, by the best judgment which we can form, to be spheres of water and of aqueous vapour, combined, it may be, with atmospheric air . . . Can we see any physical reason for the fact, which appears to us probable, that all the water and vapour of the system is gathered in its outward parts? It would seem that we can. Water and aqueous vapour are driven off and retained at a distance by any other source of heat. . . . It was, then, agreeable to the general scheme, that the excess of water and vapour should be packed into rotating masses, such as are Jupiter and Saturn, Uranus and Neptune. . . . And thus the vapour, which would otherwise have wandered loose about the atmosphere, was neatly wound into balls, which again were kept in their due place by being made to revolve in nearly circular orbits about the sun." Perhaps, when science knows a little more about the ethereal medium which fills space, and in which the heavenly bodies move, it may also learn something more about "this water and aqueous vapour," and be better able to understand the Mosaic statement about the waters above the firmament. But, however that be, Biblical usage, Jewish tradition, the reason that moved the LXX. to adopt *stereoma*, and the Vulgate *firmamentum*, the current of Protestant interpretation until a recent date, concur in proving that "the Hebrews" did not believe in a solid heaven, like the brass or iron heaven of the heathens, but in an expanse of something like the atmospheric air.* This is not contrary, but rather agreeable to the discoveries of modern science, which attributes the retardation of the heavenly bodies to some resisting medium, and light to the undulations of some subtile fluid.

16. VERSE 27. *Creation of one human pair.*—This subject has been so fully discussed by Prichard that it is not necessary to enter upon it here.† It may be

* The threat, Levit. xxvi. 19, "I will make your heaven like the iron, and your earth like the brass," also shows that the Hebrews as little looked upon the heavens as hard and solid, as they believed the earth to be brass.

† Prichard sums up his argument thus:—"On the whole it appears that the information deduced from this fourth method of inquiry is as satisfactory as we could expect, and is sufficient to confirm, and indeed by itself to establish, the inference that the human kind contains but one species, and therefore, by a second inference, but one race. It will, I apprehend, be allowed by those who have attentively followed this investigation of particulars, that the diversities in physical character belonging to different races present no material obstacle to the opinion that all nations sprang from one original, a result which plainly follows from the foregoing consideration." ('Researches into the Physical History of Mankind,' by James Cowles Prichard, M.D., vol. ii. p. 589.)

well, however, to notice a statement in 'Essays and Reviews' which says that the original formation of only one pair of human beings is taught only in the second chapter, and not in the first. "Man is said to have been created male and female, and the narrative contains nothing to show that a single pair only is intended." * "It is in the second narrative of creation that the formation of a single man out of the dust of the earth is described, and the omission to create a female at the same time is stated to have been repaired by the subsequent formation of one from the side of the man."—Note in 'Essays and Reviews,' p. 222. But the text in Gen. i., if carefully examined, proves that only one pair of human beings is intended, and that the formation of the two was not simultaneous. In verse 26 we read, "And God said, Let us make man (Adam without article) in our image, after our likeness, and let them have dominion," etc. Here the language is indefinite. It refers to the whole human race. But then follows, "And God created the man (Adam, with the article) in his image, in the image of God created He him: male and female created He them." Here the language is definite, "the man," and in the first half of the verse the pronoun is in the singular number, and the masculine gender, "In the image of God created He him." If the author had intended briefly to have stated that at first only one human being, and that one the male, was created, what other language could he have employed? Then, having spoken in the singular number, and the masculine gender, he as briefly but clearly describes the subsequent distinction into sexes. "Male and female created He them." The plan of this chapter forbade his entering into the detail of the creation of woman, just as much as it hindered him from describing the varieties of herbs or trees, or fowls or fishes, or of beasts of the earth and cattle. As he merely says that God created them, so here, after the mention of "the man," he just notices the fact that God created them male and

* Cf. 'Essays and Reviews.'

female; but in that very notice he implies that there is something peculiar, for with regard to fish or beasts or cattle he does not mention that God created them male and female, or, as it may be rendered, "a male and a female." With regard to man, short as is the notice, he does relate, first, that "in the image of God created He him," that is, one male; and then "male and female created He them." Even according to the opinion of those who make the first and second chapters of Genesis two accounts, written by two authors, the fifth chapter was written by the author who wrote the first chapter (the Elohist, as they say). But in the fifth chapter the creation of one pair only is plainly implied. "This is the book of the generations of Adam. In the day that God created Adam, in the likeness of God created He him; male and female created He them; and blessed them, and called their name Adam, in the day when they were created. And Adam lived an hundred and thirty years," etc. In all this Adam is one person, and yet the first and second verses are a recapitulation of chapter i. 26, 27, in the very words of those verses. Therefore in i. 27, the author took Adam as one individual male human being, as Knobel fairly admits in his commentary on chap. v. 1–5:—

"Adam is here a proper name, as iii. 17. . . . . The author designedly repeats the statements of i. 27, 28, as his purpose is here to narrate how the first human pair propagated the species by generation, and brought forth children of the same form which they themselves had received at the creation from God. . . . . . The passage teaches that the Elohist, who here attributes to his Adam the begetting of a son in his 130th year, also believed in one first human pair, though in i. 26 he had not plainly said so."

On this point, therefore, there is no discrepancy between the first and second chapters. The first chapter, as is proved by v. 26, 27, relates, first, the creation of Adam, and then mentions the distinction of male and female. The second chapter gives the particulars, first, of the creation of Adam, then of the creation of Eve.

17. Thus a comparison of the actual statements of Moses with the discoveries and conclusions of modern science is so far from shaking, that it confirms our faith in the accuracy of the sacred narrative. We are astonished to see how the Hebrew Prophet, in his brief and rapid outline sketched 3000 years ago, has anticipated some of the most wonderful of recent discoveries, and can ascribe the accuracy of his statements and language to nothing but inspiration. Moses relates how God created the heavens and the earth at an indefinitely remote period before the earth was the habitation of man—geology has lately discovered the existence of a long prehuman period. A comparison with other scriptures shows that the "heavens" of Moses include the abode of angels, and the place of the fixed stars, which existed before the earth. Astronomy points out remote worlds, whose light began its journey long before the existence of man. Moses declares that the earth was or became covered with water, and was desolate and empty. Geology has found by investigation that the primitive globe was covered with an uniform ocean, and that there was a long azoic period, during which neither plant nor animal could live. Moses states that there was a time when the earth was not dependent upon the sun for light or heat, when, therefore, there could be no climatic differences. Geology has lately verified this statement by finding tropical plants and animals scattered over all parts of the earth. Moses affirms that the sun, as well as the moon, is only a light-holder. Astronomy declares that the sun itself is a non-luminous body, dependent for its light on a luminous atmosphere. Moses asserts that the earth existed before the sun was given as a luminary. Modern science proposes a theory which explains how this was possible. Moses asserts that there is an expanse extending from earth to distant heights, in which the heavenly bodies are placed. Recent discoveries lead to the supposition of some subtile fluid medium in which they move. Moses describes the process of creation as gradual, and mentions the order in which living things appeared, plants, fishes,

fowls, land-animals, man. By the study of nature geology has arrived independently at the same conclusion. Where did Moses get all this knowledge? How was it that he worded his rapid sketch with such scientific accuracy? If he in his day possessed the knowledge which genius and science have attained only recently, that knowledge is superhuman. If he did not possess the knowledge, then his pen must have been guided by superhuman wisdom. Faith has, therefore, nothing to fear from science. So far the records of nature, fairly studied and rightly interpreted, have proved the most valuable and satisfying of all commentaries upon the statements of Scripture. The ages required for geological development, the infinity of worlds and the immensity of space revealed by astronomy, illustrate, as no other note or comment has ever done, the Scripture doctrines of the eternity, the omnipotence, the wisdom of the Creator. Let then Science pursue her boundless course, and multiply her discoveries in the heavens and in the earth. The believer is persuaded that they will only show more clearly that "the words of the Lord are pure words, as silver tried in a furnace of fire, purified seven times." Let Criticism also continue her profoundly interesting and important work. Let her explore, sift, analyse, scrutinize, with all her powers, the documents, language, and contents of Scripture, and honestly tell us the results. Since the day when Laurentius Valla exposed the fiction of the Imperial donation, she has contributed much to the removal of error, and the advancement of literary, patristic, and historic truth; and Divine revelation has also been illustrated by her labours. It might be shown that even the hostile and sceptical have involuntarily helped in the confirmation of the Christian verity, and that even their labours cannot be neglected without loss. But the student must carefully distinguish between the speculations of individuals and the ascertained, settled results of criticism. The theory of any one individual, however learned, laborious, and genial, is only an opinion, perhaps only one of a chaos of conflicting opinions, where sound criticism has found no sure footing. The settled results are those which, after severe testing, have been unanimously accepted by the competent, the sober, and the judicious. The former may be popular for a while, and seem to shake the faith; but they are gradually overthrown by the progress of critical investigation, and take their place in the record of things that were. The history of the last hundred years, since modern criticism took its rise, is sufficient to quiet the believer's mind as to the ultimate result. It tells of theory after theory, propounded by the critics of the day, first applauded, then controverted, then rejected, just like the philosophic systems of the same period, and yet a gradual advance from anti-Christian hostility to an effort after scientific impartiality, and a large amount of positive gain for the right interpretation of Scripture and the confirmation of the old Christian belief. Faith, therefore, feels no more fear of Criticism than of Science, being assured that neither can "do anything against the truth, but for the truth."

ESSAY VI.

ON THE GENUINENESS AND AUTHENTICITY OF THE PENTATEUCH.

CONTENTS OF ESSAY VI.

ON THE GENUINENESS AND AUTHENTICITY OF THE PENTATEUCH.

‘ Δοκεῖ οὖν πλεῖον ἢ τὸ ἥμισυ τοῦ παντὸς εἶναι ἡ ἀρχή.’—ARISTOTLE.

1. CHRISTIANITY is an historic religion. It claims to be a reasonable belief; but it does not base itself upon Reason. Its foundation is laid on the rock of Fact. God's actual dealings with the world from its creation to the full establishment of the Christian Church constitute its subject matter, and form the ground out of which its doctrines spring. The mystic spirit, which, despising the grossness and materiality of facts, seeks to form to itself a sublimated and idealized religion in which events and occurrences shall have no place, leaves the fixed and stable land to float off upon an interminable ocean of shifting and changing fancies, substituting in reality for the truth of God the mere thoughts, feelings, and opinions of the individual. If we are to maintain a Faith worthy of the name, we must plant our feet firmly on the solid ground of historic fact, and not allow ourselves to be shaken from that ground by unproved assertions, however boldly made, or however often repeated. We must give little heed to doubts, which may readily be started in connexion with any narrative, and demand of those who attack our belief, not mere ingenious speculations as to the past, but proof that the authoritative account, which has come down to us as part and parcel of our religion, and which even they profess after a certain sort to venerate, is devoid of literal truth, before we follow them in their endeavours to extract from the record some other sort of truth—not "rigidly historic"*

* Bunsen, 'Egypt's Place in Universal History,' vol. iv. p. 383.

—but ideal, poetic, symbolical. We need not, we must not, shut our eyes to any new discoveries, be they scientific or historical; but we are bound to examine the so-called discoveries narrowly, to see exactly to what they amount, and then to ask ourselves, "Do they positively conflict with the plain historic sense of Scripture or no?" If they do, it will become a question (when the presumed discovery is historical) of relative credibility. The witnesses contradict one another—which of them shall we believe? But more often it will be found that there is no such contradiction—that all which the discoveries have *established*, is compatible with the Scriptural narrative, and that the contradiction arises only where the conjectures and hypotheses of speculative minds have been superadded to the facts with which they profess to deal. Where this is the case, there need be no hesitation. "Yea, let God be true, and every man a liar!" Human speculations and conjectures, once seen to be such, cannot trouble the faith of a Christian man. Facts are stubborn things, and rightly command our respect; hypotheses are airy nothings, and may safely be disregarded and despised.

2. Among the numerous attempts made to disturb men's faith in the present day, few have seemed more plausible, or have met with a greater amount of success, than those which have grouped themselves about the Pentateuch, the foundation stone on which the rest of the Bible is built. The genuineness of the work, though it has not lacked defenders,* has been pertinaciously denied, both in Germany and in America; while the authenticity of the narrative has been assailed in various respects. It will be the aim and object of the present paper to show, first, that there is no sufficient reason to doubt the Mosaic authorship of the Pentateuch, and, secondly, that there are no sufficient historical grounds for questioning the authenticity of the narrative.

3. It is a general rule of literary criticism that, ex-

* See especially the work of Jahn, 'Aechtheit des Pentateuchs,' and Hävernick's more recent 'Einleitung,' which has been translated for Clarke's 'Theological Library.'

cept for special reasons, books are to be assigned to the authors whose names they bear. In profane literature this rule is considered sufficient to determine the authorship of ninety-nine out of every hundred volumes in our libraries. Most men, who write works of any importance, claim them during their lifetime; their claim, if undisputed, is accepted by the world at large; and nothing is more difficult than to change the belief, which is thus engendered, subsequently. Every work therefore which comes down to us as the production of a particular author is to be accepted as his production, unless strong grounds can be produced to the contrary. The *onus probandi* lies with the person who denies the genuineness; and, unless the arguments adduced in proof are very weighty, the fact of reputed authorship ought to overpower them. Sound criticism has generally acquiesced in this canon. It raises an important presumption in favour of the Mosaic authorship of the Pentateuch, anterior to any proof of the fact to be derived from internal evidence, or from the testimony of those who had special opportunities of knowing.

4. The internal evidence in favour of the Mosaic authorship is, briefly, the following:—The book is exactly such a one as a writer of the age, character, and circumstances of Moses might be expected to produce. Its style is archaic. The reader, even of the English version, feels that he is here brought into contact with a greater simplicity, a more primitive cast of thought and speech, than he meets with in any of the other sacred writings. The life described, the ideas, the characters, have about them the genuine air of primitive antiquity. The student of the original observes that the very words themselves, the constructions, the grammatical forms, bear similar traces of a remote authorship, being often such as had become obsolete even before the composition of the Book of Joshua.* It is impossible to exhibit this argument popularly in the

* See Jahn in Bengel's 'Archiv,' vol. ii., pp. 578 et seqq.; and Fritzsche, 'Aechtheit der Bücher Mosis,' pp. 174 et seqq. Compare also Marsh's 'Authenticity of the Five Books of Moses,' pp. 6 et seqq

present condition of Hebrew scholarship among us. Its weight, however, is sufficiently shown by the pressure which it has exerted upon the controversy in Germany, where the opponents of the Mosaic authorship are constrained to allow that a considerable number of "archaisms" do in fact exist in the Pentateuch, and to account for them by the supposition that genuine Mosaic documents were in the hands of its "compiler," from which he adopted the forms and words in question! * This is surely about as probable as that a modern French author, who made use of Froissart among his materials, should adopt his spelling, and form his sentences after his type.

5. Again, the writer shows a close acquaintance with Egypt, its general aspect, its history, geography, manners, customs, productions, and language, which would be natural to one so circumstanced as Moses, but which cannot be shown to belong naturally, or even probably, to any later Israelite, down to the time of Jeremiah. No doubt there was extensive commercial and political intercourse between Egypt and Judea in the age of Solomon, and in the later period of the Jewish kingdom; but such intercourse, even if direct (of which we have no proof), would fail to give that exact historic knowledge of what would then have become a remote era, which the writer of the Pentateuch displays at every turn in the most easy and natural manner possible. Laborious attempts have been made to invalidate this argument; and one writer† has gone so far as to assert that in many respects the author of the Pentateuch shows a want of acquaintance with the customs of Egypt, such as is sufficient to prove that he was not Moses. But this audacity has had the happy effect of calling forth a reply, which has established beyond all possibility of refutation the exactitude and vast extent of the author's Egyptian knowledge, which is now allowed on all hands. The work of Hengstenberg, "Aegypten und Mose," must be carefully read for the

* De Wette, 'Einleitung, in d. alt. Test.,' § 163.

† Von Bohlen.

full weight of this reasoning to be appreciated.* Its argument does not admit of compression, since it depends mainly on the multiplicity and minuteness of its detail; but the impression which it leaves may be stated, briefly, as follows:—That either a person born and bred in Egypt about the time of the Exodus wrote the Pentateuch, or that a writer of a later age elaborately studied the history and antiquities of the Egyptians for the purpose of imposing a forgery on his countrymen, and that he did this with such skill and success that not even modern criticism, with its lynx-eyed perspicacity, and immense knowledge of the past, can detect and expose the fraud or point out a single place in which the forger stumbled through ignorance.

6. To this it must be added, that the writer, who is thus intimately acquainted with the land and people of Egypt, is also fully aware of all the peculiar features of the Sinaitic peninsula; † and further (and more especially) that he has a knowledge of the ancient condition and primitive races of Canaan, which must have been quite beyond the reach of any one who lived much later than Moses. The Rephaim, Zuzim, Emim, Horim, Avim, and Anakim, who appear as powerful races in the Pentateuch, have either perished or been reduced to insignificance by the time of the Judges. The writer of the Pentateuch, however, knows their several countries, their designations in the mouths of different nations, their cities, and the peoples by whom they were severally conquered.‡ Similarly, he acquaints us with the ancient names of a number of Canaanitish towns, which had been superseded by fresh titles long before the Exodus.§ All this is natural enough, supposing that the work was composed by

* This work has been translated into English by Mr. R. D. C. Robbins, of the Theological Seminary, Andover, United States; and a reprint of this translation, with additional notes, formed the third volume of Clarke's 'Biblical Cabinet,' New Series (Edinburgh, 1845.)

† Stanley, 'Sinai and Palestine,' pp. 20–24.

‡ Gen. xiv. 5, 6; Num. xiii. 28; Deut. ii. 10–23.

§ As Mamre, which became first Kirjath-arba (Josh. xiv. 15), and then Hebron; Bela, which became Zoar (Gen. xiv. 2); Enmishpat, which became Kadesh (ib. ver. 7); Hazezon-Tamar, which became Engedi (ib.; compare 2 Chron. xx. 2); and Galeed, which became Mizpah (Gen. xxxi. 48, 49).

Moses; but it would be very forced and artificial in a writer of a later age, even if we could suppose such a writer to have any means of acquiring the information.

7. Further, the Pentateuch *professes* to be the work of Moses. Few books comparatively tell us by whom they are written. Neither Joshua, nor Judges, nor Ruth, nor the Books of Samuel, nor Kings, nor Chronicles, nor Esther, nor the first three Gospels, nor the Acts, nor the 'Commentaries' of Cæsar, nor the 'Annals,' or 'Histories,' of Tacitus, nor the 'Hellenics' of Xenophon, nor Plato's 'Dialogues,' nor Aristotle's 'Philosophical Works,' nor Plutarch's 'Lives,' nor at least nine-tenths of the other remains of ancient literature, contain within them any statements showing by whom they were written. Authorship generally is mere matter of notoriety; and usually the best evidence we have for it, beyond common repute, is the declaration of some writer, later by two or three centuries, that the person to whom a given work is assigned, composed a book answering in its subject and its general character to the work which we find passing under his name. But occasionally we have evidence of a higher order. Some writers formally name themselves as the authors of their works at the beginning, or at the close, or in the course of their narrative.* Others, without a distinct formal announcement, let us see, by the mode or matter of their narration, who the author is, using the first person, or mentioning facts of which they only could be cognisant, or otherwise implying, without directly asserting, their authorship. This last is the case of the Pentateuch. The author does not formally announce himself, but by the manner in which he writes, implies that he is Moses. This is so clear and palpable, that even the antagonists of the genuineness are forced to allow it.† "The author of the last four books," says one, "wishes to be taken for Moses." "The writer of Deuteronomy," says another,

* As Herodotus, Thucydides, Isaiah, St. Paul, Jesus the son of Sirach, &c.

† De Wette, 'Einleitung in d. alt. Test.,' §. 162, d.; Hartmann, 'Forschungen über d. Pentateuch,' p. 538; Von Bohlen, 'Die Genesis hist. krit. erläut. Einleitung,' p. xxxviii.

"would have men think that his whole book is composed by Moses." They do not indeed admit the conclusion, that what is thus claimed and professed must be true; but, on the contrary, maintain that the actual writer lived many centuries after the great Legislator. Apparently they do not see that, if their views are correct, the whole value of the work is lost—that it becomes a mere impudent fraud, utterly unworthy of credit, which cannot reasonably be attached to any statements made by one who would seek to palm on the world a gross and elaborate deception. If a work has merely gone accidentally by a wrong name, the discovery of its spuriousness need not seriously affect its authenticity; but if the writer has set himself to personate another man in order to obtain for his statements a weight and authority to which they would not otherwise be entitled, the detection of the fraud carries with it the invalidation of the document, by wholly destroying our confidence in the integrity of the author. Modern Rationalism shrinks from these conclusions. It would degrade the Sacred Books, but it would not deprive them altogether of an historic character. It still speaks of them as sacred, and as entitled to our respect and reverence, while it saps the foundations on which their claim to our reverence rests, making them at best the "pious frauds" of well-intentioned but unveracious religionists.

8. The external evidence of the Mosaic authorship of the Pentateuch is allowed to be extensive; but it is said to be of little worth, in the first place, because the witnesses are uncritical.* The Jews and Greeks, who, during eighteen centuries, without a dissentient voice ascribed the "Book of the Law" to Moses, were not acquainted with the modern Critical Analysis, which claims to be an infallible judge of the age, and mode of composition, of every literary production. It is true the witnesses include Apostles,† prophets,‡ confessors,§ our Blessed Lord Himself:‖ but the distance of these

* De Wette, § 164.
† John i. 45; 2 Cor. iii. 15.
‡ Dan. ix. 11; Mal iv. 4.
§ Acts vii. 38.
‖ Matt. xix. 7, 8; Mark x. 3; xii. 26; Luke xvi. 29; xxiv. 27; John v. 46, &c.

witnesses from the age of Moses is held to invalidate their testimony;* or if the words of One at least are too sacred to be gainsaid, He spoke (it is argued) by way of accommodation, in order not to shock the prejudices of the Jews. We are challenged to produce witnesses near the time, and told that no evidence to the Mosaic authorship "approaches within seven centuries to the probable age of Moses." † Of course, if the antiquity of the Pentateuch be denied, that of the later books of the Old Testament is not likely to pass unquestioned. But the challenge is really met, and answered fully and fairly by an appeal to those books, which are the only writings within the period named in which any reference to Moses was to be expected. The author of Joshua, by many thought to be Joshua himself, and, if not he, at least one of his contemporaries, ‡ speaks of "the Book of the Law," § — "the Book of the Law of Moses,"‖—a book containing "all that Moses commanded,"¶ with "blessings and cursings;" ** thus entirely corresponding, so far as the description goes, to the work which has always passed under Moses' name. The writer of Judges is less express;†† but he so completely agrees in his account of the Hebrew institutions with the Pentateuch, and so closely follows its diction in many places, that a candid Rationalist ‡‡ has been driven to allow, that "the arranger of this book was well acquainted with the Pentateuch in its entire extent." In Samuel, though the Pentateuch itself is not mentioned, there are at least two clear citations of it—the passage respecting "the priest's custom with the people,"§§ which follows word for word Deut. xviii. 3, and that con-

* 'Westminster Review,' No. xxxv., p. 35.

† Ibid. l. s. c.

‡ For proof of this, see the 'Bampton Lectures' for 1859, p. 83, first edition.

§ Josh. i. 8; viii. 34. ‖ Ib. viii. 31; xxiii. 6. ¶ Ib. viii. 35.

** Ib. ver. 34; compare Deut. xxvii. and xxviii. Note also the quotations in Josh. viii. 31, from Deut. xxvii. 5, 6; and in Josh. xxiii. 7, from Ex. xxiii. 13.

†† Judg. ii. 15 is probably a reference to Lev. xxvi. 16, 17; and Judg. iii. 4, to the law generally.

‡‡ Hartmann. §§ 1 Sam. ii. 13.

cerning the "assembling of women at the door of the Tabernacle of the congregation,"* which is an exact repetition of Ex. xxxviii. 8. In Kings and Chronicles —both probably compilations made from papers contemporary with the kings whose history is related—the references to the work are frequent:† and it is unhesitatingly assigned to Moses,‡ as indeed is admitted on all hands.

It thus appears that the Pentateuch is either cited, or mentioned as the work of Moses, by almost the whole series of Jewish historical writers from Moses himself to Ezra. The first testimony occurs within (probably) half a century of Moses' decease, and is by a writer who may have known him personally. It is rarely indeed that we have evidence of this satisfactory and conclusive character with respect to the genuineness of any ancient work.

9. With regard to profane testimony, it must be allowed that none of it is very ancient. But this simply results from the fact that none of the earlier authors have occasion to mention the Jews, or to touch the subject of their literature. The *first* who do so—Manetho and Hecatæus of Abdera, an Egyptian and a Greek—are in accordance with the native authorities, ascribing the law of the Jews, which is represented as existing in a written form, to Moses. And the later classical writers, with but one exception, are of the same opinion.

10. To this direct testimony the adversaries of the Mosaic authorship are wont to oppose certain difficulties, which militate (they argue) against the notion that the work is even of the age of Moses. The most important of these is the objection of De Wette, that the book is altogether beyond the literary capabilities of the age, containing within it every element of Hebrew literature in the highest perfection to which it ever attained, and thus (he thinks) necessarily belonging to

* 1 Sam. ii. 22.

† 1 Kings ii. 3; 2 Kings xxii. 8; xxiii. 3; 2 Chron. xxiii. 18; xxv. 4; xxxv. 12.

‡ 1 Kings ii. 3; 2 Kings xxiii. 25; 2 Chron. xxiii. 18, &c.

the *acmé* and not to the infancy of the nation.* Were this statement correct, we should indeed have a strange phenomenon to account for, though one which could not be pronounced impossible, if the Divine as well as the human authorship were taken into consideration. God might have chosen to assign to the first burst of written Revelation a literary perfection never afterwards to be exceeded or even equalled. He might have given to His first mouthpiece, Moses, such powers of mind and such a mastery over the Hebrew language as "to leave nothing for succeeding authors but to follow in his footsteps." The fact, however, is not really so. De Wette's statement is a gross exaggeration of the reality. Considered as a literary work, the Pentateuch is not the production of an advanced or refined, but of a simple and rude age. Its characteristics are plainness, inartificiality, absence of rhetorical ornament, and occasional defective arrangement. The only style which it can be truly said to bring to perfection, is that simple one of clear and vivid narrative, which is always best attained in the early dawn of a nation's literature, as a Herodotus, a Froissart, and a Stow sufficiently indicate. In other respects it is quite untrue to say that the work goes beyond all later Hebrew efforts. We look in vain through the Pentateuch for the gnomic wisdom of Solomon, the eloquent denunciations of Ezekiel and Jeremiah, or the lofty flights of Isaiah. It is absurd to compare the song of Moses, as a literary production, even with some of the Psalms of David, much more to parallel it with Ezekiel's eloquence and Homeric variety, or Isaiah's awful depth and solemn majesty of repose. In a literary point of view it may be questioned whether Moses did so much for the Hebrews as Homer for the Greeks, or whether his writings had really as great an influence on the after productions of his countrymen. And if his literary greatness still surprises us, if Hebrew literature still seems in his person to reach too suddenly a high excellence, albeit not so high a one as has been

* 'Einleitung,' § 163, sub. fin.

argued—let us remember, in the first place, that Moses was not, any more than Homer, the first writer of his nation, but only happens to be the first whose writings have come down to us. "Vixere fortes ante Agamemnona." Moses seems so great because we do not possess the works of his predecessors, and so are unable to trace the progress of Hebrew literature up to him. Had we the "songs" of Israel,* and the "book of the wars of the Lord," which he quotes,† we might find him no literary phenomenon at all, but as a writer merely on a level with others of his age and nation. Again, we must not forget to take into consideration the stimulus which contact with the cultivation of Egypt would naturally have given to Hebrew literature during the two centuries preceding Moses. If we may trust the modern decipherers of Egyptian papyri, literature in Egypt had reached a tolerably advanced stage in the time of the eighteenth and nineteenth dynasties, under one or other of which Moses was in all probability born and bred. "The art of writing books was invented ages before the time of Moses;" ‡ and had been carried further in Egypt than in any other country. History, epistolary correspondence, and novel-writing were known and practised; so that the composition of an extensive work possessing literary merits even of a high order would be no strange thing in the case of one bred up in the first circles of Egyptian society, and "learned in all the wisdom" of that ingenious people.

11. Besides this general objection, there are a certain number of particular passages which, it is said, record facts later than the time of Moses, and thus could not have been written by him. Such are supposed to be the mention of Dan instead of Laish in Gen. xiv. 14; of Hebron instead of Kirjath-Arba or Mamre in Genesis § and Numbers; ‖ and the list of the kings of Edom in Gen. xxxvi. Now in none of these

* Num. xxi. 17; compare Ex. xv. 1. † Num. xxi. 14.

‡ Bunsen, 'Egypt,' vol. iv. p. 384. Compare 'Cambridge Essays' for 1858, pp. 230–260.

§ Gen. xiii. 18; xxiii. 2, 19; xxxv. 27, &c. ‖ Num. xiii. 22.

cases is it really impossible that Moses may have written the passages. The Dan intended may be Dan-jaan,* and not Laish. Hebron may have been a name of the city called also Mamre and Kirjath-Arba, within the lifetime of Moses. Even the eight kings of Edom may possibly be a dynasty of monarchs intervening between Esau and Moses, the last of the eight being Moses' contemporary, as conjectured by Hävernick.† The remarkable expression, "These are the kings that reigned in the land of Edom, *before there reigned any king over the children of Israel*," may be understood prophetically. Moses may have intended in the passage to mark his full belief in the promises made by God to Abraham and Jacob;‡ that "kings should come out of their loins," a belief which he elsewhere expresses very confidently.§ There is no really valid or insuperable objection to any of these explanations; which may not strike us as clever or dexterous, yet which may be true nevertheless; for "*Le vrai n'est pas toujours le vraisemblable.*"

12. Or the right explanation may be the more commonly received one—that these words, phrases, and passages, together with a few others similar to them, are later additions to the text, either adopted into it upon an authoritative revision, such as that ascribed to Ezra, or, perhaps, accidentally introduced through the mistakes of copyists, who brought into the text what had been previously added, by way of exegesis, in the margin. Such additions constantly occur in the case of classical writers; and there is no reason to suppose that a special providence would interfere to prevent their occurrence in the Sacred Volume. We "have our treasure in earthen vessels." God gives us His Revelation, but leaves it to us to preserve it by the ordinary methods by which books are handed down to posterity. No doubt its transcendent value has caused the bestowal of especial care and attention on the transmission of the Sacred Volume; and the result

* 2 Sam. xxiv. 6.
† 'Einleitung,' § 124.
‡ Gen. xvii. 6, 16; xxxv. 11.
§ Deut. xvii. 14-20.

is that no ancient collection has come down to us nearly so perfect, or with so few corruptions and interpolations; but to declare that there are none, is to make an assertion improbable *à priori*, and at variance with the actual phenomena. The sober-minded in every age have allowed that the written Word, as it has come down to us, has these slight imperfections, which no more interfere with its value than the spots upon the sun detract from his brightness, or than a few marred and stunted forms destroy the harmony and beauty of Nature.

13. One other line of objection requires a few words of notice. The whole Levitical system, it is sometimes said, was an after-growth from the real Mosaic law, which went but little, if at all, beyond the Decalogue. This is thought to be evidenced by the scantiness of any traces of Levitical worship throughout the period of the Judges, and the infraction of various precepts of the ceremonial law from the time of Joshua to that of Nehemiah. But it has been shown* that though the Book of Judges exhibits a very disordered political and religious condition of the nation, and from its nature —biographical rather than historical—is likely to contain but little regarding the Mosaical institutions, yet it does, in point of fact, bear witness to the knowledge and practical existence during the period whereof it treats, of a very considerable number of those usages which are specially termed Levitical. The sacred character of the Levites, their dispersion among the different tribes, the settlement of the High-Priesthood in the family of Aaron, the existence of the Ark of the Covenant, the power of inquiring of God and obtaining answers, the irrevocability of a vow, the distinguishing mark of circumcision, the distinction between clean and unclean meats, the law of the Nazarite, the use of burnt-offerings and peace-offerings, the employment of trumpets as a means of obtaining Divine aid in war, the impiety of setting up a king, are severally acknowledged in the Book of Judges, and constitute together

* By Hävernick. 'Einleitung,' § 136.

very good evidence that the Mosaic ceremonial law was already in force, and, though disregarded in many points by the mass, was felt as binding by all those who had any real sense of religion. The ritual, as a whole, is clearly not of later introduction than the time of the Judges, since twelve or thirteen of its main points are noted as being at that time in force. Why, then, should we suppose, merely because the book is silent on the subject, that the other enactments which are in the same spirit and are inextricably intertwined with these, were not known at the period? It is always dangerous to build on silence. Here the silence is only partial; and the half-utterance which we have is sufficient to indicate what the full answer would have been, had it come within the scope of the writer to deliver it. There is thus ample reason to conclude that the Levitical law was complete in all its parts before the time of the Judges.

What, then, shall we say to its infractions? what to David's "priests of the tribe of Judah?" what to Solomon himself offering sacrifice? what more especially to the suspension of the Feast of Tabernacles for eight hundred years from Joshua to Nehemiah?* Are they compatible with the existence of the Pentateuch at the time, and with an acknowledgment of its Divine authority on the part of those who disobeyed its injunctions? Even if we allow them all to be infractions,†

* 'Westminster Review,' No. xxxv., p. 36. The writer gives no reference, except to Nehemiah viii. 17, which shows (he thinks) that "for 800 years, from the days of Joshua to those of Ezra, the Feast of Tabernacles was unknown in Israel." Probably he would regard "David's priests of the tribe of Judah" as mentioned in 2 Sam. viii. 18, where the Hebrew has כֹּהֲנִים, which commonly means "priests;" while for "Solomon's sacrifices" we should be referred to 1 Kings viii. 5, 62–64; 2 Chr. v. 6; vii. 4, 5; and viii. 12.

† In point of fact, none of the infractions need be allowed. David's "priests of the tribe of Judah" are probably not "priests," but "princes," or "chief rulers," as our Authorized Version renders. (See Buxtorf ad voc. כֹּהֵן, and compare Gesenius ad eand., who allows that כֹּהֵן may mean "a prince;" though he prefers in this place to translate "priests," and to understand "ecclesiastical counsellors." Note also that the LXX. give αὐλάρχαι, "chamberlains," and that in the parallel passage, 1 Chron. xviii. 17, the expression used is הָרִאשֹׁנִים לְיַד הַמֶּלֶךְ, "chief" or "first about the king.") With regard to Solomon's sacrifices, it is nowhere either stated or implied

we may still answer that undoubtedly they are. An authority may be acknowledged which is not obeyed. Precepts may be heard, read, and known, may be as familiar as household words in the mouths of persons, and yet may not be carried out in act. There would be nothing more strange in David's breaking the Levitical law with respect to priesthood in the case of his sons, than in his infraction of the moral law respecting chastity in the case of Uriah's wife. There would be no greater marvel in Solomon's taking it upon himself to offer sacrifice than in his marrying wives from the forbidden nations. There would be nothing harder to understand in the discontinuance after a while of one of the great Mosaical feasts, than in the introduction and stubborn maintenance from one generation to another of idolatrous rites. The moral law, admitted to have been given by Moses, was broken constantly in almost every clause; why then should infractions of the ceremonial law disprove its having come from him?

14. The Mosaic authorship of the Pentateuch is therefore a thing which, to say the least, has not been hitherto disproved; and the ingenious attempts of the modern reconstructive criticism to resolve the work into its various elements, and to give an account of the times when and the persons by whom they were severally composed, even if they had no other fault, must be pronounced premature; for until it is shown that the book was not composed by its reputed author, the mode and time of its composition are not fit objects of research. The theological student may congratulate himself that this is so, and that he is not called upon to study and decide between the twenty different views—each more complicated than the last—which Continental critics, from Astruc to Bunsen, have put out on this apparently inexhaustible subject.

that he sacrificed with his own hand. "The priests" are mentioned as present with him at the time (1 Kings viii. 6; 2 Chron. v. 7; vii. 2, 6), and it is most probable that he used their services. Evidently he could not himself have slain the 22,000 oxen and 120,000 sheep of one sacrifice (1 Kings viii. 63). And Nehemiah, in viii. 17, probably only means that no *such* celebration of the feast had taken place since the time of Joshua.

15. It is sometimes said that questions of genuineness are matters of mere idle curiosity, and that authenticity is alone of importance. In an historical work especially, what we want to know is, not by whom it is written, but whether the narrative which it contains is true. This last, no doubt, is our ultimate object; but it not unfrequently happens that, for the purpose of deciding it, we have to consider the other point; since the genuineness is often the best guarantee of the authenticity. How entirely would it change our estimate of Xenophon's 'Anabasis,' were we to find that it was composed under the name of Xenophon by a Greek of the time of the Antonines! No works are more valuable for history than autobiographies; and when we come upon a document claiming any such character, it is of great importance to see whether upon examination the character is sustained or no. Given the genuineness of such a work, and the authenticity follows almost as a matter of course, unless it can be shown that the writer is unveracious, and wished to deceive. Rationalists have not failed to perceive the force of this reasoning with respect to the Pentateuch; and hence their laborious efforts to disprove its genuineness. Strauss remarks naïvely enough—"The books which describe the departure of the Israelites from Egypt, and their wanderings through the wilderness, bear the name of Moses, who, being their leader, would undoubtedly give a faithful history of these occurrences, unless he designed to deceive; and who, if his intimate connection with Deity described in these books be historically true, was likewise eminently qualified, by virtue of such connection, to produce a credible history of the earlier periods." * This admission on the part of the most extreme of Rationalists is sufficient to show that, at least in the case before us, it is not irrelevant or unimportant to attempt to establish the genuineness of the record.

16. Before the final close of this portion of the inquiry, it will perhaps be best to state distinctly in what sense it is intended to maintain that Moses was the

* 'Leben Jesu,' Einleitung, § 13.

author of the Pentateuch. In the first place, it is not intended to assert that he was the original composer of all the documents contained in his volume. The Book of Genesis bears marks of being to some extent a compilation. Moses probably possessed a number of records, some of greater, some of less antiquity, whereof, under Divine guidance, he made use in writing the history of mankind up to his own time. It is possible that the Book of Genesis may have been, even mainly, composed in this way from ancient narratives, registers, and biographies, in part the property of the Hebrew race, in part a possession common to that race with others. Moses, guided by God's Spirit, would choose among such documents those which were historically true, and which bore on the religious history of the human race. He would not be bound slavishly to follow, much less to transcribe them, but would curtail, expand, adorn, complete them, and so make them thoroughly his own, infusing into them the religious tone of his own mind, and at the same time re-writing them in his own language. Thus it would seem that Genesis was produced. With regard to the remainder of his history, he would have no occasion to use the labours of others, but would write from his own knowledge.

In the second place, it is not intended to deny that the Pentateuch may have undergone an authoritative revision by Ezra, when the language may have been to some extent modernised, and a certain number of parenthetic insertions may have been made into the text. The Jewish tradition on this head seems to deserve attention from its harmony with what is said of Ezra in the book which bears his name.* And this authoritative revision would account at once for the language not being more archaic than it is, and for the occasional insertion of parentheses of the nature of a comment. It would also explain the occurrence of "Chaldaism" in the text.†

* See Lord Arthur Hervey's article on 'Ezra,' in Dr. Smith's 'Biblical Dictionary,' vol. i., p. 606.

† Hirzel, 'De Chaldaismi Biblici origine,' pp. 5 et seqq. There is also another mode in which the "Chaldaisms" may be accounted for. As

Thirdly, it is, of course, not intended to include in the Pentateuch the last chapter of Deuteronomy, which was evidently added after Moses' death, probably by the writer of the Book of Joshua.

17. The authenticity of the Pentateuch has been recently called in question, principally on the following points:—1. The chronology, which is regarded as very greatly in deficiency; 2. The account given of the Flood, which is supposed to magnify a great calamity in Upper Asia into a general destruction of the human race; 3. The ethnological views, which are said to be sometimes mistaken; 4. The patriarchal genealogies, which are charged with being purely mythical; 5. The length of the lives of the Patriarchs, which is thought to be simply impossible; and 6. The duration of the sojourn in Egypt, which is considered incompatible with the number of Israelites on entering and quitting the country. It is proposed, in the remainder of this paper, to consider briefly these six subjects.

I. According to Baron Bunsen, the historic records of Egypt reach up to the year B.C. 9085. A sacerdotal monarchy was then established, and Bytis, the Theban priest of Ammon, was the first king. Before this Egypt had been republican, and separate governments had existed in the different nomes. Egyptian nationality commenced as early as B. C. 10,000. These conclusions are vaguely said to be drawn "from Egyptian records,"* or "from the monuments and other records;"† expressions apt to beget a belief that there is really monumental evidence for them. Let us then see, in the first place, what is the true basis on which they rest.

The Egyptian monuments contain no continuous chronology, and no materials from which a continuous chonological scheme can be framed.‡ The possibility

Chaldee and Hebrew are sister tongues, having one common parent, the forms and expressions in question may have been common to both at first, but have died out in the Hebrew while they were retained in the Chaldee. Movers observes with reason:—"Aramaic forms in a book are either a sign of a *very early* or of a very late composition." ('Bonner Zeitschrift für Philosophie,' xvi. 157.) Those in Genesis may be really "Archaisms."

* 'Essays and Reviews,' p. 54. † Bunsen's 'Egypt,' vol. iv., p. 553.

‡ "The history of the dynasties preceding the 18th," says Mr. Stuart

of constructing such a scheme depends entirely upon the outline which has been preserved to us of the Sebennytic priest Manetho, who composed a history of Egypt under the early Ptolemies. This outline is in a very imperfect condition; and the two versions of it, which we find in Syncellus and in the Armenian Eusebius, differ considerably. Still both agree in representing Egypt as governed by thirty dynasties of kings from Menes to Alexander, and the sum of the years which they assign to these dynasties is a little above (or a little below) 5000. The monuments have proved two things with respect to these lists: they have shown, in the first place, that (speaking generally) they are historical—that the persons mentioned were real men, who actually lived and reigned in Egypt; while, secondly, they have shown that though all reigned in Egypt, all did not reign over the whole of Egypt, but while some were kings in one part of the country, others ruled in another. It is allowed on all hands—by M. Bunsen no less than by others—that no chronological scheme of any real value can be formed from Manetho's lists until it be first determined, either which dynasties and monarchs were contemporary, or what deduction from the sum total of the dynastic years is to be made on account of contemporaneousness. M. Bunsen regards this point as one which Manetho himself determined, and assumes that he was sure to determine it aright. He finds a statement in Syncellus,* that "Manetho made his dynasties cover a space of 113 generations, or 3555 years;" and he accepts this statement as completely removing the difficulty, and absolutely establishing the historic fact that the accession of Menes to the crown of Egypt took place more than thirty-six centuries before our era.† He then professes to follow

Poole, "is not told by any continuous series of monuments. Except those of the 4th and 12th dynasties there are scarcely any records of the age left to the present day." ('Biblical Dictionary,' vol. i. p. 509.) M. Bunsen also says, in one place, of the Egyptian monuments:—"Such documents cannot indeed compensate for the want of written history. Even Chronology, its framework, *cannot be elicited from them*."—('Egypt,' vol. i., p. 32.)

* 'Chronograph,' p. 52, D.

† 'Egypt,' vol. i. pp. 86–89. Lepsius, on the same grounds, and keeping closer to his authority, places Menes nearly 39 centuries before Christ.

Manetho for the preceding period; but here he distorts and misrepresents him. Manetho gave his Egyptian dynasties altogether about 30,000 years. This long space he divided, however, into a natural and a supernatural period. To the supernatural period, during which Egypt was governed by gods, demigods, and spirits, he assigned 24,925 years. To the natural period, which began with Menes, he gave at any rate not much more than 5000. M. Bunsen, not content with this antiquity, but determining to find (or make) a greater, changes the order of Manetho's early dynasties, and by removing to a higher position, without authority and of his own mere fancy, one which is plainly supernatural, obtains for the natural period four dynasties, covering a space of 5212 years (or, as he makes it, 5462 years), which are capable of being represented as human. This, then, is the mode in which the date B. C. 9085 is reached. It is not obtained from the monuments, which have no chronology, or at any rate none earlier than B. C. 1525. It is not derived from Manetho, for it is in direct contradiction to his views, more than doubling the period during which, according to him, Egypt had had human kings. It is a mere theory of M. Bunsen's, to square with which Manetho's lists have been violently disturbed, and above 5000 years subtracted from his divine to be added to his human period.

Even with respect to Menes, and the supposed date of B. C. 3892 (according to Lepsius), or B. C. 3623 (according to M. Bunsen), for his accession, on what does it in reality depend? Not on any monumental evidence, but simply on the supposition that in a certain passage (greatly disputed*) of Syncellus, he has correctly represented Manetho's views, and on the further supposition that Manetho's views were absolutely right. But is it reasonable to suppose that Manetho had data for determining with such exactitude an event so re-

* Böckh in Germany, and Mons. C. Müller in France, have disputed M. Bunsen's conclusions from the passage of Syncellus. The latter thinks that it is a Pseudo-Manetho to whom Syncellus refers. The former regards the passage as corrupt, and suspects that Annianus was quoted, not Manetho.

mote, even if it be a real event at all,* as the accession of Menes? It is plain and palpable, and moreover universally admitted, that between the ancient monarchy (or rather monarchies) of Egypt and the later kingdom, there intervened a time of violent disturbance—the period known as the domination of the Hyksôs—during which the native Egyptians suffered extreme oppression, and throughout Egypt all was disorder and confusion. The notices of this period are so vague and uncertain, that moderns dispute whether it lasted 500, 600, 900, or 2000 years.† Few monuments belong to it. It is extremely doubtful whether an Egyptian of Manetho's age, honestly investigating the records of the past, could have carried on chronology, with any approach to exactness, beyond the commencement of the eighteenth dynasty, which effected the expulsion of the Hyksôs or Shepherd kings. From that time Egypt had been united, and had been a tolerably settled monarchy. Previously, the country had been divided into a multitude of states, sometimes more, sometimes fewer in number, each knowing very little of the rest, all inclined to magnify their own duration and antiquity, and none able effectually to check the others. Let it be granted that Manetho honestly endeavoured to collect and arrange the lists of kings in the several states among which Egypt had been parcelled out. What a task was before him! Royal monuments, or dynastic lists of better or worse authority, might give him the names of the monarchs and the number of years that each had borne the royal title. But as "association" was widely practised in Egypt—two, three, and even more kings occupying the throne together—it would have been a work of extreme difficulty, without full and detailed records, which can scarcely be supposed to have generally survived the

* Whether Menes was an historic personage at all may reasonably be doubted. It is not pretended that he left any monuments. As a name closely resembling his is found in the earliest traditions of various nations, e. g. *Menu* in India, *Minos* in Crete, *Manis* in Phrygia, *Manes* in Lydia, and *Mannus* in Germany, there is at least reason to suspect that he belongs to myth rather than to history.

† Bunsen, 'Egypt,' vol. iv. p. 508; 'Bibl. Dict.,' vol. i. p. 508.

Hyksôs period, to make out from the length of the reigns the duration of any dynasty. And to determine what dynasties were contemporary and what consecutive would have been a still harder task. It is extremely doubtful whether Manetho really made any effort to overcome these difficulties. Setting aside the single disputed passage of Syncellus, we have no evidence that he did. His lists, as they have come down to us, both in Syncellus and Eusebius, are a mere enumeration, in a single line, of thirty dynasties of kings, with an estimate of the years of each dynasty, evidently formed by merely adding together the years of the several reigns. There is no trace in either epitome of any allowance being made, either on account of contemporary kings within a dynasty, or on account of contemporary dynasties. Apparently, Manetho either declined the task of arranging and completing the chronology as one for which he had no sufficient data, or preferred to leave the impression on foreigners that the dynasties and kings were all consecutive, and that Egypt had a history stretching back fifty centuries before Alexander! Other Egyptian priests before him had made even greater exaggerations.*

If it be still thought that the mere opinion of men so well acquainted with the Egyptian monuments, as Bunsen and Lepsius, ought to have weight, despite the weakness of the argumentative grounds on which they rest their conclusions, let it be remembered that others, as deeply read in hieroglyphic lore, and as capable of forming a judgment, have come to conclusions wholly different. Sir Gardner Wilkinson inclines to place the accession of Menes about B. C. 2690,† and Mr. Stuart Poole gives as his first year B. C. 2717.‡ These writers believe that the number of contemporaneous dynasties has been much under-estimated by the German *savans*, who have especially erred in regarding the Theban dynasties as, all of them, subsequent to the Memphite. They consider that Manetho's first and third Theban

* Herod. ii. 100 and 142, 143.
† See the writer's 'Herodotus,' vol. ii. pp. 342, 343.
‡ 'Biblical Dictionary,' vol. i. p. 508.

dynasties were contemporary with his third, fourth, and fifth Memphite; that the first and second Shepherd dynasties ruled at the same time in different parts of Lower Egypt; and that the dynasty of Choïtes (Manetho's 14th) was contemporary with the two Shepherd dynasties above mentioned, and with the second Theban. They do not deny that their arrangement of the dynasties is to some extent conjectural; but they maintain that, while the idea of it was derived from a close inspection of Manetho's lists, it is also "strikingly confirmed by the monuments."* While names of such weight can be quoted on the side of a moderate Egyptian chronology, it cannot be reasonably argued that Egyptian records have disproved the Biblical narrative.

Still less can it be argued that the records of other nations, so far as they have any pretension to be considered historical, conflict with the chronology of the Bible. The Babylonians indeed, the Indians, and the Chinese, in their professed histories of ancient times, carry back the antiquity of our race for several hundred thousand years. But it is admitted that in every case these large numbers are purely mythical; and, in truth, the authentic *histories* of all these nations begin even later than the Egyptian. India has no historical documents earlier than the third,† or China than the sixth century B.C. Indian history scarcely goes back beyond the time of Alexander; Chinese is not thought by those who place most faith in the early literature of the country to ascend any higher than the year B.C. 2637.‡ The Babylonian historian, Berosus, while he claimed for the human race an antiquity of above 466,000 years, arranged his dynasties in such a way as to make it palpable that the historic period began, at the earliest, in B.C. 2458. This is the conclusion of Sir Henry Rawlinson in England, of Gutschmid and Brandis in Germany.§ These critics divide the nine

* Ibid. p. 507.

† See the late Professor Wilson's Introduction to the 'Rig-Veda Sanhita,' pp. xlvi., xlvii.

‡ Remusat, 'Nouveaux Mélanges Asiatiques,' vol. i. p. 65; Bunsen, 'Egypt,' vol. iii. pp. 379–407.

§ Gutschmid, 'Rheinisches Museum,' vol. viii. p. 252 et seqq.; Brandis, 'Rerum Assyriarum Tempora emendata,' pp. 16, 17.

dynasties of Berosus into two mythic ones (reigning the extravagant periods of 432,000 and 34,080 years), and seven historic ones, all reigning moderate and possible periods, varying between 87 and 526 years. It might have seemed incredible that in the nineteenth century any critic could take a different view. M. Bunsen, however, believing that he has "devised a method"* whereby the historical part of the second dynasty, which he arbitrarily divides, may be reduced to 1550 years, adds that space of time to Berosus' historic chronology, and decides that the regular registration of the oldest Chaldæan kings commenced B.C. 3784. He thus assumes the partially historic character of a dynasty said to have reigned more than 34,000 years, two kings of which—Chomasbelus and Evechius—are made to occupy the throne for above 5000 years! It seems needless to examine the "method" whereby, from data thus manifestly unhistoric, an exact conclusion, claiming to be historically certain, is drawn.†

On the whole it would seem that no profane history of an authentic character mounts up to an earlier date than the 27th or 28th century before Christ. Egyptian history begins about B.C. 2700; Chinese, perhaps, in B.C. 2637; Babylonian in B.C. 2458; Assyrian in B.C. 1273; Greek, with the Trojan War, in B.C. 1250, or, perhaps, with Hercules, a century earlier; Lydian in B.C. 1229; Phœnician about the same period;‡ Carthaginian in B.C. 880; Macedonian about B.C. 720; Median not before B.C. 708; Roman in the middle of the same century; Persian in B.C. 558; Indian, about B.C. 350; Mexican and Peruvian not till after our era.§

* 'Egypt,' vol. iv. p. 411.

† One method, however, whereby M. Bunsen exaggerates his Babylonian chronology seems worthy of notice. It is the method of *mistranslation*. Philo Byblius having observed in his work about Cities that Babylon was founded 1002 years (ἔτεσι χιλίοις δύο) before Semiramis, M. Bunsen renders the words in brackets by "*two thousand* years," thus gaining for his chronology near a thousand years at a stroke. (See his 'Egypt,' vol. iv. p. 414, and again p. 491.)

‡ See the writer's 'Herodotus,' vol. iv. p. 249. The first known Phœnician king is Abibal, the father of Hiram, David's contemporary. He cannot be placed earlier than B.C. 1100.

§ See Prescott, 'History of the Conquest of Mexico,' vol. i. p. 13; 'History of the Conquest of Peru,' vol. i. pp. 10–14.

The oldest human constructions remaining upon the earth are the Pyramids, and these date from about B.C. 2400;* the brick temples of Babylonia seem, none of them, earlier than B.C. 2300;† B.C. 2000 would be a high date for the first Cyclopian walls in Greece or Italy; the earliest rock inscriptions belong to nearly the same period. If man has existed upon the earth ten or twenty thousand years, as M. Bunsen supposes, why has he left no vestiges of himself till within the last five thousand?‡ It cannot be said that his earlier works would necessarily have perished; for there is nothing to hinder the Pyramids or the Birs Nimrud from standing several thousand years longer. It is remarked that in Egypt the most ancient monuments exhibit but slight traces of rudeness, and that the arts within two centuries of Menes are in a very advanced condition, so that civilisation must have made great progress even before the age of Menes. But "the constitutional development of Egyptian life" into the condition reached in the time of the early monuments, does not require a term of five or six *thousand* years, as M. Bunsen argues,§ but rather one of five or six *hundred* years, which is what the Biblical numbers will allow. There is nothing surprising in a high civilisation, even within a very short time from the Deluge; for the arts of life, which flourished in the ante-diluvian world,‖ would have been preserved by those who survived the catastrophe, and might rapidly revive among their descendants. Rather, it is surprising that, except in Egypt, there should be so few traces of an early civilisation. Babylonian art, for many cen-

* Wilkinson in the writer's 'Herodotus,' vol. ii. p. 343; Stuart Poole in the 'Biblical Dictionary,' vol. i. p. 508.

† Sir H. Rawlinson in the writer's 'Herodotus,' vol. i. p. 435.

‡ The "flint weapons in the drift," and Mr. Horner's Egyptian pottery, will be said to be such vestiges. But the extremely doubtful age of the latter has been well shown by the 'Quarterly Review' (No. 210, pp. 419–421). The value of the former as evidence of extreme human antiquity must depend on two questions, neither of which has yet been solved—1. Are they of the same age as the formation in which they are found? and 2. Is that formation itself of an antiquity very remote? It has been clearly shown by a writer in 'Blackwood's Magazine' (No. 540, pp. 422–439), that the high antiquity of the drift is at any rate "not proven."

§ 'Egypt,' vol. iv. p. 571.

‖ Gen. iv. 20–22.

turies after the first establishment of the kingdom (B.C. 2458), is exceedingly rude and primitive; the Greek and Italian buildings, approaching to the same date, are of the roughest construction; it is not till about the year B.C. 1000 that a really advanced civilisation appears in any part of Asia, nor much before B.C. 600 that it can be traced in Europe. Thus, monumental and historical evidence alike indicate that the "Origines" of our race are recent, and the dates established on anything like satisfactory evidence, fall, in every case, within the time allowed to post-diluvian man by Scripture.

For the date of the Deluge, which we are most justified in drawing from the Sacred documents, is not, as commonly supposed, B.C. 2348, but rather B.C. 3099, or even B.C. 3159—sixty years earlier.* The modern objectors to the Chronology of Scripture seek commonly to tie down their opponents to the present Hebrew text;† but there is no reason why they should submit to this restriction. The Septuagint Version was regarded as of primary authority during the first ages of the Christian Church: it is the version commonly quoted in the New Testament; and thus, where it differs from the Hebrew, it is at least entitled to equal attention. The larger chronology of the Septuagint would, therefore, even if it stood alone, have as good a claim as the shorter one of the Hebrew text, to be considered the Chronology of Scripture. It does not, however, stand alone. For the period between the Flood and Abraham, the Septuagint has the support of another ancient and independent version—the Samaritan. It is argued that the Septuagint numbers were enlarged by the Alexandrian Jews in order to bring the Hebrew chronology into harmony with the Egyptian;‡ but there is no conceivable reason why the Samaritans should have altered their Pentateuch in this direction, and no

* See the 'Biblical Dictionary,' sub voc. CHRONOLOGY, and Mr. W. Palmer's 'Egyptian Chronicles,' p. 896.

† Bunsen, 'Egypt,' vol. iv. p. 402; 'Westminster Review,' No. 38, p. 569; 'Essays and Reviews,' pp. 54, 55.

‡ 'Westminster Review,' l. s. c.; Bunsen, 'Egypt,' vol. i. p. 185; vol. iv. p. 396.

very ready mode of accounting for the identity* of the numbers in these two versions, but by supposing that they are the real numbers of the original. This identity it has been usual to keep out of sight; but it is a most important feature in the case, and furnishes a solid ground for preferring, apart from all historical considerations, that longer system of Biblical Chronology with which Egyptian and all other profane history is found to be in accordance.

Besides the purely historic objections to the Biblical Chronology which have been here examined, another semi-historic one has been recently taken, which seems to require some notice. Languages, it is said, bear traces of having all proceeded from a common stock. Time was, when "the whole earth was of one language and of one speech."† But this time must have been immensely remote. Languages grow but slowly. It has taken nearly 2000 years to develop modern French, Italian, and Spanish out of Latin. Must it not have taken much longer to develop Latin, Greek, German, Celtic, Slavonic, Zend, Sanscrit, out of their mother-speech? And that mother-speech itself which had an affinity, and so a connexion, with the Semitic and Turanian forms of language, yet was far more widely separated from them than its daughter tongues from one another, what a vast period must have been required for its formation and divergence from the other linguistic types! Even the primitive tongue itself did not spring to its full height at once, or reach the era of decay and change till after a long term of years. Twenty-one thousand years—"the period of one great revolution of the globe upon its axis"—is (we are told) "a very probable term for the development of human language in the shortest line;" and so the conclusion is drawn, that the true era of man's creation is not B.C. 9085, when Egyptian history is said to have

* The identity is *complete*, if we reject from the Septuagint the false reading of some copies (179 for 79) in Gen. xi. 24, and omit the interpolated Cainan, who was unknown to Philo, Josephus, Theophilus of Antioch, and Eusebius. (See Clinton's 'Fasti Hellenici,' vol. i. p. 287; 'Biblical Dictionary,' vol. i. p. 819.)

† Gen. xi. 1.

begun, nor B.C. 14,000, when Hamitism and Semitism were first "deposited," but six thousand years before the earlier of these two dates—B.C. 20,000 !*

This argument claims an inductive character. It bases itself on the historical ground, that a certain number of years have been required for the development of French, Italian, Spanish, Wallachian, &c., out of Latin; and assumes that from this the rate of change or growth in language is determinately, or approximately, known. The rate is viewed as relative to the degree of change or divergence, so that as Celtic, Slavonic, German, Greek, Latin, and Sanscrit are far more unlike one another than French, Italian, and Spanish, a far longer period must be allowed for their formation.† The argument thus gathers strength at each stage; and as there are at least four stages, the formula becomes something very much like this :—$a+10a+100a+1000a=s$; so that it may seem a moderate estimate to say, that $s=21{,}000$ years.

But the following considerations detract from the force of the reasoning. The induction on which it rests is from a single instance—the case of Latin and its daughter tongues. It does not at all follow, that because a particular language under particular circumstances took a certain time to blossom into new tongues; therefore, every other language of a similar type, would, under all conceivable circumstances, do the same.

The unit which is assumed to be known, and which is made the basis of the whole calculation—the a of the above equation—is in reality unknown. It is impossible to say how long it took for Latin to change into French or Italian. Latin was probably imperfectly learnt by the Italians and the Gauls from the first, and a language far more like Italian than classical Latin was probably spoken in the provinces of Italy at a very early date. We know at the utmost what the date is

* Bunsen, 'Egypt,' vol. iv. pp. 560–566, and p. 485.

† "If the step from Latin to Italian be taken as a unit, the previous step must be reckoned *at least at ten or at twenty*." (Bunsen's 'Egypt,' vol. iv. pp. 562, 563.)

of the first extant French or Italian document. We have no means of deciding when French or Italian first began to be a spoken tongue.

The argument assumes as certain that equal linguistic changes must have occupied equal periods of time at all portions of the world's history, which is much the same as to assume that constitutional changes in states must be equal in equal times; or that, because B, a youth of eighteen, 5 ft. 10 in. high, grew half an inch between the 1st of January, 1860, and the 1st of January, 1861, therefore he grew at the same rate all his previous lifetime. Such an assumption, were it applied to discover the age of the youth by one who possessed no other data, might lead to the conclusion that he verged upon 140! It is quite possible that similar reasoning, applied to the age of language, may have produced a term of years almost equally in excess of the truth.

Not only the analogy of growth generally, but certain known linguistic facts favour the view, that when language was still young, it grew with a rapidity quite unknown to its later stages. Nothing so much tends to fix and stereotype a language as a literature. When, therefore, there was as yet no literature to keep the vagaries of speech in check, it would have been in a perpetual flux and change, and may, in a comparatively short space, have undergone the greatest modifications. Again, when literature is wanting, yet men live together in political communities of a large size, the requirements of social intercourse with a wide circle act as a safeguard against rapid dialectical change. But in the simpler and earlier times, before such communities were formed, when men were chiefly or wholly homades, and lived in small and isolated bodies without much intercourse with one another, this check would not have existed. Linguistic changes may, under such circumstances, have taken place with extraordinary quickness, and a growth equal to that, which would in later times, and under other circumstances, have required five hundred or a thousand years, may have been contained within an ordinary lifetime. "Tribes," says Professor M. Müller, "who have no literature, and no sort of intellectual occupation, seem occasionally to take a delight in working their language to the highest pitch of grammatical expansion. The American dialects are a well-known instance; and the greater the seclusion of a tribe, the more amazing the rank vegetation of their grammar. We can, at present, hardly form a correct idea with what feeling a savage nation looks upon its language; whether, it may be, as a plaything, a kind of intellectual amusement—a maze in which the mind likes to lose and to find itself. But the result is the same everywhere. If the work of agglutination has once commenced, and there is nothing like literature or society to keep it within limits, two villages, separated only for a few generations, will become mutually unintelligible. This takes place in America, as well as on the borders of China and India; and in the north of Asia, Messerschmidt relates, that the Ostiakes, though really speaking the same language everywhere, have produced so many words and forms peculiar to each tribe, that even within the limits of twelve or twenty German miles, conversation between them becomes extremely difficult. It must be remembered also, that the Dictionary of these languages is small, if compared with a Latin or a Greek Thesaurus. The conversation of nomadic tribes moves within a narrow circle; and with the great facility of forming new words at random, and the great inducement that a solitary life holds out to invent for the objects which form the world of a shepherd or huntsman, new appellations—half poetical, perhaps, or satirical—we can understand how, after a few generations, the dictionary of a nomadic tribe may have gone, as it were, through more than one edition."* These observations, which are made in reference to Turanian dialects, have a more extended bearing. They show that while the inhabitants of the earth continued nomadic, and without a literature, language would

* 'Philosophy of Universal History,' vol. iii. p. 483.

alter at a rate very much beyond that which is found to prevail since they have gathered into large communities, each with its own treasure of written law, legend, or history.

Further, it is obvious to remark that the whole argument turns upon a theory of language, which can never be anything more than an hypothesis—a theory, moreover, which ignores altogether the confusion of Babel, ascribing as it does *all* the changes and diversities of human speech to the operation of natural causes. Those persons who believe the miracle recorded in Gen. xi. 1–9, will see that if the Divine fiat produced in a moment of time a number of diversities of speech, which in the natural course of things would only have gradually been developed, language cannot but present the appearance of being older than it really is.

It seems, therefore, that nothing has really been as yet discovered, either in the facts of history, or in those of language, that militates against the chronological scheme of Scripture, if we regard the Septuagint and Samaritan versions as the best exponents of the original text in respect of the genealogy of the Patriarchs from Shem to Abraham. Whether the chronology of these versions admits of further expansion; whether, since the chronologies of the Hebrew Bible, the Samaritan Pentateuch, and the Septuagint differ, we can depend on any one of them; or whether we must not consider that this portion of revelation has been lost to us by the mistakes of copyists or the intentional alterations of systematisers, it is not necessary at present to determine. "Our treasure," as before observed, "is in earthen vessels." The revealed Word of God has been continued in the world in the same way as other written compositions, by the multiplication of copies. No miraculous aid is vouchsafed to the transcribers, who are liable to make mistakes, and may not always have been free from the design of bending Scripture to their own views. That we have a wonderfully pure and perfect text of the Pentateuch, considering its antiquity, is admitted; but doubts must ever attach to the chronology, not only because in all ancient MSS. numbers are especially liable to accidental corruption, but also, and more especially, from the fact that there is so wide a difference in this respect between the Hebrew, the Samaritan, and the Greek copies.* Still, at present, we have no need to suppose that the numbers have in every case suffered. All the requirements of profane history are sufficiently met by the adoption of the Septuagint and Samaritan date for the Deluge; and this is the date which is really most authoritative, since it has in its favour two out of the three ancient versions.

II. An authentic character is denied to the Pentateuch on account of the narrative contained in it of the great Flood. This narrative is viewed as the traditional representation of a real event, but as unhistoric in most of its details, and more especially as untrue in regard to the assertion which is so strongly made, that all mankind, except a single family, were destroyed on the occasion.† The Deluge, it is said, was local, affecting only that portion of Asia in which were located the Arians and the Semites. It did not extend to the Egyptians, or to the Chinese, or to the Turanian races generally. This conclusion is professedly drawn from "the infallible linguistic science," ‡ or, in other words, from those views of the history of language, the changes it has undergone, and the time occupied by them, which have been just shown to be arbitrary and not very tenable hypotheses. It is further regarded as confirmed by the alleged fact, that while among most of the Semitic and Arian races there was a distinct and clear tradition of the Flood, as among the Babylonians, the Indians, the Armenians, the Phrygians, the Lithuanians, the Goths, the Celts, and the Greeks; neither in China, nor in Egypt, nor among the "old Turani-

* Although in the list of patriarchs from Shem to Abraham, the Samaritan and the Septuagint coincide, they differ widely in the preceding list from Adam to Noah. The Samaritan has there a term of years even shorter than the Hebrew.

† Gen. vii. 21–23. ‡ Bunsen, 'Egypt,' vol. iv. p. 472, and p. 559.

ans" was any such tradition current. Here the argument is strong; but it attains its strength by a combination of exaggeration on the one side, with understatement on the other. It is not true that "we find allusions to the Flood *everywhere* among the Iranians and Semites."* The Flood does not appear in the Zendavesta; it was not, so far as is known, among the traditions of the Arabs, or the Phœnicians, or the Romans, or the Slaves. On the other hand, traditions of it were not entirely wanting in China, in Egypt, or among the Turanians.

The Chinese speak of a "first heaven"—an age of innocence, when "the whole creation enjoyed a state of happiness; when everything was beautiful, everything was good; all beings were perfect in their kind;" whereto succeeded a "second heaven," introduced by a great convulsion. "The pillars of heaven were broken—the earth shook to its foundations—the heavens sunk lower towards the north—the sun, the moon, and the stars changed their motions—the earth fell to pieces; and *the waters enclosed within its bosom burst forth with violence, and overflowed it.* Man having rebelled against heaven, the system of the universe was totally disordered. The sun was eclipsed, the planets altered their courses, and the grand harmony of nature was disturbed."†

In Egypt, according to Plato, the teaching of the priests was, not that there had been no Deluge, but that there had been several. They believed that from time to time, in consequence of the anger of the Gods, the earth was visited by a terrible catastrophe. The agent of destruction was sometimes fire, sometimes water. In the conflagrations, all countries were burnt up but Egypt, which was protected by the Nile; and in the deluges, all were submerged except Egypt, where rain never fell. The last catastrophe, they said, had been a deluge; it took place above 8000 years before Solon, and not only swept away the Greeks, as they were themselves aware, but permanently submerged a vast

* Bunsen, 'Egypt,' vol. iv. p. 464.
† Faber, 'Horæ Mosaicæ,' ch. iv. pp. 147, 148.

island in the Atlantic Ocean, previously the seat of a great conquering monarchy.* It does not destroy the traditional character of these latter statements, that they are coupled with a theory of repeated mundane catastrophes; neither does it much lessen the value of the evidence, in the case of a people making such absurd pretensions to antiquity as the Egyptians, that Egypt is supposed to have been exempt from the general ruin. M. Bunsen admits that the oldest traditions of Egypt "seem here and there to retain the echoes of a knowledge of some violent convulsions in nature,"† while he denies that these traditions constitute a reminiscence of the historical Flood. It is at least as reasonable to hold that the one convulsion of which they had some real knowledge was that great catastrophe, and that in regard to the rest they merely represented historically the conclusions at which they had arrived by speculation.

With regard to the belief of the Turanian races, it may be true that those of Europe and Asia have no traditions of a Deluge among them, although this point has hardly been as yet sufficiently established; but if we hold (as is now commonly done)‡ the Malays to be a Turanian offshoot, and the Polynesian islanders to be Malays, then it must be allowed that traces of a belief in the Deluge exist also in this ethnic family. "Traditions of the Deluge," says Mr. Ellis, "have been found to exist among the natives of the South Sea Islands, from the earliest periods of their history. . . . The principal facts are the same in the traditions prevailing among the inhabitants of the different groups, although they differ in several minor particulars. In one group the accounts stated, that in ancient times Taarsa, the principal god according to their mythology, being angry with men on account of their disobedience to his will, overturned the world into the sea, when the earth sunk in the waters, excepting a few projecting points, which, remaining above its surface, constituted the present clus-

* 'Timæus,' p. 21. † 'Egypt,' vol. iv. p. 559.

‡ M. Müller, in the 'Philosophy of Universal History,' vol. iii. pp. 403–429; 'Languages of the Seat of War,' p. 110, 1st edition.

ter of islands. The memorial preserved by the inhabitants of Eimeo states, that after the inundation of the land, when the water subsided, a man landed from a canoe near Tiataepua in their island, and erected an altar in honour of his god. The tradition which prevails in the Leeward Islands is intimately connected with the island of Raiatea." Here the story is that a fisherman disturbed the sea-god with his hooks, whereupon the god determined to destroy mankind. The fisherman, however, obtained mercy, and was directed to take refuge in a certain small islet, whither he betook himself with his wife, his child, one friend, and specimens of all the domestic animals. The sea then rose, and submerged the other islands, destroying all the inhabitants. But the fisherman and his companions were unharmed, and afterwards removing from their islet to Raiatea became the progenitors of the present people.* Thus, if the South Sea Islanders belong to the Turanian family, it would seem that that family, no less than the Arian and Semitic, has reminiscences of the Great Catastrophe which once befel mankind.†

The result is, that there is no marked difference, in respect of traditions of the Deluge, between the different races of men. No race is without some tradition on the subject, while in none is the tradition spread universally among all the nations into which the race subdivides. Various circumstances have caused the event to be vividly or faintly apprehended, to be stored in the memory of a nation, or to be allowed to fade from it. If the Semitic tradition is the clearest and most circumstantial, while the Turanian is the dimmest and slightest, it is probably because the Turanians generally were without a literature, while among the Semites the tradition took a written form early. If in Egypt, while the Deluge is not unknown, it makes little figure, notwithstanding the early use of letters in that country, it is perhaps because the Egyptians did not choose to keep it in mind, since,

* 'Polynesian Researches,' vol. ii. pp. 57–59.

† The Mexicans and Peruvians, who had very clear traditions of the Flood, were also probably of Turanian origin.

in their desire to be considered autochthonous and of immense antiquity, they seem to have determinately severed all the links which connected them with their primitive Asiatic abodes.* If, on the contrary, among the Arians, though they had no very early literature, the reminiscence is vivid, it may be ascribed to the liveliness, impressibility, and poetic tone of their minds, which such an event as the Deluge was calculated to affect strongly, and to their comparative honesty, which led them to cherish in most cases the traditions uniting them with primitive times.

III. The objections taken to the ethnology of Genesis are limited to two. It is allowed that a high antiquity, and a great historical value, belong to the Toldoth Beni Noah, or "Book of the generations of the sons of Noah," which forms the tenth chapter of the First Book of Moses. But it is maintained that in its present state this chapter is the work of a "compiler," who misunderstood his materials, and that it requires correction from the better knowledge of the moderns.† The two mistakes which are especially charged on the document are—first, that, by making Canaan a son of Ham, it connects the Canaanites ethnically with the Egyptians, whereas they were an entirely distinct people, not Hamites, but Semites; and secondly, that, by declaring Cush to have begotten Nimrod, it makes that conqueror and his kingdom Ethiopian, whereas they were in reality Cossæan, and so Turanian or Scythic. In the latter case it is supposed that the "compiler" was misled by a resemblance of words; in the former, that he misinterpreted a geographical fact ethnically.

But the latest research tends to vindicate the ethnol-

* "The evidence of the Egyptians," says Mr. Stuart Poole, "as to the primeval history of their race and country is extremely indefinite. .... There is a very short and extremely obscure time of tradition, and at no great distance from the earliest date at which it can be held to end we come upon the clear light of history in the days of the Pyramids. The indications are of a sudden change of seat, and the settlement in Egypt of a civilized race, which, either wishing to be believed autochthonous, or having lost all ties that could keep up the traditions of its first dwelling-place, filled up the commencement of its history with materials drawn from mythology." ('Biblical Dictionary,' vol. i. p. 507.)

† Bunsen, 'Egypt,' vol. iv. p. 417.

ogy of Genesis in both the disputed cases. The supposed Semitic character of the Canaanites rests upon two grounds—first, their presumed identity with the Phœnicians, and secondly, the Semitic etymology of certain Canaanitish names—e.g. Melchisedek, Abimelech, Adonibezek, Mamre, Eshcol, Kirjath-Arba, &c. This last argument is undoubtedly important, though it is far from decisive. For, firstly, language is not a certain sign of race, since occasionally a nation has adopted a completely foreign tongue. Secondly, the names, as given in the Hebrew Scriptures, are perhaps not Canaanitish words at all, but only the Semitic equivalents of the native (Hamitic) terms. Thirdly, the true stock of the Canaanites may have been Hamitic, yet even before the time of Abraham they may have received a Semitic infusion from the valley of the Euphrates; and Semitic names may thus have been introduced among them. As for the other argument, though it has great names in its favour, there is really very little to be said for it. Phœnicia, as a country, is distinguishable from Canaan, in which it may, perhaps, have been included, but of which it was at any rate only a part; and the Phœnician people present in many respects a strong and marked contrast to the Canaanites, so that there is great reason to believe that they were an entirely different race.* That their ethnic character was really Hamitic seems to be indicated by the Babylonian tradition in Eupolemus, † that Canaan was the grandfather of Cush and Mestraim (Mizraim). It is further evidenced by the names of various places in their country, as Baalbek, "the *house* of Baal," where *bek* is the Egyptian root found in Atarbechis, "the

* See the writer's 'Herodotus,' vol. iv. pp. 243–245, where the point is argued at length. "The Canaanites," it is noted, "are fierce and intractable warriors, rejoicing in the prancing steeds and chariots of iron, neither given to commerce nor to any of the arts of peace; the Phœnicians are quiet and peaceable, a nation of traffickers, skilful in navigation and in the arts both useful and ornamental; unwarlike except at sea, and wholly devoted to commerce. Again, whereas between the real Canaanites and the Jews there was deadly and perpetual hostility, until the former were utterly rooted out and destroyed, the Jews and Phœnicians were on terms of perpetual amity,—an amity encouraged by the best princes, who would scarcely have contracted a friendship with the accursed race."

† 'Fragm. Hist. Gr.' vol. iii. p. 212.

house of Athor"—Marathus, which seems to be *Martu*, the Hamitic term for "the West"—Beth-shan, which in Semitic was Beth-shemesh, "the house of the sun," &c. Finally, it is thought to be absolutely proved by the Hittite names, which occur abundantly in the Assyrian inscriptions, and which are found to be unmistakably of a Hamitic type and formation.

The Cushite descent of the Babylonians has still more ample evidence in its favour. Linguistic research, harmonising in this instance at once with classical tradition and with the Scriptural account, shows the *early* Babylonians to have been, not only Hamitic, but determinately of Cushite origin. * All the ancient Babylonian documents are in a dialect, the vocabulary of which has a closer connexion with the native languages of Abyssinia than with any other known form of speech. Nor is this a mere coincidence. The evidence of monuments (Himyaric, Chaldean, and Susian) shows, that a homogeneous race was spread in very ancient times from the country upon the Upper Nile, along the southern coast of Arabia, to the shores of the Persian Gulf, and thence into Susiana, whence it probably passed, by way of Gedrosia, to India. M. Bunsen decides that "an Asiatic Kush (or Ethiopia) exists only in the imagination of Biblical interpreters, and is the child of their despair." † But ancient lore and modern research are equally against this view. Homer knew the Ethiopians to be "divided," and to dwell "towards the rising and the setting sun." ‡ Hesiod made Memnon, the son of the Dawn, and the traditional founder of Susa, an Ethiopian king. § Pindar taught that this same Memnon brought an army of Ethiopians to the relief of Troy. ‖ Herodotus was told of Asiatic Ethiopians as contained within the Persian empire, and assigned them their place in the satrapies of Darius, ¶ and in the army of Xerxes.** Ephorus gave all the

* Sir H. Rawlinson, in the writer's 'Herodotus,' vol. i. p. 442, *note:* compare Kalisch, 'Comment. on Genesis,' p. 174, E. T.

† 'Philosophy of Universal History,' vol. iii. p. 191.

‡ 'Odyssey,' i. 23, 24.

§ 'Theogonia,' 984, 985.

‖ 'Nemea,' iii. 62, 63.

¶ Herod. iii. 94.

** Ibid. vii. 70.

shores of the Erythræan Sea, or Southern Ocean, to the Ethiopians;* and so, according to Strabo, did the ancient Greek writers generally.† The names Kissia, and Kossæa, Kusan,‡ and Kutch or Kooch, which have clung to portions of the south coast of Asia, from the time of Herodotus to the present day, confirm the classical belief—a belief which is further evidenced by the genealogists, who almost universally connect Belus, the mythic progenitor of the Babylonians, with Ægyptus and Libya.§ Thus the Asiatic Ethiopia, which is mentioned more than once in Scripture,‖ is no guess or myth, but an established fact; and to this Ethiopia it appears that both early Babylon and the neighbouring countries of Susiana and Southern Arabia belonged.

The "Toldoth Beni Noah," therefore, instead of proving incorrect on the two points where its accuracy has been most recently challenged, is found in regard to them singularly to accord with the latest results of philological and ethnological research.¶ Indeed that document, which has been well called "the most authentic record that we possess for the affiliation of races,"** is continually receiving fresh illustration and confirmation from the progress of modern discovery, and is probably destined to become, as time goes on, a continually stronger evidence of the historic accuracy of Genesis.

IV. Of all the attempts made to invalidate the historical character of the Pentateuch, the boldest is that which, starting from an observation of the resemblance of the names given in the two genealogies of the Sethites and the Cainites,†† proceeds to argue that they are

* Ap. Strab. i. 2, § 28. † Strab. i. 2, § 27.

‡ Kusan was the name given to the country east of Kerman throughout the whole of the Sassanian period.

§ Pherecyd. Fr. 40; Charax Perg. ap. Steph. Byz. s. voc. Αἴγυπτος; Apollodor. ii. 1, § 4; Eupolemus ap. Alex. Polyhist. Fr. 3; Johann. Antiochen. Fr. 6, § 15.

‖ Gen. ii. 13; Ezek. xxxviii. 5.

¶ In connexion with this subject Mr. R. S. Poole's articles on 'The Canaanites,' and 'Cush' in Dr. Smith's 'Biblical Dictionary,' are recommended to the reader's attention.

** Sir H. Rawlinson in the 'Journal of the Asiatic Society,' vol. xv. p. 230.

†† Gen. iv. 17–22; Gen. v. 3–32.

really representations of one and the same list, with variations in the order and in the orthography, which variations destroy the authority of both, and show that nothing has come down to us but a document founded on "a misunderstanding of the earliest records."* "Not having one tradition, but two," we have, it is argued, in reality, "no historical account." We may, therefore, suppose that neither list contains any actual genealogy at all. We may view the names as ideal or mythical, significative of notions, nations, or epochs; and we may then construct a history of the Old World according to our fancy, with very little check indeed upon our faculty of invention.

Now the facts of the case are simply, that in the two genealogies, which differ both at the beginning and at the end, six consecutive names occur, of which two are identical, while the remaining four have more or less of resemblance. These names are Cain, Enoch, Irad, Mehujael, Methusael, and Lamech in the one list; Cainan, Mahalaleel, Jared, Enoch, Methuselah, and Lamech in the other. The names Enoch and Lamech (it will be seen) occur in both lists; of the rest, Cain resembles Cainan; Irad, Jared; Mehujael, Mahalaleel; and Methusael, Methuselah. The resemblance, however, is in the Hebrew scarcely so great as in the Authorized Version. Irad differs from Jared by an initial letter of peculiar importance, the Hebrew *ain* (ע), which had a strong guttural sound, and is rarely lost.† Mahalaleel differs from Mehujael by one entire element out of the two which make it up; it is really no nearer to Mehujael than Theodosius to Theophilus, or Jeroboam to Jerubbaal. In Methusael, and Methuselah, again, the concluding element is different, there being probably no connection between the *sael* or *sha'el* of the one and the *selah* or *shelach* of the other. Further, there is a considerable difference in the order which

* 'Egypt's Place,' vol. iv. p. 395.

† In the LXX. the *ain* is represented by the Greek γ. There the two names scarcely retain any resemblance at all, being respectively Iared (Ἰάρεδ) and Gaïdad (Γαϊδάδ). The copies used by the LXX. evidently had ד in the place of ר.

the names hold in the two lists; and of this difference no account has been even attempted. The second name in the Cainite list is the fourth in the list of the Sethites; and conversely the fourth among the Cainites is a name resembling the second name among the Sethites. Hence, if we allow the names to correspond, we must say that the two lists agree in no single relationship, except only that of the last pair. Cain is the son of Adam and father of Enoch; but Cainan is the son of Enos and father of Mahalaleel. Enoch the Cainite is the son of Cain and father of Irad; but Enoch the Sethite is the son of Jared and father of Methuselah. Irad is son of Enoch and father of Mehujael; but Jared is son of Mahalaleel and father of Enoch. Finally, Methusael is son of Mehujael, but Methuselah of Enoch; and Lamech the Sethite is father of Noah, but Lamech the Cainite, of Jabal, Jubal, and Tubal-Cain. Altogether, while the amount of resemblance in the two lists is certainly remarkable, the amount of diversity is such as very clearly to distinguish them from one another. Where confusion was most likely to ensue—that is to say, in the cases of the two identical names of Enoch and Lamech—the narrative in one or the other list is fuller and more detailed than usual, apparently for the very purpose of guarding against the mistake of identification. All, therefore, that can fairly be concluded is, that in the two families of the Sethites and the Cainites, as in the two kingdoms of Israel and Judah,* similar appellations, and to some extent the same appellations, prevailed. It would seem that at first men were slow to invent new names, and either used the old names over again or modified them slightly. Thus we have *Enos* and *Enoch*, *Adam* and *Adah*,† *Jabal*, *Jubal*, and *Tubal*-Cain, where no one suggests an identification. Probably names were considered of great importance, and the experiment of an entirely new name was not readily made.

* Taking the five consecutive and contemporary monarchs of these two kingdoms, who follow upon Ahab and Jehoshaphat, we find three names common to the two lists.

† The resemblance is less in the Hebrew, but still it is real.

The mythical character of this same portion of the Biblical history has been further based upon certain supposed etymologies. Seth, we are informed, represents, not a man, but God Himself, since Set or Sutekh was an old Oriental root for God, and Set or Suti continued to be an Egyptian deity.* Enos is the same as Adam, since in Aramaic it means "man," as Adam does in Hebrew.† Neither are real names of persons, but only ideal appellations for the first founder of our race. Enoch, "the seer of God," represents a religious period intervening between the time of the marauder Cain, and that of the agricultural builder of cities Irad.‡ At the same time he is "the solar year," since the number of years which he is said to have lived coincides exactly with the number of days in that division of time.§ Cain and Irad are the respective types of the nomadic shepherd races and the agricultural dwellers in towns. The other patriarchs also represent epochs; and Nahor, the grandfather of Abraham, is the first real Biblical man.‖

It is clear that all history whatsoever may be made to evaporate under such treatment as this. If we may guess at etymologies, and then at once assume our guesses to be coincident with truth; if we may regard all significant names as mythic, and the personages to whom they are assigned as ideal, there is no portion of the world's annals which may not with a very little ingenuity be transferred to the region of myth. A witty writer noted some ten years since the certainty that, if such views prevailed, a famous passage from the ecclesiastical history of our own time would be relegated by posterity to that shadowy region; for how could it be doubted that such names as Newman, Wiseman, Masterman, Philpotts, Wilde, were "fictitious appellations invented by an allegorist, either to set forth certain qualities or attributes of certain persons whose true names were concealed, or to embody certain tendencies

* Bunsen, 'Egypt,' vol. iv. p. 208.
† Ibid. p. 385.
‡ Ibid. p. 390.
§ Ibid. p. 389.
‖ Ibid. p. 409.

of the times, or represent certain party characteristics?"* Similarly it might be argued that Athenian history, from Draco to Pericles, is mythical—that Draco was intended to represent the bloody and cruel spirit of the old aristocracy, Cylon their *crooked* courses, Solon the first establishment of a *sole* authority (for it would seem to be thought allowable to draw a derivation from a cognate dialect), Pisistratus the usurpation in which a chief *persuaded an army* to help him, Hippias, Hipparchus, and Thessalus, the time when, with the aid of *Thessaly*, the *cavalry* service was first fully organised, Isagoras the establishment of *democracy*, Clisthenes the *triumph of physical strength*, Themistocles the *ascendancy of law*, Aristides the completion of the *best form* of government, Pericles the age when Athens attained her *full glory*. Where names are significant, and their etymology is accurately known, it is generally easy to bend them into agreement even with the actual history of the time. How much more easy must it be, when their signification is unknown, to affix a meaning on plausible grounds which shall square with our historical fancies!

But, it is said, the histories of all other nations run up into myth. Can the Hebrews be a solitary exception? This is simply to ask: Can there be direct revelation at all; or, in other words, can God or a Divine messenger speak to man face to face, as the prophets declare they were spoken to? If He can, there is certainly nothing to prevent the subject matter of His revelation from being historical. And the beginnings of human history might in this way be as well communicated as any other facts, past, present, or future. Nor is it at all impossible that the true history may have been handed down in one line by an undefiled tradition, while in all other lines it was corrupted. The laws which govern human action are general, not uni-

* 'Eclipse of Faith,' pp. 347, 348. The significance of two of the names belonging to this passage of our history gave occasion to the following couplet, written by a living scholar at the time of the "Papal Aggression":—

"Cum Sapiente Pius nostras juravit in aras:
Impius heu Sapiens insipiensque Pius!"

versal; and an exception is so much a matter of course that some regard it as "proving the rule." It is unphilosophical to assume, merely on the analogy of other nations, that the Hebrew "beginnings" are mythic. At the least, they ought first to be formally compared with the "beginnings" of those other nations, and only pronounced mythic if found to resemble them. Such a comparison has not been made at all fully as yet; and, if it were made, would exhibit the most striking diversity.* The "beginnings" of other races have an air of extravagance about them, a tone of quaintness and grotesqueness utterly alien from the "Origines" of the Hebrews. In the former gods have their heads cut off, or devour their children, or undergo marvellous transformations, or marry their mothers, or are fished up out of the sea by fishermen, or are otherwise set before us in ludicrous aspects, which take away all solemnity and seriousness from the narrative. How different from this is the simple and awful grandeur of Genesis! What a deep and solemn earnestness greets us in the very first words! What sustained seriousness do we find throughout! How evident that we are on holy ground, in the hands of a writer who does not dare to jest or sport with things divine, who is no fanciful allegorizer, weaving quaint fables to delight us as he instructs, but one who speaks as in the presence of God, with a simple reverent solemnity, incompatible with any conscious departure from literal truth! It is impossible to illustrate this subject to any large extent here; but the reader may gain, from the two passages placed below in parallel columns, a tolerably fair notion of the extent to which the "Origines" of other nations differ in tone from Genesis.

ACCOUNT OF THE CREATION FROM BEROSUS.†	ACCOUNT OF THE CREATION FROM GENESIS.‡
"In the beginning all was darkness and water, and therein	"In the beginning God created the heaven and the earth.

* M. Bunsen makes a very incomplete comparison in the fourth volume of his 'Egypt' (pp. 364–375). He cannot, however, even proceed so far as he has gone without being struck with the diversity here spoken of. (See p. 374.)

† Ap. Syncell. 'Chronograph.' vol. i. p. 53; compare Euseb. 'Chron. Can.' i. 2; pp. 11, 12, ed. Mai.

‡ Gen. i. 1–8; 24–27; ii. 7.

were generated monstrous animals of strange and peculiar forms. There were men with two wings, and others even with four, and with two faces: and others with two heads, a man's and a woman's, on one body; and there were men with the heads and the horns of goats, and men with hoofs like horses, and some with the upper parts of a man joined to the lower parts of a horse, like centaurs; and there were bulls with human heads, dogs with four bodies and with fishes' tails, men and horses with dogs' heads, &c., &c. A woman ruled them all, by name Omorka, which is the same as 'the sea.'

And the earth was without form and void; and darkness was upon the face of the deep. And the Spirit of God moved upon the face of the waters.

"And God said, Let there be light; and there was light. And God saw the light that it was good; and God divided the light from the darkness. And God called the light Day; and the darkness he called Night. And the evening and the morning were the first day.

"And Belus appeared, and split the woman in twain; and of the one half of her he made the heaven, and of the other half the earth; and the beasts that were in her he caused to perish. And he split the darkness, and divided the heaven and the earth asunder, and put the world in order; and the animals that could not bear the light perished.

"And God said, Let there be a firmament in the midst of the waters; and let it divide the waters from the waters. And God made the firmament, and divided the waters which were under the firmament from the waters which were above the firmament; and it was so. And God called the firmament Heaven. And the evening and the morning were the second day.

"And God said, Let the earth bring forth the living creature after his kind, cattle and creeping thing and beast of the earth after his kind; and it was so. And God made the beast of the earth after his kind, and cattle after their kind, and everything

	that creepeth upon the earth after his kind: and God saw that it was good.
"Belus, upon this, seeing that the earth was desolate, yet teeming with productive power, commanded one of the gods to cut off his head, and to mix the blood, which flowed forth, with earth, and form men therewith, and beasts that could bear the light. So man was made, and was intelligent, being a partaker of the Divine wisdom."	"And God said, Let us make man in our image, after our likeness; and let them have dominion over the fish of the sea, and over the fowl of the air, and over the cattle, and over all the earth, and over every creeping thing that creepeth upon the earth. So God created man in his own image; in the image of God created he him; male and female created he them. "And the Lord God formed man of the dust of the ground, and breathed into his nostrils the breath of life. And man became a living soul."

V. The longevity of the Patriarchs appears to modern critics "at variance with all the laws of human and animal organism," and therefore "as contrary to common sense as the notion of there being any real chronology in astronomical cycles of hundreds of thousands of years." * Men, we are told, *cannot ever* have lived more than 150, or, at the most, 200 years; and a document which assigns them lives of 300, 600, 800, and even 900 years, *must* be unhistorical, and is either, in respect of its numbers, worthless, or to be explained in some not very obvious way. This argument is supposed to be drawn from physiology, another of the "infallible sciences," which are held to lay down laws, not only for our practical guidance at the present day, but for our intellectual belief as to the occurrences of all past ages. In truth, however, the science of physiology has not spoken on the point before us. Its problem has been, not what length of time it is possible for man ever to have lived, but how long it is possible for him now to live under the present

* Bunsen, 'Egypt,' vol. iv. p. 391; compare Winer, 'Realwörterbuch,' vol. ii. p. 207; Bauer, 'Hebr. Mythologie,' vol. i. p. 197; Bredow, 'Untersuchungen,' vol. i. p. 1, &c.

circumstances of the earth, and in the present known condition of human bodies. And even this question it can only answer empirically. It finds the body to be a machine which wears out by use; but it fails to discover any definite rate at which the process of wearing out must proceed. In this difficulty, comparative physiology does not help it, for the law of longevity in the brute creation is capricious in the extreme. All the proposed standards of measurement—the period of gestation, the time occupied in growth, the size of the full-grown body—when applied to species severally, fail in certain instances. Physiology then can only say: These human bodies are mortal; death is inevitable; and, so far as modern testimony goes, men do not seem now able to resist the tendency to decay beyond the term of 150, or at the utmost 200 years. But the possible duration of life, when the species was but recently created, and had its vigour unimpaired by the taint of hereditary disease, is beyond the cognizance of physiological science, which, by the mouth of its most celebrated professors, declines to pronounce a positive judgment. The great Haller, when led to speak on the subject, declared the problem one which could not be solved, on account of the absence of sufficient data,* while Buffon accepted the Scriptural account, and thought he could see physical reasons why life should in the early ages have been so greatly extended.†

It cannot, therefore, be said with truth that the longevity of the Patriarchs is "at variance with all"—or indeed with any—"of the laws of human and animal organism." We do not know on what longevity depends; we could not possibly tell *à priori* whether man, or any other animal, would live one, ten, twenty, fifty, a hundred, or a thousand years. The whole question is one of fact, and so of evidence. Men now do not, except in very rare instances, exceed 100 years.

* "Problema ob paucitatem datorum insolubile." ('Element. Physiolog.' viii. § 21.)

† 'Histoire Naturelle de l'Homme,' Œuvres, vol. iv. pp. 358–361.

Was this always so, or was it once different? The Bible answers this question for us very clearly and decidedly, showing us that human life gradually declined, beginning with a term little short of a millennium, and by degrees contracting, till, in Moses' time, it had reached (apparently) its present limits — the days of man's age having become then "threescore years and ten," and only a few, "by reason of strength," reaching to fourscore years.* Does other historical testimony really run counter to this, and render it even hard to believe? or is it not the fact that all the evidence we have is in accordance with the Scriptural narrative, and strongly confirmatory of the statement that in the early ages human life was prolonged very much beyond its present term?

In the Hindoo accounts there are four ages of the world. In the first, man was free from diseases, and attained to the age of 400 years; in the second the term of life was reduced to 300 years; in the third it became 200; and in the fourth 100. The Babylonian traditions gave to their early monarchs reigns of between two and three thousand years. The Greeks told of a time when men were children till they reached a hundred.† Pliny mentions a number of authors, according to whom men had lived 300, 500, 600, and 800 years.‡ Josephus relates that the Egyptian, Phœnician, Babylonian, and Grecian historians united in declaring that there had been cases of persons living nearly 1000 years.§ It seems to be quite certain that a very wide-spread tradition existed in the ancient world, to the effect that the term of human life had been greatly abbreviated since man's first appearance upon the earth.

VI. The duration of the sojourn in Egypt, whether taken as 430 years, according to the apparent meaning of Ex. xii. 40, 41, or as 215 years, according to the traditional explanation of that passage, is thought to be unhistorical because of the impossibility (as it is

* Ps. xc. 10. The title of this psalm is "a prayer of *Moses*, the man of God."

† Hesiod, 'Op. et Dies,' 130, 131.

‡ 'Hist. Nat.' vii. 48.

§ 'Ant. Jud.' i. 3.

said) of a family of seventy persons having, even in the longer of the two periods, multiplied into two millions of souls. So strongly is this difficulty felt, that for a theologian not to perceive its force, is regarded as "one of the most melancholy signs of the times," reducing modern exegesis to a level with the absurdities of Rabbinical comment.* The chronology, it is argued, must of necessity require a very considerable expansion; and this it is proposed to give by substituting for the 430 years of Moses and St. Paul,† 1400, or (more exactly) 1427 years (!) as the real length of the interval between the going down of Jacob into Egypt and the Exodus under Moses.‡ But it is more easy to make a vague and general charge of absurdity against an adversary than to point out in what the absurdity with which he is taxed consists.§ No one asserts it to be naturally probable that such a company as went down with Jacob into Egypt would in 215, or even in 430 years, have become a nation possessing 600,000 fighting men. Orthodox commentators simply say that such an increase of numbers was *possible* even in the shortest of these terms. They note that Jacob brought into Egypt fifty-one grandsons, and that if, under the special blessing of God so repeatedly promised to Abraham,‖ his male descendants had continued to increase at the same rate, they would long within the specified period have reached the required number. In point of fact, they would in the fifth generation have exceeded 850,000, and in the sixth have amounted to six millions.¶ If God can bless

* Bunsen, 'Egypt,' vol. i. p. 179. † Gal. iii. 17.

‡ Bunsen, 'Egypt,' vol. iv. pp. 492, 493.

§ When M. Bunsen condescends to particularize, he falls himself into a remarkable error. Baumgarten had observed that, "if we deduct from the 70 souls who came into Egypt 14, viz. Jacob, his 12 sons, and Dinah, there remain 56 pair who produced children." M. Bunsen says this reminds him of Falstaff's mode of reckoning. But the reckoning is perfectly correct, since the "56 pair" who remain consist of the 56 *male* grandchildren and great-grandchildren of Jacob (who, together with the 14 deducted, make up the 70 souls), *and their wives*, who were additional to the 70. (See Gen. xlvi. 8–27.)

‖ Gen. xii. 2; xiii. 16; xvii. 4–6; xxii. 17.

¶ The average increase of the males in the two generations had been *more than* sevenfold each generation. A sevenfold increase would have given 857,157 males in the fifth generation, and 6,000,099 in the sixth.

with increase, if fecundity and life are His gifts, He might, by making every marriage fruitful and every child grow up, raise, even with greater rapidity than the record declares to have been done, a family into a nation. At the same time, as we are bound not to exaggerate the Divine interference with the ordinary course of nature beyond what is actually stated or implied in Scripture, it ought to be borne in mind that we have no need to suppose the 600,000 fighting men who quitted Egypt, though they are all called Israelites, to have been all descendants of Jacob. The members of the Patriarch's family came down into Egypt *with their households*.* What the size of the patriarchal households was, we may gather from that of Abraham, whose "trained servants born in his house" amounted to 318.† Nor was this an exceptional case. Esau met Jacob on his return from Padan-aram with 400 men, who were probably his servants, ‡ and Jacob at the same meeting had such a number that he could divide them into two "bands," or "armies" (מַחֲנוֹת). § It is not unlikely that the whole company which entered Egypt with Jacob amounted to above a thousand souls. ‖ As all were circumcised,¶ all would doubtless be considered Israelites; and their descendants would be reckoned to the tribes of their masters. Again, we must remember that polygamy prevailed among the Hebrews; and that though polygamy, if a nation lives by itself, is not favourable to rapid increase, yet, if foreign wives can be obtained in any number,** it is an institution by means of which population may be greatly augmented. A recent Shah of Persia is said to have left at his death nearly three thousand descendants; and it is a well-known fact that one of his sons had a body-guard of

* Gen. xlv. 18; Ex. i. 1.

† Gen. xiv. 14.

‡ Gen. xxxii. 6.

§ Gen. xxxii. 7.

‖ Kurtz thinks they must have consisted of "several thousands." ('Hist. of Old Covenant,' vol. ii. p. 149, E. T.)

¶ Gen. xvii. 12.

** The Israelites could probably have obtained wives from the lower castes of the Egyptians; also from the Midianites (Ex. ii. 21), the Libyans, and others.

sixty grown men, who all called him father.* Egypt, moreover, was a country where both men and animals are said to have been remarkably prolific;† where, therefore, natural law would have tended in the same direction as the special action of Divine Providence at this time. These considerations do not indeed reduce the narrative within the category of ordinary occurrences; but they diminish considerably from its extraordinariness. They show that at any rate there is no need to extend the period of the sojourn beyond the 430 years of the Hebrew text, unless we seek to deprive the increase of that special and exceptional character which is markedly assigned to it by the sacred historian.‡

It is further maintained, that, even apart from the entire question of the rapid increase of the Israelites in Egypt, the Biblical number, 430, cannot be historical, because it is the exact double of the period immediately preceding it, that, namely, between Abraham's entrance into Canaan and Jacob's journey into Egypt. It is "repugnant," we are told, "to any sound critical view," to believe the one period to have really been exactly the double of the other.§ The nature and ground of the repugnancy are not stated; but apparently the principle assumed must be, that numerical coincidences are in no case historical, and that where they occur we are justified in assuming that one or other of the two numbers is purely artificial—the invention of a writer not honest enough to admit his ignorance. But is this principle really sound? Will there be no numerical coincidences in historical chronology? What, then, shall we say to the ready acceptance by the writer who takes this view, of a statement made by Manetho,

* Sir H. Rawlinson in the writer's 'Herodotus,' vol. i. p. 277.

† Aristot. 'Hist. An.' vii. 4; Strab. xv. 1, § 22; Plin. 'H. N.' vii. 3; Senec. 'Quæst. Nat.' iii. 25; Columell. 'de Re Rust.' iii. 8.

‡ "And the children of Israel were fruitful, and increased abundantly, and multiplied, and waxed exceeding mighty; and the land was filled with them." (Ex. i. 7.) "But the more they afflicted them the more they multiplied and grew; and they (i.e. the Egyptians) were grieved because of the people of Israel." (Ib. verse 12; compare also verse 20.)

§ Bunsen, 'Egypt's Place,' vol. i. p. 173.

that during a certain period of 151 years there reigned in different parts of Egypt two contemporary dynasties consisting of exactly forty-eight kings each? Yet this is exhibited as part of a "clear historical picture" in the very same work which proclaims the belief in a less exact coincidence repugnant to all sound criticism.* The truth is, that a certain number of these coincidences will be presented by the historical chronology of any nation. For instance, from the commencement of the Persian to the end of the Peloponnesian war—a very marked period of Grecian History—was eighty-six years; and from the end of the Peloponnesian war to the termination of the struggle between Sparta and Thebes—the next marked period—was exactly half the time, or forty-three years. At Rome, from the beginning of the disturbances caused by the Gracchi to the first civil war between Sylla and Marius was forty-four years, and from the breaking out of this war to the death of Julius Cæsar was likewise forty-four years. (It was also exactly forty-four years from the death of Julius Cæsar to the reputed year of the birth of Christ.) In the Mohammedan Caliphate the family of Mohammed occupied the throne from B.C. 632 to B.C. 661, or (inclusively) thirty years; and the succeeding dynasty of the Ommiades held it from B.C. 660 to B.C. 750, or just ninety years, thrice the time of their predecessors. Again, in the portion of Jewish history with respect to which there is no dispute, the length of the period of independence intervening between the Syrian and the Roman servitudes is exactly equal to that of the servitude under Rome, which began with Antipater and terminated with the destruction of Jerusalem by Titus.† But it is needless to multiply instances. Common sense assures us that such accidental coincidences must occasionally take place; and no chronology claiming to be historical is to be rejected on account of them, unless they are of

* Bunsen, 'Egypt,' vol. iv. p. 510.

† Judas Maccabæus revolted B.C. 166. Antipater was made Procurator of Judæa by Julius Cæsar in B.C. 48. Jerusalem was destroyed A.D. 70. But 166−48=118, and 48+70=118.

more frequent occurrence in it than can be accounted for by the doctrine of chances. It is not pretended that they are frequent in the Pentateuch; nor indeed in the whole of the five books of Moses is there any other instance of a recurring number that has given rise to any suspicion.

18. It appears, then, from this whole review, that there is nothing in the history of the world, so far as it is yet known, that forms even a serious objection to the authenticity of the Pentateuch. Were we bound down to the numbers of the Hebrew text in regard to the period between the Flood and Abraham, we should, indeed, find ourselves in a difficulty. Three hundred and seventy years would certainly not seem to be sufficient time for the peopling of the world, to the extent to which it appears to have been peopled in the days of Abraham, and for the formation of powerful and settled monarchies in Babylonia and Egypt. But the adoption of the Septuagint numbers for this period, which are on every ground preferable, brings the chronology into harmony at once with the condition of the world as shown to us in the account given in Scripture of the times of Abraham, and with the results obtainable from the study, in a sober spirit, of profane history. A thousand years is ample time for the occupation of Mesopotamia, Syria, and Egypt, by a considerable population, for the formation of governments, the erection even of such buildings as the Pyramids, the advance of the arts generally to the condition found to exist in Egypt under the eighteenth dynasty, and for almost any amount of subdivision and variety in languages. More time does not seem to be in any sense needed by the facts of history hitherto known to us. The world, generally, is in a primitive and simple condition at the time of the call of Abraham. Men are still chiefly nomades. Population seems sparse; for Abraham and Lot find plenty of vacant land in Palestine, and the descendants of Abraham experience no difficulty in overspreading several countries. Settled kingdoms appear nowhere, except in Egypt and in

Babylonia; and there the governments are of the simplest form. Art in Babylonia is in a poor and low condition, the implements used being chiefly of stone and flint. Yet Babylon is much superior to her neighbours, holds Assyria in subjection, and claims the second place in the history of the world. Her historical beginnings reach back, at the utmost, to B.C. 2458, while those of Egypt are probably but a very little earlier. All other nations acknowledge themselves younger than these two, and have no traditions even of their existence much before B.C. 2000. The idea that the Biblical chronology is too narrow, that it cramps history, and needs to be set aside in favour of a scheme which puts 10,000 years between the Deluge and the birth of Christ, is not one which has grown upon men gradually through the general tenor of their inquiries into the antiquities of different nations. It is merely the dream of a single historical enthusiast, who, devoting himself to the history of one country, and pinning his faith on one author—whom after all he exaggerates and misrepresents—has come to imagine that the additional time is required by the history of his favourite, and has then forced and strained the histories of other countries, with which he has no special acquaintance, into a distant agreement with the chronological scheme formed upon the supposed necessities of a single kingdom and people. As for the further requirement of another 10,000 years between the Deluge and the creation of man, it rests upon linguistic phantasies of the most purely speculative character. The remainder of the historical objections to the authenticity of the Pentateuch, though sometimes ingenious, have in them nothing to alarm us. Profane history is decidedly favourable to a Deluge extending to all races of men, and to the greater longevity of man in the earlier ages. Ethnological research tends continually more and more to confirm, instead of shaking, the account given of the affiliation of nations in the tenth chapter of Genesis. The more accurately old myths are examined, the more evident does it become that their tone and spirit are wholly different from the tone and spirit of Scripture. The Pentateuch has the air and manner of history; the Jews have always regarded it in that light; and modern historical and geographical inquiries, whenever they afford an opportunity of testing the accuracy of the narrative, are found to bear witness to its truth. Whatever may be the scientific difficulties in the way of a literal reception of some portions, historical difficulties of any real magnitude there are none. Internally, the narrative is consistent with itself; externally, it is supported by all that has any claim to be considered sober earnest in the histories of other nations. The Christian world, which has reposed upon it for nearly 2000 years, as an authentic record of the earliest ages, is justified, by all the results of modern historical research, in still continuing its confident trust. There is really not a pretence for saying that recent discoveries in the field of history, monumental or other, have made the acceptance of the Mosaic narrative in its plain and literal sense any more difficult now than in the days of Bossuet or Stillingfleet.

ESSAY VII.

INSPIRATION.

CONTENTS OF ESSAY VII.

INSPIRATION.

1. As in the natural world wisdom and intelligence are among the signs of life in an intelligent being, so in the spiritual world a spiritual understanding follows on the possession of spiritual life. As the Divine Spirit gives life, so He inspires wisdom. Indeed all spiritual gifts flow equally from the same Spirit. St. Paul says that "there are diversities of gifts, but the same Spirit," who gives to one the word of wisdom, to another the word of knowledge, to another faith, to another miracles and gifts of healing, to another prophecy, to another divers kinds of tongues, to another the interpretation of tongues. So he describes the influence of that one and the selfsame Spirit on the early disciples in the Church of Corinth. Are we to take this literally? Are we to believe that, whilst some had spiritual wisdom and understanding—and that in larger or less degrees—others were enabled to work miracles, others to prophesy; that whilst to some there was only the common understanding of spiritual truths and mysteries, such as an enlightened mind among ourselves could penetrate, to others there was given an infallible knowledge of future events or of Divine truths otherwise unknown to man? Or, on the other hand, shall we think no more than this—that the Holy Spirit, who is the inspirer of all wisdom, by regenerating the heart, purifying the soul, exalting the affections, and quickening the intuitions of the mind, gives to some men more than to others an insight into things heavenly, and so enables them in all times and in all ages of the Church to be exponents of the Divine will? —that He reveals God and Christ in their inmost con-

sciences, inspiring them with all high and holy thoughts, and that thus they can utter things which would be deep mysteries to other men, and which are, indeed, the oracles of God?

2. This is pretty much the question concerning inspiration so much agitated now. When we come to consider it, there can be no doubt but that we must admit a human and a Divine element. There is the mind of the Prophet or Apostle to be enlightened, and the Holy Spirit, the inspirer or enlightener. The question will be, in what manner and in what proportion these two elements coexist. We may suppose the human mind perfectly passive, acting simply under a mechanical influence of the Holy Spirit, speaking or writing not its own thoughts or its own words, but only the thoughts and words of the Spirit of God. Or we may suppose the mind of the writer or speaker acting altogether freely, speaking entirely its own thoughts and words, but having derived from Divine communion and enlightenment a higher tone, having acquired a correcter judgment, and, from a deep spiritual insight, able to speak spiritual things such as the natural man receiveth not. These are the two extremes. The one is verbal inspiration, simple dictation, so that the lips of the Prophet and the pen of the Evangelist are but mechanical organs moved by the Spirit of God. The other is no more than an exaltation of the natural faculties by the influence of the same Spirit, such an exaltation as we must believe all wise and holy men to have received, an inspiration such as that by which a Hooker or a Butler wrot ethe works which bear their names. There are many intermediate steps between these two, but no one can exceed either of these extremes and yet call himself a Christian.

3. Many causes have brought this subject into controversy at present. It has, however, occupied the thoughts of thoughtful men, and has been debated and disputed on in earlier times; and a rapid glance at the history of the question may be a help to giving it its true place, and perhaps to finding its true solution.

The reverence which the ancient Jews felt for the Jewish Scriptures, must have sprung from the highest theory of verbal inspiration. Their care to count every verse and letter in every book of the Old Testament, to retain every large or small letter, every letter above or below the line, their belief that a mystery lurked in every abnormal state of letter, jot, or tittle, cannot have resulted from any lower principle. Later Jews, like the Cabbalists or Maimonides, may have become Pantheists or Rationalists; but the more ancient have left us the clearest proof that they esteemed the Scriptures as the express word of God Himself. The well-known tradition amongst the Alexandrian Jews concerning the verbal agreement of all the LXX. translators, though working in seventy separate cells, looks the same way. There is considerable reason to believe that the distinction between the different books of scripture—the Hagiographa being esteemed inferior to the Prophets, and the Prophets inferior to the law—was at least much magnified, if not wholly invented, by the later Jews. So far, however, as such a distinction and such difference of estimation existed at all, so far we must perhaps believe that there was a notion of something like degrees of inspiration.

The earlier Christian Fathers seem to have followed much the same course as their Jewish predecessors. Clemens Romanus calls the Holy Scriptures "the true words of the Holy Ghost" (c. 45). No definite theory of inspiration would be likely to be propounded; but the general reverence for the words of Holy Writ, and the deep significance believed to exist underneath the letter, prove the belief in inspiration to have been very strong and universal. Justin Martyr, and his Jewish opponent, seem fully agreed in their appreciation of the Old Testament. "No Scripture can be opposed to any other Scripture" ('Dialog.' p. 289). Irenæus saw in our Lord's promise to his Apostles—"He that heareth you, heareth Me" (Luke x. 16)—an assurance of their infallibility in the Gospel. "After the Lord's resurrection they were indued with the power of the Holy

Ghost, and had perfect knowledge of the truth. He, therefore, who despises their teaching despises Christ and God" (Iren. iii. 1). Still it may be fairly said that Irenæus, in his accounts of the composition of the Gospel, seems to combine a human element with the Divine. (See Iren. iii. 11.)

Tertullian embraced the Montanist belief, that Divine communications were made to man by means of a condition of trance or ecstasy. In this trance the prophet was supposed to lose all sense, like a Pythoness under the influence of the Divine afflatus (c. Marcion. iv. 22). This was the highest kind of inspiration. Yet he seems to have thought that the Apostles were at times allowed to speak their own words, and not the words of God, as where St. Paul (1 Cor. vii. 12) says, "To the rest speak I, not the Lord" ('De Monogam.' c. 3).

The Alexandrian Fathers, Clement and Origen, though adopting somewhat of the Neo-Platonic views of the soul, as receiving an enlightenment by communion with the Divine Logos, appear to have held firmly the infallibility of every word of Scripture; and the Mystical sense which they attach to the history and the language of the Old Testament seems to point even to verbal inspiration. (See Lumper, 'Historia Theologico-critica,' vol. 9. c. 4. § iii. art. 2.) Origen was, however, the first great Biblical critic: few things have tended more than Biblical criticism to modify the theory of verbal inspiration: and this appeared even in the patristic ages and among some of the most illustrious of the patristic writers. The critical labours of Chrysostom and Jerome, in the beginning of the fifth century, made them observe the apparent discrepancies in the account of the Evangelists, and other like difficulties in Holy Writ. Such observations led to a greater appreciation of the human element in the composition of Scripture. St. Chrysostom could see that some slight variations in the different narratives of the same event were no cause for anxiety or unbelief, but rather a proof that the Evangelists were independent witnesses. And St. Jerome could discern in the New Testament writers a dialect inferior to the purest Greek, and even at times a mixture of human passion in the language of the Apostles.* All this, however, these Fathers clearly held to be subjected and subordinate to the general Divine influence of the guiding and overruling Spirit.

4. No argument against a high doctrine of inspiration, as held by the Fathers, can be fairly deduced from the fact that they were disposed to admit the inspiration of other writings besides the Canonical Scriptures. Many of them knew the Old Testament only in the Greek translation, and were inclined to pay the same reverence to that which may have been due only to the Hebrew original. The writings of Clement and Hermas were at first received as canonical, though more careful inquiry excluded them from the Canon of the New Testament. This may be an argument against the critical accuracy of the Fathers, but is none against their belief in the inspiration of the Bible. Nor, again, are we warranted in thinking that they confounded natural enlightenment with spiritual inspiration, because some of them speak as if prophetic powers and supernatural illumination were vouchsafed to others besides the Apostles of Christ. There can be no question that the earlier Fathers believed in the continuation of the miraculous powers of the Apostolic age down to their own times, and hence they looked themselves for a special illumination from the Holy Ghost. Yet, even so, they distinguished carefully between the gift of infallibility in things spiritual vouchsafed to the writers of the New Testament, and the gift of Divine illumination to themselves and their own contemporaries.†

* Neander, 'History of Doctrines,' i. 280. (Bohn.)

† Ignatius claims for himself that he knew the doctrines which he taught, not from man, but from the testimony of the Spirit ('ad Philadelph.' 7); but then he clearly distinguishes between himself and the Apostles. "I do not enjoin you as Peter and Paul; they were Apostles, I a condemned man." ('Ad. Eph.' 15.) And Tertullian, who took a peculiarly high view of the Divine illumination of the true Christian, says distinctly that "all the faithful have the Spirit of God, but all are not Apostles." "The Apostles have the

5. The Church of the middle ages had, for the most part, a belief similar to that of the earlier Fathers. Visions, and dreams, and sensible illuminations were still expected. Miraculous powers and Divine inspiration were still believed to reside in the Church; but the Scriptures were not the less esteemed as specially, and in a sense distinct and peculiar, the lively oracles of God. Still the bold speculations of Abelard, in the twelfth century, reached the doctrine of inspiration as well as other deep questions of theology. The Prophets, as he taught, had sometimes the gift of prophecy and sometimes spoke from their own minds. The Apostles too were liable to error, as St. Peter on the question of circumcision, who was reproved by St. Paul.* Abelard's tendency was rationalistic. But here a very important phenomenon, not confined to the middle ages, but very apparent then, deserves our careful attention. In all ages of the Church we find frequent tendencies to mysticism. The desire for a kind of ecstatic vision of things Divine, of abstraction from the external world, and an absorbed contemplation of the Deity, is natural to enthusiastic temperaments, and is not uncommon in times of dogmatic controversy. The state so sought after seems to offer a refuge from the strife of tongues, from the din and noise and uncharitableness of the world and the Church without. Those who have taken this line, indulged in this spirit, have, of course, a firm belief in the communion of the Christian soul with the Spirit of God, and look for constant revelations from the Divine to the human intelligence. The mystic is transported out of self, and aims at frequent supernatural communion with God. To such a person the condition of the devout soul is a condition of constant inspiration. It is very true that the Holy Spirit is ever present with the Church, ever dwells in the souls of Christians, is our teacher and guide in all things, is ever ready to enlighten our understandings, as

Holy Spirit in a peculiar sense." ('De Exhortatione Castitatis,' 4.) See Westcott, 'Introd. to the Gospels,' pp. 386, 400.

* 'Sic et Non.' Ed. Hencke, p. 10. See Neander, 'Hist. of Doctrine,' vol. ii. p. 492.

well as to convert our hearts. But this truth of Scripture, pressed to the extent of mysticism, breaks down the boundary between the inspiration of Prophets or Apostles, and the enlightenment of the Christian soul. The genuine mystic is himself in a state of the highest inspiration. The intuitions of his spirit enable him to see things invisible. High doctrine concerning the Church is favourable enough to such a view of things. Belief in the infallibility of the existing Church, in its miraculous powers, and in frequent revelations to the higher Saints, looked all this way. Again, it is well known how mysticism tended to Pantheism. Striving after absorption in God, men learned to identify their own minds, more or less, with Deity. The Divine Spirit was believed to dwell in all human souls, and needed only to be stirred up within them. The inclination to look wholly within, neglect of the objective, cultivation only of the subjective—all this too readily takes a pantheistic direction. And so we find many sects of medieval mystics lapsing at length into pure Pantheism—a state of belief in which it is plain enough that anything like the Christian doctrine of the inspiration of the Scriptures is impossible, as it cannot be distinguished from the illumination of any devout mind, or from the inspirations of genius. This is a thing of great importance to observe, as it shows itself in subsequent ages of Church History. Mysticism and extreme spiritualism destroy any definite doctrine of the inspiration of Scripture, and they very readily glide into Pantheism.

6. The Reformation, of course, introduced much thought and controversy about Scripture. "The sufficiency of the Scriptures for salvation" became a Reformation watchword: Scripture, the written word of God,—not the unwritten record of the Church, Tradition. The natural inclination was to a very high esteem of the Bible, as the definite deposit of Christian truth, in contradistinction to the indefiniteness of the traditions of the Church, and of that teaching of the Holy Spirit ever present with the Church, on which the Roman divines insisted. Nevertheless, the tendency

of the Reformation was to boldness of thought and freedom of inquiry. Erasmus, the great forerunner of Luther, had from his critical investigations been led to a somewhat freer view of inspiration than had been common before him. He thought it unnecessary to attribute everything in the Apostles to miraculous teaching. Christ suffered the Apostles to err, and that too after the descent of the Paraclete, but not so as to endanger the faith.* Even Luther, the great master mind of the age, with his strong subjective tendency, and with his indomitable boldness, ventured to subject the books of the New Testament to the criterion of his own intuition. The teaching of St. Paul penetrated and convinced his soul; St. James seemed to contradict St. Paul; and his Epistle was rejected as an Epistle of straw. There is reason to believe that he afterwards regretted and retracted; but words once spoken reach far and wide, and can never be unsaid again.

7. The tendency of Calvin and the Calvinist reformers was less subjective and more scholastic than that of Luther and the Lutherans. Their distinct and definite system of doctrine, like that of their forerunners Augustine and Aquinas, naturally found a place for the plenary and even verbal inspiration of the Scriptures, so that some of the Swiss Confessions speak of simple dictation by the Holy Ghost. The Remonstrants or Arminians, on the other hand, were more disposed to Rationalism than the generality of the reformed; and writers, like Grotius and Episcopius, made clear distinctions between the Divine and the human elements in the writers of the Old and New Testaments.†

The Socinians were, of course, the most rationalising sect of those which early sprang from the Reformation, a fungus-growth, rather than one of the natural branches. At first, however, they took the same view

* Non est necesse ut quicquid fuit in Apostolis protinus ad miraculum vocemus. Passus est errare suos Christus, etiam post acceptum Paracletum, sed non usque ad fidei periculum.—Erasm. *Epistt.*, lib. ii., tom. iv. Edit. Basil.

† *E. g.* A Spiritu Sancto dictari *historias* non fuit opus. Satis fuit scriptorem memoriâ valere.—Grotius, *Vot. pro pace Eccles.*, tom. iii. p. 672. Lond. 1679.

as other Protestant writers of the authority of Holy Writ, only they were less sensitive about difficulties and apparent discrepancies in Scripture, and more disposed to cut and square it so as to accord with what appeared to them to be reason and common sense. This tendency more and more fully developed itself. The modern Unitarian is a genuine Rationalist, often little different from a Deist.

The mystical spirit, which had long been swelling up under the weight of the Medieval Church, sometimes wholly within it, sometimes bursting forth from the pressure, showed itself in many places and many forms, after the triumph of the Reformation. Its elevation of the subjective over the objective, of the inward life over the outward letter, led insensibly to a disregard of the Bible in comparison with the internal testimony and the intuition of the soul. The Anabaptists of Germany were of the coarsest class of mystics. Among the best have been the Quakers in this country. The leading principle of George Fox, their founder, was the doctrine of the Inward Light. This is the true principle of all knowledge of religion. The outward Word is chiefly valuable as it stirs up the Word within. The highest source of knowledge is this inward illumination. All outward forms, all outward tests, all creeds and confessions, are strictly forbidden. Even the Bible must be subordinated to the light of God within. It is evident that, on this principle, there can be no distinction between the inspiration of Prophets and Apostles and the inspiration of every devout soul. It is also observable how this theory produces results like those which spring from the Roman doctrine of tradition. The written Word of God is no longer the final court of appeal in controversies of doctrine. The Church of Rome finds an infallible interpreter in that Divine Spirit which ever dwells in and guides the Church. The mystic has an infallible interpreter in his own bosom, who not only opens his understanding that he may understand the Scriptures, but communicates directly and sensibly truth to the soul. It is also very deserving of remark, however painful it may be, that at one time the Quakers were rapidly hurrying into Rationalism, and even Socinianism—the coldest forms of unbelief—from the warm mysticism of their first founders.

To come nearer to our own times, the whole spirit of the last century in Germany was subjective. There seemed a reaction from the positive spirit of the seventeenth century, which has been called the middle age of the Reformation. Pietism was the form taken by the religious revival, a form which was eminently subjective, and whch partook much of the mystical. The philosophical spirit was of the same character. The very principle of illuminism (auklärung) was, that there is in man's inmost consciousness an intuitional knowledge of truth. Its motto—"Wahr ist was klar ist," "that is true which is clear,"—sufficiently indicates its character. Proceeding from such a ground, and raising Natural Religion to the rank of a Revelation, Töllner, the disciple of Wolff, reduced Scripture to the level of a natural light.* At the same time, the Pietists used the Bible, not so much to be the source of truth and the fountain of faith, as for a book of devotion and to raise pious emotions.† In both ways there was a move towards the confounding of the light of Nature with the light of Revelation, of the light of the Spirit in the devout or illuminated soul with the light which had been specially vouchsafed to Prophets and Apostles for communicating God's truth to the world.

8. In the latter half of the eighteenth century, the Deism, which had been troubling England, had passed through the alembic of French scepticism, and now settled down in a shower of Rationalism on Germany. The Rationalism of Paulus, the Pantheism of Hegel, the historical myth of Strauss, derive their pedigree from the writings of Lord Herbert of Cherbury, Toland, Tindall, and other English Deists of the seventeenth

* See Kahnis, 'Hist. of German Protestantism,' English Translation, by Meyer, p. 116.

† Ib., pp. 100, 116.

and early eighteenth centuries, through the school of Rousseau and Voltaire.* The special principle of Lord Herbert and his followers, the Deists, was that there were several positive religions—Christianity, Judaism, Mohammedism, &c. In the main all these are the same. The *general* religion is at the bottom of all of them, i. e., the Religion of Nature, a religion founded in the natural perception of truth, the intuitional consciousness of the human mind. Positive religions may be very good for practical purposes; but all that is positive in them is evil, or at the best worthless; the valuable part being that which they hold in common of the general religion. It was this principle which passed through the various forms of French infidelity, German Rationalism and Pantheism, and which has been brought back to us, as the highest result of modern discoveries in science and mental philosophy. How it was calculated to act upon the theory of inspiration, and to unsettle it even with those who had not become either Rationalists or Deists, it is needless to remark. Where a shadow of infidelity is obscuring the light, many, who are not wholly under its darkness, will yet pass through the penumbra that surrounds it. Even the apologist in the last century, from the wish to take positions which were impregnable, surrendered, at least for argument's sake, the higher ground of their forerunners in the faith. And, in the like manner, among the German divines, who still held Christian and orthodox opinions, there was a tendency to depart from the higher doctrine of inspiration held by the Church and the Reformers; to speak of degrees of inspiration, of fallibility in things earthly, of a Divine influence elevating the mental faculties of the sacred writers; not simply to ascribe all to the direct teaching of the Spirit of God.†

9. Distinct theories of inspiration were in old times seldom propounded, even where some attention was

* See Kahnis as above, p. 31, &c. McCaul's 'Rationalism and Deistic Infidelity,' passim.

† See Kahnis, pp. 116, 117.

directed to the question. Definite controversies upon it scarcely arose. The present century has been rife in both; and they have prevailed not a little among ourselves. Several causes have contributed to call them forth. First, and chiefly, the spread of rationalising speculations, and the consequent unsettling of faith.* Next, the greater attention which has been paid to the criticism of the Bible, and especially of the New Testament, has exposed to view some of the difficulties concerning the origin of the books of the Bible, concerning the historical accuracy of some statements, concerning the slight apparent variations in the testimony of the Evangelists. In ordinary historians these would puzzle no one. The strictest integrity is compatible with slight inaccuracy or divergence of testimony; but if all was the work of God's Holy Spirit, speaking through human agents, the least discrepancy is formidable. Hence the human element has been thought more of among modern critics, and by some has been elevated above the Divine. Thirdly, the rapid discoveries of modern science have been supposed to contradict the records of the Old Testament Scriptures; and, in order to account for such a contradiction, efforts have been made to interpret anew the words of Moses; and, where these have proved unsatisfactory, many have more or less believed that the writers of the historical books were merely chroniclers of historical events or collectors of ancient records, the providence of God having watched over the preservation of such records, but the Spirit of God having in no sense dictated them. Still freer views have been propounded; but this may suffice as the expression of the thoughts of serious men.

10. One of the first among ourselves to put forth a bold theory of inspiration was Coleridge. His 'Confessions of an Enquiring Spirit' was indeed not pub-

* It is important to observe, that this was first in *time* as well as in importance. Dr. McCaul has shown clearly ('Rationalism and Deistic Infidelity') that the spread of unbelieving opinions in Germany was first, the criticism came afterwards. Faith in Revelation was shaken by Deism and Rationalism, and then the unfriendly criticism was brought to bear upon the records of Christianity.

lished till after his death; but the tone of many former writings is much the same. In the posthumous work just mentioned he unfolds his theory pretty freely. Of the Bible he speaks as a library of infinite value, as that which must have a Divine Spirit in it, from its appeal to all the hidden springs of feeling in our hearts. "In short," he writes, "whatever *finds* me bears witness that it has proceeded from a Holy Spirit." (Letter i.) "In the Bible there is more that finds me than I have experienced in all other books put together; the words of the Bible find me at greater depths of my being; and whatever finds me brings with it an irresistible evidence of its having proceeded from the Holy Spirit." (Letter ii.) But then he protests against "the doctrine which requires me to believe that not only what finds me, but all that exists in the sacred volume, and which I am bound to find therein, was not only inspired by, that is, composed by men under the actuating influence of, the Holy Spirit, but likewise dictated by an Infallible Intelligence; that the writers, each and all, were divinely informed, as well as inspired." The very essence of "this doctrine is this, that one and the same Intelligence is speaking in the unity of a person, which unity is no more broken by the diversity of the pipes through which it makes itself audible, than is a tune by the different instruments on which it is played by a consummate musician equally perfect in all. One instrument may be more capacious than another, but as far as its compass extends, and in what it sounds forth, it will be true to the conception of the master." Such a doctrine, he conceives, must imply infallibility in physical science and in everything else as much as in faith, in things natural no less than in spiritual. He expresses a full belief "that the word of the Lord came to Samuel, to Isaiah, to others, and that the words which gave utterance to the same are faithfully recorded." But for the recording he does not think that there was need of any supernatural working, except in such cases as those in which God not only utters certain express words to a prophet, but also enjoins him to record them. In the latter case he accepts them "as supernaturally communicated and their recording as executed under special guidance." The arguments of Coleridge are calculated rather to pull down than to build up. He brings many reasons against a rigid mechanical theory, against a belief that the Bible is simply the voice of God's Holy Spirit uttered through different organs or instruments; but he does not fix any limit, he does not say how far he admits Divine teaching or inspiration to extend, nor does he apparently draw any line of distinction between the inspiration of holy men of old and the spiritual and providential direction of enlightened men in every age and nation.

Wherever Coleridge has trodden Mr. Maurice follows him; not that he is a servile imitator, but he is a zealous disciple, and one who generally outdoes his master. In his 'Theological Essays' he begins to speak of the inspiration of poets and prophets among the Greeks; he speaks again of the quickening and informing spirit, to which all good men ascribe their own teaching and enlightenment; he quotes the language of our Liturgy as ascribing to "God's holy inspiration" the power of "thinking those things that be good;" and then he asks the question, "Ought we in our sermons to say, 'Brethren, we beseech you not to suppose the inspiration of Scripture to at all resemble that for which we have been praying; they are generically and essentially unlike; it is blasphemous to connect them in our minds; the Church is very guilty for having suggested the association?'" Proceeding in this course he naturally arrives at the conclusion that all which is good and beautiful comes from the inspiration of the Spirit of God, and that the sacred words of Scripture came in the same manner from the same Spirit. (See Essay xiii.) In some of his writings, especially in his work on 'Sacrifices,' he appears to have carried his disbelief of a more *special* inspiration of Holy Scripture to a greater length than in his 'Theological Essays,' as where God's tempting of Abraham to slay his son is attributed to a horrible thought coming over him and haunting him.

A very able and interesting writer on the same side of the same subject is Mr. Morell in his 'Philosophy of Religion.' The work is one of considerable acuteness and philosophical power. The writer's theory of inspiration is based on his theory of the human mind. The different powers of consciousness he classes thus:

Powers of Consciousness ..	to which correspond ..		Emotions.
1. The Sensational	"	"	The Instincts.
2. The Perceptive	"	"	The Animal Passions.
3. The Logical	"	"	Relational Emotions.
4. The Intuitional	"	"	Æsthetic, Moral, and Religious Emotions.

Now, the intuitional consciousness, he contends, is that which alone is properly susceptible of religious impressions and religious truths. Revelation he considers to involve an immediate intuition of Divine realities. All revelation implies an intelligible object presented, and a given power of recipiency in the subject, which power is lodged in the intuitional consciousness. In distinguishing revelation and inspiration, he defines "revelation, in the Christian sense, as that act of the Divine power by which God presents the realities of the spiritual world immediately to the human mind, while inspiration denotes that especial influence wrought upon the faculties of the subject, by virtue of which he is able to grasp these realities in their perfect fulness and integrity" (p. 150). "God made a revelation of Himself to the world in Jesus Christ; but it was the inspiration of the Apostles, which enabled them clearly to discern it."

Mr. Morell argues that "the canonicity of the New Testament Scriptures was decided upon solely on the ground of their presenting to the whole Church clear statements of *Apostolical* Christianity. The idea of their being written by any special command of God, or verbal dictation of the Spirit, was an idea altogether foreign to the primitive Christians" (p. 165). "The proper idea of inspiration, as applied to the Holy Scriptures, does not include either miraculous powers, verbal

15*

dictation, or any distinct commission from God." (*Ib.*) On the contrary, it consists "in the impartation of clear intuitions of moral and spiritual truth to the mind by extraordinary means. According to this view of the case, inspiration, *as an internal phenomenon*, is perfectly consistent with the natural laws of the human mind—it is a higher kind of potency, which every man to a certain degree possesses" (p. 166). This view, he thinks, "gives full consistency to the *progressive* character of Scripture morality" (p. 167). "It gives a satisfactory explanation of the minor discrepancies to be found in the sacred writers" (p. 170), whether those discrepancies be between Scripture and science, or in statements of facts, or in reasoning. In every case in which the moral nature is highly purified, and so a harmony of the spiritual being with the mind of God produced, a removal of all outward disturbances from the heart, "What," he asks, "is to prevent or disturb the immediate intuition of Divine things? 'Blessed are the pure in heart, for they shall *see* God'" (p. 186).

It is clear that this theory makes great purity of heart, or high sanctification, equivalent to, or the unfailing instrument of, inspiration. If one man is a better Christian than another, and so has a purer heart, he must be more inspired than the other. Hence, if a man of modern times could be found of a higher religious tone and character than an Apostle, he would have a higher intuition of Divine things, and therefore would know Christian truth more infallibly. Moreover, it appears that the value of the Scriptures consists, not in their proceeding from any direct command of God, or from any infallible guidance of His Spirit, but in their embodying the teaching and experience of men whose hearts were elevated, and so their understandings enlightened; to this it being added, in the case of the New Testament, that the writers were such as were specially qualified to represent the Apostolical Church, and so to transmit its spirit and teaching to us.

A writer of less ability, but more boldness, Mr. Mac Naught of Liverpool, has carried the same theory to its furthest limits. He defines inspiration to be "that action of the Divine Spirit by which, apart from any idea of infallibility, all that is good in man, beast, or matter, is originated and sustained" (p. 136, Second Edition). He denies all distinction between genius and inspiration. He doubts not that "David, Solomon, Isaiah, or Paul would have spoken of everything, which may with propriety be called a work of genius, or of cleverness, or of holiness," as "works of the Spirit of God, written by Divine inspiration" (p. 132).

11. The historical sketch thus rapidly given seems to show that there have always been some slight differences of tone and opinion touching this important question, but that these differences have never so markedly come out as in the nineteenth century. The subject at present causes great anxiety, and not without reason. Many feel that, if they must give up a high doctrine of inspiration, they give up Christianity; and yet they think that a high doctrine is scarcely tenable. Such a feeling is not unnatural, and yet it is not wholly true. All the history, and even all the great doctrines of the Gospel, might be capable of proof, and so deserving of credence, though we were obliged to adopt almost the lowest of the modern theories of inspiration. For instance, all, or almost all, the arguments of Butler, Paley, Lardner, and other like authors, are independent of the question, "What is the nature and degree of Spiritual inspiration?" Paley, for instance, undertakes to prove the truth of Christ's resurrection and of the Gospel history, and thence the truth of the doctrines which Christ taught to the world. But this he argues out, for the most part, on principles of common historical evidence. He treats the Apostles as twelve common men, of common honesty and common intelligence. If they could not have been deceived, and had no motive to deceive the world, then surely we must accept their testimony as true. But if their testimony is true, Jesus Christ must have lived, and taught, and worked miracles, and risen from the dead, and so in Him we have an accredited witness sent from God. His teach-

ing, therefore, must have been the truth; and if we have good grounds for believing that His disciples carefully treasured up His teaching, and faithfully handed it on to us, we have then in the New Testament an unquestionable record of the will and of the truth of God. Even if the Apostles and Evangelists had no special inspiration, yet, if we admit their care and fidelity, we may trust to their testimony, and so accept their teaching as true.

So, then, even if we were driven to take the lowest view of inspiration, we are not bound to give up our faith. External evidence must almost of necessity begin by taking low ground. It must treat nothing as certain until it is proved. It must not, therefore, even presume that witnesses are honest till it has found reason to think them so; and, of course, it cannot treat them as inspired till it meets with something which compels an acknowledgment of their inspiration. This is taking the extremest case, one in which we altogether doubt the inspiration of the Apostles. *A fortiori*, we need not throw away all faith, if we should be led to think that some books of the Old Testament are only historical records, collected by Jewish antiquarians, and bound up with the writings of prophets, as venerable and valuable memorials of the peculiar people of God. All this might be, and yet God may have spoken by holy men of old, and afterwards more fully by His Son.

Some Christian controversialists, who take high ground themselves, write as if they thought that Christianity was not worth defending, unless it was defended exactly on their principles. The minds of the young more especially are sometimes greatly endangered by this means. The defender of the Gospel may be but an indifferent reasoner. He fails to make his ground sure and strong. His reader finds more forcible, at least more specious, arguments elsewhere. He thinks the advocate he rested on defeated, his arguments answered and upset, and Christianity itself seems lost. Now, we may surely begin by saying, that the question of inspiration is, within certain limits, a question *internal* to Christianity. No doubt, it may materially affect the evidences of Christianity; but the questions of verbal inspiration, mechanical inspiration, dynamical inspiration, and the like, are all questions on which persons believing in the Gospel may differ. There is a degree of latitude which must be fatal to faith; but within certain limits men may differ, and yet believe. We shall be wise to take safe ground ourselves, and to bear as charitably as we can with those who may take either higher or lower. Only it cannot be concealed that the temper of mind which disposes to a very low doctrine of inspiration is one that may not improbably lead in the end to the rejection of many religious truths —to scepticism, if not to unbelief.

12. It seems pretty generally agreed among thoughtful men at present, that definite theories of inspiration are doubtful and dangerous. The existence of a human element, and the existence of a Divine element, are generally acknowledged; but the exact relation of the one to the other it may be difficult to define. Yet some thoughts may aid us to an approximation to the truth, perhaps sufficiently clear for practical purposes.

13. In the first place, then, let us consider for a moment what is the real principle which seems to actuate those writers and thinkers, of the present day especially, who endeavour to root out all distinction between the inspiration of the Apostles and Prophets, and the ordinary illumination of good and wise men. Is it not that morbid shrinking from a belief in anything miraculous in religious history, now so commonly prevalent? that fear to admit the possibility that the Creator of the universe should ever specially interfere with the universe which He has created? There can be no question but that that inspiration of Holy Scripture in which the Church has generally believed is of the nature of a miracle; and so its rejection follows upon the rejection of miracles in general. Many marvellous things exist in nature, things at least as marvellous as any miracles recorded in Scripture. It is mar-

vellous that the worlds should have come into being, and should all be under the government of the strictest laws and the most undeviating rules—that life should exist at all—that new life should be constantly bursting forth—that eyes should open curiously formed to see, and ears curiously constructed to hear;—all this, and much beside, is as marvellous as the suspension of a natural law, as the restoring life to the body from which it had gone forth, as the giving sight to the blind, or hearing to the deaf. But the latter startles us into conviction that some living personal being of creative power has newly put forth his strength; the former state of things is so general, uniform, and constantly recurring, that we can go on as usual without much thinking of it, call it Nature, or perhaps Deity, or any other abstract generality, and so rest satisfied.

14. Without doubt we witness in the universe the constant prevalence of general laws, and the regulation of all things by them. In proportion to this general constancy is our natural expectation that it will continue. And, moreover, even though we may be led to believe that the whole must have been framed, and that the laws must have been given by a creative intelligence; still the uniform operation of those laws disposes us to doubt the probability that they will ever be interfered with by the hand that first ordered them. This doubt is strengthened by the belief that the wisdom, which first gave being to an universe, could never have wrought so imperfectly as that its active interference should afterwards be needed, to remedy defects or to repair the machinery. And all this might perhaps be probable enough, if we could see but a natural creation, and if there were no moral and rational creation too. But suppose it to be true, that there is in the physical universe, and more or less connected with matter and the laws of matter, a multitude of intelligent, rational, moral, and accountable beings; some more powerful than others; some, the angels, wholly good; some, the evil angels, wholly bad; some of a mixed character, like man; all capable, more or less, of communication

with each other — those indeed of mixed character closely connected with matter, joined to material bodies, whilst the more powerful intelligences, good and evil, are freer and more independent of mere physical influences: suppose, too, that there is one great Intellect, one Sovereign Mind, who made all, and who governs all; with premises like these, where is the improbability that there should be occasional interferences with natural laws? Life does not exist at all without producing some interference with the mere laws of matter and motion. Where intelligent beings exist capable of acting on material substances, they ever do mould those material substances to their will, and make the laws of nature serve them. If created intelligences superior to man have any power to act through material instruments, we should expect that they could only act, as man does, by taking advantage of the laws by which matter is guided, and so controlling one law by bringing a more powerful law to bear upon it. Even of the providence of the Supreme Being, if that providence be continually at work, controlling the moral and intellectual, and upholding the material creation, it is most probable that such providential agency would be exercised in overruling and directing natural causes and laws rather than in displacing or superseding them. But there certainly seems no *à priori* improbability that the Creator should be also the Ruler of the universe; that where the creation is moral and intelligent, He should rule and interfere as He might not where it was simply material or animal; that, where moral, personal beings were acting upon one another, striving to benefit, and striving to ruin one another, He too at times should be at hand, to punish or to protect. And so the doctrine of a special providence seems only consistent with the belief in a personal God. But the step from thence to a belief in miracles is no great stride. For, if the great personal Creator rules and guides and interferes in the affairs of His creation, though he would be likeliest to do so commonly by mere guidance of natural laws, yet, if there were need or occasion for it, it must be quite as easy for Him to interfere by the entire suspension of those laws, or by a temporary alteration of them.*

15. Indeed it is hard to see how miracles should appear either impossible or improbable; but either on the theory that what we see commonly we must see always, or else on the theory that there is no personal providence of God. And, in short, is it not true, that the natural tendency of those who try to get rid of miracle and special inspiration is to the resolving of providence into law, and of God into simple intelligence? We are all well aware that we see the government of law, not only in the physical, but even in the intellectual world; and there are those, who, from observing this, have been led to a belief in law, and nothing but law. God with them is but law; and providential or moral government gives place to mere necessity. Of course, this is simple Atheism, and involves all the difficulties, as well as all the miseries, of Atheism. And yet, surely it is more consistent and logical than the system, which does not deny the wisdom that seems to have planned and still seems to order all things, but which yet shrinks from acknowledging the distinct, individual personality of the Creator, His personal presence to all the universe which He has created, His superintending providence over it, and His active interference in it. Unquestionably this latter is the doctrine of the Hebrew Bible, and that which Jesus Christ taught in the Sermon on the Mount. But philosophic religion talks to us of a general principle of intelligence diffused throughout all things, moving, and breathing in, and animating all beings. Now this general principle of intelligence sounds philosophical enough; but how can it be reconciled with what Eng-

* Of course, if Professor Baden Powell's theory be true, that the physical and the spiritual worlds are so separate that they can never come into contact, then all this is impossible. But then all creation is impossible. The spiritual could never have created the material. Indeed, the union of soul and body must be impossible; at all events, all religious knowledge must be impossible. It can be founded on no evidence, and can result only from certain convictions of the mind, wholly incapable of being tested as to their truth.

lishmen call common sense? What, on principles of common reason, can be meant by intelligence where there is no intellect, or a great principle of mind where there is no personal mind at all? We know what is meant by the intelligence of a man, or the intelligence of a beast—intelligence being the power of perceiving, understanding, and reasoning predicable of the mind of that man or that beast. In like manner we can understand, that if there be one great infinite mind, then infinite intelligence may be predicable of that infinite mind. But to say that there is any general principle of intelligence separable and distinguishable from any particular mind, is surely to palter with us in a double sense. We can no more appreciate intelligence as separated from the intellect of which it is a quality or attribute, than we can understand agency without an agent, potency without a power, sight without a seer, thought without a thinker, or life without that which lives. In short, may we not demur altogether to mere abstractions, except as they may exist in the mind, or in systems of philosophy? And so, is not the conclusion inevitable, that our real alternative lies between a mere Stoical law, a Buddhist Kharma, blind and inexorable, working in matter, it is useless to inquire whence or how—between this and a belief in a God, personal, present, Maker, Ruler, Guider of all things, and of all men?

16. Give us this, as the Bible gives Him to us: and though we should never expect Him to be perpetually setting aside the laws which He has made for the universe, yet we need not—rather we cannot—believe, that He should be so inevitably fettered by them, as that He should not continually guide them for the good of His intelligent and moral creatures—guide them as in a less degree those creatures themselves can guide them, or that, when He may see fit, He should not suspend, or even for a season alter them. And if this latter contingency should ever take place, we should naturally expect that it would be never so probable as when it was His pleasure to communicate to rational

beings some special revelation of His will, and to teach them concerning Himself what they might not be able to learn from mere natural phenomena.

Can there be any inconsistency in such a putting aside of the veil of nature, and giving man a somewhat clearer vision of God? Doubtless, other courses are possible. God might be pleased, instead of making any objective communications to mankind, to breathe silently into each individual spirit, and to teach separately each one of His will and of Himself. But no one has a right to say that such must be God's plan of action—that such only is consistent with Divine wisdom, or human capacity, or philosophical theology. If God be not the mere pervading intelligence, which informs the universe, but which can exert itself only through the medium of things in the universe; if, on the contrary, He is a personal, present ruler and guide, there can be no inconsistency in the belief that He may at times let Himself be heard by those who can hear Him—in other and clearer tones than the voices of mere natural phenomena, or even of the intuitional consciousness.

17. Now, the common course which we see philosophic scepticism taking at present is this: First, there is a doubt about miracles, then about special inspiration. To build our faith in any degree on miracles is unwise. Inspiration is wholly a question of degree. One man has by the teaching or breathing of God's Spirit greater insight into spiritual truth than another. The Apostles, doubtless, had an unusual brightness of such vision, and so we may truly call their writings inspired; but the difference between their inspiration and that of St. Augustine, or even of Plato, is but a difference of degree. Next comes a doubt or a denial of the existence of personal spiritual beings. The devil, Satan, wicked spirits are but names for a general evil principle, which we cannot but see and feel influencing and pervading ourselves and all things around us. Angels are soon placed in the same category; and the last step of all reduces God Himself to a principle of intelligence,

if it does not go yet farther, and make Him but a law.

But in all honesty, is there a middle course? Does not the Bible at all events—Old Testament and New alike—speak of a present, personal God, of a multitude of personal spiritual beings—some good and others evil —working around us and within us, of miracles wrought by teachers sent from God, of predictions uttered before the event, of holy men of old moved by the Spirit of God to speak things, which could be known to none but God Himself? It is quite impossible to get rid of all this, and to retain the Bible as in any proper sense true. Let it be said, that good men who wrote books of the Bible were good men, but spoke according to the prejudices of their times. They believed in prophecies and miracles, and evil spirits, and so spoke of them. Their inspiration quickened their intuitions, but it did not make them infallible, and so in these matters they may have erred. But, if Christianity be Christianity, and not a system of mere morals and philosophy, there was One Man, who was so much more than man, that if we disbelieve Him, we make God Himself a liar. And may we not ask, if His discourses be not so unfaithfully handed down to us that we might as well or better not have them at all, whether He did not perpetually appeal to miracles, whether He did not continually quote prophecies as fulfilled or soon to be fulfilled, whether He did not speak much of angels and devils, whether He did not in the most signal manner promise to His disciples the guidance and teaching of His Holy Spirit, to bring to their remembrance all that He had said to them, and to lead them into all truth? Is it possible to reject all this without rejecting Christ?

18. And so much of miracles and inspiration generally. Now let us take a few facts, and see what they seem to teach us. We have a number of different books written in different styles, indicating the different characters of the writers. At times, too, there appear slight diversities of statements in trifling matters of

detail. Here we mark a human element. If God spoke, it is plain that He spoke through man; if God inspired, He inspired man. Even the Gospel *miracles* were often worked with some instrumental means; no wonder, then, that when God would teach men, He would teach through human agency. And the difference of style—perhaps the slight discrepancies in statements—seem to satisfy us that some portions at least of the Bible were not simply dictated by God to man; there was not what is called mere mechanical or organic inspiration; God did not simply speak God's words, using as a mere machine man's lips to speak them with. Of course, we must not forget the benefit we derive from these differences between writers of the same narrative. The apparent or trifling discrepancies in the statements of the different Evangelists, for instance, convince us that they were independent witnesses, and that the whole story did not arise from some well concerted plan to deceive the world: the homely and even barbarous style of some of the writers proves to us that they were really fishermen, and not philosophers; and so we have a convincing evidence that the deepest system of theology, and the noblest code of ethics ever propounded—the one stirring the depths of the whole human heart, the other guiding all human life—came, not from the profound speculations of the wisest of mankind, but either from God Himself, or else from a source more inexplicable and impossible; from the poor, the narrow-minded, and the untaught. But whilst we see the benefit of all this, and admire the wisdom which so ordered it, we learn from it that there must have been a human element in Scripture; that God may, nay must, have spoken, but that he dealt his own common dealing with us—that is, He used earthly instruments for giving heavenly blessings, human means for communicating Divine truth.

Now, let us look the other way. Scripture is not a mere system of theology, nor is it a mere historical record. If it were either or both of these, and nothing more, of course we could believe that nothing might be needed, beyond the quickening of the intuitional consciousness, to enable men to conceive its truths and to communicate them to others. There is, however, as has been already noticed, a distinctly miraculous element in it; and here, if we admit its existence, we cannot fail to see the working of a present, personal God. Take away the miraculous element, and we may easily get into any kind of philosophical abstraction. Admit it, and we are brought back again into the intelligible region of common, plain sense.

If anything in the world can be supernatural or miraculous, it surely must be the infallible foreknowledge of future events. No elevation of the intuitional consciousness can account for such foreknowledge. None can certainly foretell the future, but one who can certainly guide the future. Do we, then, admit that any of the prophets in the Old Testament were enabled to foretell coming events, the events of the Gospel history in particular? Some modern writers go so far as to deny this *in toto*. According to them every prophecy of the Old Testament concerned, primarily at least, contemporaneous history, or history so nearly contemporaneous, that it required only common foresight and "old experience" to look into it. Burke early shadowed forth the French Revolution: Isaiah, on the same principle, could forewarn Israel of its dangers, threaten sinners with punishment, and promise protection to penitents. Of course, we can understand such a view; but can we admit it and not reject Christianity? And let us remember that, in arguing on the nature of inspiration, we are not arguing in proof of Christianity; but that, admitting the truth of Christianity, we are inquiring into somewhat which, as has been already observed, is really internal to Christianity. Most Christians are ready to believe that the passages of the Old Testament to which our Lord and his Apostles appealed, as proofs of His Divine mission and of the truth of their teaching, were really predictions, and not guesses. This is not the place to enter at length into such a question. But, if we just think of what Jacob said of Shiloh—Moses, of a prophet like himself—David and others, of a great Son of David—Isaiah, in his ninth and fifty-third chapters, of a Child born, a Son given, called Mighty God, Eternal Father, Prince of Peace, and of a righteous Servant, on whom the LORD should lay the iniquity of us all—Daniel, of Messiah the Prince, cut off, but not for Himself, and of one like a Son of Man, to whom a kingdom is given by the Ancient of days, an everlasting kingdom, a dominion that shall not pass away—Haggai, of the glory of the second temple, so much surpassing that of the first—Malachi, of the forerunner of the Messiah—and many prophecies of like kind; we shall feel that the burden of proof must lie with those who deny, not with those who believe, that there were prophets, who bore witness to the coming of the Christ centuries before His birth.* We may remember that these predictions have been preserved to us both in the original Hebrew, and in translations made from the Hebrew before the birth of Christ, made, not by Christians, but by Jews—that the more ancient Jews did undeniably interpret these prophecies, as pointing forward to a prince who should be sent from heaven to save their own nation, and to bless other nations in them. Comparatively modern Jews have explained some of these prophecies away, because they too manifestly favour the Christians; but even so, they continue to believe that the Scriptures foretold a Messiah. Moreover, we have the clearest testimonies from Jews and Gentiles alike (Jews and Gentiles who never became Christians, and so are independent witnesses) that in the East generally, *Oriente toto*, and especially among the Israelites themselves, there had prevailed an ancient and constant persuasion that by Divine appointment a Deliverer was to

* It matters little to this argument whether all the books of the Old Testament were written by those whose names they bear; whether, for instance, the last chapters of Isaiah were Isaiah's or some other's; whether the book of Daniel was written at the time of the captivity, or not collected till some centuries later. It is certain they were all written before Christ; and if in them there be found prophecies of the Messiah, prophecies, be they many or few, like precious stones imbedded in a rock; we have then the phenomenon existing, and we have to explain how it came. Idoneum, opinor, testimonium divinitatis veritas divinationis. (Tert. *Apolog.* c. 20.)

arise out of Judea, who should have dominion; and, moreover, that he was impatiently expected in the reigns of the early emperors of Rome. Jews, who have lived since those times, have confessed that the period presignified is apparently past. Now, it is quite certain that the most remarkable and most influential religious teacher that ever lived in any nation upon earth did arise and live in Judea, at the time so marked and agreed on. It is undoubted that He declared the predictions in question to have pointed to Him. His followers have always claimed them as fulfilled in Him. Of all religious revolutions, nay, of all revolutions, moral, spiritual, social, or political, ever produced in the world, He has produced the greatest, the most influential, the most extensive. As Christians, we, of course, believe that He was the Christ; and we are justified in urging on the Jews such considerations as the above, in proof that their own cherished Scriptures pointed to Him.

Now, if the prophets really did centuries before foresee an event, most unlikely, but which we have witnessed as true, they must have had something more than the inspiration of genius, or than the exalting of their intuitional consciousness. For, whatever degree of insight into the truth of things spiritual we may attribute to such intuitional consciousness, and whatever communion it may give with the mind of God, it can hardly be said to make us partakers of God's omniscience, or to endue us with His powers of foresight.

One of the favourite modes of evading such conclusions as this, and so one of the favourite positions of the low inspirationists is, that *Nihil in scripto quod non prius in scriptore;* a man can speak nothing but what he thinks. In a sense this is true enough; and, as a general rule, we may suppose the holy men of old, who spake as they were moved by the Holy Ghost, to have been first gifted with the knowledge of the future, and then moved to communicate that knowledge to others. But still, if there be an overruling and over-guiding Providence as well as an informing and inspiring Spirit, may not a man be guided to speak unconsciously words of deep import? We see this in the Old Testament in the case of Balaam. If the history of him be not a false legend or a mere myth, the Almighty told him that he was to speak to Balak that word which was put into his mouth. His will was quite the other way. He willed to curse Israel, and so to obtain from Balak the wages of unrighteousness; but his own will was overruled by the direct command of God. If Balaam prophesied, if he prophesied, as most Christians have believed, not only of the future fortunes of Israel, but of the future coming of Christ; it is certain that his extraordinary knowledge could not have been the result of his purity of heart qualifying him to see God, could not have come from the clearing away of those clouds of sin, and therefore of error, which darken the mental vision; for his heart was set upon covetousness, and he perished with the enemies of God. The same, or much the same, may be said of Caiaphas, who was altogether bent on evil, and yet of whom the Evangelist testifies that "being High Priest that year he prophesied." If miracles are impossible, of course all this is impossible. But how miracles can be impossible, unless God is impossible, it seems that we have yet to learn.

Though, therefore, we may not generally look for a work of the Spirit through the mere bodily organs of men, without an elevation of their souls; we surely have no power to limit the operations of God, or to say that He may not, if He will, use the very unconscious words of wicked men as well as the heart service of pious men.

19. But farther, is it not true that Almighty God has made even acts and histories to prophesy, independently of any utterance of men's mouths? Are there not types in the Law, and through all the Old Testament history, which have their antitypes in the New Testament? There are those, no doubt, who will say that we can find historical parallels in profane, as readily as in sacred, history. But are these really to be compared with the sacrifice of Isaac typifying the

death and resurrection of Christ—with the history of Joseph, sold by his brethren, and then exalted to be their prince and saviour—with the brazen serpent, lifted up to heal all that looked on it—with the passage of the Red Sea, and other parables put forth by the history of the Exodus—with the priesthood of Aaron, the passover, the ceremonies on the day of atonement, and the many Levitical rites forepicturing Christ—with the kingly types, such as David and Solomon—with the prophetic parallelism of Elijah and John the Baptist—and the many others, too many to enumerate now?* If there be, as the writers of the New Testament all assert, and as Christians have ever hitherto believed, a complete system of type and antitype in the Old and New Testament respectively; to what can we attribute this, but to an overruling Hand guiding the fortunes of the chosen race, and of individuals in that race, and to the continual presence of that Holy Spirit who divideth to every man severally as He will? Is not all this to be esteemed a special inspiration? And if all this is in the Old Testament, then, whatever human elements there be in it, there is surely such a Divine element as to make its books emphatically the "Oracles of God," to which we may look as unmistakably embodying His will and word. We may admit that the word of God so embodied in the Scriptures was designed to communicate to us great moral and spiritual truths, that there was no purpose to give any revelation of physical science or of mere general history. Yet if we have abundant evidence that Almighty God chose the prophets and the books of the Bible as channels for communicating His will to mankind, we have surely abundant evidence that they

* Professor Jowett thinks we must give up the types appealed to in the New Testament, just as we do not press the patristic appeal to the scarlet thread of Rahab, or the 318 followers of Abraham. That is to say, we must attach no more importance to the language of the Apostles, or of our blessed Lord Himself, than to the language of any Christian writer in the earlier days of Christianity. The New Testament has appealed to types of Christ in the Old Testament. The early Christians universally acknowledged such types, but perhaps unwisely found moreover certain fanciful resemblances unknown to the Apostles and Evangelists. Because the latter were fanciful, must we conclude that the former were false?

would not be permitted to err in things pertaining to God. It may not be proof that their language will not be popular, and so possibly inaccurate, in matters of science, or that their statements will be infallible in the matter of a date or in other things immaterial; but it is surely proof enough that they would never be permitted to mislead us in questions of faith; for otherwise they would bring us credentials to their faithfulness from God Himself, and with these credentials in their hands, deceive, and mislead, and delude us.

And here may we not see the fallacy of Coleridge's view, who accepts Scripture where it "finds" him, but not in its less interesting and merely historical records? If we go on this principle, where are we to stop? If we read the second book of Chronicles, perhaps we may discover very little which "finds" us; whereas, if we read Baxter's 'Saint's Everlasting Rest,' it may "find" us in nearly every page. To carry out Coleridge's principle, we ought to uncanonize, or reject the inspiration of, the book of Chronicles, and set up as canonical the book of Baxter. But, if our former arguments be correct, and the general belief of Christians in all ages be true, the whole historical record of the Old Testament is part of the great depository of God's revealed will. One part may be more important than another. But when we see that God spoke by words of man, and also by acts of man—that even actions were predictions—when we find Christ Himself and His Apostles citing the books of the Old Testament, as the "Scriptures," as the "Oracles of God," as "God-breathed" (Θεόπνευστα)—surely we have no right to say that one part "finds me" and another does not, and to settle our own Canon accordingly. The whole collection of the books of the Old Testament comes to us with Divine credentials—prophecies in it fulfilled after they were uttered—Christ's attestation to them, that they all testified of Him—St. Paul's testimony to them that they were "given by inspiration of God"—and, having such Divine credentials, we cannot suppose that any of these books would mislead us, at least in things heavenly.

20. If all this holds of the Old Testament, it holds, *à fortiori*, of the New; for probably no one will contend that the Apostles, with Christ's own mission, with the gift of tongues and miraculous powers, with the special promise of the Comforter and of guidance by Him into all truth, with the assurance of Christ's own presence, and with the command to preach on the house-tops what He had told them in the ear,—were in a worse position or more liable to error than the prophets of the Old Testament. And, though we may well believe that each individual Apostle, like every Christian man, may have grown in grace and in the knowledge of our Lord and Saviour Jesus Christ; yet this belief need in no wise interfere with our acknowledgment that messengers, specially accredited by God to man, would never be permitted to deliver a false message, or to mislead those whom they were so signally commissioned to lead.*

For Mr. Maurice's question, as to whether we ought not to consider the inspiration of Holy Scripture like to that inspiration for which all of us pray, there seems but little difficulty in the reply. Undoubtedly, the

* Revelation has all along been progressive, but not on that account self-contradictory. Abel offered the firstlings of his flock; Abraham offered a ram instead of his son; Moses instituted the Paschal sacrifice; John the Baptist pointed to "the Lamb of God, which taketh away the sin of the world;" St. Paul spoke of "Christ our Passover;" St. Peter of "the precious blood of Christ, as of a lamb without blemish and without spot." There is the same testimony here through a course of at least four thousand years; but yet the knowledge was progressive. John the Baptist knew more of Christ than all that before him had been born of woman, but less than the least in the kingdom of the Saviour. What is true of the knowledge of the Church may be equally true of the knowledge of the Apostles. If they had not been capable of growth in wisdom, they would not have been human; but no proof whatever has yet been given that the testimony of one Apostle is, on points of Christian doctrine, in conflict with the testimony of another, or that the more matured knowledge of any particular Apostle ever led him to contradict, in the least degree, his own former witness to the truth. Certainly they themselves always appeal to the consistency of their own teaching, and denounce all teaching which is inconsistent with their own. "Though we or an angel from heaven preach any other Gospel unto you than that which we have preached unto you, let him be accursed." (Gal. i. 8.) "If there come any unto you, and bring not this doctrine, receive him not into your house, neither bid him God speed." (2 John 10.)

inspiration for which we pray is the same as the inspiration of the writers of Scripture—that is to say, it is the inspiration of God's Holy Spirit which guides not only into holiness, but also into truth. Probably pious men in general never begin any work of importance without praying for grace and guidance; but when they do so, they do not expect to be answered with, for instance, the gift of tongues. They ask for the word of wisdom or the word of knowledge, not for the working of miracles; yet they look for it from one and the selfsame Spirit. And surely we may admit that that great Teacher of the Church may teach one in one way and another in another. It may be His will to give one a deep insight into spiritual mysteries, but yet not to give him a knowledge of future events. To another, at a particular period of the Church, or under a peculiar dispensation, he may give the power of prophecy, or the gift of tongues, or the working of miracles, or such guidance and direction as shall render his testimony, as to things heavenly, infallibly true. Are we to deny that God can do so? Or again—is it impossible for him to give such a knowledge except in the way of giving a higher degree of sanctification, purifying the soul from all that may darken the understanding, and so sharpening the spiritual insight? Such a view of things is surely in direct opposition to the constant record of the Bible. If it be true, it must convict the writers of the books of the Bible of false testimony. Is it not clearly set down that Balaam—that "the man of God, who was disobedient to the word of the Lord"—that Jonah, who fled from God's presence—that Caiaphas, even when compassing Christ's crucifixion—were all empowered to speak of future things, and some of them sorely against their wills? Although it is most likely that God would in general use sanctified instruments to speak to man of sacred things, yet, if the record of the Bible be true, there may be a revelation to the mind, and so through the mouths of men, which is not the result of high sanctification, of purifying the heart that it may see God. A man may have "the gift of prophecy and understand all mysteries and all knowledge," may "speak with the tongues of men and angels," and yet lack charity and be nothing.

21. And so, to pass to another view of the question, Mr. Morell argues that the Divine or religious truth can only be revealed to our highest and deepest intuitional consciousness. It is not to be received by the senses, by the understanding, or by the reason, but deeper down still in our inmost being. There is no reason to quarrel with this statement so far as it goes. Its fault is, that it is one-sided. "When it pleased God to reveal his son in" St. Paul, doubtless the revelation was not to the intellect only, but to the very heart of hearts. But there may be abundant head-knowledge without any such revelation to the soul and spirit. And must we not distinguish here between objective and subjective revelation? Of course objective revelation must suppose a subject; that is to say, if an object is to be revealed, there must be a subject by which that object may be embraced and conceived. But is it not plain to common sense, setting aside all logical subtilty, that there may be an outward manifesting (*φανέρωσις*, if *ἀποκάλυψις* be ambiguous) of God to man, without any inward reception of Him to the soul? And if so, may not a man be taught, as Daniel or St. John, by a vision of God, and yet, like Balaam or Jonah, not have his soul converted to God? He may "see the vision of the Almighty, falling into a trance, and having his eyes open;" and yet his heart may not be opened to know and to love God. It really seems as if Mr. Maurice, Mr. Morell, and others of similar sentiments, deny the possibility of this.* But on what principle can it be denied, except on a principle which rejects all that is miraculous, and which makes God, not a Personal Being, but an impersonal influence?

* Of course, Professor Baden Powell must have held this impossible, because he held that there was no contact point between the spiritual and the physical worlds. They lie, according to him, in two distinct planes, which can never come in contact. But to what must such a theory lead short of Materialism and Atheism, in minds of the common stamp?

22. But if we believe that God has in different ages authorized certain persons to communicate objective truth to mankind, if in the Old Testament history and the books of the prophets we find manifest indications of the Creator, it is then a secondary consideration, and a question on which we may safely agree to differ, whether or not every book of the Old Testament was written so completely under the dictation of God's Holy Spirit, that every word, not only doctrinal, but also historical or scientific, must be infallibly correct and true. The whole collection of the books has been preserved providentially to the Church as the record of God's early dealings with mankind, and especially with one chosen race, as the collection of the prophecies and of the religious instruction which God was pleased to communicate to man in the preparatory dispensations of His grace: and with these there is a book of sacred psalmody, embodying the religious experience of men living under the Theocracy, some at least of the hymns contained in it evincing the power of prophecy in their writers. Whatever conclusion, then, may be arrived at as to the infallibility of the writers on matters of science or of history, still the whole collection of the books will be really the oracles of God, the Scriptures of God, the record and depository of God's supernatural revelations in early times to man. And we may remember that our Blessed Lord quotes the Psalms as the Scripture, adding, "And the Scripture cannot be broken."

23. It has been already observed that what holds good of the Old Testament holds *à fortiori* of the New. If the writers of it were the accredited messengers from God to man, taught by Christ, assured by Him of the teaching of His Holy Spirit, sent to bring to man the knowledge of God and of His highest truths, we cannot doubt that that Spirit, who was to guide them into all truth, would never let them err in things pertaining to God. This is really what we want. We want to be assured that we have an *infallible* depository of *religious* truth. And if we are satisfied that the Apostles

were accredited messengers for delivering God's message and communicating God's truth to the world, clearly we have this assurance. It may, no doubt, be true that all ministers of Christ in all ages are God's accredited messengers; but the difference is this: the Apostles had new truths to deliver direct from heaven; other ministers of Christ have old truths to impress—truths which may perhaps be new to their hearers, but which are old to the Church. In the one case there is a direct commission with a need of infallibility in things spiritual; in the other the mission is through the intervention of others, and with the power of correcting errors by appealing to the authority of the written record.

If we can establish this much, then there seems no need to fear the admission of a human element, as well as a Divine, in Scripture. The Apostles had the treasure of the Gospel in earthen vessels. The Holy Spirit taught the Churches through the instrumentality of men of like passions with ourselves. The difficulty of enunciating a definite theory of inspiration consists exactly in this—in assigning the due weight respectively to the Divine and the human elements. A human element there clearly was. Though in instances like those of Balaam and Caiaphas we seem to have something more like organic inspiration, yet in ordinary cases God was pleased to take the nobler instruments of man's thoughts and hearts through which to communicate a knowledge of Himself to the world, rather than to act through the organs of speech, moving men's mouths as mere machines. With all the pains and ingenuity which have been bestowed upon the subject, no charge of error, even in matters of human knowledge, has ever yet been substantiated against any of the writers of Scripture. But, even if it had been otherwise, is it not conceivable that there might have been infallible Divine teaching in all things spiritual and heavenly, whilst on mere matters of history, or of daily life, Prophets and Evangelists might have been suffered to write as men? Even if this were true, we need not be perplexed or disquieted, so we can be agreed that the Divine element was ever such as to secure the infallible truth of Scripture in all things Divine.

24. All this, of course, is applicable to questions of physical science. Scripture was not given to teach us science, but to teach us religion; it may not have been needful that the inspired writers should have been rendered infallible in matters of science, nor is it at all likely that they should have been directed to teach to the ancient world truths which would anticipate the discoveries either of Newton or of Cuvier. It would have been almost as strange if they had not used popular expressions in writing on such subjects, as if they had written not in the tongue of their own people, but in a new dialect more refined and philosophical. But may we not ask, whether in this question of physical science, as in many like things, sceptical writers have not been sharp-sighted on minute discrepancies, whilst they have been blind to the great general harmony of truth? It is ever so; each petty difference of date, each little inconsistency in two concurrent narratives, every, the slightest appearance of doubtful morality, anything like a supposed repugnance to what we consider the necessary attributes of the Most High, have been dwelt on and magnified, and used as objections to the inspiration of Holy Writ; whilst the general truth of its history, the purity and holiness of its general moral teaching, the grandeur and sublimity of its doctrines concerning God, are altogether forgotten or concealed. Yet is it not true that, both in moral and in physical science, nothing short of miraculous inspiration can account for the superior knowledge of the writers of the Old Testament compared with the most enlightened sages of heathen antiquity? The Jewish philosophers, like Philo, felt that the Scriptures of their own prophets had brought in simple language to their unlettered fellow-countrymen moral and spiritual truths, after which the Platonists had been "seeking, if haply they might feel after them and find them." Greeks, like Justin

Martyr, who had tried one school of philosophy after another, discovered in the Gospel all that was most valuable in the teaching of all schools. And may not we, who have come upon an age of rapid discovery in physical science, confess that the account given of the Creator and His works in the Bible was an anticipation and is an epitome of all that has lately come to light? The telescope has revealed to us worlds and systems of worlds rolling in unbroken order through infinity of space; the microscope has shown us living and organised beings so small as to bewilder the mind with their minuteness as the suns and planets bewilder it with their vastness; the geologist takes us back through countless ages, the records of which are indelibly engraven "as with lead in the rock for ever." And the Bible, but no other ancient book that is written, had told us that the Being who created all things was such that the Heaven and the Heaven of Heavens could not contain Him, that He was the High and lofty One inhabiting eternity, but that though He had His dwelling so high, yet He humbled Himself to behold the things that are in heaven and earth, that a sparrow did not fall without Him, that the very hairs of man's head were numbered by Him. Infinite greatness, infinite minuteness, infinity of duration, infinity of action, eternity of past existence and of past operation, as well as an eternity of the future, are all distinctly predicated in the Scriptures of the mind of Him who made us all. And here for the first time, now in the nineteenth century, we find the same infinity in heaven and in earth, and in the sea, and under the earth.

Why, then, must we be puzzled because some recently discovered geological phenomena seem hard to reconcile with a few verses in one chapter of Genesis? Are we to forget the marvellous harmony between God's word and His works, which a general view of both convinces us of, because there are some small fragments of both, which we have not yet learned to fit into each other? Nay! even here, we may fairly say, that the harmony already found is greater than the as yet unexplained discord. For, putting aside all doubtful interpretations and difficult questions concerning the six days of creation and the like, these two facts are certain; all sound criticism and all geological inquiry prove them alike; viz., first, that the original creation of the universe was at a period indefinitely, if not infinitely, distant from the present time; and secondly, that of all animated beings, the last that came into existence was man. Geology has taught us both these facts; but the first verse of Genesis clearly teaches the first, and the twenty-sixth verse teaches the second.

To touch but for a moment on one other subject which has been so strongly pressed of late, the uniform prevalence of law, not only in things inanimate, but where there is life and even reason and morality—can anything be more consistent than this with the whole of the Old Testament? Indeed its peculiar teaching from first to last may be said to have been that God is a God of order; that He has impressed His law on all creation; that all things serve Him, all things obey Him; that to break laws, whether moral or physical, is inevitably to entail suffering; and that even rational and spiritual beings, even in their rational and spiritual natures and capacities, are subject to laws which cannot be broken; that the sins of the fathers go down in sin and sorrow to the children; and that even repentance, though it may save the soul, cannot undo the sin or avert the suffering. There is nowhere in creation or in history written more plainly the record of order and law.

25. Surely such thoughts as these seem fit to satisfy us, that God's works rightly read are not likely to contradict God's word rightly interpreted. There will be for a time, perhaps for all time, apparent difficulties. When new questions arise, at first many will feel that it is hopeless to attempt to solve them. Some will despair, some will try to smother inquiry; some will rush into Atheism, and others will fall back into superstition. Patience is the proper temper for an age like our own, which is in many ways an age of transition.

The discoveries of Galileo seemed more alarming to his contemporaries than any discoveries in geology or statistics can seem to us. We see no difficulty in Galileo's discoveries now. Such things, then, are probably the proper trials of our faith. Sober views, patience, prayer, a life of godliness, and a good conscience, will, no doubt, keep us from making shipwreck of faith. What now seems like a shadow may only be the proof that there is a light behind it. And even if at times there should come shadows seeming like deep night, we may hope that the dawn of the morning is but the nearer.

ESSAY VIII.

THE DEATH OF CHRIST.

CONTENTS OF ESSAY VIII.

THE DEATH OF CHRIST.

Jesus, the Son of God, died on the Cross to redeem mankind from sin and death. This is the truth which for eighteen centuries has been preached to Jew and Gentile; the truth which the Apostles took in their mouths when they went to teach Christianity to nations who had never heard of Christ before. The doctrine of Reconciliation has not escaped the fate of other Christian truths: it has done and is doing its work in converting the world, and consoling many a crushed heart; but at the same time the terms in which it should be set forth have been disputed, and sometimes the doctrine itself denied. Recent writers have discussed the subject, avowing for the most part the wish to preserve the tenet itself; but in some cases dealing so hardly with the evidence on which it rests, as to leave an impression that the doctrine of the Atonement is a modern invention, which can well be dispensed with in teaching Christianity; and some even speak of it as a dishonour to God the Father, in that it represents Him as accepting the sufferings of the innocent for the guilty. The present Essay is directed to those who profess to attach to the sufferings of the Redeemer some preternatural efficacy, beyond that of mere example, yet who would substitute for the received account of their effect some other doctrine. With those who utterly deny the doctrine of Atonement we have nothing here to do, except to wish them an increased consciousness of the need of a purgation from sin: for when Christ is needed, then, and not sooner, He will be found; when man sees the serpent twining round his limbs, and feels serpent-poison beating in his blood, and sees over all his beauty and glory the serpent's defiling trail, he will look to the Son of Man lifted up, and be healed. But the promise that the doctrine shall in spirit be preserved, but heightened and spiritualized, has much attraction for the inquiring. In approaching them with the key of a profounder gnosis, men profess to give to the well-worn pages of the Bible the freshness and originality which is all they need. And the attempt in this Essay will be to show that the doctrine of the Atonement, although a mystery, is made known to us in the Bible in certain strong and definite touches which allow of no mistake; that this doctrine has been, in fact, continuously held and taught in the Church, altering from time to time in form, but in substance neither gaining anything nor losing anything; and that the difficulties, which beset this as they do other mysteries, are not at all lightened by the remedies proposed on behalf of human reason, but rather increased.

I. Much has been made of the supposed silence of our Lord as to the atoning virtue of His death; and it has even been hinted that in this respect the words of Jesus are at variance with those of His Apostles.* If these were so, the question would bear no discussion; and much else would fall to the ground at the same time. The only proof of it which we are offered is, that Christ Himself "never uses the word sacrifice"† as applied to His own life or death. But this is a purely artificial test. It remains still to inquire what the Lord does say of that death; for such is the copiousness of language, that an act which has the nature of a sacrifice may be described without the use of that particular word. When He speaks of "My blood of the new Covenant," no doubt the word sacrifice is dispensed with; but there must be very few, we should

* Professor Jowett on the Epistles, ii. 556. "In [the words of Christ] is contained the inner life of mankind and of the Church; there too the individual beholds, as in a glass, the image of a goodness which is not of this world. *To rank their authority below that of the Apostles and Evangelists,* is to give up the last hope of reuniting Christendom in itself, and of making Christianity an universal religion."

† Ibid.

hope, who cannot discern in such words the "sacrificial allusion."

1. The three first Evangelists, as we know, agree in showing that Jesus unfolded His message to the disciples by degrees. He wrought the miracles that were to be the credentials of the Messiah; He laid down the great principles of the Gospel morality until He had established in the minds of the Twelve the conviction that He was the Christ of God. Then as the clouds of gloom grew darker, and the malice of the Jews became more intense, He turned a new page in His teaching. Drawing from His disciples the confession of their faith in Him as Christ, He then passed abruptly, so to speak, to the truth that remained to be learnt in the last few months of His ministry, that His work included suffering as well as teaching.* He was instant in pressing this unpalatable doctrine home to His disciples, from this time to the end. Four occasions when He prophesied His bitter death are on record, and they are probably only examples out of many more.† We grant that in none of these places does the word sacrifice occur; and that the mode of speaking is somewhat obscure, as addressed to minds unprepared, even then, to bear the full weight of a doctrine so repugnant to their hopes. But that He must (δεῖ) go and meet death; that the powers of sin and of this world are let loose against Him for a time, so that He shall be betrayed to the Jews, rejected, delivered by them to the Gentiles, and by them mocked and scourged, crucified, and slain; and that all this was done to achieve a foreseen work, and accomplish all things written of Him by the prophets—these we do certainly find. They invest the death of Jesus with a peculiar significance; they set the mind inquiring what the meaning can be of this hard necessity that is laid on Him. For the answer we look to other places; but at least there is here no contradiction to the doctrine of sacrifice, though the Lord does not yet say, "I bear the wrath of God against your sins in your stead; I

* Matt. xvi. 20, 21. † Matt. xvi. 21.

become a curse for you." Of the two sides of this mysterious doctrine,—that Jesus dies for us willingly, and that He dies to bear a doom laid on Him as of necessity, because some one must bear it,—it is the latter side that is made prominent. In all the passages it pleases Jesus to speak not of His desire to die, but of the burden laid on Him, and the power given to others against Him.

2. Had the doctrine been explained no further, there would have been much to wait for. But the series of announcements in these passages leads up to one more definite and complete. It cannot be denied (we might almost say that before Mr. Jowett it never was denied) that the words of the institution of the Lord's Supper speak most distinctly of a sacrifice. "Drink ye all of this, for this is My blood of the new covenant," or, to follow St. Luke, "the new covenant in My blood." We are carried back by these words to the first covenant, to the altar with twelve pillars, and the burnt-offerings and peace-offerings of oxen, and the blood of the victims sprinkled on the altar and on the people, and the words of Moses as he sprinkled it: "Behold the blood of the covenant which the Lord hath made with you concerning all these words."* No interpreter has ever failed to draw from these passages the true meaning: "When My sacrifice is accomplished, My blood shall be the sanction of the new covenant." The word sacrifice is wanting; but sacrifice and nothing else is described. And the words are no mere figure used for illustration, and laid aside when they have served that turn, "Do this in remembrance of Me." They are the words in which the Church is to interpret the act of Jesus to the end of time. They are reproduced exactly by St. Paul.† Then, as now, Christians met together, and by a solemn act declared that they counted the blood of Jesus as a sacrifice wherein a new covenant was sealed; and of the blood of that sacrifice they partook by faith, professing them-

* Exod. xxiv.

† 1 Cor. xi. 25.

selves thereby willing to enter the covenant and be sprinkled with the blood.

3. So far we have examined the three "synoptic" Gospels. They follow a historical order. In the early chapters of all three the doctrine of our Lord's sacrifice is not found, because He will first answer the question about Himself, "Who is this?" before he shows them "What is his work?" But at length the announcement is made, enforced, repeated; until, when the feet of the betrayer are ready for their wicked errand, a command is given which secures that the death of Jesus shall be described for ever as a sacrifice and nothing else, sealing a new covenant, and carrying good to many. Lest the doctrine of Atonement should seem to be an afterthought, as indeed De Wette has tried to represent it, St. John preserves the conversation with Nicodemus, which took place early in the ministry; and there, under the figure of the brazen serpent lifted up, the atoning virtue of the Lord's death is fully set forth. "As Moses lifted up the serpent in the wilderness, even so must the Son of Man be lifted up; that whosoever believeth in Him should not perish, but have eternal life."* As in this intercessory act, the image of the deadly, hateful, and accursed † reptile became by God's decree the means of health to all who looked on it earnestly, so does Jesus in the form of sinful man, of a deceiver of the people,‡ of Antichrist,§ of one accursed,‖ become the means of our salvation; so that whoever fastens the earnest gaze of faith on Him shall not perish, but have eternal life. There is even a significance in the word זקף, which in older Hebrew meant to lift up in the widest sense, but began in the Aramaic to have the restricted meaning of lifting up for punishment.¶ With Christ the lifting up was a seeming disgrace, a true triumph and elevation. But the context in which these verses occur is as important

* John iii. 14, 15.
† Gen. iii. 14, 15.
‡ Matt. xxvii. 63.
§ Matt. xii. 24; John xviii. 33.
‖ Gal. iii. 13.
¶ So Tholuck and Knapp, 'Opuscula,' p. 217. The treatise of Knapp on this discourse is valuable throughout.

as the verses themselves. Nicodemus comes as an inquirer; he is told that man must be born again, and then he is directed to the death of Jesus as the means of that regeneration. The earnest gaze of the wounded soul is to be the condition of its cure; and that gaze is to be turned not to Jesus on the mountain, or in the temple, but on the Cross. This, then, is no passing allusion, but it is the substance of the Christian teaching addressed to an earnest seeker after truth.

Another passage claims a reverent attention—"If any man eat of this bread he shall live for ever, and the bread that I will give is My flesh, which I will give for the life of the world."* He is the bread; and He will give the bread.† If His presence on earth were the expected food, it was given already; but would he speak of "drinking His blood" (ver. 53), which can only refer to the dead? It is on the Cross that He will afford this food to His disciples. We grant that this whole passage has occasioned as much disputing among Christian commentators as it did among the Jews who heard it; and for the same reason—for the hardness of the saying. But there stands the saying; and no candid person can refuse to see a reference in it to the death of Him that speaks.

In that discourse, which has well been called the Prayer of Consecration offered by our High Priest, there is another passage which cannot be alleged as evidence to one who thinks that any word applied by Jesus to His disciples and Himself must bear in both cases precisely the same sense, but which is really pertinent to this inquiry:—"Sanctify them through Thy truth: Thy word is truth. As Thou hast sent Me into the world, even so have I also sent them into the world. And for their sakes I sanctify Myself, that they also might be sanctified through the truth.‡ The word

* John vi. 51.

† Some, omitting ἣν ἐγὼ δώσω, would read, "And my flesh is the bread that I will give for the life of the world." So Tertullian seems to have read "Panis quem ego dedero pro salute mundi caro mea est." The sense is the same with the omission; but the received reading may be successfully defended.

‡ John xviii. 17–19.

ἁγιάζειν, "sanctify," "consecrate," is used in the Septuagint for the offering of sacrifice,* and for the dedication of a man to the Divine service.† Here the present tense, "I consecrate," used in a discourse in which our Lord says He is "no more in the world," is conclusive against the interpretation "I dedicate My *life* to thee;" for life is over. No self-dedication, except that by death, can now be spoken of as present. "I dedicate Myself to Thee, in My death, that these may be a people consecrated to Thee;" such is the great thought in this sublime passage, which suits well with His other declaration, that the blood of His sacrifice sprinkles them for a new covenant with God. To the great majority of expositors from Chrysostom and Cyril, the doctrine of reconciliation through the death of Jesus is asserted in these verses.

The Redeemer has already described Himself as the Good Shepherd who lays down His life for the sheep,‡ taking care to distinguish His death from that of one who dies against his will in striving to compass some other aim: "Therefore doth my Father love Me, because I lay down My life that I might take it again. No man taketh it from Me, but I lay it down of Myself. I have power to lay it down, and I have power to take it again."

Other passages that relate to His death will occur to the memory of any Bible reader. The corn of wheat that dies in the ground to bear much fruit,§ is explained by His own words elsewhere, where He says that He came "to minister, and to give His life as a ransom for many."‖

4. Thus, then, speaks Jesus of Himself. What say His witnesses of Him? "Behold the Lamb of God," says the Baptist, "which taketh away the sins of the world."¶ Commentators differ about the allusions implied in that name. But take any one of their opinions, and a sacrifice is implied. Is it the Paschal lamb that is referred to? Is it the lamb of the daily sacrifice?

* Levit. xxii. 2. † Numb. iii. 15. ‡ John x. 11, 17, 18.
§ John x. 24. ‖ Matt. xx. 28. ¶ John i. 29.

Either way the death of the victim is brought before us. But the allusion in all probability is to the well-known prophecy of Isaiah (liii.), to the Lamb brought to the slaughter, who bore our griefs and carried our sorrows.*

5. The Apostles after the Resurrection preach no moral system, but a belief in and love of Christ, the crucified and risen Lord, through whom, if they repent, men shall obtain salvation. This was Peter's preaching on the day of Pentecost;† and he appealed boldly to the Prophets on the ground of an expectation of a suffering Messiah.‡ Philip traced out for the Eunuch, in that picture of suffering holiness in the well-known chapter of Isaiah, the lineaments of Jesus of Nazareth.§ The first sermon to a Gentile household proclaimed Christ slain and risen, and added "that through His name whosoever believeth in Him shall receive remission of sins."‖ Paul at Antioch preaches "a Saviour Jesus;"¶ "through this Man is preached unto you the forgiveness of sins, and by Him all that believe are justified from all things from which ye could not be justified by the law of Moses."** At Thessalonica all that we learn of this Apostle's preaching is "that Christ must needs have suffered and risen again from the dead: and this Jesus, whom I preach unto you, is Christ."†† Before Agrippa he declared that he had preached always "that Christ should suffer, and that He should be the first that should rise from the dead;"‡‡ and it was this declaration that convinced his royal hearer that he was a crazed fanatic. The account of the first founding of the Church in the Acts

* See this passage discussed fully in the notes of Meyer, Lange (*Bibelwerke*), and Alford. The reference to the Paschal Lamb finds favour with Grotius and others; the reference to Isaiah is approved by Chrysostom and many others. The taking away of sin (αἴρειν) of the Baptist, and the bearing it (φέρειν, *Sept.*) of Isaiah, have one meaning, and answer to the Hebrew word נָשָׂא. To take the sins on himself is to remove them from the sinners; and how can this be through his death except in the way of expiation by that death itself?

† Acts ii.

‡ Acts iii. 18.

§ Acts viii.; Isai. liii.

‖ Acts x.

¶ Acts xiii. 23.

** Acts xiii. 38, 39.

†† Acts xvii. 3.

‡‡ Acts xxvi. 23.

of the Apostles is concise and fragmentary; and sometimes we have hardly any means of judging what place the sufferings of Jesus held in the teaching of the Apostles; but when we read that they "preached Jesus," or the like, it is only fair to infer from other passages that the Cross of Christ was never concealed, whether Jews, or Greeks, or barbarians were the listeners. And this very pertinacity shows how much weight they attached to the facts of the life of our Lord. They did not merely repeat in each new place the pure morality of Jesus as He uttered it in the Sermon on the Mount: of such lessons we have no record. They took in their hands, as the strongest weapon, the fact that a certain Jew crucified afar off in Jerusalem was the Son of God, who had died to save men from their sins; and they offered to all alike an interest, through faith, in the resurrection from the dead of this outcast of His own people. No wonder that Jews and Greeks, judging in their worldly way, thought this strain of preaching came of folly or madness, and turned from what they thought unmeaning jargon.

6. We are able to complete from the Epistles our account of the teaching of the Apostles on the Doctrine of Atonement. "The Man Christ Jesus" is the mediator between God and man, for in Him the human nature in its sinless purity is lifted up to the Divine, so that He, exempt from guilt, can plead for the guilty.* Thus He is the second Adam that shall redeem the sin of the first; the interest of men are bound up in Him, since He has power to take them all into Himself.† This salvation was provided by the Father, to "reconcile us to Himself;"‡ to whom the name of "Saviour" thus belongs;§ and our redemption is a signal proof of the love of God to us.‖ Not less is it a proof of the love of Jesus, since He freely lays down His life for us—offers it as a precious gift, capable of purchasing all the lost.¶ But there is another side of the truth more

* 1 Tim. ii. 5; 1 John. ii. 1, 2; Heb. vii. 25.
† Eph. v. 29, 30; Rom. xii. 5; 1 Cor. xv. 22; Rom. v. 12, 17.
‡ 2 Cor. v. 18. § Luke i. 47. ‖ 1 John iv. 10.
¶ 1 Tim. ii. 6; Tit. ii. 14; Eph. i. 7. Compare Matt. xx. 28.

painful to our natural reason. How came this exhibition of Divine *love* to be needed? Because wrath had already gone out against man. The clouds of God's anger gathered thick over the whole human race; they discharged themselves on Jesus only. God has made Him to be sin for us who knew no sin.* He is made "a curse" (a thing accursed) for us, that the curse that hangs over us may be removed.† He bore our sins in His own body on the tree.‡ There are those who would see on the page of the Bible only the sunshine of the Divine love; but the muttering thunders of Divine wrath against sin are heard there also: and He who alone was no child of wrath, meets the shock of the thunderstorm, becomes a curse for us, and a vessel of wrath; and the rays of love break out of that thunder-gloom and shine on the bowed head of Him who hangs on the Cross, dead for our sins.

We have spoken, and advisedly, as if the New Testament were, as to this doctrine, one book in harmony with itself. That there are in the New Testament different types of the one true doctrine, may be admitted without peril to the doctrine. The principal types are four in number.

7. In the Epistle of James there is a remarkable absence of all explanations of the doctrine of the Atonement. But this admission does not amount to so much as may at first appear. True, the key-note of the Epistle is that the Gospel is the Law made perfect, and that it is a practical moral system, in which man finds himself free to keep the Divine law. But with him Christ is no mere lawgiver appointed to impart the Jewish system. He knows that Elias is a man like himself; but of the Person of Christ he speaks in a different spirit. He calls himself "a servant of God and of the Lord Jesus Christ," who is "the Lord of Glory." He speaks of the Word of Truth, of which Jesus has been the utterer. He knows that faith in the Lord of Glory is inconsistent with time-serving and "respect of per-

* 2 Cor. v. 21. † Gal. iii. 13. ‡ 1 Pet. ii. 24.

sons." * "There is one lawgiver," he says, "who is able to save and to destroy;" † and this refers no doubt to Jesus, whose second coming he holds up as a motive to obedience. ‡ These and like expressions remove this Epistle far out of the sphere of Ebionitish teaching. The inspired writer sees the Saviour, in the Father's glory, preparing to return to judge the quick and dead. He puts forth Christ as Prophet and King, for he makes Him teacher and judge of the world; but the office of the Priest he does not dwell on. Far be it from us to say that he knows it not. Something must have taken place before he could treat them with confidence, as free creatures, able to resist temptations, and even to meet temptations with joy. He treats "your faith" as something founded already, not to be prepared by this epistle. § His purpose is a purely practical one. There is no intention to unfold a Christology, such as that which makes the Epistle to the Romans so valuable. Assuming that Jesus has manifested Himself, and begotten anew the human race, he seeks to make them pray with undivided hearts, and be considerate to the poor, and strive with lusts, for which they and not God are responsible; and bridle their tongues, and show their fruits by their works. ‖

8. In the teaching of St. Peter the doctrine of the Person of our Lord is connected strictly with that of His work as Saviour and Messiah. The frequent mention of His sufferings shows the prominent place he would give them; and he puts forward as the ground of his own right to teach, that he was "a witness of the sufferings of Christ." ¶ The atoning virtue of those sufferings he dwells on with peculiar emphasis; and not less so on the purifying influence of the Atonement on the hearts of believers. He repeats again and again that Christ died for us; ** that He bare our sins in His

* James i. 1, ii. 1, i. 18.

† James iv. 12.

‡ James v. 7–9.

§ James i. 2, 3, 21.

‖ See Neander, 'Pflanzung,' b. vi. c. 3; Schmid, 'Theologie der N. T.,' part ii.; and Dorner, 'Christologie,' vol. i. p. 95.

¶ 1 Pet. v. 1.

** 1 Pet. ii. 21, iii. 18, iv. 1.

own body on the tree.* He bare them; and what does this phrase suggest, but the goat that "shall bear" the iniquities of the people off into the land that was not inhabited? † or else the *feeling the consequences* of sin, as the word is used elsewhere? ‡ We have to choose between the cognate ideas of sacrifice and substitution. Closely connected with these statements are those which connect moral reformation with the death of Jesus. He bare our sins that we might live unto righteousness. His death is our life. We are not to be content with a self-satisfied contemplation of our redeemed state, but to live a life worthy of it. § In these passages the whole Gospel is contained; we are justified by the death of Jesus, who bore our sins that we might be sanctified and renewed to a life of godliness. And from this Apostle we hear again the name of "the Lamb," as well as from John the Baptist; and the passage of Isaiah comes back upon us with unmistakable clearness. We are redeemed "with the precious blood of Christ as of a lamb without blemish and without spot." ‖ Every word carries us back to the Old Testament and its sacrificial system: the spotless victim, the release from sin by its blood (elsewhere, i. 2, by the *sprinkling* of its blood), are here; not the type and shadow, but the truth of them; not a ceremonial purgation, but an effectual reconcilement of man and God.

9. In the inspired writings of John we are struck at once with the emphatic statements as to the Divine and human natures of Christ. A right belief in the incarnation is the test of a Christian man; ¶ we must believe that Jesus Christ is come in the flesh, and that He is manifested to destroy the works of the devil.** And, on the other hand, He who has come in the flesh is the One who alone has been in the bosom of the

* 1 Pet. ii. 24. If there were any doubt that "for us" (ὑπὲρ ἡμῶν) means "in our stead" (see verse 21), this 24th verse, which explains the former, would set it at rest.

† Lev. xvi. 22.

‡ Lev. xx. 17, 19.

§ 1 Pet. ii. 21–25, iii. 15–18.

‖ 1 Pet. i. 18, 19, with Isaiah liii. 7.

¶ 1 John iv. 2; John i. 14; 2 John 7.

** 1 John iii. 8.

Father, seen the things that human eyes have never seen, and has come to declare them unto us.* This Person, at once divine and human, is "the propitiation for our sins," our "advocate with the Father," sent into the world "that we might live through him;" and the means was His laying down His life for us, which should make us ready to lay down our lives for the brethren.† And the moral effect of His redemption is, that "the blood of Jesus Christ cleanseth us from all sin."‡ The intimate connection between His work and our holiness is the main subject of his first Epistle: "Whosoever is born of God doth not commit sin."§ As with St. Peter so with St. John, every point of the doctrine of the Atonement comes out with abundant clearness. The substitution of another who can bear our sins, for us who cannot; the sufferings and death as the means of our redemption, our justification thereby, and our progress in holiness as the result of our justification.

10. To follow out as fully in the more voluminous writings of St. Paul the passages that speak of our salvation would far transgress the limits of our space. Man, according to this Apostle, is a transgressor of the law. His conscience tells him that he cannot act up to that law which, the same conscience admits, is divine, and binding upon him. Through the old dispensations man remained in this condition. Even the law of Moses could not justify him: it only by its strict behests held up a mirror to conscience that its frailness might be seen. Christ came, sent by the mercy of our Father who had never forgotten us; given to, not deserved by us. He came to reconcile men and God, by dying on the Cross for them and bearing their punishment in their stead.‖ He is "a propitiation through faith in his blood:"¶ words which most peo-

* 1 John i. 2, iv. 14; John i. 14–18.

† 1 John ii. 1, 2, iv. 9, 10, v. 11–13, iii. 16, v. 6, i. 7; John xi. 51.

‡ 1 John i. 7.

§ 1 John iii. 9.

‖ 2 Cor. v. 14–21; Rom. v. 6–8. These two passages are decisive as to the fact of substitution; they might be fortified with many others.

¶ Rom. iii. 25, 26. Compare Levit. xvi. 15. Ἱλαστήριον means "victim for expiation."

ple will find unintelligible except in reference to the Old Testament and its sacrifices. He is the ransom, or price paid, for the redemption of man from all iniquity.* The wrath of God was against man; but it did not fall on man. God made His Son "to be sin for us" though He knew no sin; and Jesus suffered though men had sinned. By this act God and man were reconciled.† On the side of man trust and love and hope take the place of fear and of an evil conscience; on the side of God, that terrible wrath of His, which is revealed from heaven against all ungodliness and unrighteousness of men, is turned away.‡ The question whether we are reconciled to God only, or God is also reconciled to us, might be discussed on deep metaphysical grounds; but we purposely leave that on one side at present, content to show that at all events the intention of God to punish man is averted by this "propitiation" and "reconcilement."

11. Different views are held about the authorship of the Epistle to the Hebrews, by modern critics. But its numerous points of contact with the other Epistles of St. Paul must be recognized. In both, the incompleteness of Judaism is dwelt on; redemption from sin and guilt is what religion has to do for men, and this the law failed to secure. In both, reconciliation and forgiveness and a new moral power in the believers are the fruits of the work of Jesus. In the Epistle to the Romans, Paul shows that the Law failed to justify; and that faith in the blood of Jesus must be the ground of justification. In the Epistle to the Hebrews the same result follows from an argument rather different: all that the Jewish system aimed to do is accomplished in Christ in a far more perfect manner. The Gospel has a better Priest, more effectual sacrifices, a more profound peace. In the one Epistle the Law seems set aside wholly for the system of faith; in the other the Law is exalted and glorified in its Gospel shape. But

* Titus ii. 14. Still stronger in 1 Tim. ii. 6, "ransom instead of" (ἀντίλυτρον). Also Eph. i. 7 (ἀπολύτρωσις); 1 Cor. v. 20, vii. 23.

† Rom. v. 10; 2 Cor. v. 18–20; Eph. ii. 16; Col. i. 21.

‡ Rom. i. 18, v. 9; 1 Thes. i. 10.

the aim is precisely the same, to show the weakness of the Law and the effectual fruit of the Gospel.

12. We are now in a position to see how far the teaching of the New Testament on the effects of the death of Jesus is continuous and consistent. Are the declarations of our Lord about Himself the same as those of James and Peter, John and Paul? and are those of the Apostles consistent with each other? The several points of this mysterious transaction may be thus roughly described:—

1. God sent His Son into the world to redeem lost and ruined man from sin and death, and the Son willingly took upon Him the form of a servant for this purpose; and thus the Father and the Son manifested their love for us.

2. God the Father laid upon His Son the weight of the sins of the whole world, so that He bare in His own body the wrath which men must else have borne, because there was no other way of escape for them; and thus the Atonement was a manifestation of Divine justice.

3. The effect of the Atonement thus wrought is, that man is placed in a new position, freed from the dominion of sin, and able to follow holiness; and thus the doctrine of the Atonement ought to work in all the hearers a sense of love, of obedience, and of self-sacrifice.

In shorter words, the sacrifice of the death of Christ is a proof of Divine *love* and of Divine *justice*, and is for us a document of *obedience*.

Of the four great writers of the New Testament, Peter, Paul, and John set forth every one of these points. Peter, the "witness of the sufferings of Christ," tells us that we are redeemed with the blood of Jesus, as of a lamb without blemish and without spot; says that Christ bare our sins in His own body on the tree. If we "have tasted that the Lord is gracious,"* we must not rest satisfied with a contemplation of our redeemed state, but must live a life worthy of it. No

* 1 Pet. ii. 3.

one can well doubt, who reads the two Epistles, that the love of God and Christ, and the justice of God, and the duties thereby laid on us, all have their value in them; but the love is less dwelt on than the justice, whilst the most prominent idea of all is the moral and practical working of the Cross of Christ upon the lives of men.

With St. John, again, all three points find place. That Jesus willingly laid down His life for us, and is an advocate with the Father; that He is also the propitiation, the suffering sacrifice for our sins; and that the blood of Jesus Christ cleanseth us from all sin, for that whoever is born of God doth not commit sin; all are put forward. The death of Christ is both justice and love, both a propitiation and an act of loving self-surrender; but the moral effect upon us is more prominent even than these.

In the Epistles of Paul the three elements are all present. In such expressions as a ransom, a propitiation, who was "made sin for us," the wrath of God against sin, and the mode in which it was turned away, are presented to us. Yet not wrath alone. "The love of Christ constraineth us; because we thus judge, that if one died for all, then were all dead: and that He died for all, that they which live should not henceforth live unto themselves, but unto Him which died for them, and rose again."* Love in Him begets love in us, and in our reconciled state the holiness which we could not practise before becomes easy.

The reasons for not finding from St. James similar evidence, we have spoken of already.

Now in which of these points is there the semblance of contradiction between the Apostles and their Master? In none of them. In the Gospels, as in the Epistles, Jesus is held up as the sacrifice and victim, quaffing a cup from which His human nature shrank, feeling in Him a sense of desolation such as we fail utterly to comprehend on a theory of human motives. Yet no one takes from Him His precious redeeming life; He

* 2 Cor. v. 14, 15.

lays it down of Himself, out of His great love for men. But men are to deny themselves, and take up their cross and tread in His steps. They are His friends only if they keep His commands and follow His footsteps.

II. We must consider it proved that these three points or moments are the doctrine of the whole New Testament. What is there about this teaching that has provoked in times past and present so much disputation? Not, I am persuaded, the hardness of the doctrine,—for none of the theories put in its place are any easier,—but its want of logical completeness. Sketched out for us in a few broad lines, it tempts the fancy to fill it in and lend it colour; and we do not always remember that the hands that attempt this are trying to make a mystery into a theory, an infinite truth into a finite one, and to reduce the great things of God into the narrow limits of our little field of view. To whom was the ransom paid? What was Satan's share of the transaction? How can one suffer for another? How could the Redeemer be miserable when He was conscious that His work was one which could bring happiness to the whole human race? Yet this condition of indefiniteness is one which is imposed on us in the reception of every mystery: prayer, the incarnation, the immortality of the soul, are all subjects that pass far beyond our range of thought. And here we see the wisdom of God in connecting so closely our redemption with our reformation. If the object were to give us a complete theory of salvation, no doubt there would be in the Bible much to seek. The theory is gathered by fragments out of many an exhortation and warning; nowhere does it stand out entire, and without logical flaw. But if we assume that the New Testament is written for the guidance of sinful hearts, we find a wonderful aptness for that particular end. Jesus is proclaimed as the solace of our fears, as the founder of our moral life, as the restorer of our lost relation with our Father. If He had a cross, there is a cross for us; if He pleased not Himself, let us deny ourselves; if He suffered for sin, let us hate sin.* And the question ought not to be, What do all these mysteries mean? but, Are these thoughts really such as will serve to guide our life and to assuage our terrors in the hour of death? The answer is twofold—one from history and one from experience. The preaching of the Cross of the Lord even in this simple fashion converted the world. The same doctrine is now the ground of any definite hope that we find in ourselves, of forgiveness of sins and of everlasting life.

Now, in examining the history of the Doctrine we shall expect to find, as in the case of other doctrines, that attempts have been made to force from Scripture a clearer and more definite statement than is found there at first sight. We should also expect that these attempts at greater precision had been accompanied often, if not always, with the loss of some element on which the Bible insists.

But we are told at the outset that the position which this doctrine holds in the history of early controversies is far from being so prominent as that which we assign it now. The answer is, that in the first ages the disputes which prevailed about the Person of Jesus superseded the discussion of the Atonement, because they contained and implied it. More than once, when the ostensible argument was the nature of the Redeemer, Athanasius insisted that if the Son of God had been such a one as Arians and Sabellians dreamed of, He could not have redeemed the world. How could a man who was only one among other men have power to redeem them all? It needed the Son of God, who had power over all men, to redeem them.† And

* Pages might be filled with examples of this, and yet Mr. Garden ('Tracts for Priests and People,' iii. p. 4) starts back from one of them as Crusoe did from the footprint in the sand. "In 1 Pet. i. 18, we have an impressive sentence, which we read on in our habitual key of thought, but are surprised to find that it does not end on the key-note:—'Forasmuch as ye know that ye were not redeemed with corruptible things, as silver and gold, from [it is here that modern ears and thoughts will anticipate a different ending] your vain conversation received by tradition from your fathers.'" This is the usual key-note of Scripture, but not the only note. The same Epistle speaks of redemption from wrath and eternal death (1 Pet. i. 5, ii. 10, iv. 17, 18).

† Cont. Arian. i. § 49. Comp. i. §§ 19, 37, ii. § 14, 20.

Arians, conscious of this, rested the redemption of men, not on any power inherent in the Saviour's nature, but on the simple declaration of God that the curse was removed.* Cyril objects to Nestorius that his doctrine makes the Atonement meaningless, for it refers it, not to one who is God and man, but to a man, whose relation to God the Word is only external.† When the whole doctrine of the Person of Christ was the subject of searching controversy, the doctrine of Atonement did not emerge as the subject of a separate dispute; but we may be sure that it was never far off. And it may be that this is the clue to our present discussions about the Atonement. As of old it was involved in another controversy, so now the subject of that other controversy is involved in this; and when we are invited to discuss whether one man can ever bear the sins of another, and whether vicarious punishment could ever be agreeable to God's justice, we cannot but notice that the divine nature of Christ is never strongly asserted on that side, or assumed as an element in the argument. The death of Jesus is discussed as the death of a mere man. The most incautious rhetorical flights of orthodox sermons are selected for assault, in which a substitution of the innocent for the guilty is spoken of under the forms and phrases of human law, in the very points where human law is not applicable; and the more deliberate expositions of faith are put on one side. We are accused of making that the corner-stone of the Christian faith which no creed fully defines. The necessity of our position compels us to make the Atonement prominent. But all the faith is involved in the discussion. When the views of Socinus on the Atonement are brought forth again, his notions as to the Redeemer's person are probably not far off.

In modern writers who have touched the subject, an undue prominence is given to one feature of the patristic teaching, the notion that the ransom paid by our Lord was paid to the Devil, into whose power man had

* Cont. Arian. ii. § 68.

‡ Adv. Nestorius, III. 2.

passed through sin.* Thus what is for the most part rhetorical playing with words, is put forward as if it were the sole and the serious belief of these writers. The story bears a very different telling. There is not space for it here; but a few quotations may be useful. The old Epistle to Diognetus † tells how God gave His Son a ransom for us; and we are to rejoice that the Holy One died for the evil-doers, the sinless for the sinful; for what was there, short of His righteousness, that would cover our sins? Clement of Rome ‡ sees the truth not less clearly. According to Ignatius, § we owe our salvation to Christ crucified for us in the flesh, and to His "God-blessed passion." To the Jewish objection that the cross is accursed, and therefore unworthy of Messiah, Justin Martyr retorts that this is matter for those to be ashamed of who inflicted the death, when the Father of all had "willed that His Christ should take the curses of all for the whole race of man, knowing that He would raise Him up after He had been crucified and put to death." ‖ By Irenæus the Scriptural accounts of the Redemption are prominently put forward. As a man caused the fall, a man must cause the restoration; he must be a man able to *sum up* (*recapitulare*) all the human species in himself, so as to bear the punishment of all, and to render an obedience that will compensate for their innumerable acts of disobedience. It suits not with the Divine nature to effect His will by force, but rather by love and influence; hence came the voluntary self-sacrifice, out of exceeding love, of the divine Son of Man, who is truly God and man; and hence too men are not dragged, but drawn back to God from sin, embracing by an act of their will the offers of mercy made them through Christ. But, combined with these statements, there are indications at least of the idea that Christ died to redeem men from a real objective power which Satan had acquired over them, so that the redeeming price was paid, not so

* Professor Jowett, ii. 572. Mr. Gardner (p. 4) devotes seventeen lines to the subject of the Fathers, and this theory occupies the whole of them; as if there were no other opinions worth mentioning.

† Ch. ix. ‡ Ch. l. § Ad Smyrn. ch. i. ‖ Dial. Tryph., § 95.

much by way of debt due to the righteousness and justice of God, as by way of ransom to release them from a conqueror, and to restore them to God, to whom they originally belonged. "Since," says he, "the apostasy [the Devil] unjustly got the dominion over us, and, though we belonged by nature to the omnipotent God, alienated us against nature and made us his own disciples, the Word of God [Christ], powerful in all things and perfect in justice, acted justly in regard to the apostasy [the Devil], redeeming from it that which was His own; not by force, in the way that it got dominion over us in the beginning, when it carried off insatiably that which belonged not to it, but by persuasion (*secundum suadelam*), as it became God to receive what He would, by the use of persuasion, not of force, that justice should not be infringed, nor yet that which God created of old should perish." * Some have supposed that the words "by persuasion" mean by a way which the Devil himself must be convinced was right and reasonable, but this would be strangely inconsistent with the general views of the writer. The apostate spirit, as he says in another place, persuaded men to transgress, but he used fraud and wrong to compass his purpose; and here Irenæus contrasts with this false persuasion, which he calls force and injustice, the fair and just persuasion by which the Son of Man, who has been lifted up, draws all men back to Him. The persuasion is addressed to lost men, and not to Satan. With Irenæus the redemption was not a friendly treaty between two powers for the release of prisoners; he says that Christ contended with, repulsed, conquered, despoiled, and bound the enemy of God and man. The point on which he lays most stress is certainly not the power which Satan has acquired, but the power that belongs inherently to our Redeemer of summing up in Himself the interests of the whole human race. He sees that to offer a sacrifice for all mankind is a privilege that can belong only to man on one side, for man's fault is in question; only to the Divine Son of God on the other, for only He can

* Adv. Hær. v. i. 1.

control the destinies of all men. If the "persuasion" has been rightly referred to *man*, and not to Satan (and Dorner seems to have clearly established it*), then Irenæus goes very little beyond Holy Scripture in his attempt to explain the mystery of the power of the Evil One over us. In both we are to be redeemed from Satan and from death, in both the offering of One whose power over the human race is unlimited shall procure deliverance. The doctrine of the Atonement is knit up with that of the Incarnation; and he does not ask whether one man can suffer for another, but what manner of person He must be whose sufferings can have power over all others to save them.

The doctrine of Athanasius will furnish another sample of patristic teaching. Man fell through sin, says this great teacher; and the righteousness of God was thus brought into conflict with His goodness. According to His righteousness and truth, He who has given the law must inflict the allotted punishment on those who break it: but then His goodness could not suffer that man, made in his own image, should perish through the deceit of the Devil and his angels. It were better he had not been created. How shall this contradiction be solved? By man's repentance? Simple repentance would be insufficient on two grounds; because the Divine veracity, which had promised death, would not have been satisfied, and because this would not free man from the physical corruption (ἡ κατὰ φύσιν φθορά) which he had incurred. The Word of God, the Son, who created the world, can alone restore it. He is above all, and can suffer and satisfy for all, and free all from their natural corruption; for He indeed created them at first, and so can re-create. In order to this restoration, He, the incorporeal and incorruptible Word, made for Himself a temple, a house, in a human form and flesh. Now and then the expressions of Athanasius savour of Apollinarian views, as though Christ were the nature of God in the form of man, the human mind

* 'Person Christi,' vol. i., p. 479, note against Baur, 'Versöhnung,' p. 85; compare notes in Thomson's 'Bampton Lectures,' p. 287.

being left out of the account; but in other places no one has more strongly expressed himself against this very error, and his comment on the words "Let this cup pass from me," and on "The spirit is willing, but the flesh is weak," is that they reveal two wills in man —the human, that is of the flesh, and the Divine, which is from God. The analogy between the creation and the restoration of man is closely pursued by Athanasius. He describes the redemption more as a mere renewal than as a development and completion of the creation of man; and here lies the peculiarity of his system. The curse of death is taken away; but more than this, the Word becomes, through the Holy Ghost, a living principle diffused through the hearts of men, freeing them from the power of sin, and enduing them with immortality. What part the death of the Lord bears in our restoration will appear from such expressions as these. His death is "a sacrifice offered on behalf of all and instead of all;"* and it reconciles us to the Father,† for in it Jesus took on Him the punishments to which we were liable, and, by suffering in His own body our punishment, conferred salvation on us.‡ His death paid a debt,§ and was a ransom for us.‖ As our High-Priest He brought Himself as an offering to the Father, to purge us from our sins by His own blood.¶ The power of this sacrifice to reconcile for the whole human species arose from the position in which Jesus stands to us all; He is the Creator, and again He is the Ruler of all the world and of mankind, and so nothing that He does but must influence all. When a king comes into a great city, and takes up his dwelling in a single house of it, the honour of the visit is reflected on all the city; enemies and robbers desist from their work, and, through the presence in one house, the whole city is protected. So it is with the presence of our King.** Who can fail to see in this system all the Scriptural elements of the Atonement faithfully pre-

* De Incar. 20.
† De Decr. 14.
‡ Cont. Ar. i. 60.
§ Cont. Ar. ii. 66.
‖ Cont. Apol. ii. 12.
¶ Cont. Ar. ii. 7.
** De Incar. ix.

served? More than this might be proved if space and time allowed: the anxious recurrence to Holy Writ as the rule of faith, the correction by the light of Scripture of statements that run perilously close to error. In the Fathers the various representations of the work of the Lord,—the ransom, the sacrifice, the conflict with Satan,—all have reference to His death. We have seen this in Athanasius. Tertullian uses the phrase that Christ is "the universal Priest of God,"* in reference to His offering of Himself for men. No doubt the theories on this subject were indefinite and incomplete; but a greater mistake could not be made than to suppose that the doctrine of satisfaction and substitution was absent from the patristic writings, and lay dormant till the voice of Anselm woke it. Origen, who is often said to know nothing of the substitutive sufferings of the Lord, asserts them expressly in several passages.† Cyril of Jerusalem not less so:—"We were enemies of God through sin, and God had appointed the sinner to die. One of two things therefore must needs have happened,—that God keeping His word should destroy all men, or that in His loving kindness He should cancel the sentence. But behold the wisdom of God; He preserved both the truth of His sentence and the exercise of His loving kindness. Christ took our sins in His own body on the tree, that we, being dead to sin, should live to righteousness."‡ So Cyril of Alexandria:—"Since they who were the servants of sin were made subject to the punishment of sin, He who was free from sin, and had trod the paths of all righteousness, underwent the punishment of sinners, destroying by His Cross the sentence of the old curse . . . 'being made a curse for us.'"§ The same doctrine is found in Augustine, Hilary of Poitiers, and Ambrose. None of these writers worked out into a system the doctrine of the

* Cont. Marc. iv. 9.

† Cont. Cels. ii. 23, and vol. xviii. 14, Explan. in Epist. ad Rom. iii. 8. Compare Möhler, Symbolik. p. 247.

‡ Catech. xiii. 33.

§ De Incarnatione, ch. xxv. in Mai's Patrum Bibliotheca. It is doubtful whether this work is Cyril's, but it is of about the same date, and other passages as express are quoted from Cyril's acknowledged works.

substitutive sacrifice of Christ; but it is absurd to pretend, with these passages before us, that Anselm was the inventor of the doctrine, and the destroyer of another which is supposed to have usurped dominion over the minds of all the Fathers. It is something more than absurd when words are put into the mouth of Gregory Nazianzen which he never spoke, to the effect that there is no danger in errors about the mode of our redemption.*

* By what means a weak cause may be supported will appear from the history of a spurious quotation. Mr. Garden, in his tract already quoted, says: "In the strong language of Gregory Nazianzen, we may affirm that 'the mode in which Christ has redeemed us is a matter in which we may err without danger.'" If Gregory the Theologian had made such an assertion, no doubt the language would have been as strong as it was startling. But he never did. Mr. Garden follows Professor Jowett, who says: "Gregory of [*sic*] Nazianzen numbers speculations about the sufferings of Christ among those things on which it is useful to have correct ideas, but not dangerous to be mistaken." Professor Jowett has followed F. C. Baur, who, however, quotes the whole passage, and not a fragment of a sentence, and admits that it is not in harmony with the rest of Gregory's views. The passage in question comes from the first of the 'Theological Orations' of Gregory (Orat. xxvii. [xxxiii.]), in which he is inveighing against the Eunomians for the length to which they carry their speculations on the nature and counsels of God. He suggests other subjects of discussion from profane philosophy, in which they may show off their skill and eloquence without wronging God by irreverence. He then says: "But if you think these things unworthy of discussion, as trifling things that have been often refuted, and desire to employ yourself on your own subjects, and seek the distinction that may arise from these, I will afford you even here a wide field. Philosophize about the world or worlds, about matter, the soul, about reasonable creatures higher and lower, about resurrection, judgment, retribution, *the sufferings of Christ; for in these things to attain our object is not useless, and to fail of it is free from peril* (τὸ ἐπιτυγχάνειν οὐκ ἄχρηστον καὶ τὸ διαμαρτάνειν ἀκίνδυνον)." Here there is not a word about "the mode in which Christ has redeemed us;" the nature of our Lord's sufferings is what they are allowed to discuss, and not the consequences of those sufferings, of which no hint is given. As well say that the passage tells us it is safe to err on the side of materialism, because matter is mentioned; or safe to deny the soul's immortality, because the soul is mentioned. There are questions, physical and metaphysical, about all these things, which admit of discussion, and yet need not trench on vital Christian truth. The origin and duration of the world, the nature of matter, the soul's connexion with the body, the nature of reason, the state of the body in the resurrection, the nature of future rewards and punishments, the sufferings of the Lord, how far physical and how far mental, are all questions of this sort. It is not even clear that the word διαμαρτάνειν means "to err from the truth;" it may be, as Leunclavius renders it, "to fail of your object," and the object in this case is success in disputation. But on this I do not insist. We have here the solitary patristic quotation by which lax views about the Atonement are supposed to be encouraged; and Mr. Jowett prints part of the sentence, when the whole would have at once disarmed his argument, whilst Mr. Garden puts words into the mouth of this Father which he never used, which he could not and would not have used. We are thankful for the admission that this is the best that can be done on that side

7. But it is time to pass to Anselm, the reputed parent of our modern teaching; and we ought to be thoroughly satisfied upon the question whether he has or has not supplanted the Bible in our pulpits and treatises, and in our thoughts. The *Cur Deus Homo*, of this great and truly humble writer, is an attempt to answer the question, Why was it requisite for man's salvation that God should become man? Considering the Divine omnipotence, we might expect that the mere fiat of His will or the acceptance of some lower sacrifice than that of the only begotten Son of God might have sufficed to effect the reconciliation. The incidents of the Incarnation and the Crucifixion seem derogatory to God; the Infinite Spirit clothing Himself with a finite nature, and allowing finite men and the power of evil to assail and triumph over Him, these are representations that may shock our reverence. If redemption was required at all, why was it not effected by means of a sinless man who was no more than man? A mere man caused the fall, a mere man might have sufficed for the restoration. Anselm replies that this would not have procured man's perfect restoration, for it would have left men dependent on one of themselves; he to whom they owed redemption would have been in some sense their master instead of God. But why, it may be urged, was there any need of redemption at all? When we speak of God's anger, we mean neither more nor less than His will to punish. The moment that will is withdrawn, there is neither anger nor punishment to fear; and so it might appear that a mere revocation of the will to punish would of itself constitute salvation. The argument that God gave His Son as a ransom for man from the power of Satan, because it was right

of the argument. Let us put a true quotation from Gregory in the place of the sham one: "... the very sufferings of Christ by which all of us, without exception, were restored (ἀνεπλάσθημεν) who partake of the nature of the same Adam, and were deceived by the serpent and brought into the death of sin, and were saved again by the heavenly Adam, and were brought back to the tree of life whence we had fallen, by means of the tree of ignominy" (Orat. xxxiii. p. 609, ed. Paris, 1840). This is one among many statements as to "the mode in which Christ redeemed us."

and just to recover by fair means a race who had freely and voluntarily given themselves over to his power, is at once dismissed: for the true reasons, namely, that the Devil cannot properly have either merit or power or right over man; that the power which in one sense he exerts against mankind was only permissive, and that it expired when the permission was withdrawn. He then proceeds to establish the need of redemption on purer grounds. Every creature that can will and act owes to God an entire obedience, as the honour due to Him. All sin, then, is a wrong done to His honour, of what kind soever the offence is. Punishment must attach to sin invariably, in order to mark the difference between sin and holiness; it would not only encourage sin, if men thought that the Almighty were blind to it, but would obscure and distort our views of the Divine nature itself, if we conceived of Him as one to whom sin and its opposite are both alike. We should thus regard God as admitting sin into the order of the universe without dissent or protest, whereas we know that the very nature of sin is disorder. God, however, cannot suffer disorder; for though sin could not really detract from His power and dignity, its aim and intent are to dishonour and deface, as far as may be, the beauty of the Divine government. If it may do this and yet draw at pleasure on the Divine but free forgiveness, unrighteousness is more free and unshackled than obedience. Now no man can render for his brethren the full obedience required: "a sinner cannot justify a sinner." Even if a man with his heart full of love and contrition were to renounce all earthly solaces, and in labour and abstinence to strive to obey God in all things, and to do good to all and forgive all, he would only be doing his duty. But he is unable to do even this; and it is his misery that he cannot plead his inability as an excuse, because that proceeds from sin. He must be of the same nature as those for whom he renders the obedience, in order that it may be accepted as theirs; and yet if the satisfaction is to be complete, he must be able to render to God something greater than every created thing, for among men pure righteousness is not to be found; and if so, he must be God, for what is there above the creature but God Himself? Therefore he must be God and man, whose life far exalted above all created things must be infinitely valuable. As to the manner of this redemption, Anselm uses these words, which bear on a controverted point in his theory:—"If man sinned for pleasure, is it not consistent that he should make satisfaction by hardness? And if he were most easily overcome by the Devil, so as to dishonour God by sin, is it not just that man, making satisfaction to God for sin, should conquer the Devil, for the honour of God, in the most difficult manner?" If he departed from God completely by sin, the mode of making satisfaction should be by a complete devotion to God. Now man can undergo nothing harder or more difficult, for the honour of God, than death; nor can he devote himself to God more completely than when he delivers himself to death for His honour.* But Anselm insists more on the *life* of obedience which was acted out by Jesus, and which no other could have rendered, as the satisfaction which was rendered to God. He made atonement for men, by rendering through life a perfect obedience, in lieu of theirs, and by a death which, as sinless, He did not owe, and as God He might have escaped. Thus is the Divine mercy, which seems to be excluded when we think of the Divine justice and of the infinite amount of sin, brought into perfect harmony with justice, so that the reason can discern that no better scheme of redemption could have been devised.

8. This is a rough sketch of the system to which, as we are often told, modern theology is indebted for the theory of satisfaction which it teaches. We are

* II. 11. I find in this passage the doctrine of vicarious retribution, which Baur fails to find in the *Cur Deus Homo*. Mr. Garden (p. 5), in deciding between us on this point, thinks it enough to quote a passage in the next chapter (II. 12) which is supposed to preclude the doctrine. The passage, however, seems to me wholly irrelevant, referring merely to the question whether what one does willingly can be the cause of misery.

supposed by many to owe the doctrine of the Cross to a pious Christian writer, as late as the eleventh century. Let us sift the claim.

The foundation of Anselm's theory is found in Athanasius. Both these writers view the Atonement habitually as a transaction before the bar of Divine justice in heaven; both seek the explanation of its possibility in the divine nature of him who atones; both conceive it as the payment of a debt due to God. It would have been equally hard for both to admit the force of the modern objection that it is not lawful for one *man* to be punished for another; for while the perfect human nature of the Lord was essential to complete the Atonement, the human nature is dwelt in by the divine, and the will that chooses to suffer for man is divine. With both these writers the great moment of the Atonement is found in the Incarnation; in the presence in human flesh of one able to act for men. What we owe to Anselm is not so much the general plan of salvation as the minute and careful delineation of it. Nowhere else is there such logical precision, such a continuous chain of deduction. This is the kind of originality which we ought to attribute to him.

9. Anselm has indeed introduced a word, which has ever since been associated with the dogma of the Atonement—the word satisfaction. But a new word is not necessarily an innovation in thought. The legal sense of the word satisfaction is the appeasing a creditor on the subject of his debt, not necessarily by the payment of it (solutio), but by any means that he will accept. It is used more than once by Tertullian, but not in the sense of *vicarious* satisfaction; in that sense no doubt it owes its currency to Anselm. It has gone far to replace the word sacrifice. But the fundamental ideas of the two words are not so far apart as is often assumed. Sacrifice, in the usage of the Bible, is the appointed rite by which a Jewish citizen, who has broken the law and forfeited thereby his position within the pale of the Covenant, is enabled to procure

his restoration. It is a Jewish word, and belongs to the positive provisions of the Jewish polity, and not to general ethics. Still, as the Jewish constitution reflected the general dealings of God with all the world, the term sacrifice applies to the restoration of all men who have strayed from God by their sins. With thankful hearts we may look up to Christ as the lamb of our paschal sacrifice; since by His death and resurrection, and without any merit or effort of our own, we are restored to the place before God which we had lost. The word satisfaction, on the other hand, implies a debt which we have not the means of paying, a debt of punishment in consequence of our sins, or of obedience to compensate former disobedience. Both terms imply a restoration through something which is not us nor ours. Whether we speak of it as a sacrifice or a payment, the same thought may be present to our minds; a reconcilement of God and us, wrought not by us but by our Redeemer. It is a gain to us, as sacrificial usages become forgotten, to acquire a term which expresses the same idea appealing to the principles of general ethics. But facts, and not words, are the subject of revelation; what we believe is that the death of the Redeemer purchased our life, our reconciliation, that without His obedience our sins would have borne their natural fruit of death. And whether we call this act a sacrifice, on account of its being an offering to appease the Divine wrath, or a satisfaction, as it is a mode of payment which God accepts instead of the debt of obedience that we cannot render, is of less importance than might at first appear. So long as we believe that the wrath of God because of our disobedience fell in the shape of affliction on Him who alone had so acted as to please God, the terms in which it may be expressed may be suffered to vary.

10. The system of Anselm is indeed open to criticism, but not for the introduction of the word sacrifice. So far is it from being an undue development of Holy Writ, that it falls far short of it in the completeness of its statements. As the Atonement transcends all our

means of exposition, it must needs be that, the more exactly it is fitted to any analogous human affairs, the more entirely will some of its complex elements be omitted from the description. Hence, for example, there is the danger lest the Atonement degenerate into a transaction between a righteous Father on the one side, and a loving Saviour on the other, because in the human transaction from which the analogy is drawn two distinct parties are concerned; whereas in the plan of salvation one will operates, and in the Father and the Son alike justice and love are reconciled. Again, the reconciliation effected by Christ appears rather as a bringing God into harmony with Himself, His mercy with His justice, than as a reconciliation of man with God. The passages of Scripture that speak of the wrath of God against man are not explicable of Anselm's system. The exclamation of the Baptist, that Jesus is the Lamb of God, that taketh away the sin of the world; the prophecy of His sufferings by Isaiah (ch. liii.); the words of Peter that He "his own self bare our sins in his own body on the tree;"* and passages of like import in St. Paul's writings,† can only find place with Anselm by a very forced interpretation. His scheme is mainly this, that the merit of the perfect obedience of Jesus was so great as to deserve a great reward, and that in answer to the prayer of the Lord this reward was given in the form of the salvation of His brethren. But Christ does not appear in this system as groaning and suffering under the curse of the world, as He does in Holy Scripture. Until the time of Anselm the doctrine of the Atonement had within certain limits fluctuated with the change of teachers; the doctrine itself was one and the same, but this or that aspect of it had been made prominent. Anselm aimed at fixing in one system the scattered truths; and the result has been that he, like his predecessors, made some parts of the truth conspicuous to the prejudice of the rest.

11. Looking fairly at the whole period from Igna-

* 1 Pet. ii. 24. † Gal. iii. 13. 2 Cor. v. 21.

tius to Anselm, we are obliged to own that the efficacy of the death of the Lord was always believed, and that of the three parts or moments of this doctrine, the love, and the justice, and the practical obedience, not one fell to the ground. The theory of a victory over Satan, gained by deceit, shrinks into its proper proportions; it is an excrescence on the truth, and not a leprosy turning all the truth into corruption.

III. 1. Holy Scripture contains the doctrine, and the Church has always taught it. Whence, then, the repugnance to it which some persons of serious and devout minds have expressed? The objections for the most part take the form of a denial that it is possible that one man should suffer for the sin of another; that the wrath of God could be appeased by the sacrifice of one who had done no sin in the place of the sinful. A thorough-going sense of man's responsibility for his own acts, and a reluctance to own that the sufferings of the just can ever be the consequence of the sins of others, are the two principal motives at work. How can these be most easily dealt with?

2. All the difficulties that belong to this question are introduced prior to it by a consideration of sin itself. The conscience of man admits that there is such a thing as guilt; and so strong, decided, and constant is its witness, that there is no fear that mankind in the long run will attempt to explain away the fact that sin exists. But when I am asked to believe that it is against the Divine plan that any other being should take away from me any of the consequences of my guilt, I think myself entitled to say that it is the correlative of this proposition that no one should have brought upon me any of the guilt and its consequences. It is surely not more repugnant to God's justice that another should bear my guilt than that I should be guilty because of another; nay, Divine justice will be more readily reconciled with a plan in which One who is entirely willing to bear my sin should take off its intolerable burden from me who am earnestly desirous to get rid of it, than with a plan in which sinfulness

devolves from one who did not mean his own faults to do me harm, upon me who by no means wished to inherit them. But this kind of devolution, or transmission, is a fact of constant occurrence of which no man can be ignorant. We open the works of writers like Broussais and Büchner, and find such importance given to the influence on moral habits of hereditary transmission, of age, sex, maladies, mode of living, and climate, that the doctrine of individual responsibility seems for the moment to be in peril. We need to retire within, and take counsel of conscience, in order to resist the invitation to believe "that what we call free-will is nothing but our being conscious of a will, without being conscious of the antecedents that determine its mode of action," which, translated into plainer nonsense, would mean—being conscious of our will without being conscious that we did not possess one. But all are agreed that outward circumstances and inward constitution derived from parents and ancestors by physical laws, have a great influence upon the character of men. In extreme cases this may be true to the extent of paralysing the will altogether. If a young man has sprung from parents of intemperate habits, who lived by stealing, and has been brought up among companions of the same sort, we shall hardly look to find him any better than the soil in which he grew; and any efforts to amend him and call forth his moral nature would be preceded by the effort to transplant him. Alike in the good and evil qualities of men the effect of hereditary transmission comes under daily notice. And since we are always invited in this question to discuss it in forensic language, and are told that no man can be allowed before a human tribunal to take upon himself the position of the criminal and suffer the punishment of another, because every one arraigned there must bear his own burden, we must remark that, if every one did actually bear his own burden there, human justice would have attained a perfection which it has never yet boasted. In graduated punishments for the same offence there is a rough attempt to take into account the antecedents of the criminal and the amount of his temptation; but these palliations are not proved in evidence, and it is by a rough guess only that an equitable apportionment of punishment is attempted. In defining the line at which mental imbecility extinguishes all sense of responsibility laws have utterly failed, and tribunals have stultified themselves by conflicting decisions. But the arguments on these cases prove that all believe in a class of minds where guilt is just imputable and no more,—where the mental debility, often congenital, all but extinguishes the moral offence. In cases of such nice difficulty, mistakes must be made; punishment must fall on the wrong man. Nor is this mere speculation; a man has been decided insane at one place for a crime for which another man at another place has been hanged, according as the judge and jury made prominent in their minds the safety of society or consideration for the supposed criminal. Capital punishment has fallen upon men who, upon the same facts before a different tribunal, would have been judged to have exercised no choice at all, but to have acted out the course to which birth and disease and the like compelled them. Absolute compulsion of this kind is no doubt rare; but absolute freedom is more than rare, it is impossible. Men enter this world the heirs of passions, perhaps cultivated in the last generation to an unnatural height; they are nurtured on bad examples and a low morality, so that they cannot do the things that they would. And it is the rule, and not the exception, that men's moral actions are tinctured with the colour of the actions of others before and around them, which they could not possibly have caused. Now, if these facts are admitted,—if, instead of that perfect isolation of responsibility which some insist on, a joint responsibility is the universal rule,—with what show of reason can they pretend that it is on this ground that the Christian scheme is untenable? Look into the black London alleys teeming with ignorance, improvidence, and vice; do you not see written in those faces eloquent in wretchedness, "We did not place ourselves here: were the choice given us freely, we would not be as we are"? Then what do we think of the consistency of those who see guilt brought on by others, but think it revolting that another should take it off? Living comments upon the words "In Adam all die" abound, and cannot be blotted out: it ought not then to revolt our moral sense that those other words are added, "In Christ shall all be made alive." The latter words, in fact, go far to solve the mystery of the former. For the constant transmission of sinfulness, the heritage of sins bequeathed from the fathers to their children, is revolting to the moral sense when severed from the thought of a Deliverer. The message of Heaven to us is, "Ye are all of one family, partakers of the family heritage of sin, and wretchedness, and ruin; and yet every one of you driven by the stimulus of conscience to protest against the ruin, and to erect yourselves above it. Ye are accustomed to this derived destruction, this hereditary partnership in guilt; lift your eyes one step further back, to that common Father from whom ye sprung, from whom ye have lived in separation. By taking your nature I will re-establish that lost connection, I will make the Father's lost favour accessible to you again. I will undo the curse, by placing myself under it. I will sanctify the flesh, which the sin of generations has made unclean. For I am partaker of the Father's nature, and the power over you which belongs to Him is mine also; and I am partaker of your nature in all save in the sin of it; and thus I am the Mediator between God and man."

3. There is then nothing new or startling in the revelation of a great moral good bestowed on us without our effort; it is in harmony with the system under which we live, as members of a great family having common interests even in things belonging to the soul. But, beside the general fact, the mode of our redemption, mysterious as it must be, should still be in harmony with our mental constitution; it should be such as not to shock our natural expectation. We cannot

possibly hope to understand it; but it must not be such that we can understand it ought not to be. The question—Why should Jesus have died for our sins instead of simply declaring forgiveness? Why was not He the ambassador of forgiveness instead of the artificer of it?—will obtrude even upon submissive minds. Now the death of Jesus, after such a life as His, was the crowning act and achievement of sin; and so showed to man the extent of his own corruption. Here was one whose every act went to deserve the titles of "the Holy One, and the Just," whose love for His own people gushed forth through the openings of a hundred miracles wrought for their good: whose speech was meek, and whose life could provoke no jealousy, nor threaten the foundations of any lawful power; who had fed, or healed, or taught many thousands of the people that ought to have been ready witnesses in His behalf; whose doctrines seldom failed to produce on the hearers a profound impression in favour of a teacher different from and far above all others; yet whose goodness quickened the hatred of those in authority, and was the direct cause of reviling, persecution, and death. By how much the example of the sinless Jesus is conspicuous, by so much is the sin of His persecution and death intensified. Had there been in the Lord (the supposition must be pardoned) one trace of human folly or sin, high-priest and Pharisee would have been more tolerant, because the contrast that rebuked them would have been less violent. But that shining armour showed no flaw nor stain. Their hatred was pure hatred of goodness; their sentence of death was passed because there was no crime; the death itself was the first death that was the wages of no sin. And so the Apostles, in preaching the Gospel, wanted no better arguments for condemning sin: that men had imbrued their hands in the blood of One who was sinless and who loved them, was enough to abase any candid spirit. As when some man of doubtful repute becomes suddenly recognized as the author of some enormous crime, and all his fellows recoil from him, and will not give him a cup of water lest they seem to countenance his evil deed, so, when mankind saw that the blood of the sinless Jesus was red on the hand of the rulers and the people, they were pricked to the heart by the spectacle, and fled from a haunt of guilt too horrible for them to live in longer. "Men and brethren, what shall we do? . . . . . . Save yourselves from this untoward generation."* In the death of Jesus sin stood revealed to itself. In that deed it first reached its full height; it brought forth into act all the potential consequences of ages of lust and malice. The devil was a liar and a murderer from the beginning, and men obeyed him in all falsehood and wrong. But he never showed what he was capable of till he murdered the sinless Redeemer in the name of God. And with that crowning act his power was scattered and overthrown. We are almost tempted to recur to the language of the Fathers, as to the delusion into which Satan was betrayed. Satan as lightning fell from heaven, just as he stood upon the highest heap of ruin. And out of the discord and the darkness of that hour, the most terrible in human history, was heard a voice proclaiming peace to man, just when Satan's foot was planted most firmly on his neck.

4. "But," it is answered, "what we object to is the use of such words as imply that Jesus fell under the wrath of God and became a curse for us. These cannot be applied properly to our Lord; but if at all, only in a loose and figurative way." Now what are the tokens of the curse under which man labours?† It shows itself in his social relations, in his relation to nature, and in his relation to God.

The contrast between our aspirations after social progress and the actual state of society marks strongly the effect of sin and wrath upon it. Whilst we sigh after a reign of industry and peace and love, the thunders of a causeless and profitless war mutter again in the air, and portend the loss of the fruits of fifty years of progress to the devoted nations engaged in it. We

* Acts ii. 37, 40.
† See Gess, Lehre, v. d. 'Versühnung.'

would befriend and raise the poor, but the necessities of their position are a chain round them that seems to make us and them helpless for good. For want of a little more food and a little more room in their dwellings, the sublimest truths fall dead upon their ears. Every great step of social progress, however plainly good and just, has had its battlefields or its scaffolds. Doubt, and suffering, and selfishness abound. Commercial speculations, founded in sheer fraud, collapse and bury the trusting multitude in their ruins. Life must be for most of our population a constant struggle against starvation. The complaints against our present social condition come not from Christian writers only, but from social reformers of every degree and creed.*

The relations of man to nature are likewise "out of joint." The high purposes that the soul is able to conceive are thwarted by the body. Hereditary indolence, or temper, or desire, stands across the path; and men despair when they measure their meagre performance with their high promise, and find too often the evil habit growing on them and checking their pace, as the cheetah pulls down the running deer. And the bodily organism, crippled at the outset with the faults perhaps of a former generation, breaks down prematurely; and "the night when no man can work" overtakes the pilgrim when morn has scarcely passed.

But the third effect of the curse is worse than these; the relation between God and man is broken by sin. "Sin is a great ditch and wall, dividing us from God."† The law of God is lost, and the soul becomes dark and self-seeking, and without purposes of good. Sometimes extravagant and nameless horrors of vice show what man without God may be capable of:‡ but always the want of God has been accompanied by want of love and of good purposes and of self-government. And the wages of sin have been death; a death of the spirit in men that seemed to live.

5. Now it is idle to discuss whether we ought to say

* For example, see the opening chapter of Buchez, 'Science de l'Histoire.'
† Theophylact. in Luc. 14.
‡ Rom. i. 28. Gal. v. 19.

that our Lord became a curse for us, if we have not exhausted the direct evidence of what He became and suffered for us. Did He or did He not put His neck under the yoke of this curse and bear His share of it?

Did He claim any social exemption? He accepted the evils of poverty; it followed Him from the manger to the carpenter's workshop, to the wilderness. For thirty years He dwelt with a family that did not understand Him, in a city that despised Him and would rebel against His first efforts to teach. His conversation was not among scholars* nor statesmen; but with lepers and lunatics, with halt and maimed, with men afflicted and possessed. All the sufferings of our social state, all that makes the aspect of society painful to a feeling heart, were brought around Him, and He showed no repugnance. The twelve whom He chose for His friends, to receive His constant teaching, were dull scholars, who knew Him not, even to the end. At last a disciple betrayed Him; the priest of His Father pronounced that it was good that He should die for the people; the Prince of the chosen people was delivered up by them to the Gentiles, and put to death; and His disciples fled in terror from His side.

But it is to be observed that, even if the death of our Lord had not taken place, even if He had ascended in glory without being put to death in shame, it would have been true that He became a curse for us. In point of justice there would be no question of degree; and even if there had been no death, that Jesus should have suffered even one look of scorn from some proud Nazarene who knew him as the carpenter's son, and this on our account, would involve the whole discussion of the Divine justice. The sinless and the just has suffered something which He did not deserve, be it little or great. If we are so rash as to impugn the Divine justice at all, understanding it so little, we must begin before the cross, with the first indignity, with the first pressure of earthly want. It is, perhaps, natural that the shocking discrepancy between the Divine sufferer

* Luke iv. 28.]

and the mode of His death should shock our sense of justice more than all that had gone before; because death awakens our sympathies more powerfully than the less harrowing incidents of a life of hardship. But if we are to appeal to a metaphysical theory of Divine justice, we must analyze our facts more exactly; and then one of our first admissions must be, that if it is unjust to slay it is unjust to smite or to degrade. And in order to set our theory going, we shall have to soften with docetic glosses not only the account of the passion, but that of the whole life of the Redeemer.

But he tastes also the bitterness of death. Death came by disobedience; and the fear of death, and of all the possible consequences of death, has been one of the burdens of the human race ever since. "Through fear of death" men "were all their lifetime subject unto bondage." * One who should be exempt from the fear of death would not bear the whole burden of man's condition. How far was the Redeemer partaker of this fear? Perhaps it is difficult to sever the dread of death from the burden of sin which was in death to be born; but towards the close of the history we see the Redeemer girding Himself for the terrible suffering, "steadfastly setting his face to go to Jerusalem,"† expressing His state of pain until the baptism that He must be baptized with could be accomplished.‡ Tears had fallen from His eyes at seeing the stroke of death take effect on Lazarus his friend; and from the thought of His own death there was that shrinking which belongs to a man. He shared our curse in tasting the bitterness of death.

And with the thought of death must have mingled a still more gloomy thought—the sense of the weight of sin. It is at this point that some will cease to go along with us. That any true feeling of sin, as of a burden on His own spirit, can ever have belonged to Jesus, is what some, careful for the honour of their Lord, will not admit. Let us refrain from theories on such a subject on both sides. But there are two places

* Heb. ii. 15. † Matt. x. 32. ‡ Luke xii. 50.

of the Gospel history that cannot be understood except on the supposition that sin and the power of darkness were suffered to press upon Him with a terrible weight. The scene in Gethsemane is one which Christians would fain keep out of their disputes; * yet it is described for our instruction, and we must venture to enter there. And it seems to me that those who would place all the import of the Lord's death in its being a heroic termination of a heroic and devout life, and an example of a faith true to itself even in extremity, receive under these olive-trees their most complete refutation. For, first, the Redeemer here appears harrowed by a misery which many a martyr has been free from, utterly perturbed by a prospect which a Stephen, an Ignatius, a Ridley viewed without dismay. If no more than death is in question, we should expect an example of calm reliance on the present help of God. But we find the unaccountable agony, the bloody sweat, the prayer for deliverance: all fortifying and calming influences seem withdrawn for a time from Him who through His life so constantly enjoyed them. We are astonished that the curse of our race should be suffered to press in all its terrible reality upon the sinless and divine Son. Yet there is the description of His great struggle. We cannot refuse to see that it relates to One utterly broken down for a time in a wretchedness beyond our conception, a prey to thoughts which, judging by their outward effects, were far darker than those of the felon the night before his execution, when He counts the quarters of each hour, and hears the hammers that are busy at his scaffold. If our salvation is to be made an easier work, if the price paid is to be abated, we must forget Gethsemane or deny it.† But if we believe with the

* "A feeling always seizes me," says Krummacher, "as if it were unbecoming to act as a spy on the Son of the living God in His last secret transactions with His heavenly Father; and that a sinful eye ventures too much in daring to look upon a scene in which the Lord appears in such a state of weakness and abandonment that places Him on the same footing with the most miserable among men."

† Mr. Garden, whose theory is that the Lord would never have felt misery, is here consistent. He forgets Gethsemane altogether: he quotes only our Lord's words upon the Cross.—Tracts, &c., p. 10.

Apostle that "God hath made Him to be sin for us Who knew no sin, that we might be made the righteousness of God in Him,"* then the terror and the agony become accountable. All the inner horror of sin is revealed to Him. Sin in its nakedness is more horrible than death. And He sees it as it is; the blasphemous self-worship that it is, the revolt against God, the violation of order, the death in life. And all this sin is His, though He is sinless of it: for He has thrown in His lot with men, and has proposed to Himself the task of breaking down this foul and destroying tyranny. The mystery of that agency lies in the completeness of His humanity. He is no bystander, watching how men sin. He is one of themselves, but with the power of God over them to make their interests His own. In Him, as God, they live, and move, and have their being: and now the power of darkness is let loose to show Him all the sin and misery, and defiance of God, that He, by clothing Himself with human nature, has taken into His bosom. The words of the Lord upon the cross are an echo from the garden of agony: "Why hast Thou forsaken me?" These words from the twenty-second Psalm, uttered at such a moment, are of course no mere ejaculation of pain; they recall a Psalm which, as any one may see, contains matter that can apply to Messiah only. But the words themselves express a sense of desertion by God: they can have no other meaning. Vain would it be to attempt to explain how He, one with the Father, and never severed from Him by spot or stain of guilt, could have admitted such a feeling. But there are the words: we dare not deny them. They belong to Him, not as Son of God, but as burdened with the sins of the world. They express perhaps the complete separation which sin makes between man and God. He is now the Advocate of all mankind; and their separation from God because of sin extends itself to Him for a season. It appears, then, that the question whether the wrath of God can be said to have fallen upon the Son, who has done no sin, is no

* 2 Cor. v. 21.

verbal question, but a question of fact. Jesus did suffer all those things which are the evident tokens of wrath against us. He tried the sufferings of our disjointed social state; He knew the fear of death, and the anguish of sin which separates from God. The motives of those who would protect his name from the supposed contamination of sin, are not unworthy of respect. "Be it far from thee, Lord!" came from one who loved his Lord sincerely; but "Get thou behind me, Satan!" was the answer he received. When the Son of God is minded, of His own free will and His exceeding love towards our race, to come down from heaven, and in the form of a servant to explore all the secrets of our vile condition, it is more reverent in us to observe and love His condescension, than to say, out of some private text-book of morality, "This shall not be unto thee!" The mystery of evil is far beyond our rules and measures. There must be a cause when such a great act of condescension had to be done. But done it was; and when all the vials of wrath were poured out upon His head, and when He did not shrink from receiving them, it is idle to discuss whether this shall be called wrath or love; when He smarted under all that we call punishment, it is idle to say that it must have another name.

But you that are so jealous lest the name of sin should attach to the sinless One, carry the jealousy another step. When the Pharisees revile and the Priests entrap the Lord, and when the scourging, and the buffets, and the spitting mangle and defile His innocent frame, you think that nature itself should give tokens of indignation. And yet, how close to God sin has ever come! how sins have ever polluted and defiled the world, which is His temple! and you have not conceived of the sins in that light, as sins that touch Him. When a man slays his brother, or pollutes the virtue of a women, and each is dear to the Almighty Maker, does not the murderer smite God, and the betrayer spit upon Him? and the long-suffering Ruler of the world bears, as in His bosom, all our wayward sins, and weaves them into the web of His providence, and contrives an order of things in which these evil elements may work and not destroy. Jealous of the Son's contact with sin, can we not, by a larger reach of the same morality, conceive that the Father's contact with, and permission of sin, is a profound mystery? Can you not see in this fact a greater hideousness in evil, since every day that it is permitted seems to impugn the justice or the power of Him who could abolish every sin, with the doers of it, by the breath of His mouth? If so, let us at least assent to the position that a disease so utterly past our comprehension may require means to cure it that shock the ordinary conclusions of our conscience; and that a wider view, if we could stand high enough to take it, might correct our crude impressions.

6. The doctrine of Atonement is many-sided, as all mysteries are when we try to express them in the forms of human thought. And no doctrine has suffered so much, on the part both of friend and foe, from a one-sided treatment. "It has been said, that this doctrine represents the Almighty as moved with fury at the insults offered to His Supreme Majesty, as impatient to pour forth His fury upon some being, as indifferent whether that being deserves it or not, and as perfectly appeased upon finding an object of vengeance in His own innocent Son. It has been said, that a doctrine which represents the Almighty as sternly demanding a full equivalent for that which was due to Him, and as receiving that equivalent in the sufferings of His Son, transfers all the affection and gratitude of the human race from an inexorable Being, who did not remit any part of His right, to another being who satisfied His claim. It has been said, that a translation of guilt is impossible, because guilt is personal; and that a doctrine which represents the innocent as punished instead of the guilty, and the guilty as escaping by this punishment, contradicts the first principles of justice, subverts all our ideas of a righteous government, and, by holding forth an example of reward and punishment dis-

pensed by Heaven, without any regard to the character of those who receive them, does encourage men to live as they please."* So the objections were summed up many years since, and there is little to alter after the recent controversy. Now, most of these objections have arisen from a crude and one-sided way of stating the doctrine on the part of its friends, and disappear when all the elements of the truth are taken in. Sin exists; and therewith must enter a host of contradictions. Sin is that which turns the love of God into wrath; not into the passion of wrath as men feel it, but to the intention of visiting with punishment. With sin, the face of God is altered against us and turned away. We know the theological objections to this mode of speaking, but there is no other open to us. God cannot change; but yet His purpose towards us is changed in its workings by ourselves. And this enormous power all classes of Christians assign to sin, that it can dam up and divert the current of Divine love, that set so strongly towards us. We are obliged to pick our expressions, whenever we touch the subject, lest sin itself should be laid to the account of Him who is the governor of the world, and suffers sin in the world. Sin turns love to wrath, the life of our souls to the death of them, our light to darkness, our free adherence to God to enmity against Him. From this view of sin, as something which is suffered to thwart the free workings of God's love, and which casts shadows as of the darkness of Gethsemane over all the scenes of history, where evil is suffered to come in and overcloud the good, there is no escape except in the pantheistic view, which reads all sin and evil as good in a transition state. And against that view conscience will ever protest; for it is the best proof of our still retaining vestiges of good that conscience finds all the suggestions of physiological materialists, and of metaphysical pantheists, powerless to lull to sleep the sense of individual guilt, which yet she has so strong an interest in getting

* Rev. Dr. Hill's Lectures, b. iv., ch. 3, quoted by Dr. Candlish.

rid of. To remove sin and its consequences God sent His Son, the Eternal Word of the Father, to become truly man as He was truly God, and to mediate between men and Him for their relief. It is not true, whatever friend or foe shall say it, that God looked forth on His works to find some innocent man able and willing to bear the weight of His wrath, and found Jesus and punished Him. It is all false, because it is only half true. The Son of God took our nature upon Him, and therewith the sins of it, at least in their consequences; not because He became one man among many, but because when God takes man's nature He still has divine right and power over all, and so manhood is taken into God. That sinfulness should press upon the Son of God, in any of its consequences, revolts us at first; nay, it was intended to revolt us and thereby to secure our repentance: and jealous for His honour we protest that of sin He shall know nothing. Yes: but we have been flaunting our sins in the face of the Father, to His displeasure, ever since we were born; using the limbs He makes and keeps strong, for purposes of lust and violence; quickening the pulses that He controls, with draughts of passionate excitement: in a word, sinning before God's face and under His hand. Is it less shocking that sin should be in the world which is God's, than that it should be in the manhood which is Christ's? No: both before and after the incarnation sin is a contradiction; and it is less difficult to conceive sin taken by the Son upon Himself for a time and by way of remedy, than it is to understand it as suffered by the Father always as a permitted destruction. The punishment in this transaction falls on the innocent. And we are told that such a doctrine is cruel, unjust, and useless: cruel, because it punishes where it could forgive; useless, because it misses the true end of punishment in striking the guiltless, which can never deter from guilt; and unjust, because it falls on one who knows no sin. But it is not cruel, if it thereby marks for ever the enormity of sin which needed such a sacrifice; it is not useless, if it changed the relation of man to God, and if in fact it has ever since been turning men to holiness and "drawing all men unto" Jesus;* and it is not unjust, because the Father's will to punish never outstripped the Son's to suffer, and because His death was a solemn offering of Himself in love, for man's redemption. Nor can there be any tendency to transfer from the severe Father to the loving Son, the love we owe to both; for the mode of our redemption was designed by both, and the Son adopts the Father's and the Father sanctions the Son's loving self-sacrifice. Nor is there the least pretext for saying that this doctrine encourages men to live as they please, by holding forth the spectacle of rewards earned for those who do not deserve them and punishments warded off from those who deserve them well: since the blood of the Redeemer, all-sufficient as it is to cleanse the sins of the world, saves from wrath only those who repent and turn to Him. The power of the doctrine of the Atonement has been felt wherever the Gospel has come. It has carried comfort to sinners where nothing else could do so. Wherever the conviction of sin has been deepest, the power of the Cross has been most conspicuous; and this in the face of objections which it was not left to modern times to suggest, against such a punishment for such a deliverer. Let it still be preached; and our lesson from these controversies be that we preach the whole of it, so far as Scripture informs and our mind comprehends. Let us not so exalt the justice of God that we seem to record the harshness of a tyrant, and not the device of a Father seeking to bring His children back. Let us not so dwell on the love of Christ as to forget that one great moral purpose of this sacrifice was to set the mark of God's indignation upon sin. Let us not so offer the benefits of the Cross to our people as to lose sight of it as a means of their crucifying their own flesh and dying to their own sins. He bare our sins in His own body on the tree; He is our ransom, our propitiation; He is made sin for us; because

* John xii. 32.

God is just. He laid down His life for the sheep, out of love, and God so loved the world that He gave Him for this labour; because God is love: and we are to run with patience the race that is set before us, looking unto Jesus the Author and Finisher of our faith; because the work of justice and love has restored us to our position of moral freedom and moral life, and we must live as the redeemed servants of our Lord.

ESSAY IX.

SCRIPTURE, AND ITS INTERPRETATION.

CONTENTS OF ESSAY IX.

SCRIPTURE, AND ITS INTERPRETATION.

§ 1.

1. It can hardly be considered strange that great differences of opinion should exist respecting the interpretation of Scripture. When we consider the nature of the Sacred Writings, their number, their variety, the different epochs to which they belong, and the vast period of time over which they extend, we can hardly be surprised to find the opinions concerning the interpretation of the Volume into which they are collected not only to be various, but even conflicting. When we turn from the outward to the inward, and ponder over "that inexhaustible and infinite character" of the Sacred Writings, which even the better portion of our opponents are not unwilling to concede,—when we observe that "depth and inwardness," which, it has been rightly considered, require something corresponding in the interpreter himself,—when we reverentially recognize throughout the Volume references alike to the past, the present, and the future; teachings in history only partly realised, lessons in prophecy "not yet learned even in theory," germs of truth which, we are told, have yet to take root in the world,—when we consider all this, are we to wonder that differences of opinion exist concerning the interpretation of a volume so ancient, so wondrous, and so multiform?

It would indeed be strange if it had been otherwise; it would be a phenomenon in the literary or mental history of Christianity not easy to account for, if expounders of Scripture had been found always accordant in their views; nay, it may even be considered a subject for surprise, though for thankfulness, that the differences of opinion about the interpretation of a volume such as we have described are not greater than we find them to be.

When, however, we are thus speaking of the differences of opinion respecting the interpretation of Scripture (and we are using the language of opponents), let us, from the very outset, agree to avoid all ambiguities in language. Let us be careful not to fall into an error which we may fairly impute to those with whom we are contending,—the error, to choose the mildest expression, of using terms of a vague and undefined character, and, as the sequel will show, of a somewhat convenient elasticity. What do we mean by differences respecting the interpretation of Scripture? We may mean two things. Either we may mean that there have been differences of opinion about the meanings of the actual words of Scripture, or we may mean that there have been differences of opinion about the manner in which those meanings have been obtained. We may include both if we choose in the same form of words, but in so doing let us not fail to apprise the reader, and in conducting the argument let us act with fairness. Let us be careful to recognize the clear logical difference between these two meanings, and avoid that really culpable method of dealing with a momentous subject which does not scruple to mix up illustrations or arguments derived from one of its aspects with those which really and plainly belong to the other. There may have been from the very first many methods of interpreting Scripture: allegory may have prevailed in one age, mysticism in another; scholastic methods of interpretation may have been succeeded by rhetorical, and these again may both have given place to methods in which grammar and history may have borne a more prominent part. All this may have been so, but it still does not necessarily follow that the meanings actually assigned to any given text have been as manifold or as discordant as the methods which may have been adopted to obtain them. The modes and principles of interpretation may have been very different, and yet, in the main, they may have led to very accordant results. Such a probability, however, is now somewhat studiously passed over in silence, or mentioned only to be dismissed as unworthy of serious consideration. The object, we fear, is to create anxiety and uneasiness, to unfix and to unloosen, to awaken a general feeling of distrust in current interpretations, and, in the case of doctrinal statements and every form of exposition that involves a reference to the analogy of faith, to arouse even hostility and antagonism. This has been done of late, as we have already implied, by a judicious combination of two methods of proceeding,—on the one hand, by calling attention to the discordances of interpretation in a few extreme cases where such discordance is sure to be a maximum; on the other, by dwelling exclusively on the varieties of the different systems and methods of interpretation, and leaving it to be inferred that the results arrived at are as various and diversified as the methods by which they have been obtained. In a word, such a phenomenon as a Catholic interpretation, substantially the same under all systems but varied only in details or application, is assumed to be an exegetical impossibility. The true state of the case we are told is this,—that Scripture has had every possible variety of meaning assigned to it, that it has been understood to say this to one age and that to another, that all hitherto has been conflict or uncertainty. We learn, however, that now a better era is dawning; that a fundamental principle, viz., that Scripture has one meaning and one meaning only, has at length clearly been made out; and that a little "free-handling," a few assumptions, and a free use of a so-called "verifying faculty," will finally adjust all difficulties and discordances in the interpretation of the Book of Life.

There is obviously something very attractive in all this. There is a fascination in the whole procedure that imperfectly disciplined or willingly sceptical minds find it impossible to resist. There is the charm of the alleged discovery that criticism at last has made, the attractiveness of the generalization, the variety of the modes of applying the principle so as to meet all needs, whether of the reader, the preacher, the missionary, the teacher, or the interpreter,—and then the retrospect, the backward look of serene triumph over the accumulated errors and prejudices of eighteen long Christian centuries, all chased away by the brightness of this second Reformation and the "burst of intellectual life" that is at last becoming visible above the clouded horizon of Scriptural interpretation. One topmost stone, and the monument of our exegetical successes must be pronounced complete. Philosophy and Theology claim of us, we are told, as of value to themselves a history of the past. Be it so. Let us take the pen of the historian and sit down and trace the record of our own mental supremacy in a history of the prejudices and errors of the Exegesis of the past. Let us show by this tacit comparison how "great names must be accounted small," how few ever "bent their mind to interrogate the meaning of words," how men who were accounted benefactors of the human race have yet only left to us the heritage of erring fancies and party-bias, —let us write the history of all this littleness, confusion, and bondage to the letter, and the fabric of our own greatness, harmony, and intellectual freedom will appear by the contrast only the more stately and unique.

Such is the dream of the present. Such, stated in no exaggerated or unkindly terms, is the course which men whose general goodness and high principles we have no cause to doubt or deny are now inviting us to follow. What are we to say of all this? The comment rises to the lips, but we suppress it. We may feel, perhaps, that as in Corinth of old so now in nineteenth-century England, vain knowledge may puff up, yet remembering that "love edifieth," we sit by silent and wondering, even though the fire is kindling within, and silence is becoming a pain and a grief to us. At first perhaps we prepare to answer the call to join the wise and tranquil few, who, knowing that the Eternal Spirit has been ever present with the Church, and that what things were written aforetime were written, not for our contempt but for our learning, smile pensively at these childish exultations and straw-woven crowns, and see in them only one more of the premature triumphs that have been claimed for some shifting form of the errors or heresies of the time. We feel tempted to join this quiet company, and calmly to smile as they alone can smile whose feet stand within the sheltering walls of the City of God, and whose faith is that which was not only delivered but handed down to the saints in each age of the Church of Christ. What can we do but smile, when we recognize old quibbles and difficulties all mustered up again, disguised in new trappings, and arranged in new combinations,—but yet the same, the very same that have been dispersed a hundred times over, and which the very generation to which we now belong will see dispersed again, though it may be to ally themselves finally with powers and principles of which at present they are only permitted to act as the scout and the courier?

But with this last thought the smile fades away. When we remember that the forms of error which of late have been reappearing among us may belong, consciously or unconsciously, to the great apostasy of the future,—when we observe how they instinctively associate themselves with masked or avowed denyings of the Divinity of our blessed Lord, and of the full efficacy of His sacrifice,—when we mark how their vanities and self-confidences bear a strange family likeness to that Pelagian pride in the perfectibility of our corrupted nature which tears open the wounds of a crucified Lord more heartlessly than the hands that first inflicted them,—when we ponder over that puffed up and unyoked spirit of the day that is now calling on us to clear away the remains of dogmas and controversies, and when we see, as we must see, with a shudder, that it is but the harbinger of him who is to set himself against everything "that is called God or that is worshipped" (2 Thess. ii. 4),—then it does seem our duty to play our part in the great controversy, to quit ourselves like men, and to strive with all Christian earnestness, with stern brow yet with true and loving heart, to rescue the endangered souls of our own time and age, and to bring them back into the City of God.

2. The position of the defender of the faith in the present day is that of one whose home and citizenship is in the City "that lieth four-square," whose builder and whose maker is God. The storm of battle has often raged round those massive walls, wild rout and turmoil have often striven to shake those solid gates. Passwords have been tried; treachery has played its dastardly part,—but all stands firm and sure. The rising sun that smites on the broad front of those fair walls and towers, beholds them as stately in their strength and their beauty as they were ever of old; the shadows they cast when day declines are as many and as lengthened as they were of yore. Who within would wish to see a stone displaced, who would fain see one battlement laid low? Perhaps none who are really and truly within the circuit of those sheltering walls. But there are voices without that we know full well, voices of those with whom we have dwelt as friends, whose God has been our God, and whose Lord has been our Lord,—men who went from among us on strange missions, and are come back to tell us strange tidings, and to bid us do strange deeds. That beleaguering host whose flaunting standards we can see on every wooded knoll around, and whose open or covert assaults our fathers and forefathers have experienced so often, and resisted so sucessfully and so long,—that motley eager host they tell us is not composed of foes but of friends and well-wishers, changed by civilization and the glory of human development, eager to meet us as kindred and brothers if we will but remove the envious barriers that separate us, relics of a religious feudalism, as they term it, long passed away. Shall creeds separate brothers? Shall doctrines divide those whom unity of race and shared civilizations plainly declare to be one and inseparable? Shall we churlishly strive any

longer to stint the growth of the ideal man? Shall the orient and glowing future be darkened with jealousies of sects and rivalries of religions? "We are couriers," they impetuously cry aloud; "ambassadors, friends of both, friends of truth, friends of Christ. Unbar, then, these envious gates; down with these unfriendly walls; let us learn from each other the great lesson of mutual concessions, and so at last realize the great hope of the future, the fabled restitution of theologians, and at last, all in fraternal triumph, merge into the one great family of Truth and of Love." Such are the voices now sounding in our ears; voices that the young and the generous, as well as the godless and the worldworn, give ear to with ready sympathy. But shall the true defenders of the ark of their God, that ark of the New Covenant wherein lie the written words of life, yield it and themselves up to this stratagem which one "whose time is short" has put into the hearts of unconscious instruments? Never. God defend us from such fearful, such frantic disloyalty! God indeed forbid that, in any sense, however modified, it should hereafter be the boast of the spirits of perdition, that it was with the City of the hills even worse than it was with a city of the plain,—that the host wound round it, that sounding brass brayed forth and eager voices shouted, and that, mined by traitorous occupants, wall and tower fell flat as those of Jericho, and fell never to rise again!

Such, it would seem, is the allegory of our own times—such no overdrawn picture of the exact attitude in which true believers now appear to stand. We are called upon by specious words to give up every defence which the mercies of God have permitted to be reared up around us; and our reward is to be a bondage, to which the bondage of the worst age of the Church of Rome would be found light and endurable. There is no bondage like that of scepticism. There is no intolerance more intolerable than that of those who are themselves the servants of a hard master. It may be a bondage different to bondages of the past in its mode of being brought about, but it is no less complete and coercive. It is the bondage of contempt and of scorn. Do we doubt it? Are there not writings of our own times, writings that claim scholars and ministers of the Gospel for their authors, that show, only too painfully, what we have to expect if we allow such to be leaders of thought among us, if wall and tower are to be thrown down to let such men come in and have the rule over us? Granted that there may be numerous exceptions, that there may be those who, even while we are compelled to number them among our secret foes, we may be free to own have many kindly and elevated sympathies,—granted that there may be silver sounds heard amid all this clanging brass, yet does not common sense, does not history itself tell us, that the voices of this better part will be the first to be silenced; that their kindly idealisms will be rudely swept aside to make room for varied and repulsive forms of aggressive materialism; that they will themselves be the earliest victims of the Frankenstein their own hands have helped to shape into existence? Let the thoughtful reader pause only for a moment to muse upon some of the present aspects of modern society as revealed by, as commented on, and sometimes even as defended by, our public papers, and then answer to his own heart what he thinks must be the issue if laxity of religious thought seriously increase among us. Vice will borrow its excuses from scepticism; lawlessness of act will become the natural sequel of lawlessness of thought; and the end will be, no noble, colossal, heavenward-looking, ideal man, but a grovelling satyr, the slave of his own appetites, and the vassal of his own abominations.

But we must pass on to, or rather return to, the subject which lies more immediately before us. Enough, perhaps, has been said to show that there can be no safe compromise, no over-liberal parleying with those without, be they the kindliest or the most silver-tongued of the children of men. The believer of the present day must put himself in the attitude of an opponent, kind indeed it may be, and large in heart and sympathies, ready and anxious to rescue, prompt to spare,—yet an opponent; one who, when asked to give up old principles, may not, for the sake of others, wholly refuse to hear the nature of the demand, but who hears it with a full knowledge of the true attitude and posture of those by whom it is urged. We are asked especially to give up old principles in the interpretation of the Word of God. Some concession, we are warned, is almost imperatively demanded. We ask why. We bid our opponents state their reasons for a demand so sweeping and comprehensive. One of these reasons we have heard already, and we have already observed that it involves an ambiguity. We are told that the differences respecting the interpretation of Scripture are such that they show that prejudice rather than principle is the true mainspring of Scriptural exegesis. Pictures are held up to us of the successive schools of interpreters, their follies and their fallacies, their bondage to the influences of the age in which they lived, their hostility to all intellectual freedom. Be it so; but is it proved that the interpretations which they actually advanced are as varied as their methods of procedure are so confidently alleged to be? Whether a great deal too much has not been said even on this subject, whether the diversities or antagonisms of early systems of explaining Scripture have not greatly been exaggerated, is a question into which here we will not enter. Our inquiry is simply, whether the differences of interpretation are at all more than the nature and importance of the subject-matter would lead us to expect, and whether a great deal that has been said about the differences of interpretation does not wholly belong to the differences of the modes of procedure. It is, of course, quite natural and conceivable that the spirit of each age may have swayed teacher and preacher more to this method than to that; that passing controversies may have left their traces, and that declarations which seemed of great moment to one generation may not have been found equally so to another. All this may be so, but with this we are now only partially concerned. If we were endeavouring to form an estimate of the variety of deductions that have been made from the words of Scripture in different ages of the Church, or were discussing the varying applications that the same sentiment has been found to bear, much that has been said on the subject might pass unchallenged. We should probably account for these varied forms of application or deduction on different principles to our opponents; we might see, for instance, in all this diversity of application only evidences of "the manifold wisdom of God," and of that hidden life with all its varying aptitudes to human needs which we know to be in the Written Word. Our opponents, on the contrary, might see in it only evidences of the folly, ignorance, prejudice, or bad faith of successive expositors: we might differ widely in our manner of accounting for these different applications of Scripture, but we might to a great extent agree as to their number and variety. This, however, is not the question between us. What we are now told is not merely that the applications or adaptations of Scripture have been very varied, but that the difference of actual meaning assigned to the words of Scripture by expositors of different ages is so suspiciously excessive, that the duty of purging our minds from past prejudices is imperative, and that Scripture must henceforth be explained on sounder principles. The one true meaning must be discovered and adopted, the many disregarded or rejected. The first question between us, then, is a question of amount and of degree. Our opponents assert that Scripture has had so many meanings, often too so hostile and suicidal, that it presents one meaning to the Frenchman, another to the German, and another to the Englishman. We are asked if this is not in itself an utter absurdity, and if it is not time to enter upon some more reasonable course. That assumed reasonable course is sketched out; canons of interpretation are laid down; appeals are not wanting to current prejudices; disinclination or inaptitude for that wrestling with the Word of God which marked earlier and better ages of the

Church is dealt gently with; disregard of the great exegetical writings of the past is not only excused but commended; we are advised wholly to trust to ourselves, and are cheered by the assurance that "if we will only confine ourselves to the plain meaning of words and the study of their context," we may beneficially dispense with all the expository labours of the past or of the present. Such is the modern mode of dealing with one of the most momentous subjects of our own times, and with which personal holiness and man's salvation are more intimately connected than with any other that can be specified. Is it unfair to characterize the whole as nothing more than positive assertions, resting on ambiguities of language, or on the assumed identity of things logically different, and supported by covert appeals to the idleness, vanity, and self-sufficiency of the day?

3. We revert, however, to the preliminary question before us. Are the differences of meaning that have been assigned to Scripture such in amount as they are said to be, and such as to demand the rehabilitation of Scriptural interpretation which is now proposed? Are they such that, as it has been asserted, Scripture bears an utterly different meaning to men of different ages and nations? Assuredly not. No statement seems more completely at variance with our general Christian consciousness; no assertion can more readily be disproved when we come to details. These, however, can never be made palatable to the general reader, nor are they commonly convincing, unless carried out much further than would be possible in an Essay of this nature. To prove clearly and distinctly that there is *not* this great amount of discordance in the interpretations of Scripture, it would be necessary to compare, and that not in a few selected cases, but in a portion of Scripture of some length, the results arrived at by commentators of different ages and countries. Less than this would fail to convince; for in the case of a few prerogative instances, which would be all we should have space for, the feeling is ever apt to arise that lists equally telling

and convincing could be made out on the other side. We have, therefore, as it would seem, little left us than to meet assertion by counter-assertion, and leave each reader to ascertain for himself on which side the truth lies,—whether the differences in the interpretations of Scripture (except in a comparatively few cases) have been thus excessive, or whether there has not been a very considerable amount of accordance in general matters, and variations only in details. Those who are acquainted with the subject, and have had experience in referring to expository treatises belonging to different ages and countries, will have no difficulty in pronouncing which is the true state of the case, and whether assertion or counter-assertion is to be deemed most worthy of credit. As, however, the general reader is not always likely to have it in his power to decide between the two statements, and as the mere denial of the major in an opponent's syllogism is never satisfactory without some reasons being assigned, we will mention one or two general considerations which, though not amounting to a positive proof that Scripture has *not* been interpreted as diversely as has been asserted, may yet render it probable that such is the case, and supply some grounds for the counter-assertion above alluded to.

In the first place, we may perhaps with justice appeal to the Ancient Versions, especially when combined with some of the best Modern Versions, as tending to show that the amount of variety in interpretation is not so great as has been imagined. Let us take, for example, seven of the best Ancient Versions of the New Testament—the Syriac (Peshito), the Old Latin (as far as it has been ascertained), the Vulgate, the Gothic, the Coptic, the Ethiopic (Pell Platt's), and the Armenian, and with them let us associate the Authorized English Version and Luther's German Version, and then proceed to inquire what general opinion a comparison of the characteristics of these Versions leads us to form as to the question of a prevailing unanimity, or a prevailing discordance, of interpretation, as far as it can be evinced by a Version. Now, admitting on the one hand that there may be such relations existing between some of these Versions, that each can hardly be considered an independent witness,—that the Vulgate, for example, is but an amended form of the Old Latin, that the Ethiopic sometimes seems to indicate dependence on the Syriac, that the Armenian was retouched at a late period, and possibly that the Vulgate was in the hands of the reviser,—admitting all this, and making also a deduction for the influence of the Vulgate, and, perhaps, to some small extent, of the Syriac over the two Modern Versions, we may still most justly point to these nine Versions, of ages and countries so different and distant, as evincing an unanimity in their renderings, not only of general but even of disputed passages, far beyond what could have been expected *à priori*, or can in any way be accounted for by the admissions we have already made. If it be said this must necessarily be the case in Versions which are all strictly literal in their character, these two remarks may be made by way of rejoinder: first, that the very fact that nine Versions of different ages and countries should agree in this important feature, that not one of them should in any respect be paraphrastic,* and that some, as for instance the Old Latin, should almost be barbarous in their exactness, does seem to show that not only in later ages, but even in the earliest, the very letter of Scripture was regarded as of the utmost importance, and treated with the most scrupulous accuracy. Where Versions were so punctilious, it does not seem natural to expect that interpretation would have been very wild or varied, except when it was allowed to degenerate into applications, or busied itself with minutiæ and details. Secondly, it may be added, that even the most literal Versions involve interpretation in the fullest sense of the word, especially in the opinions they necessarily express on the connexion of clauses, and in the renderings of words of disputed meaning. A good

* It may be noticed that we have specified the Ethiopic Version as that edited by Mr. Pell Platt. The Ethiopic found in Walton's 'Polyglott' often degenerates into a paraphrase, especially in difficult passages. The Peshito is sometimes idiomatically free, but never paraphrastic.

translation is often the very best of commentaries, and it was a full appreciation of this fact that led a venerated scholar and divine, when asked what he judged to be the best commentary on the New Testament, to name the Vulgate. The general unanimity of the early as well as later Versions is thus a testimony, at any rate, of some little weight, in favour of the belief that the amount and degree of differences of interpretation in earlier, when compared with later ages, have been much overstated.

Still it may be urged, that whatever may be the case with Versions, it is perfectly certain that, in the results at which commentators of different ages have arrived, there is a vast amount not only of variety but of antagonism. In reference to a certain number of difficult passages this may be true; if, however, this be intended as a general statement referring to Scriptural interpretation at large, it must be regarded as open to considerable doubt. Let us endeavour to show this in the following way. It is said that there is an increasing agreement between recent German expositors, and it is also implied that the results at which they have arrived are far more consonant with truth than any that have preceded. Of these expositors, De Wette and Meyer are often mentioned with respect by modern writers. Let us agree to take them as two fair representatives of the exegesis of our own times. Let us now go to a remote past, and choose two names to compare with them as representatives of the interpretation of a former day. Let us take for example Chrysostom and Theodoret. They belonged to an age sufficiently distant; they shared in its feelings and sympathies; they took part in its controversies. They were not specially in advance of their own times. One of them had, what many will judge to be not always compatible with calmness of interpretation, a strongly rhetorical bias; the other did not escape some suspicion of heresy. Such as they were, or have been judged to be, let us compare them, in some portion of Scripture (St. Paul's Epistles for example), on which all have written, with the two modern commentators above specified, and state what seem to be the general results of the comparison. We naturally set out with the expectation of finding very great diversity. If all that has been said on this subject be true; if the fourteen centuries which lie between the two pairs of men be as plentifully diversified as they are said to have been by changes in methods of interpretation,—changes, too, asserted to have been gradually leading us up to more perfect principles of interpretation,—we must expect to find a very great amount of discordance between them. Yet what do we discover when we actually institute the comparison? To speak very generally, it would seem to be as follows. There will be found in the first place a considerable amount of variety in matters of detail, the older interpreters more commonly giving what may be termed an objective reference to words and expressions, where the two modern writers will be found agreeing to adopt a more subjective view. In the second place, differences will be observed in the treatment of doctrinal passages; the older interpreters usually expounding them with reference to the great controversies of their own times, and to points of polemical detail; the modern interpreters usually trying to generalize, and not unfrequently to dilute and explain away, whenever doctrinal statements appear to assume a very distinctive or definite aspect. In a word, the tendency of the two earlier writers is to what is objective and special; of the two later to what is subjective and general. These distinctions will certainly be observed, especially in the two departments above alluded to—matters of detail and matters of doctrine, and may perhaps be deemed sufficient to justify the recognition of some clear lines of demarcation between earlier and more modern interpretation. When, however, these points of difference are set aside, there will be found remaining in the great bulk of Scripture, and in all general passages, an amount of accordance so striking and so persistent, that it can only be accounted for by the assumption that these four able expositors all instinctively recognized one common and sound principle of Scriptural interpretation. The precise nature of that principle will become apparent as we advance further in our investigations.

4. Believing that these remarks are just, and capable of being fully substantiated, we may claim to have at least made it probable, that the extent of the alleged differences in the interpretation of Scripture between our own times and the past has been unduly exaggerated. Here we might pause as far as the present portion of our subject is concerned. It may be well, however, to take one step further, and show, what fairly can be shown, that from the very earliest times, the literal and historical method of interpreting Scripture, now so often claimed as the distinguishing characteristic of our own times, has ever been recognized in the Church as the true method on man's side of interpreting the Oracles of God. On this subject, owing to the small amount of exact knowledge, even among more professed students, and to the currency which a few popular comments readily obtain among those whose acquaintance with these ancient writers must ever be second-hand, many questionable statements are allowed to pass unchallenged. It would, perhaps, seem hopeless to attempt to say one word in favour of the method of interpretation adopted by Origen. Every writer of the day uses that great name to illustrate what is to be regarded as wild and fanciful. And yet, what is the opinion which any real student of Origen's exegetical works would certainly give us? What, for instance, would be the statement of an unbiassed scholar who had thoughtfully read what remain to us of his commentaries on St. Matthew and St. John? Would he not tell us that in these portions of his works, whatever may have been his theories elsewhere, Origen rarely failed to give the first place to the simple and literal interpretation, and that his divergencies into allegory far more often deserve the name of applications than of actual expositions? Allegory seems really and primarily to have commended itself to Origen as the

readiest method of dealing with those difficulties which his acute mind almost too quickly recognized as transcending human reason and explanation. The remark of one who has carefully read and well used one portion of his works—the expositor Lücke—is probably not wholly unjust, that a tendency to rationalize, of which Origen himself was unconscious, may to a great degree account for his bias to allegory and mystical modes of interpretation, whenever the difficulties of the passage seemed to rise above the usual level. Where there was no necessity for this, where there were no historical details which seemed at issue with human reason, or with received views of morality and justice, Origen shows plainly enough what method of interpreting the Word of God he deemed to be the true and correct one. We may abundantly verify this from his extant writings. We may also further judge from fragments preserved in Catenæ (his scattered comments, for example, on the Epistle to the Ephesians) what were really his leading principles; and we may fairly ask if they were so very different from the principles of interpreting Scripture which all parties, friends and foes, seem now in the main agreed in regarding as reasonable and correct.

We might extend these remarks almost indefinitely by discussing the true nature of the leading methods of interpreting Scripture—these methods which we are told are so strangely discordant—in the case of each one of the more distinguished expositors of different ages of the Church. We might show, for instance, that no amount of strong polemical bias prevented Cyril of Alexandria from expounding portions of Scripture (the Gospel of St. John for example) with what, even in our own critical days, must be called felicity and success. We might make it clear that the rhetorical turn of Chrysostom's mind never prevented him from fully discussing verbal distinctions, analysing the meanings of prepositions, estimating the force of compound forms, and so placing before his reader as calm, clear, and persuasive a view of the passage under consideration as we may find in the best specimens of modern interpretation. We might turn to the West, and in spite of some growing disposition to admit more generally those studied distinctions in reference to threefold or fourfold senses of Scripture which Origen bequeathed to his successors, we might still appeal to Augustine as a writer, whose special interpretations can never be spoken of without respect, and whose perceptions of the inner mind of Scripture, and of the true bearing of its deeper declarations, remain to this very hour unequalled for their perspicuity and truth. Nay, we might even show that the studied recognition of several senses in Scripture was rather a form of *application* than of definite and genuine interpretation. We might even go onward, and pass into those ages which have become very bywords for perverted interpretation of Scripture—the ages of the earlier and later schoolmen—and even in them, amid subtile and narrow logic on this side, and a wild and speculative idealism on that, we should have no difficulty in showing that there was a *via media* of sound principles of interpretation which was both recognized and proceeded on. It is perfectly true that at this period not only the earlier threefold and fourfold senses of Scripture were re-asserted and re-applied, but that even sevenfold, eightfold,* and, if we choose to press the words of Erigena, infinite senses of Scripture were admitted by mediæval interpreters; but it is also perfectly true and demonstrable, from passing comments and cautions, that the simple, plain, and literal sense was always admitted to be the basis, and that other forms of interpretation were commonly regarded more in the light of deductions and applications. The rule laid down by Aquinas was clear enough, and expresses fairly the general feeling of the interpreters of his own time,—"In omni-

* The enumeration may amuse the reader: (1) Sensus literalis vel historicus; (2) allegoricus vel parabolicus; (3) tropologicus vel etymologicus; (4) anagogicus vel analogicus; (5) typicus vel exemplaris; (6) anaphoricus vel proportionalis; (7) boarcademicus vel primordialis (*i.e.* quo ipsa principia rerum comparantur cum beatitudine æterna et tota dispensatione salutis); see *Bibl. Max. Patr.* tom. xvii. p. 315 seq. (Lugd 1677).

bus quæ Scriptura tradit, pro fundamento est tenenda veritas historica, et desuper spirituales expositiones fabricandæ" (*Summa Theol.* Pars. 1, Qu. 102, Art. 1): the literal and historical came first, the rest were forms of application. It is not, however, merely from passing comments, or from asserted, but really neglected principles, but from the general tenor of the better expositions of the time that the full force of the above remarks will best be felt. Let a fair and intelligent reader consent to give a little time to some of the interpretations of difficult passages in St. Paul's Epistles as put forward by Lombard or Aquinas, and then tell us his impressions. We will venture to state what his report would be,—that it was a matter of surprise to him, in an age which has ever been a very byword for subtilties and pedantry, to find such a large amount of reasonable and intelligent interpretation of the Word of God.

5. To gather up, then, our preceding comments, may we not fairly say,—*first*, that much that has been said about the extent and variety of interpretations of Scripture is exaggerated; *secondly*, that even the various methods of interpretation—which, when it serves a purpose, our opponents regard as meaning the same as the results arrived at—may in many, perhaps most, cases be regarded as modes of applying or expanding the primary sense, rather than of eliciting substantive and independent meanings; *thirdly*, not only that God has never left Himself without a witness, and that in every age there have been a few faithful representatives of faithful principles of interpretation, but further, that there has been from the very earliest times, not only in theory but in practice, a plain, literal, and historical mode of interpreting Scripture; and *finally*, that there may be traced so great an identity in the results arrived at by successive interpreters, that we have full warrant for using the term Catholic in reference to a far larger portion of what may be considered current orthodox interpretations than the mere popular disputant is at all aware of? Let the inquiry be put

with all simplicity to those, whether in this country or abroad, who have made Ancient Versions and expositors their study, and, however different their opinions may be on other points, on this they will be agreed,—that there is such a *concordia discors* in the results obtained, that in very many passages we can produce interpretations which may stand even the test of Vincent of Lerins, and may justly be termed the traditional interpretations of the Church of Christ.

We know, of course, how these statements both have been and will be disposed of by the impatient and the confident. It will be said, probably, that granting merely for the sake of argument, that there is that species of concord of interpretation in many important passages, it has been only the result of traditional prejudices from which it is now our duty to make ourselves free. It will be added that any form of such consent is in itself suspicious, and that if our intuitions run counter to it we are at once to listen to the voice of reason within us, and reject the interpretation of every Church and every age of the world, if it does not approve itself to our own convictions. Brave and buoyant in our own self-esteem, we shall perhaps never pause to ask how far the so-called voice of reason may not be the voice of prejudice,—how far convictions may not be merely the results of secret influences within, and of some half-consciousness that what we reject bears aspects or involves conclusions sadly at variance with our habits or our propensions. We may at last perceive that it is the Word of God in its dreaded function of searching the intents of the heart that is now being brought home to us, and in our very dismay and perplexity we may have felt forced to come to the determination that every interpretation, be it of Church or of Council, that makes us thus tremble for ourselves, both must be and shall be either rejected or ignored. Thus, perhaps, will all that has been urged be disposed of. Be it so. There is a proud and confident spirit abroad; there is a love of self, self in its more purely intellectual aspects, above measure painful and revolting; there are forms bearing the names of moral goodness and freedom, and yet involving the denial of the essence of both, that bring an Apostle's predictions sadly and strangely to our thoughts,—and we feel it must be so, and that there are some whose ears must be and will be turned away from the truth. Yet there are others—especially the young, the ardent, the inexperienced—to whom what has been thus far urged may not have been urged in vain. To them our arguments are mainly addressed, to them we are speaking, for them we are pleading. "Young man, true in heart and earnest in spirit, honest searcher, anxious yet prayerful inquirer, let not thy eyes be holden by proud, unkindly hands, judge for thyself. Believe not every one that tells thee that the records of the Church are scribbled over with every form of strange, idle, and conventional interpretation of the Word of God. Judge for thyself, but judge righteous judgment. If there be fuller concords in the voices of the past than thou hast believed, close not thine ears to them because as yet they sound not fully harmonious to thee. Wait, ponder, pray: ere long, perchance thine own voice will spontaneously blend with what thou hearest; thou thyself, by the grace of God, may at length hear sounding round thee, and by thine own experience make others hear with thee, the holy accords and harmonies of the deep things of the Word of God."

§ 2.

6. We now pass naturally onward to another portion, or rather to another, and that at first sight an opposed, aspect of our present subject. Hitherto we have shown not only that the amount of the differences of interpretation has been clearly over-estimated, but even that the true and honest method of interpreting the Word of God—the literal, historical, and grammatical —has been recognized in every age, and that the results are to be seen in the agreement on numberless passages of importance that may be found in expositors

of all periods; in other words, that the illuminating grace of God has ever been with His Church. This being so, it is but waste of time to consider the causes that have been alleged for the existence of the multitude of interpretations, when that multitude has been proved to a great extent to be imaginary. We will not, then, pause to discuss the amount of varying interpretations that have been ascribed, whether, on the one hand, to rhetoric and desires to edify, or, on the other, to party feeling and efforts to wrest the meanings of Scripture to different sides. We deny not that both have produced some effect on the interpretation of Scripture. We do not deny that the Christian preacher may have often urged meanings that do not lie in the words, and that these may have been adopted by contemporaries and echoed and reproduced by those that have followed. We deny not, again, that the natural meaning of many texts may have been perverted by prejudice on one side or other, and that traces of this may still remain in some of the current interpretations of our own times. All this we deny not, but, on the other hand, we confidently assert that the effects have been limited, and that all the assumptions that the contrary has been the case fall with the fallen assumption, viz., that the discordance of Scripture interpretations is excessive, and that all methods hitherto adopted have been uncertain or untrustworthy.

But we now come to what at first sight may appear a reversed aspect of our subject. While, on the one hand, we consider it proved that there has been from the first a substantial agreement, not only in the mode of interpreting Scripture, but in many of its most important details, we are equally prepared, on the other hand, to recognize the existence of great differences of opinion about the meanings of individual passages, and even in reference to the methods by which these meanings may be best obtained. No one who has had any experience in the interpretation of Scripture can with honesty assert the contrary. It may be true that in the great majority of all the more important passages careful consideration will show that what logic, grammar, and a proper valuation of the significance of words, seem to indicate as the principal and primary meaning of the passage, will be found to have been recognized as such ages before, and has substantially held its ground to our own times,—still experience teaches us that there is a very large residuum of less important passages in which interpreters break up into groups, and in which the expositor of the nineteenth century has to yield to the guidance of principles perhaps but recently recognized, yet, from their justice and truth, of an influence and authority that cannot be gainsaid. There are, indeed, even a few cases, but confessedly unimportant, where the modern interpreter has to oppose himself to every early Version and every patristic commentator, and where it is almost certain he is right in so doing. Let the connexion of the concluding portion of Gal. iv. 12 be cited as an example. Such instances are, however, very rare, and need hardly be mentioned, save to show that principles can never be dispensed with, and that, though we yield all becoming deference to interpretations in which antiquity is mainly agreed, we yet by no means pledge ourselves unreservedly to accept them. All these differences, then, in the interpretations of individual passages, we frankly recognize; nay more, we may in many cases admit that there are clearly defined differences in the method of interpreting—perhaps an extended context. Last of all, it is not to be suppressed that there is a somewhat large class of passages so far-reaching, so inclusive, and so profound, that not only are all the better interpretations remarkable for their varied character, but for their appearing, perhaps each one, to represent a portion of the true meaning, but scarcely, all of them together, what our inner soul seems to tell us is the complete and ultimate meaning of the words that meet the outward eye.

7. We are thus admitting the existence of diversity of interpretation, especially in individual passages and details, as readily and as frankly as we have argued for

the existence of a far greater prevailing unity both in the meanings themselves, and the methods of arriving at them in all more important passages, than is willingly recognized by popular writers. The question then naturally arises, how do we account for these apparently reversed aspects? How can we in the same breath assert prevailing unity, and yet admit diversity? How do we account for a state of things which in Sophocles or Plato would be pronounced incredible or absurd? Our answer is of a threefold nature. We account for this by observing, *First*, that the Bible is different to every other book in the world, and that its interpretation may well be supposed to involve many difficulties and diversities. *Secondly*, that the words of Scripture in many parts have more than one meaning and application. *Thirdly*, that Scripture is inspired, and that though written by man, it is a revelation from God, and adumbrates His eternal plenitudes and perfections.

On each one of these forms of the answer we will make a few observations.

I. On the first, perhaps, little more need be said than has been incidentally brought forward in earlier parts of this Essay. It is, indeed, most unreasonable to compare, even in externals, the Bible with any other book in the world. A collection of many treatises, written in many different styles, and at many different ages, can never be put side by side with the works of a single author, nor will any canons of interpretation which may be just and reasonable in the latter case, be necessarily applicable to the former. What, for instance, can really be more strange than to lay down the rule that we are to interpret the Scripture like any other book, when, in the merest rough and outside view, the Scripture presents such striking differences from any book that the world has ever seen? The strangeness becomes greater when we look inward, and observe the varied nature of the contents,—prose and poetry, history and prophecy, teachings of an incarnate God, and exhortations and messages of men to men. How very unreasonable to insist on similar modes of interpreting what our very opponents rightly term "a world by itself"—a world from which foreign influences are to be excluded—and any other documents or records that have come from the hand of man! How can we with justice require that amount of exegetical agreement in the former case that might naturally be looked for and demanded in the latter? How very reasonable, on the other hand, is the supposition that in the interpretation of a collection of treatises of such varied and momentous import we may have to recognize both unities and diversities,—unities as due to the illuminating grace of the one and self-same Spirit similarly vouchsafed to all meek and holy readers of Scripture in every age of the Church,—diversities as due to the profundity and variety that must ever mark the outpourings of the manifold wisdom of God! It seems, indeed, idle to dwell upon what is thus obvious and self-evident; but it has been rendered necessary by what we are obliged to term the unfairness of our opponents. At one time, when the argument seems to require it, the Scripture is considered as a single book, to be dealt with like other books, subject to the same critical canons, amenable to the same laws of interpretation: at another time it emerges to view as a collection of records, unconnected and discordant, which it is desirable to keep thus divided, that they may be the more readily disposed of; and, whenever it may seem necessary, the more successfully pitted against one another in contradictions and antagonisms.

II. We pass onward to our second form of answer. Here we find ourselves, as might have been foreseen, in undisguised conflict with the sceptical writers of our own time. That Scripture has one meaning, and one meaning only, is their fundamental axiom: it is seen to be, and felt to be, one of the keys of their position. When, however, we pause to ask how that one meaning is to be defined, we receive answers that are neither very intelligible nor consistent. If we are told that it is "that meaning which it had to the mind of the Prophet or Evangelist who first uttered or wrote, to the hearers or readers who first received the message," we may justly protest against an answer involving alike such assumptions and such ambiguities. What right have we to assume that the speaker knew the full meaning which his own words might subsequently be found to bear? A very little reflection will show the justice of this query. What right, again, have we to assume that the meaning which the Prophet or Evangelist designed to convey was identical with that which the hearers or readers who first received the message conceived to be conveyed in its words? Assuming even that it was so, how are we to arrive at this one meaning common to hearer and speaker? How are we to recognize it, when the words before us may bear two or more meanings, each, perhaps, equally probable and supported by arguments of equal validity? It will be said that this is precisely the duty of the Interpreter; that it is for him to disengage himself from the trammels of the present, and free from the bondage of prejudices and creeds to transport himself back into the past, to mingle in spirit with those who first heard the words, to feel as they felt, to hear as they heard, to recover the one, the true, and the original meaning, and to bring it back to the hearer or reader of our own times. All this is high-sounding and rhetorical; it is sure to attract the young and the enthusiastic, and by no means ill-calculated to excite and delude the inexperienced. But it is rhetoric, and nothing more. No one who has had genuine experience in the interpretation of Scripture would hesitate to pronounce such "magnifyings of an office" as completely delusive, if even not deserving the graver term, mischievous. Delusive they certainly are, because all this self-projection into the past is in reality, and ever has been, unostentatiously practised by all better interpreters—by all who have sought with humility and earnestness to catch the spirit and mind of the writer whom they are striving to expound. All this has been practised, almost from the first. Chrysostom spoke of it, Augustine commended it, and yet what has been the result of experience? Why, that passage after passage has been found to be so pregnant with meaning, so mysteriously full, so comprehensively applicable, that the most self-confident interpreter in the world could scarcely be brought to declare his complete conviction that the one view out of many which he may have adopted was certainly the principal one, much less that it was the only meaning of the words before him.

But to give up such attitudes of delusive self-confidence, and to return to modesty and reason, we may now proceed to illustrate our first assertion, that Scripture has frequently more than one meaning, by references to three particulars in which this is very clearly exemplified,—double meanings, or applications of prophecy, types, and deeper senses of simple historical statements. A few remarks shall be made on each.

(1.) On the first so much has been said of late that it might almost seem pure knight-errantry to undertake the advocacy of what (we are told) ought now to be regarded as a mere outworn prejudice. And yet what is more thoroughly consonant with reason, and, we might almost add, experience, than such a belief? We say experience,—for there must be few calm observers of the course of events around them who can fail to have been struck with the curious re-appearance, under unlikely circumstances, of former combinations, and who have not occasionally been almost startled by the recurrence of incidents in relations and connexions that could never have been reasonably expected again. It does not seem too much to say that in many instances nations and individuals alike seem moving as it were in spirals, constantly returning, not exactly to the same point, but to the same bearings and the same aspects,—not precisely to a former past, but to a present that bears to it a very strange and wholly unlooked-for resemblance. If this be true in many things that fall under our own immediate observation (and very unobservant must he be who has not often verified it for himself), if we often seem to ourselves to recognize this principle of events becoming in many respects doubles of each other, and that not only in minor matters, but even in circumstances of some historical importance,—if this be so, is it strange that in the spiritual history of our race there should be such parallelisms; that words apparently spoken in reference to a precursory series of events should be found to refer with equal pertinence to some mysteriously similar combinations that appeared long afterwards? Are we to think that counsels sealed in silence from eternity, that purposes of the ages formed before the worlds were made, that dispensations of love and mercy laid out even before the objects for whom they were designed had come into being, were not over and over again reflected, as it were, in the history of our race, and that the events of a former day were not often bound in mystical likenesses and affinities with the events of the future by that principle of redeeming love which permeated and pervaded all? Unless we are prepared plainly to adopt some of the bleakest theories of the scepticism of these later days; unless we are determined to find civilization and development and not God in history; unless we have resolved to see in the Gospel no fore-ordered dispensation, but only a system of morality, unannounced, unforeshadowed, as strange in its isolated and exceptional character as it has been strange in its effects,—then, and then only, can we consistently deny the likelihood and probability of God's purposes to the world having imparted to events seemingly remote and unconnected, and to issues brought about by varied and dissimilar circumstances, real and spiritual resemblances. Then only can we justly deny that the word of prophecy might truly, legitimately, and consistently be considered to refer as well to earlier as to later events, wherever such resemblances could be reasonably demonstrated to exist.

To illustrate the foregoing comments by an example, let us take an instance which our opponents are never wearied with bringing forward,—our Lord's prophecy relative to the fate of Jerusalem and the end of the world. Here it is said that the system of first and second meanings, which we are now defending, is most palpably nothing whatever else than an attempt to help out the verification and mitigate the incoherence of a somewhat confused and partially unrealized prophecy. Now, in disposing of this idle but painfully familiar comment, we will make no allusion to the question of the four Apostles, which, it may be observed, necessitated in the answer reference to the end of the world as well as to the end of the Theocracy (Matt. xxiv. 3); we will only take the prophecy as we find it, with its mingled allusions to a near and to a remote future, and simply inquire whether there is any such resemblance, spiritual or otherwise, as might make expressions used in reference to the one almost interchangeably applicable to the other. Who can doubt what the answer must be? Who that takes into consideration the true significance of the fall of Jerusalem, who that sees in it, as every sober reader must see, not merely the fall of an ancient city, but the destruction of the visible seat of Jehovah's worship, the enforced cessation of the ancient order of things, the practical abrogation of the Theocracy,—all closely synchronous with the Lord's first coming,—who is there that will take all these things fairly into consideration and not be ready to acknowledge resemblances between the end of the fated city and the issues of the present dispensation, sufficiently mysterious and sufficiently profound to warrant our even alternating between them (we use the studiedly exaggerated language of opponents) the verses of the Lord's great prophecy? Till it can be shown that the course of things is fortuitous, that providential dispensations are a dream, and the gradual development of the counsels of God a convenient fiction—till it can be made clear to demonstration, that there are no profound harmonies in the Divine government, no mystical recurrences of foreordered combinations, no spiritual affinities between the past and the present, no foreseen resemblances in epochal events, and no predestined counterparts, the ground on which the reasonable belief in double meanings and double applications of prophecy has been rightly judged to rest will remain stable and unshaken; the perspective character that has been attributed to Scriptural predictions will still claim to be considered no idle or unreal imagination.

(2.) The subject of *types* has been much dwelt upon by modern writers, and in most cases with singular unfairness. The popular mode of arguing on this subject is to select some instances from early Christian writers which are obviously fanciful and untenable, to hold up the skirts of their folly, to display their utter nakedness, and then to ask if a system of which these are examples either can or ought to be regarded with any degree of favour or confidence. If Justin tells us that the king of Assyria signified Herod, and Jerome was of opinion that by Chaldæans are meant Demons, if the scarlet thread of Rahab has been deemed to have a hidden meaning, and the number of Abraham's followers has been regarded as not wholly without significance, we are asked whether we can deem the whole system otherwise than precarious and extravagant, whether we can at all safely attribute to the details of the Mosaic ritual a reference to the New Testament, or really believe that the passage of the Red Sea can be very certainly considered a type of baptism. The ultimate design of this mode of arguing will not escape the intelligent reader;—it is simply an endeavour by slow sap to weaken the authority of some of the writers of the New Testament, and to leave it to be inferred that our Lord Himself, in recognizing and even giving sanction to such applications of Scripture (Matt. xii. 40, John iii. 14; comp. ch. vi. 58), either condescended to adopt forms of illustration which He must have felt to be untrustworthy, or else really in this did not rise wholly above the culture of His own times. Now at present, without at all desiring to press what we have not yet discussed—the inspiration of Scripture—we do very earnestly call upon those who are not yet prepared wholly to fling off their allegiance to Scripture, to bear in mind the following facts:—(*a*) That our Blessed

Lord Himself referred to the Brazen Serpent as typical of His being raised aloft, and that He illustrated the mystery of His own abode in the chambers of the earth by an event of the past which He Himself was pleased to denominate as a sign,—the only sign that was to be vouchsafed to the generation that then was seeking for one; (*b*) that the Evangelists recognize the existence and significance of types in reference to our Lord (Matt. ii. 15; John xix. 36); (*c*) that the teaching of St. Paul is pervaded by references to this form of what has been termed "acted prophecies" (Rom. v. 14 *seq.*; 1 Cor. v. 7, x. 2 *seq.*; Gal. iv. 24 *seq.*; Col. ii. 11); (*d*) that the greater part of the Epistle to the Hebrews is one continued elucidation of the spiritual significance of the principal features of the Levitical law: its sacrifices, rites, and priests were all the shadows and typical resemblances of good things to come (Heb. x. 1); (*e*) that St. Peter plainly and distinctly declares that the water of the Flood is typical of baptism (1 Pet. iii. 21); (*f*) that in the last and most mysterious revelation of God to man the very realms of blessedness and glory are designated by a name and specified by allusions (Rev. xxi. 22) which warrant our recognizing in the Holy City on earth, the "Jerusalem that now is," a type of that Heavenly City which God hath prepared for the faithful (Heb. xi. 16), a similitude of the Jerusalem that is above, a shadow of the incorruptible inheritance of the servants and children of God.

When we dwell calmly upon these things, when we observe further how, not only thus directly and explicitly, but how, also, indirectly and by allusion, nearly every writer in the New Testament bears witness to the existence and significance of types, how it tinges their language of consolation (Rev. xxi. 2 *seq.*), and gives force to their exhortations (Heb. iv. 14); when we finally note how the very Eternal Spirit of God, by whom they were inspired, is specially declared to have vouchsafed thus to involve in the ceremonies of the past the deep truths of the future (Heb. ix. 8),—when we calmly consider the cumulative force of all these examples and all these testimonies, we may perhaps be induced to pause before we adopt the sweeping statements that have been made in reference to the whole system of typology. We may admit that types may have been often injudiciously applied, that it may be difficult to fix bounds to their use or to specify the measure of their aptitude, and yet we may indeed seriously ask for time to consider whether such recognitions of the deeper meanings of Scripture thus vouchsafed to us, and thus sanctioned by our Lord and His Apostles, are to be given up at once because they are thought to come in collision with modern views of Scripture and modern canons of interpretation. Our opponents may well be anxious to get rid of the whole system of types; we can understand their anxiety, we can even find reasons for the sort of desperation that scruples not to represent what was once sanctioned by our Lord and His Apostles as now either mischievous or inapplicable. It is felt that if typology is admitted, the assertion that Scripture has but one meaning is invalidated. It is seen clearly enough that if it can be shown, within any reasonable degree of probability, that the details of a past dispensation were regarded by the first teachers of Christianity as veritable types and symbols of things that had now come, then the recognition of further and deeper meanings in Scripture, of secondary senses and ultimate significations, must directly and inevitably follow, and the rule that the Bible is to be interpreted like any other book at once be shown to be, what it certainly is, inapplicable. Need we wonder then that every effort has been made to denounce a system so obstructive to modern innovations; need we be surprised that the rejection of what is thus accredited has been as persistent as it would now seem proved to be both unreasonable and without success?

(3.) Our third subject for consideration, the existence of deeper meanings in Scripture, even in what might seem simple historical statements, follows very naturally after what has been just discussed. Here again we can adopt no more convincing mode of demonstration than is supplied by an appeal to Scripture. Yet we may not unprofitably make one or two preliminary comments. In the first place, is not this assertion of a oneness of meaning in the written words of an intelligent author open to some discussion? Is it at all clear, even in the case of uninspired writers, that the primary and literal meaning is the only meaning which is to be recognized in their words? Is it so wholly inconceivable that more meanings than one may have been actually designed at the time of writing, and that, conjointly with a leading and primary meaning, a secondary and subordinate meaning may have been felt, recognized, and intended? Nay, can we be perfectly certain that even words may not have been specially or instinctively chosen which should leave this secondary meaning fairly distinct and fairly recognizable? It would not be difficult to substantiate the justice of these queries by actual examples from the writings of any of the greater authors whether of our own or some other country. Still less difficult would it be to show that in very many passages meanings must certainly be admitted which it may be probable were not intended by the writer, but which nevertheless by their force and pertinence make it frequently doubtful whether what has been assumed to be the primary meaning of the words is really to be deemed so, and whether what is judged to be an application may not really represent the truest aspects of the mind and intentions of the author.

Let us add this second remark, that the instances in which words have been found to involve meanings, not recognized at the time by reader or by writer, but which after-circumstances have shown were really to be regarded as meanings, are by no means few or exceptional. The whole group of illustrations supplied by "ominata verba," the whole class of cases which belong to that sort of unconscious prescience which is often found in minds of higher strain, the various instances where glimpses of yet undiscovered relations have given a tinge to expressions which will only be fully understood and realized when those relations are themselves fully known,—all these things, and many more than these, might be adduced as illustrative of the deeper meanings that are often found to lie in the words of mere uninspired men. Such meanings neither they nor their own contemporaries may have distinctly recognized, but meanings they are notwithstanding; not merely applications or extensions, but meanings in the simple and regular acceptation of the term. How this is to be accounted for, we are not called upon to show. We will not speculate how far the great and the good of every age and nation may have been moved by the inworking Spirit of God to declare truths of wider application than they themselves may have felt or realized; we will not seek to estimate the varying degrees of that power of partially foreseeing future relations which long and patient study of the past and the present has sometimes been found to impart. All such things are probably beyond our grasp, and would most likely be found to elude our present powers and present means of appreciation. With reasons we will not embarrass ourselves; we will be satisfied with simply calling attention to the fact that the existence of such phenomena as that of words having deeper and fuller meanings than they were understood to have at first is not only not to be denied, but may even be deemed matter of something more than occasional experience.

The two foregoing observations will, perhaps, have in some measure prepared us for forming a more just estimate of the further and second meanings that have been attributed to the words of Scripture. If it be admitted that some of the phenomena to which we have alluded are occasionally to be recognized in purely human writings, is it altogether strange that in a revelation from God the same should exist in fuller measures, and under still clearer aspects? If the many-sidedness, mobility, and varied powers of combination existing in the human mind, appear at times to invest words written or spoken with a significance of a fuller and deeper kind than may at first be recognized, are we to be surprised if something similar in kind, but higher in degree, is to be observed in the language of Holy Scripture? Is the Divine mind not to have influences which are conceded to the human? Are the words of Prophets or Evangelists to be less pregnant in meaning, or more circumscribed in their applications, than those of poets and philosophers? Without assuming one attribute in the Scripture beyond what all our more reasonable opponents would be willing to concede, without claiming more for it than to be considered a revelation from God, a communication from the Divine mind to the minds and hearts of men, we may justly claim some hearing for this form of the *à priori* argument; we may with reason ask all fair disputants whether they are prepared positively to deny, in the case of a communication directly or even indirectly from God, the probability of our finding there some enhancement of the higher characteristics and more remarkable phenomena that have been recognized in communications of man to men?

When we leave these *à priori* considerations, and turn to definite examples and illustrations, our anticipations cannot be said to have disappointed us. We have really an affluence of examples of second and deeper meanings being deliberately assigned to passages of Scripture that might have been otherwise deemed to have only the one simple or historical meaning that seems first to present itself. Let us select two or three instances. Is it possible to deny that our Lord Himself discloses, in what might have been deemed a mere title of Jehovah under His aspects of relation to favoured worshippers, a meaning so full and so deep that it formed the basis of an argument (Matt. xxii. 31 *seq.*; Mark xii. 24 *seq.*; Luke xx. 37 *seq.*)? The familiar titular designation is shown to be the vehicle of a spiritual truth of the widest application; the apparently mere recapitulation of the names of a son, a father, and a grandfather, in connexion with the God whose servants they were, and whom they worshipped, is not only urged as proving a fundamental doctrine, but is tacitly acknowledged to have done so by gainsayers and opponents (Luke xx. 39). And further, let it be observed, that it is clearly implied that this was no deeply-hidden meaning, no profound interpretation, which it might require a special revelation to disclose, but that it was a meaning which really ought to have been recognized by a deeper reader,—at any rate that not to have done so argued as plain an ignorance of the Written Word as it did of the power and operations of God (Matt. xxii. 29). Let this really "prerogative" example be fairly considered and properly estimated, and then let it be asked if the existence of deeper meanings in Scripture can consistently be denied by any who profess a belief in our Lord Jesus Christ. It seems to us that this is a plain case of a dilemma: either with Strauss and Hase we must regard the argument as an example of Rabbinical sophistry,—and so, as Meyer reminds us, be prepared to sacrifice the character and dignity of our Lord,—or we must admit that, in some cases at least, there is more in Scripture than the mere literal sense of the words.

Such an example opens the way for the introduction of others, which, without this prerogative instance, could not have been strongly urged, except on assumptions which, in our present position in the argument, it would not be logically consistent to make. By being associated, however, with the present example, they certainly seem to be of some force and validity in confirming our present assertion, and, to say the very least, can be more easily explained on that hypothesis than on any other that has yet been assigned. Let us specify Matt. ii. 15. Now the question presents itself in the following form:—Is not this an example furnished by the Apostle of what we have already seen must be recognized in an example vouchsafed by his Lord? Is not this a case of deeper meaning? Do not the words of Hosea, the second meaning of which was doubtless not more apparent even to the prophet himself than it was to his earlier readers, seem only to have a simple historical reference to the earthly Israel? and yet do they not really involve a further and typical reference to Him who was truly and essentially what Israel was graciously denominated (Exod. iv. 22; comp. Jerem. xxxi. 9), and of whom Israel was a type and a shadow? So, at any rate, St. Matthew plainly asserts. Which, then, of these hypotheses do we think most probable,—that St. Matthew erroneously ascribed a meaning to words which they do not and were not intended to bear, that the two chapters are an interpolation (for such an hypothesis has been advanced), or that they supply an instance of a second and typical meaning in words of a simply historical aspect, and that a truth is here disclosed by an Apostle similar to what we have already seen has been clearly disclosed by our Lord?

Let us take yet another, and that, as it might be thought, a very hopeless instance. St. Paul, in his Epistle to the Ephesians (ch. iv. 8), not only makes a citation from a Psalm, which at the part in question appears to have a simple historical reference to some event of the time (perhaps the taking of Rabbah), but even alters the words of the original, so as to make its application to our Lord more pertinent and telling. What are we to say of such a case? Does it not really look like an instance of almost unwarrantable accommodation? Does it not seem as if we had now fairly fallen upon the point of our own sword, and that, in citing an example of a second meaning, we had unwittingly selected one in which the very alteration shows that the words did not originally have the meaning now attributed to them? Before we thus yield, let us at any rate state the case, and leave the fair reader to form his own opinion. Without at present assuming the existence of any influence which would have directly prevented the Apostle from so seriously misunderstanding and so gravely misapplying a passage of the Old Testament, and only assuming it as proved that there is one authentic instance of words of Scripture bearing a further meaning than meets the eye, we now ask which is to be judged as most likely: that the

Apostle to substantiate a statement, which could have been easily substantiated by other passages, deliberately altered a portion of Scripture which had no reference to the matter before him, or that he rightly assigned to a seemingly historical passage from a Psalm, which (be it observed), in its original scope, has every appearance of being prophetic and Messianic, a deeper meaning than the words seem to bear (such a meaning being in one case, at least, admitted to exist), and that he altered the form of the words to make more palpable and evident the meaning which he knew they involved? We have no anxiety as to the decision in the case of any calm-judging and unbiassed reader. . . . . . One further remark we may make in conclusion, and it is a remark of some little importance, viz., that if the present instance be deemed an example of Scripture having a second and deeper, as well as a first and more simple meaning, it must also be regarded as an example of an authoritative change in the exact words of a quotation,—the change being designed to bring up the underlying meaning which was known to exist, and to place it with more distinctness before the mind of the general reader.

III. Having thus, as it would seem, substantiated our assertion that deeper meanings lie in Scripture than appear on the surface, and that this may be properly considered as in part accounting for the existence of some of those difficulties and diversities which are met with in Scripture interpretation, we now pass to the third assertion relative to the subject, viz., that Scripture is *divinely inspired.*

Here we enter upon a wide subject, which may with reason claim for itself a separate and independent essay, and which certainly ought fully to be disposed of before any rules bearing upon interpretation can properly be laid down. As a longer discussion of this subject will be found in another portion of our volume, we will here only make a very few general remarks upon inspiration as immediately bearing upon interpretation, and more especially upon the estimate formed of its nature and extent by the advocates of the system of Scriptural exegesis now under our consideration.

In the outset, let it be said that we heartily concur with the majority of our opponents in rejecting all theories of inspiration, and in sweeping aside all those distinctions and definitions which, only in too many cases, have been merely called forth by emergencies, and drawn up for no other purpose than to meet real and supposed difficulties. The remark probably is just, that most of the current explanations err more especially in attempting to define what, though real, is incapable of being defined in an exact manner. Hence all such terms as "mechanical" and "dynamical" inspiration, and all the theories that have grown round these epithets,—all such distinctions as inspirations of superintendence, inspirations of suggestion, and so forth,—all attempts again to draw lines of demarcation between the inspiration of the books of Scripture themselves and the inspiration of the authors of which those books were results, may be most profitably dismissed from our thoughts, and the whole subject calmly reconsidered from what may be termed a Scriptural point of view. The holy Volume itself shall explain to us the nature of that influence by which it is pervaded and quickened.

8. Thus far we are perfectly in accord with our opponents. We are agreed on both sides that there *is* such a thing as inspiration in reference to the Scriptures, and we are further agreed that the Scriptures themselves are the best sources of information on the subject. Here, however, all agreement completely ceases. When we invite our opponents to go with us to the Scriptures to discuss their statements on the subject before us, and to compare the inferences and deductions that either side may make from them, we at once find that by an appeal to Scripture we and our opponents mean something utterly and entirely different. *We* mean a consideration of what Scripture says about itself: we find that *they* mean a stock-taking of its errors and inaccuracies, of its antagonisms

with science and its oppositions to history,—all which they tell us must first be estimated, and with all which they urge, that inspiration, be it whatever it may, must be reconcilable and harmonized. In a word, both sides have started from the first on widely different assumptions. *We* assume that what Scripture says is trustworthy, and so conceive that it may be fittingly appealed to as a witness concerning its own characteristics; *they* assume that it abounds in errors and incongruities, and suggest that the number and nature of these ought to be generally ascertained before any further step can be taken, or any opinion safely arrived at on the whole subject. Such seems a fair estimate of the position and attitude of the two contending parties.

If this statement of our relative positions be just, it seems perfectly clear that several different lines of argument may be adopted. We may examine the grounds on which their assumption rests, or endeavour to establish the validity of our own. We may deny that any errors or inaccuracies exist, and throw upon them the *onus probandi*, or we may take the most popular and telling instances in their enumeration and endeavour to discover by fair investigation how far they deserve their position, and how far prejudice and exaggeration may not have been at work on their side, as conservatism and accommodation on ours. All these are courses which may be adopted with more or less advantage, but any one of which would occupy far more space than we can afford for this portion of our subject. We must satisfy ourselves, on the present occasion, with making, on the one hand, a few affirmative comments upon the nature, degree, and limits of the inspiration which we assign to the Scripture; and on the other hand, a few negative comments upon counter-statements advanced by opponents, which seem more than usually untrustworthy.

To begin with the negative side, let us observe, in the first place, that nothing can really be less tenable than the assertion that there is no foundation in the Gospels or Epistles for any of the higher or supernatural views of inspiration. It is a perfectly intelligible line of argument to assert that for the testimony of any book upon its own nature and characteristics to be worth anything, it must first be shown that the book can fully be relied on: it is quite consistent with fair reasoning to refuse to accept as final or conclusive the evidence of what it may be contended has been shown to be a damaged witness. Such modes of argument are quite fair and intelligible, and as such we have no fault to find with them; but to make at the outset an assertion, such as we are now considering,—to prejudice the minds of the inexperienced by an affirmation, which, if believed, cannot fail to produce the strongest possible effect, and which all the time is the very reverse of what is the fact, is indeed very like that "random scattering of uneasiness" which has been attributed to our opponents,* and which such cases as the present go very far to substantiate. It is scarcely possible that those who make such assertions can be ignorant of the terms in which our Lord is represented by the Gospels to have spoken about the Scriptures of the Old Testament. It cannot surely be forgotten that He said that they "could not be broken" (John x. 35), and that when he so spake He was using Scripture in a manner that almost vouched for its verbal and literal infallibility. It cannot have been overlooked that when He was citing the words of David He defined the divine influence under which those words were uttered (Mark xii. 36). Does not an Evangelist record His promise to His Apostles that the Holy Ghost "should teach them all things, and bring all things which He said to them to their remembrance" (John xiv. 26)? and does not that same Evangelist mention the yet more inclusive promise that the same Eternal Spirit should lead the Disciples into "the whole truth" (John xvi. 13)? and are such words to be explained away or to be limited? Does not the same writer further tell us that the Holy Ghost was almost visibly given to the Apostles by the

* See Moberly, Preface to 'Sermons on the Beatitudes,' p. ii.

Lord Himself (John xx. 22)? and does not another Evangelist tell of the completed fulness of that gift, and of men so visibly filled with the Holy Spirit that the lips of bystanders and strangers bore their ready and amazed testimony? Have we no foundation for asserting a higher inspiration when eleven men are told by a parting Lord that they are to be his witnesses, and that they are to receive supernatural assistance for their mission? Is testimony to be confined to words spoken, and to be denied to words written? Did the power that glowed in the heart of the speaker die out when he took up the pen of the writer? Was not, again, the "demonstration of the Spirit" laid claim to by St. Paul (1 Cor. ii. 4); was it not "God's wisdom" that he spake (ver. 7)? Does he not plainly say that the things "which God prepared for those that love Him," His purposes of mercy and counsels of love, were revealed to him by God through the agency of the Spirit (ver. 10)? and does he not enhance his declaration not only by affirmatively stating from whom his teaching was directly imparted, but by stating, on the negative side, that to man's wisdom he owed it not? Yea, and lest it should be thought that such high prerogatives belonged only to words spoken by the lips, does not the same Apostle guard himself, as it were, by claiming for his written words an origin equally Divine? and does he not make the recognition of this a very test of illumination and spirituality (1 Cor. xiv. 37)? We pause, not from lack of further statements, but from the feeling that quite enough has been said to lead any fair reader to pronounce the assertion of there being "no foundation" in the Gospels or Epistles for any of the higher or supernatural views of inspiration contrary to evidence, and perhaps even to admit that such assertions, where ignorance cannot be pleaded in extenuation, are not to be deemed consistent with fair and creditable argument. To deny the worth or validity of such testimony is perfectly compatible with fair controversy; to deny its existence in the teeth of such evidence, — and such evidence is known and patent,—can only be designed to give a bias to a reader, and to raise up antecedent prejudices in reference to subjects and opinions afterwards to be introduced. How far such a mode of dealing with grave questions is just or defensible, we will leave others to decide.

Let us make a second remark of a somewhat similar character, and earnestly protest against hazy and indefinite modes of speaking about the testimony of the Church in reference to the doctrine of inspiration. Whether the Church is right or wrong in its estimate of the nature and limits of this gift, is certainly a question which those who feel the necessity of inquiry are perfectly at liberty to entertain. We may pity a state of mind that is not moved by such authority, and we may suspect it to be ill-balanced; but we do not complain of such a mode of proceeding. If a man wishes to find out whether the Early Church, for instance, is right or wrong in its estimate of a principle or a doctrine, let him (in a serious and anxious spirit) commence his investigation, but let him not seek by vague and indefinite language to make it first doubtful whether the Early Church really did form any estimate at all,—when that estimate is plainly set down in black and white in fifty different treatises. Let us, at any rate, have a clear understanding on the question at issue, and agree as honest men to throw no doubts upon simple matters of simplest fact. Now, when we are told that the term inspiration is but of yesterday, and more especially that the question of inspiration was not determined by Fathers of the Church, we do seem justified in protesting against such really unfair attempts to gain over those who have neither the time, the knowledge, nor perhaps the will, to test the truth of the assertion. Let there be no mistake on this subject. The Fathers of the Church may be right or they may be wrong; but, at any rate, on this topic they have spoken most frequently and most plainly, and if any question in the world may be considered determined by them this certainly is one. The Apostolical Fathers term the

Scriptures "the true sayings" of the Holy Ghost (Clem. Rom. *ad Cor.* i. 45). In quoting passages from the Old Testament they often use the significant formula "the Holy Ghost saith." Those that followed them used their language. Justin Martyr describes the nature of inspiration, and even hints at its limits (*Cohort.* § 8); Irenæus speaks of the Scriptures as "spoken by the Word of God and His Spirit" (*Hær.* ii. 28. 2); and even attributes to the foresight of the Eternal Spirit the choice of this rather than that mode of expression in the opening words of St. Matthew's Gospel (*Hær.* iii. 16. 2). In quoting a prophet, Clement of Alexandria pauses to correct himself, and say it was not so much the prophet as the Holy Spirit in him (*Cohort.* § 8, p. 66), and on the question of Scripture infallibility and perfection he is no less precise and definite (*Cohort.* § 9, p. 68; *Strom.* ii. p. 432, vii. p. 897, ed. Potter). Tertullian and Cyprian carry onward the common sentiment; those who follow them reiterate the same so frequently and so definitively that we become embarrassed by the very affluence of our examples. Eusebius of Cæsarea deals even with technicalities, and brands those who dared to say that the writers of Scripture put one name in the place of another (*Comment. in Psalm.* xxxiii., ed. Montf.). Augustine states most explicitly his views on the whole subject, and asserts the infallibility of Scripture in language which the strongest asserter of the so-called bibliolatry of the day could not desire to see made more definite or unqualified (see for example *Epist.* lxxxii. 3, *tom.* ii. p. 285, ed. Bened. 2). . . Again we pause. We could continue such quotations almost indefinitely. We could put our fingers positively on hundreds of such passages in the writings of the Fathers of the first five or six centuries; we could quote the language of early Councils; we could point to the silent testimony of early controversies, each side claiming Scripture to be that from which there could be no appeal; we could even call in heretics, and prove from their own defences of their own tenets, from their own admissions and their own assumptions, that the inspiration of Scripture was of all subjects one that was conceived thoroughly settled and agreed upon. Enough, however, has perhaps been said, enough quoted, to place the matter beyond doubt, and to make this perfectly certain,—that what are called high views of inspiration were entertained almost unanimously by the earlier writers of the Church. So obvious, indeed, is the fact that writers like Gfrörer not only concede the fact of the agreement of the early writers, and admit the strong opinions they held on the subject, but use it as a very ground of reproach against them, and call upon us to wonder how men who entertained such high views on the inspiration of Scripture could possibly be such arbitrary and unfaithful interpreters.

A third remark may be made on the negative side by way of complaint that we find so little weight assigned to the subjective argument, as it may be termed, for the inspiration of Scripture. In the sceptical writings of the day the argument is rarely stated except to be dealt with as a form of a natural but not very harmless illusion. Yet it is an argument of the greatest force and importance, and an argument which, if rightly handled, it is much easier to set aside than to answer. Is it nothing that the Bible has spoken to millions upon millions of hearts, as it were with the very voice of God Himself? Have not its words burned within till men have seen palpably the Divine in that which spake to them? Is it not a fact that convictions on the nature of the Scriptures deepen with deepening study of them? Ask the simple man to whom the Bible has long become the daily friend and counsellor, who reads and applies what he reads as far as his natural powers enable him; ask him whether longer and more continued study has altered to any extent his estimate of the Book as a Divine revelation. What is the invariable answer? The Book "has found him;" it has consoled him in sorrows for which there seemed no consolation on this side the grave; it has wiped away tears that it seemed could only be wiped away in that far land where sadness shall be no more; it has pleaded gently during long seasons of spiritual coldness; it has infused strength in hours of weakness; it has calmed in moments of excitement; it has given to better emotions a permanence, and to stirred-up feelings a reality; it has made itself felt to be what it is; out of the abundance of his heart the mouth speaks, and he tells us with all the accumulated convictions of an honest mind, that if he once deemed the Bible to be fully inspired on the testimony of others, now he knows it on evidence that has been brought home to his own soul. He has now long had the witness in himself, and that witness he feels and knows is unchangeably and enduringly true.

Ask, again, the professed student of Scripture, the scholar, the divine, the interpreter, one who, to what we may term the testimony of the soul, in the case of the less cultivated reader, can add the testimony of the mind and the spirit,—ask such a one whether increased familiarity with Scripture has quickened or obscured his perception of the Divine within it, whether it has led him to higher or to lower views of inspiration. Have not, we may perhaps anxiously ask, the difficulties of Scripture wearied him, its seeming discordances perplexed, its obscurities depressed him? Have not the tenor of its arguments, and the seeming want of coherence and connexion in adjacent sentences, sometimes awakened uneasy and disquieting thoughts? What is almost invariably the answer?—"No; far otherwise." Deepened study has brought its blessing and its balm. It has shown how what might seem the greatest difficulties often turn merely upon our ignorance of one or two unrecorded facts or relations; it has conducted to standing-points where in a moment all that has hitherto seemed confused and distorted has arranged itself in truest symmetry and in the fairest perspective. In many an obscure passage our student will tell us how the light has ofttimes suddenly broken, how he has been cheered by being permitted to recognize and identify the commingling of human weakness and Divine power, the mighty revelation almost too great for mortal utterance, the "earthen vessel" almost parting asunder from the greatness and abundance of the heavenly treasure committed to it. He will tell us, again, how in many a portion where the logical connexion has seemed suspended or doubtful,—in one of those discourses, for instance, of his Lord as recorded by St. John,—the true connexion has at length slowly and mysteriously disclosed itself, how he has perceived and realized all. For a while he has felt himself thinking as his Saviour vouchsafed to think, in part beholding truth as those Divine eyes beheld it; for a brief space his mind has seemed to be consciously one with the mind of Christ. All this he has perceived and felt. And he will tell us, perchance, what has often been the sequel; how he has risen from his desk and fallen on his knees, and with uplifted voice blessed and adored Almighty God for His gift of the Book of Life.

The cold-hearted may smile at such things, the so-called philosophical may affect to account for them; they may be put aside as illusions, or they may be explained away as projections of self on the passive page, unconscious infusion of one's own feelings and emotions in the calm words that meet the outward eye. All this has been urged against such testimony, and will ever be urged even to the very end. But when the end does come the truth will appear. That witnessing of soul and spirit will, it may be, rise up in silent judgment against many a one who now slights it; that testimony so often rejected as self-engendered and fanciful, will be seen to have been real and heaven-born, a reflex image of an eternal truth, a part and a portion of the surest of the sure things of God.

9. But let us now pass from the negative to the positive, and make a few affirmative observations on the subject before us. Let us begin, not with a theory, but with a definition and a statement of the belief that is in us. If asked to define what we mean by the inspiration of Scripture, let us be bold, and make answer —that fully convinced as we are that the Scripture is

the revelation through human media of the infinite mind of God to the finite mind of man, and recognizing as we do both a human and a Divine element in the written Word, we verily believe that the Holy Ghost was so breathed into the mind of the writer, so illumined his spirit and pervaded his thoughts, that, while nothing that individualized him as man was taken away, everything that was necessary to enable him to declare Divine Truth in all its fulness was bestowed and superadded. And, as consonant with this, we further believe that this influence of the Spirit, whether by illumination, suggestion, superintendence, or all combined, extended itself—*first*, to the enunciation of sentiments and doctrines, that so the will and counsels of God should not be a matter of doubt, but of certain knowledge; *secondly*, to statements, recitals, facts, that so the truth into which the writer was led should be known and recognized; *thirdly*, to the choice of expressions, modes of speech, and perhaps occasionally even of words (the individuality of the writer being conserved), that so the subject-matter of the revelation might be conveyed in the fittest and most appropriate language, and in the garb best calculated to set off its dignity and commend its truth.

Let such be our definition. If asked how we justify it, how we prove our assertions, we answer in two ways: first, by *à priori* arguments of great force and validity; secondly, by *à posteriori* arguments of equal or even greater strength—arguments which our preceding remarks on the negative side have been designed indirectly to set forward and substantiate. Into these arguments we do not intend to enter, but we may profitably pause to specify them. On the *à priori* side, and especially in reference to the Old Testament, we may specify evidences of inspiration derived from the clear accordance of various events with prophecies special or general that can be proved to have been uttered before the events in question. Among instances of this nature the history and present state of the Jews have been always rightly and confidently appealed to.* Again, on the same side, but more in reference to the New Testament, it has been fairly urged that, if we admit the general truth and Divine character of the Christian dispensation, we can hardly believe that those who were chosen to declare its principles and to make known its doctrines were not especially guarded from error in the execution of their weighty commission, and were not divinely guided both in the words they uttered and the statements they committed to writing. On the *à posteriori* side we may specify the three great arguments to which we have already alluded: the direct declarations of Scripture, the trustworthy character of Scripture having been first demonstrated;† the unanimous consent of the early writers, and unchanging testimony of the Catholic Church; and, lastly, the inward and subjective testimony to the Divine nature of the Scripture yielded by the soul and spirit of the individual. Other arguments there are, especially on the *à priori* side, of varying degrees of strength and solidity, appealing in different ways to different minds; but the chief perhaps have been specified, and on these we may safely and securely base our preceding assertions, and our unhesitating and unqualified belief in the full inspiration of the Word of God.

But it may be asked, how do we conceive that this inspiration took place? What is our theory of the process? what do we conceive to be the *modus agendi* of the Holy Spirit in the heart of man? This we plainly refuse to answer. We know not, and do not presume to inquire into the manner; we recognize and believe in the fact. Individual writers may have speculated; imagery, suitable or unsuitable, may have been introduced as illustrative by a few thinkers in early ages; but the Catholic Church has never put forward a theory. On this subject she has always maintained

* See Moberly, Preface to 'Sermons on the Beatitudes,' p. xxxii.

† Thus to appeal to Scripture to define its own character in reference to inspiration seems perfectly fair, when the trustworthy character of the volume has been properly denonstrated; compare the remarks of Chalmers, 'Christian Evidences,' iv. 2. 26, vol. iv., p. 390. (Glasgow ed.)

a solemn reserve; she declares to us that in the Scripture the Holy Ghost speaks to us by the mouths of men; she permits us to recognize a Divine and a human element; but, in reference to the nature, extent, and special circumstances of the union, she warns us not to seek to be wise above what has been written, not to endanger our faith with speculations and conjectures about that which has not been revealed. Theories of inspiration are what scepticism is ever craving for; it is the voice of hapless unbelief that is ever loudest in its call for explanation of the manner of the assumed union of the Divine with the human, or of the proportions in which each element is to be admitted and recognized. Such explanations have not been vouchsafed, and it is as vain and unbecoming to demand them as it is to require a theory of the union of the Divinity and Humanity in the person of Christ, or an estimate of the proportions in which the two perfect natures are to be conceived to co-exist.

Not much more profitable is the inquiry into the exact limits of inspiration, whether it is to be considered in all cases as extending to words, or whether it is only to be confined to sentiments and doctrines. At first sight we might be inclined to adopt the latter statement, and such, to some extent, would certainly seem to have been the view of a writer of no less antiquity and learning than Justin Martyr; still when we remember, on the one hand, that there are instances in Scripture in which weighty arguments have in some degree been seen to depend on the very words and expressions that are made use of (John x. 34: Gal. iii. 16), and on the other, that many important truths must have lost much of their force and significance if they had not been expressed exactly with that verbal precision which the subject-matter might have demanded, we shall be wise either to forbear coming to any decision, or else to adopt that guarded view which we have already indirectly advocated, viz., that in all passages of importance, wheresoever the natural powers of the writer would not have supplied the befitting word or expression, there it was supplied by the real though probably unperceived influence of the Spirit of God.

A question of far greater moment, and far more practical importance, is that which relates to the exact degree of the inspiration, the fallibility or infallibility of the Sacred Records. Was the inspiration such as wholly to preclude errors and inaccuracies, or was it such as can be compatible with either one or the other? This is clearly the real anxious question of our own times, and one to which we must briefly return an answer, as general canons of interpretation must obviously to some extent be modified by the opinions we form on a subject which so seriously affects the character of the documents before us. Let us pause for a moment to consider the answer that is now commonly returned by those among us who claim to be considered of advanced thought and intelligence. They tell us, in language of unrestrained confidence, that no man of candour can fail to acknowledge the existence not only of mistakes as to matters of minor importance, but of such positive "patches of human passion and error," such "weakness of memory," or such "mingling of it with imagination," such "feebleness of inference, such confusion of illustration with argument," and such variations in judgment and opinion, that in the study of Scripture we must continually have recourse to a "rectifying or verifying faculty," that we may properly be enabled to separate the Divine from the human, —what is true, real, and unprejudiced, from what is perverted, mistaken, and false. In a word, the Sacred writers now stand charged with errors of two kinds,—errors of mind and judgment, and errors in matters of fact, but on evidence (as the following remarks will tend to show) which cannot be regarded either as sufficient or conclusive.

To substantiate the first class of errors we may commonly observe two modes of proceeding: on the one hand, the more reckless method of citing difficult texts, assuming that they contain a meaning arbitrarily fixed on by the critic, and probably not intended by the writer, and then censuring him for not having intelligibly expressed it; on the other hand, the more guarded but equally mischievous suggestion that the logic of the Scriptures is *rhetorical* in character, and that such passages as Rom. i. 16 *seq.*, Rom. iii. 19, al., are examples of some forms of error in reasoning, and such oppositions as "light and darkness," "good and evil," "the Spirit and the flesh," "the sheep and the goats," oppositions of ideas only, which are not realized in fact and experience. With regard to these methods, we will say briefly that the first is unfair and discreditable; the second, simple assertion that can either be disproved in detail, or that fairly admits of counter-assertion of greater probable truth.

The second class of alleged errors is, at first sight, of more importance and plausibility. It professes to include oppositions to science, oppositions to received history, and cases of direct mutual contradiction. Of these three forms we may again briefly say that instances of the first kind, far from increasing, are steadily decreasing under a just comparison of the true meaning of the words of Scripture with the accredited conclusions of science. Recent discussions of the subjects of controversy by men of acknowledged scientific attainments have tended to show that the oppositions of Scripture and science are really far more doubtful than they are assumed to be, and that though they still hold a very prominent place on the pages of the charlatan, they one by one disappear from the treatises of men of real science who have scholarship sufficient to extract the real meaning of the language of Scripture in the passages under consideration. . . . Much the same sort of remark, *mutatis mutandis*, may be made on alleged oppositions to received History or Chronology; many of the supposed oppositions held in former times to be inexplicable have now entirely passed away from the scene, and have alike ceased to stimulate the sceptic or to disquiet the believer; others, like the case of Cyrenius (Luke ii. 2), are all but gone; and as to what remain there is a growing feeling among unbiassed scholars and historians that if we could but obtain the knowledge of a few more facts relative to the various points at issue, the oppositions of Scripture and History would wholly cease to exist. . . . In regard of mutual contradictions, it might be thought a better case has been made out. Writers from whom we might have looked for more guarded comment have done much to exaggerate the so-called discrepancies of the Scripture narrative, and have somewhat too emphatically denounced modes of explanation that, both from their simplicity and, not unfrequently, their antiquity, have very great claims on our consideration. Sceptics have not been slow to take advantage of this ill-advised course. When, however, all these so-called contradictions are mustered up, they are but a motley and an enfeebled host. We survey them, and we observe some as old as the days of Celsus, and as decrepit as they are old; others vainly hiding all but mortal wounds received in conflicts of the past, and now only craving a *coup de grace* from some combatant of our own times; some of a later date, and a more aspiring air, recruited from Deistical controversies of a century or two back, but all marked with uncomely scars, and armed with nothing better than broken or corroded weapons. There they stand; the discrepancy between two Evangelists about the original dwelling-place of Mary and Joseph, explained and well explained fourteen hundred years ago; the two genealogies, fairly discussed in ancient times, and in our own explained in a manner that approaches to positive demonstration; the blasphemy of the *two* thieves, disposed of very reasonably by Chrysostom, and since his time on the same or a similar principle by every unprejudiced commentator; the narrative of the woman who anointed our Lord's feet, first prepared for the occasion by the assumption that the narratives in all the four Gospels relate to the *same* woman,—an assumption regarded even by Meyer, and apparently De Wette, as plainly contrary to the fact. And so on. When we survey such a company, and are told that, at any rate, we should respect their numbers, their aggregate authority, their cumulative weight, an uneasy feeling arises in the mind that those who parade them must really be aware that there is something amiss with each case, that, however numerically strong they may be, it is disagreeably true that as individual instances they are disabled or weak. If so, is there not a great responsibility resting on those who bring forward catalogues of such instances, and yet do not apprise the simple and the inexperienced that each supposed difficulty has most certainly been met over and over again, and with very reasonable success; that this array, so to be respected for its numbers, is really strong in nothing else,—a mere rabble of half-armed or disarmed men?

But finally, it may be said, are we prepared to assert that no inaccuracy, even in what all might agree in regarding as a wholly unimportant matter of fact,—a date, for instance, or a name, or a popular statement of an indifferent matter,—either has been, or can ever be, found in the whole compass of Scripture? To that question, in its categorical form, we should perhaps be wise in refusing positively to return any answer. We have no theory of inspiration, we only state what we find to be a matter of fact, we only put forward what those facts and the testimony of the Church alike warrant us in defining as the true and Catholic doctrine. We have no means of settling definitely whether a *posse peccare* in minor matters may, or may not, be compatible with a Divine revelation communicated through human media; but certainly till inaccuracies, fairly and incontestably proved to be so, are brought home to the Scripture, we seem logically justified in believing that as it is with nine-tenths of the alleged contradictions in Scripture, so is it with the alleged inaccuracy. Either the so-called inaccuracy is due to our ignorance of some simple fact, which, if known, would explain all; or it is really only an illustration of one of those very conditions and characteristics of human testimony, however honest and truthful, without which it would cease to be human testimony at all. If positively forced to state our opinion, we will express what we believe to be the true doctrine of inspiration in this particular by an example and a simile. As in the case of the Incarnate Word we fully recognize in the Lord's humanity all essentially human limitations and weaknesses, the hunger, the thirst, and the weariness on the side of the body, and the gradual development on the side of the human mind (Luke ii. 40),—in a word, all that belongs to the essential and original characteristics of the pure form of the nature He vouchsafed to assume, but plainly deny the existence therein of the faintest trace of sin, or of moral or mental imperfection,—even so in the case of the written Word, viewed on its purely human side, *and in its reference to matters previously admitted to have no bearing on Divine truth*, we may admit therein the existence of such incompleteness, such limitations, and such imperfections as belong even to the highest forms of purely truthful *human* testimony, but consistently deny the existence of mistaken views, perversion, misrepresentation, and any form whatever of consciously committed error or inaccuracy.

10. We have thus at length touched upon all the main points in which the doctrine of the inspiration of Scripture is in any degree likely to come in contact with rules and principles of interpretation. Less than this could not have been said. Less it was not logically consistent to say. It may, indeed, seem plausible to urge that we have no right to express any prior opinion on such subject; that we have only to apply to Scripture the ordinary rules of interpretation which we observe in the case of other books, and that we ought to leave the question of inspiration to be settled by the results we arrive at. Is it not, however, abundantly clear that if there be even a low presumption, arising from external or internal evidence, for supposing that the Scripture *has* characteristics which render it very unlike any other book, then it is only right and reasonable to examine that evidence before we apply rules of interpretation which, perhaps, may be found in the sequel to be inadmissible or inapplicable? Surely, on the very face of the matter it seems somewhat strange to

be told to interpret the Scripture like any other book, while in the same breath it is avowed that there are many respects in which Scripture is unlike any other book. It is really very much the same as being told to ascertain with a two-foot rule the precise linear dimensions of a room of which it is known or admitted that the sides are not always straight, but variously curved and embayed. The application of our two-foot rule would doubtless put very clearly before us, if we had ever doubted it, not only the fact that bays and curvatures really did exist, but also that the instrument in our hands was a singularly unfit one for measuring what it was plain required something less rigid and impracticable. The duty of the two-foot rule would really then be over, unless we chose to reserve it for those parts where the walls somewhat more nearly conformed to the straight line. If, however, we desired properly to complete our task, we should have to go home for our measuring-tape. The nature and application, first of the two-foot rule and then of the measuring-tape, may now very fitly engage our attention, and occupy the remaining portion of the present essay.

§ 3.

11. Hitherto we have been engaged in two very important departments of the subject before us. In the first part of our paper we have done our best to clear away some of the errors and misrepresentations connected with the great alleged variety of Scripture interpretations. In the second portion we have endeavoured to arrive at a just estimate of the nature and characteristics of Scripture, which must be recognized by the careful and reverent interpreter. We have seen that variety is to be expected, and difficulties to be prepared for in the interpretation of Scripture, and we have further seen that this variety and these difficulties are to be ascribed, first, to the real difference between Scripture and every other book; secondly, to the existence in it of deeper meanings, as shown in its prophetic,

typical, or even historical portions; and thirdly, to the fact of its being a volume written under the influence of an inspiration which we have endeavoured briefly to explain and substantiate. These two portions of our subject being finished, we now proceed to the third portion,—a discussion of what appears generally to be the true and right method of interpreting a volume characterized as we have found the Scripture to be; and a statement of a few principles, rules, and observations, which may be of some service to younger students, and which experience has certainly shown to be sound and trustworthy.

This forms the main department of our subject, and admits of several subdivisions. Perhaps our simplest course will be to devote the present section to a discussion of general rules of interpretation—the really important portion of the subject; and to append in concluding sections a few comments, on the one hand, upon the application of Scripture, and, on the other, upon the grammar and laws of the letter. In so doing we confine ourselves principally to the New Testament, but we shall perhaps be found not unfrequently to allude to canons and principles that will apply to all parts of the Sacred Volume, and may benefit the student of the Old as well as of the New Testament. Ere, however, we enter into these discussions, let one point be clearly understood,—that there is a requisite, a necessary preparation for the study of the Scripture, which we assume throughout, a preparation of more value than a knowledge of all the rules and canons of the wisest interpreters of the world: that requisite and preparation is preliminary prayer. It is not necessary to enlarge upon a subject which speaks for itself; it is not necessary to commend what the very instincts of the soul tell us is a preparation simply and plainly indispensable. We allude to it as by its very mention serving to hallow our coming remarks, and as useful in reminding us, in the pride and glory of our intellectual efforts, that it is more than probable that the very simplest reader that takes his translated Bible on his knees, and reads with prayer that he may understand, will attain a truer and more inward knowledge of the words than will ever be vouchsafed to him who, with all the appliances of philology and criticism, reads the original but forgets to mark its holy character, and to pray that he may not only read, but may also learn and understand. Would to God that this rule were of more universal adoption, and had been of late more regularly observed; for then we may be well assured that none of the scornfulness and rash modes of interpretation against which we have now to protest would ever have been put forth, and have tried, as they now are trying, both the faith and the patience of humbler students of the Word.

One further preliminary and requisite in the case of the interpreter of Scripture we must here allude to, both on account of its own intrinsic importance, and still more in consequence of the startling way in which it has been recently neglected. That requisite is candour. Next, in the work of interpretation, to a prayerful and humble stands a candid and honest spirit,—a brave and faithful spirit that, knowing and believing that God is a God of Truth, hesitates not to state with all clearness and simplicity the results to which humble-minded investigation seems in each case to lead,—that scorns to palter and explain away, to gloss or to idealize,—that shrinks not from frankly specifying all the details of the apparent discrepancy, be it with other portions of Scripture, with science, or with history, believing thus that the true reconciliation will hereafter be more readily discovered,—in a word, that has faith clearly to tell the dream, and patience to wait for the interpretation thereof. We cannot but observe that even sounder interpreters both of our own and other times have often sadly failed in this particular. We own with sorrow that there have ever been over-eager Uzzahs among us that have sought to upbear the endangered truth with aids that have brought on themselves their own chastisement. We admit, alas! that good and earnest men have sometimes been driven by anxieties and antagonisms into patently inadmissible solutions; we know that they have urged untenable accommodations, and we are even willing to believe, as our opponents tell us, that they have dwelt on evidence that was in their favour, and have been very insufficiently sensitive to that which was against them. This we know and admit, but at the same time we fail not to observe that, as our coming examples will show, they who have brought this charge against others lie grievously open to it themselves, and that it is indeed time that both parties should desist from courses which do such deep dishonour to the Word of God, and imply such an utter want both of faith and integrity.

Let the interpreter then resolve, with God's assisting grace, to be candid and truthful. Let him fear not to state honestly the results of his own honest investigations; let him be simple, reverent, and plain-spoken, and, above all, let him pray against that sectarian bias which, by importing its own foregone conclusions into the word of Scripture, and by refusing to see or to acknowledge what makes against its own prejudices, has proved the greatest known hindrance to all fair interpretation, and has tended, more than anything else in the world, to check the free course of Divine Truth. To illustrate our meaning by examples. Let the interpreter in the first place be seduced by no timidity or prejudices from ascertaining the true text. Let him not fall back upon the too often repeated statement that, as readings affect no great points of doctrine, the subject may be left in abeyance. It is indeed most true, that different readings of such a character as 1 Tim. iii. 16, or interpolations such as 1 John v. 7, are few and exceptional. It is indeed a cause for devout thankfulness, if not even for a recognition of a special providence, that out of the vast number of various readings so few affect vital questions; still it is indisputably a fact that but few pages of the New Testament can be turned over without our finding points of the greatest interest affected by very trivial variations of reading. On the presence or absence of an article in John v. 1 the whole chronology of our Lord's ministerial life may be said almost entirely to depend. A very slight alteration in Mark vii. 31 opens out a fact of deep historical interest, and is of very great significance in reference alike to commands subsequently given to the Apostles to preach the Gospel, and to former prohibitions (Matt. x. 5). The absence of two words in Eph. i. 1 (now rendered *somewhat* more probable by the testimony of the Codex Sinaiticus) gives a fresh aspect to an important Epistle, disposes at once of several *primâ facie* difficulties, and further must be taken greatly into account in the adjustment of some subordinate but interesting questions with which the Epistle has been thought to stand in connexion (Col. iv. 16). The presence or absence of a few words in Matt. xxviii. 9 affects considerably our ability to remove one of the many seeming discrepancies in the narratives of the first hours of the morn of the Resurrection. We could multiply such examples, but perhaps enough has been said. There are indeed several grounds for thinking that there is an improved feeling on the whole subject; and there seem some reasons for hoping that though no authoritative revision is likely to take place, nor, at present perhaps, even to be desired, yet that the time is coming when there will be a considerable agreement on many of the results of modern criticism, and when it will be as startling to hear a sermon deliberately preached on Acts viii. 37, as it would be now on the Heavenly Witnesses. There are, alas! still many signs of uneasiness and obstruction; but we do entreat and conjure those who would only too gladly put the whole question in abeyance to pause, seriously to pause, before they do such dishonour to the words of inspiration, and leave clinging to our Church both the reproaches which are now so pitilessly cast upon us all by the gainsayer, and that still deeper reproach of our own hearts,—that, believing the Bible to be a special, direct, and inspired revelation from God, we have yet not used the means now at hand of ascertaining the exact language in which that revelation is vouchsafed. Mournful indeed will be the retrospect, and gloomy indeed the future, if unbecoming anxiety or a timid conservatism is to tempt honest hearts to show sadly lacking measures of faith, and to deal deceitfully with the Oracles of God.

If this be the first form in which candour is to be shown, let the second be the fearless statement of the apparent results of investigation, whether on this side or on that, in the case of collective or individual passages. A few remarks will illustrate our meaning, and will incidentally substantiate what we have stated above, viz., that those who have recently most inveighed against want of candour in others are grievously lacking in it themselves.* What, for instance, can be more uncandid than to imply that justification by faith may mean "peace of mind or sense of Divine approval," when against it we have not only the current of two important Epistles, but observe that in the very passage from which such a perverted view might have been derived (Rom. v. 1) the mention of the Saviour as the medium shows in what sense the Apostle meant his words to be understood, and how consistently he could state eight verses afterwards that we were justified in and by the blood of Christ (ἐν τῷ αἵματι), and were reconciled by His death (ver. 10)? How really unpardonable to hint that resurrection may mean "a spiritual quickening," and to stamp the exact meaning of the hint by the subsequent assertion, that Heaven is not a place so much as fulfilment of the love of God, when this is a perversion of the word against which an Apostle has left a special and determinate protest! How opposed to all principles of honest explanation to imply that propitiation is the recovery of a peace with God which sin has interrupted, and to follow it up by the supplementary assertion that negation of "rite of blood" belongs essentially to a spiritual God, when we have the drift of part of a long Epistle opposed to such a view, and when we further observe that a mention of the material element "blood" in connexion with our

* For the culpable statements and insinuatious reprehended in the text, see 'Essays and Reviews,' p. 80 *seq.*

redemption and our Lord's atonement (Eph. i. 7, ii. 13; 1 Pet. i. 2, 19, al.) is in the New Testament so perpetual and pervasive that he who denies it must be prepared to deny the evidence of his own senses! Such melancholy perversions of Scripture may perhaps be extreme cases, but they may suitably serve as examples of the lengths to which prejudice and want of candour may at last proceed, and may incidentally warn us that the dread term "judicial blindness" expresses no mere fancy of theologians, but a frightful and a substantive truth.

With such painful examples before us, surely the duty of resolving at all costs to be candid, to estimate fairly the details, and state honestly the results of investigations, be the apparent tenor of those results whatever it may, seems to press itself upon us with redoubled force. Never was there a time when candour on all sides seemed more necessary, never a period in the history of our Church when a frank recognition of points of difficulty and difference seemed likely to be productive of more real good. Above all things, let us not yield to the temptation of holding back what we believe to be the true aspect of a passage because it may be thought to lend a passing countenance to the tenets of opponents. Let us be fair to all sides. While then, for example, we justly protest against the use of 1 Cor. iii. 13 to establish Purgatory, because, on the one hand, perspicuity, and, on the other, details (*ἐν πυρί*), as illustrated by parallel passages (2 Thess. i. 8; Dan. vii. 9, 10; Mal. iv. 1), alike seem to point to *ἡ ἡμέρα* (previously agreed upon by both sides to be "dies Domini," Vulg.) being the nominative to *ἀποκαλύπτεται*; so, in the case of 2 Tim. i. 16 (comp. ch. iv. 19) we do not shrink from giving the opinion that the terms of the verse seem to imply that Onesiphorus was dead at the time that the Epistle was written, though we may know the use that will be made of the statement. While, again, we deny the fairness of using Gal. v. 6 to support the theory of a *fides formata*, we are not deterred by the known use of the text in support of Tradition from stating the opinion that, in the case of 2 Thess. ii. 15, the use of ἐδιδάχθητε and the general tenor of the context justify the reference of παραδόσεις to matters, not only of discipline, but *also* of doctrine. . . . To pass to other opponents: we fear not, on the one side, to give up several of the examples said to fall under Granville Sharp's rule, as, for example, Eph. v. 5, 2 Thess. i. 12, deeming the application of the rule in words like Θεὸς and Κύριος to be, grammatically considered, precarious; on the other side, we feel the contextual allusions to be so distinct in Tit. ii. 13, that we have no hesitation in stating our firm belief that the title "Great God" is there applied to the Lord Jesus. Again, we are not afraid to own that ὑπέρ, though apparently so used in Philem. 13, is not safely to be pressed in every doctrinal passage similar to Gal. iii. 13, or 1 Pet. iii. 18, as serving to establish the doctrine of our Lord's vicarious sufferings: we claim however, in return, the same candour at the hands of our opponents in the interpretation of such passages as 1 Tim. ii. 6 (ἀντίλυτρον), 1 Pet. ii. 24, which, if words mean anything, do assuredly imply that doctrine in the most plain and unqualified way. We deny not all the *fair* inferences that flow from such passages as—"every soul shall bear its own iniquity,"—but we do justly complain, with such words before us as τέκνα ὀργῆς (Eph. ii. 2; actually rendered by one living writer "children of *impulse*" *), and with a variety of similar allusions positively pervading the New Testament, that we should be told that the Christian scheme of redemption "has been staked" on two so-called figurative expressions of St. Paul, as found in Rom. v. 12 and 1 Cor. xv. 22. We draw back with positive repugnance from such a gloss as that of Beza ("quosvis homines") on the holy inclusiveness of the πάντας in 1 Tim. ii. 5, yet again we do not shrink from a single inference that legitimately comes from the ἐξελέξατο in such passages as Eph. i. 4, nor do we deny that few topics have been more overlooked, and few which throw

* See Maurice, 'Unity of the New Testament,' p. 538.

a greater light on the final adjustment of all things, than the circumstances, characteristics, and prerogatives of the elect. Few perversions, again, have been more decided than the change of nominative in Heb. x. 38, yet this ought all the more to urge us, on the other side, to set an example of candour in the interpretation of the ἐπιτελέσει in Phil. i. 6, and not to tamper with the tense of *βεβαιώσει*, or the meaning of ἕως τέλους in 1 Cor. i. 8. So again, though we may use Calvin's own words, and regard it in truth as a *horribile decretum* that would involve in a predetermined perdition the darkened nations of a pagan world, we yet refuse to interpret against the *usus scribendi* of an inspired author, and in a passage like Rom. i. 24 we dare not regard a grammatical formula which appears in almost all cases to mark *purpose*, as in this case only indicative of issue and result. Lastly, to gather up a handful of passages with which party bias has dealt deceitfully,—if we regard it as unprincipled that such a word as ἱλαστήριον should be explained away in Rom. iii. 25, perverse that such a plain and positive concrete term as λοῦτρον should be volatilised in Eph. v. 26, Tit. iii. 5, or such a passage as John iii. 5 toned down, monstrous that such a clear prohibition as that in Col. ii. 18 should be evaded by an unauthorized limitation of one word (θρησκείᾳ), or a non-natural explanation of another (ἀγγέλων),—if, again, we recoil from the expressed or implied denials of the typical relations of circumcision and baptism, when we can put our fingers on such verses as Col. ii. 11, and the explanatory verse which follows it,—if we start to find the use of a strong word (ὁρκίζω), where we should not have expected it (1 Thess. v. 27), suggest the assumption that an Apostle at times was not master of, or did not know the value of, the words which he was using,—if, with reason, we shrink from and even denounce all such instances of prejudice and want of candour in our opponents; yet let us also remember that on the side of over-anxious orthodoxy every instance could find its exact parallel, and that we may be well reminded ourselves to take good heed that we be not ensnared by perverted principles of interpretation that have thus long retained such a baneful ascendency. On reviewing such a list, does not the conviction arise that the "speaking the truth in love" of the Apostle is a principle that needs anew to be commended to every interpreter of Scripture? and does not also the melancholy reflection rise with it that it is, perhaps, almost exclusively owing to the long neglect of this principle that we must ascribe the present state of parties, and their present attitudes of increasing hostility and antagonism?

12. But to pass from these preliminary comments to the main question with which we are now more especially concerned, let us proceed to consider what, judging from the experiences of the past and the present, seems to be the most befitting and trustworthy method of interpreting a Volume bearing such striking and unique characteristics as we find in the Holy Scriptures. The answer, it can hardly be doubted, after what has been said in the earlier portion of this essay, must be—"the literal and historical method," that method which not only concerns itself with the simple and grammatical meaning of the words, but also with that meaning viewed under what may be termed, for want of a better word, its historical relations, viz., as illustrated by facts, modified by the context, substantiated by the tenor of the Holy Book, and receiving elucidation from minor specialities and details. On the general propriety of such a method there will not be, perhaps, any very great differences of opinion. On the particular rules for carrying out the method we must naturally expect considerable debate and disagreement. For example, the seemingly comprehensive and plausible rule which has been lately so much pressed upon our attention—"Interpret Scripture like any other book"—has already been seen to be at best only of limited application, and to involve assumptions —e.g. the resemblance of Scripture to other books in respect of its having one and only one meaning—which we have apparently had the fullest reasons for refusing

to concede. Many just objections may also be urged against other rules that have been proposed, especially against those which, tacitly assuming an exaggerated amount of figurative language in the Scriptures, tend to exempt many portions of the inspired Volume from being regarded to mean what they actually say, and many declarations from having assigned to them their real force and significance. It is scarcely too much to say, that most of these modern rules have involved some sinister tendency, and have been based on very thinly covered assumptions of an amount of error in the Scriptures that is totally undemonstrable. In this real difficulty of accepting what has hitherto been advanced, we will ourselves venture to propose for consideration a few short canons of a very simple nature, which, perhaps, may be found practically useful in carrying out the method of interpretation above alluded to. Not to be unnecessarily minute, we may first specify, with illustrations, four rules or principles, two of which relate rather more to the letter, two rather more to the spirit and applications of it. Whether we need any further rule will be best seen as we proceed.

The first rule is an extremely obvious one, yet a rule which, if it had been always followed, would have spared the Church a large amount of bitterness and controversy. It is simply this,—*Ascertain as clearly as it may be possible the literal and grammatical meaning of the words:* in other words, ascertain first what is the ordinary lexical meaning of the individual words; and next, what, according to the ordinary rules of syntax, is the first and simplest meaning of the sentence which they make up. . . . We almost turn away with a smile from such a thread-bare rule, and yet there is really no rule that has been less followed in the interpretation of the New Testament; and none which in spite of all boasted recent improvement, it is more necessary calmly to restate and enhance. The full force of Hermann's almost indignant protest* against the principles, or rather absence of all principles, on which the New

* In his edition of 'Viger's Idioms,' p. 788.

Testament was interpreted during all the earlier portions of his life, is now happily rendered somewhat unnecessary. A pupil of the great scholar was among the first to restore the more reverent and accurate exegesis of an earlier day, and since that time there has been a continuance of efforts in the same direction. Still it must be clear to every quiet observer, that there is a strong desire evinced in many quarters to evade the rule, and, under cover of escape from pedantry, to endeavour to make Scripture mean what we think, or what we wish, not what it really says to us. The mode of procedure is simple, but effective. We are first told, as Chrysostom told us long ago,* that we are to catch the spirit of the author, and next invited to take a step onward, and do what that great interpreter neither did nor sanctioned—rectify by the aid of our own "verifying faculty" the imperfect utterance of words of which it is assumed we have caught the real and intended meaning. No mode of interpretation is more completely fascinating than this intuitional method, none that is more thoroughly welcome to the excessive self-sufficiency in regard to Scriptural interpretation of which we are now having so much clear and so much melancholy evidence. To sit calmly in our studies, to give force and meaning to the faltering utterances of inspired men, to correct the tottering logic of an Apostle, to clear up the misconceptions of an Evangelist, and to do this without dust and toil, without expositors and without Versions, without anxieties about the meanings of particles, or humiliations at discoveries of lacking scholarship,—to do all this, thus easily and serenely, is the temptation held out; and the weak, the vain, the ignorant, and the prejudiced are clearly proving unable to resist it. Hence the necessity of a return to first principles, however homely they appear.

To set forth, if need be, still more clearly the practical value of the foregoing rule, let us take a few, almost chance-met examples, in which attention to grammatical accuracy often serves to remove difficulties or

* See Chrysostom, 'Comment. on Gal.', tom. x., p. 801 B (ed. Bened. 2).

misapprehensions of old standing, and that, too, in questions of considerable importance. Let us observe, for instance, how an attention to the force of a tense removes all possible difficulty from such a verse as Acts ii. 47, and adds a deepened significance to the weighty words we find in such passages as 2 Cor. ii. 15. How simply, yet how instructively, the simple participles place the two classes before us, each under its aspects of progress and development, each capable of reversed attitudes and directions, but each at the time of consideration wending its way; the one silently moving onward to light and to life, the other turning its sad steps to darkness and to death! The mere tense is in itself a sermon and a protest: a sermon of blended warning, consolation, and hope, to those who will pause to meditate on its significance; a protest, and a very strong protest, against those who tell us that the existence of "two classes of men animated by two opposing principles," though the teaching of Scripture, "is contrary to the teaching of experience." Let us observe again how, upon a due recognition of the very same grammatical fact, the imputation of mistaken expectations in an Apostle (1 Thess. iv. 17) becomes almost wholly wiped away,—how some details of the Last Supper (*δείπνου γινομένου,* John xiii. 2: even with the ordinary reading *γενομένου,* the correct translation removes difficulties) supposed to be conflicting or impossible to arrange, admit of easy and natural explanation; and how, to take a last instance, the innocent but pointless imagery of the "cloven" tongues (Acts ii. 3) passes at once into something pertinent and intelligible, and especially consonant with the workings of that Eternal Spirit that divideth "to every man severally as He will." Under the application of similar principles of accuracy, much of the verbal difficulty disappears in Mark xi. 13, the true force of the *ἄρα* combined with the known fact of leaves being posterior to the fruit, making the reader feel how it was the unseasonable display that led to *the inference*, and how the Saviour drew nigh to see if an inference so just was to be substantiated. To add two or three more instances: the great exegetical difficulty in John xx. 17 appears modified, if not removed, by taking into consideration the tense of the verb ἅπτου (not ἅψῃ); a train of profound speculation is suggested by the accurate translation of one word in Col. ii. 15 (ἀπεκδυσάμενος), and relations, if not established, yet rendered probable between the act specified in that mysterious clause and the last three hours of darkness on Golgotha. The recent controversy relative to the precept in Matt. v. 32 is almost settled when we pause to recognize the difference between the nature of the predications respectively conveyed by the participle with and the participle without the article; and, to conclude with an instance of a similar application of the same grammatical principle, a very great amount of difficulty is removed in the interpretation of the very obscure passage, 1 Pet. iii. 18 *seq.*, if, besides adopting the true reading πνεύματι (not τῷ πνεύματι, *Rec.*) and referring it to the Saviour's human spirit, we also observe that the participle ἀπειθήσασιν involves no direct predication ("*who* were"), but partially discloses the reason of the gracious procedure ("*inasmuch as* they were"), and causes the difficulty ever felt in the specification of this one class in some degree to disappear.

We now pass to a second rule, equally simple and homely with that which we have just considered and exemplified, and to which it may be considered to form a kind of supplement or corollary. It is, in fact, involved in the very definition of the true method of interpreting Scripture, and is simply as follows:—*Illustrate, wherever possible, by reference to history, topography, and antiquities.*

On a rule so very natural and obvious little more need be said than this, that the ordinary reader can scarcely form any conception of the strangely different aspects which many of the leading events in Scripture —for example, many of the scenes in our Lord's life— will be found to assume when the rule is carefully observed. We may especially remark this in reference to illustrations from topography. To modern travellers in Palestine the student of Scripture is under obligations which as yet have not by any means been fully recognized. By the aid of their narrative we can sometimes almost place ourselves in the position of the first beholders, and see the whole scene of mystery or mercy disclose itself before our eyes. The Triumphal Entry becomes almost an event in which we ourselves have borne a part when we read the narrative with all the illustrations that have been furnished by the traveller or the antiquary. We can feel ourselves almost led to the spot where the opening view of the Holy City called forth the first shouts of the jubilant multitude; we can realize the strange pause, and feel the naturalness of the transition from meek triumph to outgushing tears, when some turn in the rocky road made the City of the Great King rise up suddenly, even as the modern traveller tells us it still is found to do, in all its full extent, and in all that stateliness and beauty which was so soon to pass away. All the scenes near to or connected with the Lake of Gennesareth will be found to be brought home to us by any of the better recent descriptions of the locality, in a manner and to a degree that we could scarcely have conceived possible beforehand. We seem, for example, to appreciate, for the first time in all its fulness, the allusion to the "city on a hill" (Matt. v. 14) when we are told that from the horned hill that has been lately almost agreed on as the probable scene of the Sermon on the Mount, the heights on which Safed stands are distinctly visible, and form the striking object in the distant landscape. We feel, again, the force of the κατέβη in Luke viii. 23, when we recall what we may perhaps have read but yesterday of the low-lying lake, and the deep-cut ravines and gorges in the vast and naked plateau behind, down which the storm-wind rushes as fiercely and as continuously as of old.* We pause with interest on what otherwise might have seemed a mere question of criti-

* See the remarkably interesting description in Dr. Thomson's 'The Land and the Book,' vol. ii., p. 32.

cal detail, when we read in the traveller's journal that round a few scattered ruins in a lonely wady still lingers a name which brings up the Gergesa of the first Evangelist's narrative, and which almost forces us to muse on the extreme naturalness of the circumstance that he who knew the lake so well should almost instinctively be specific, and that the other two narrators should use names of a wider reference, and more familiarly known to their Greek or their Roman readers.* How interesting again, in the hands of an interpreter who will make it his duty to gather up all the items of antiquarian information, is the narrative of the Lord's presence among the Doctors in the Temple, or even the briefly mentioned circumstances of His hastened Burial! How well an expositor like Meyer, who never fails to use this mode of illustration in a very telling way, brings at once up before us the scene and circumstance of the healing of the paralytic! How the narrative gains in freshness and interest; how much nearer we seem brought to the past! Till we made use of this form of illustration, the events of the Gospel history, to use the words of a popular writer when commenting on this very subject, are almost regarded as if they had taken place in heaven: now they seem, as they truly were, done on this very work-day earth we tread on, under circumstances which the mind can be brought fully to realize, and amid scenes which, if the bodily eye has not beheld, the imagination can readily depict to itself when stimulated and quickened by the narrative of the graphic observer. The real and vital effect that is thus produced on the heart,—especially of the young,—the positive increase to our faith that is supplied by this mode of illustration, has been far too much undervalued by the modern interpreter.

A third rule of very great importance, and of a very wide range of application, may be stated as follows:—*Develop and enunciate the meaning under the limitations assigned by the context*, or, in other words, *Interpret contextually*.

† See Thomson, 'The Land and the Book,' vol. ii., p. 33 *seq.*

The value of this rule and its true and real importance will be sensibly felt in all the various forms of applying Scripture, and giving its doctrines or precepts their true and proper significance. As we have already remarked, the present rule has rather more to do with the spirit and general sentiment of the passage than with the immediate elucidation of the letter. Its application, however, is extremely varied and extensive. In really numberless cases we have nothing to guide us in our decisions except the connexion and the general aspect of the passage. Whenever we are in difficulty as to the justice or pertinence of a deduction, or find, as we often do find, that grammatical considerations leave us in a state of uncertainty, the context is that which acts as the final arbiter. Our rule has thus two great uses,—the one on the negative side, the other on the affirmative. Under the first aspect, it serves to restrain improper deductions or applications; under the second, it helps in deciding between two or more competing interpretations, each supposed to be grammatically tenable. We will give a few examples of its use and application in both cases. To take a first instance, is it often that a text has been considered as more thoroughly inclusive in its application than the latter part of Rom. xiv. 23 ("for whatsoever is not of faith is sin")? Is there any text that in certain controversies is more frequently appealed to as final and absolute? The mere English reader sees in the very argumentative mode in which the words are introduced, a strong confirmation of the axiomatic character of the words, and estimates their force, and extends their application accordingly. The inaccuracy of the translation of the particle (δὲ) that connects the words with what precedes seems to make certain what might otherwise have appeared doubtful, and the clause is used without hesitation in its full and unlimited force. On the exact extent of the application of such a statement, it may not be easy, nor indeed are we called upon, to express any very definite opinion; but with regard to its plain, primary, and general meaning, we can scarcely be in difficulty or hesitation. When we look back at the context and consider the subject-matter, we may surely say, without fear of contradiction, that the words in the passage before us were not meant to be applied to every imaginable case, but to be restricted to scruples or cases of conscience that bear some analogy to the instances which the Apostle is discussing. Take, again, on the other side, such a text as Phil. ii. 12. The concluding clause is doubtless most useful as a corrective to the many unlicensed estimates of the course of the Divine procedure in man's salvation, but to dwell upon such a text as in any degree favouring the idea that, in the fullest sense of the words, our salvation is in our own hands, is simply to ignore the important fact that the next verse supplies the confirmatory ground (γὰρ) of the command, by stating that it is God that supplies both the will and the energy. To take a last instance: Can anything really be more unreasonable than what has been lately said about our practical neglect of certain commands given by our Lord, especially such a command as Matt. v. 34? If we look only at the verse by itself, dislocated from the context, it might reasonably be thought to be a command which was designed to include every form of adjuration, judicial or otherwise. When, however, we look at the verse in its proper connexion, the limitation becomes apparent,—*Ἔστω δὲ ὁ λόγος ὑμῶν, Ναὶ ναί, Οὒ οὔ* (ver. 37). Surely, without any casuistry or subtilty, these last words, with their plainly implied reference to general life and conversation, may be rightly urged by the interpreter as showing the true and real aspects of the prohibition, and may exempt the Saviour from the charge of having, by an acceptance of the form of adjuration used by Caiaphas (*Σὺ εἶπας*, Matt. xxvi. 64), practically violated his own command.*

To exemplify the second aspect of the rule, we may take almost any disputed text that suggests itself to the

* See Archdeacon France, 'The Example of Christ and Service of Christ, p. 109.

memory, and we shall at once see the use and application of the rule. Let us take, for instance, the contested words διὰ τῆς τεκνογονίας, 1 Tim. ii. 15. Here we have at least two competing translations: the one which gives the substantive a somewhat vague but still plausible application, the other which connects it with the great Promise. The article, especially when thus present after a preposition, throws some weight in the scale; the context, in which the allusion is specially to Gen. iii., and to the circumstances of woman's first transgression, seems to decide the question. So, again, to take another example out of the same Epistle, it has long been doubted whether the command in ch. v. 22, refers to Ordination or to Absolution. In favour of the former there is a very general consent among the oldest and best interpreters, and much may be urged in its favour; when, however, we carefully consider the context, the preponderance seems so much on the side of the latter, that, in spite of the amount of authority on the other side, we shall perhaps find it difficult to resist coming to the decision to which a due observance of the rule of contextual interpretation seems certainly to lead us. To take a last instance: the exact meaning of the formula δοκιμάζειν τὰ διαφέροντα, used on two occasions by St. Paul (Rom. ii. 18, Phil. i. 10), has always been considered very doubtful, owing to the differences of meaning which each of the two verbs will fairly admit of. As far as lexical usage goes, the words may be understood to imply a discrimination between things that are different, or a proving, and thence approval, of what is excellent. Which meaning are we to adopt? In the first passage where the words are used we have but little to guide us either way; but in Phil. i. 9, the prayer for an increase of love in knowledge and moral perception expressed in the preceding verse seems to decide us in favour of the latter view,—love being more naturally shown in approval of what is excellent, and so worthy of love, than in a mere discrimination between elements or principles that involve distinctions or degrees of difference.

We now come to the fourth rule, which, as the very terms in which it is expressed will sufficiently show, is of an importance not inferior to that of any one of those which have preceded. It may be thus expressed: —*In every passage elicit the full significance of all details.*

The rule seems to speak for itself. Under one aspect it bears a kind of supplemental relation to the first and second rules; under another it will be found to assist in applications of the third rule, as being frequently concerned with the meanings of connecting particles, and so with the contextual relations of the passage, and its general logical or historical drift. It thus, though at first sight a mere rule of detail and of the letter, has much to do with the spirit of the passage, and will be found eminently useful in suggesting deductions. As the third rule served to regulate the *applications* of Scripture, so this fourth rule will be found to have much to do with the incidental *inferences* which may be drawn from it. Further comments seem unnecessary. Let this one remark, however, be made,—that the rule, besides being obviously a rule of common sense, is really, in the case of the Scripture, a rule of necessity and duty. If we believe the Scripture to be inspired of God, then it surely follows that we must never rest satisfied till we have elicited the fullest and most complete significance of every item of the heavenly Revelation thus mercifully vouchsafed to us. It becomes positive unfaithfulness not to dwell upon every clause, every word, every particle, if we have any real and heart-whole belief that what we are permitted to read are indeed, as they were rightly termed by an Apostolical Father, "the true sayings of the Holy Ghost." It is not that we are hampered with any theory of verbal or mechanical inspiration; it is not that we completely sympathize with the somewhat restricted view (noble, however, in its very restrictedness) of a great Biblical critic* of our own day, that every individual word of Scripture is written by the very

* Dr. Tregelles, Preface to 'The Book of Revelation.'

finger of God; it is simply because we know that in every case words are the appointed media of ideas and sentiments, and believe, in the case of Scripture, that both the ideas are heaven-sent and the sentiments inspired. Knowing this, and believing this, can we deem it otherwise than our highest duty and privilege to exhaust the fullest significance of the outward letter, when it contains enshrined in it an inward spirit thus holy and Divine?

To come to examples. The first and largest class of cases which may be alluded to, as exemplifying the value and usefulness of the rule, are those in which much depends on the true force and meaning of the various connecting particles, whether of cause, inference, or consequence. These, however, we must be content merely to allude to, as examples of this kind can scarcely be adduced without fuller remarks on the general bearings of the passage than our limits will permit. Let one instance, however, be given, and that in one of the most important of the doctrinal passages of the New Testament,—Phil. ii. 6. Here it is scarcely too much to say that the interpretation turns mainly on the proper recognition of the use and force of *ἀλλὰ* when following a negative, and on the remembrance that in such cases it marks a full and clear antithesis between two members of a clause, "not this—*but* that." Apply this to the passage before us, and we see that the words *οὐχ ἁρπαγμὸν ἡγήσατο κ. τ. λ.* must be understood to convey some idea distinctly antithetical to *ἀλλὰ ἑαυτὸν ἐκένωσε,* and that no interpretation can be safely regarded as admissible in which this condition is not fully satisfied. Let this one example be sufficient; but let it carry with it both a suggestion and a protest: a suggestion, that in many a contested passage similar methods of grammatical generalization may be applied with equal simplicity and success; and a protest against mere assumptions that the particles of the New Testament can ever be safely neglected, or quietly disposed of as mere "excrescences" of a vitiated style.

A second and large class of instances to which the

rule applies, are passages in which simple and comparatively insignificant details are found, when properly considered, to supply some fact of real historical interest. The Gospels, especially, supply us with a vast list of striking and suggestive examples. To name only a few. Of what importance, historically considered, is the simple addition of the word Ἱερουσαλήμ in Luke v. 17, as showing the quarter whence the spies came, and marking, throughout this portion of the narrative, that most of the charges and machinations came, not from the natives of Galilee, but from emissaries from a hostile centre! What a picture does the ἦν προάγων αὐτοὺς of Mark x. 32 present to us of the Lord's bearing and attitude in this His last journey, and how fully it explains the ἐθαμβοῦντο which follows! How expressive is the single word καθήμεναι (Matt. xxvii. 61) in the narrative of the Lord's burial, as depicting the stupefying grief that left others to do what the sitters-by might in part have shared in! How full of wondrous significance is the notice of the state of the abandoned grave-clothes in the rock-hewn sepulchre (John xx. 7)! what mystery is there in the recorded position and attitude of the heavenly watchers (ver. 12)! What a real force there is in the simple numeral in the record of the *two* mites which the widow cast into the treasury! she might have given one (in spite of what Schoettgen says to the contrary); she gave her all. How the frightful ἔα of the demoniac (Luke iv. 34) tells almost pictorially of the horror and recoil which was ever felt by the spirits of darkness when they came in proximity to our Saviour (comp. Matt. viii. 29; Mark i. 23, v. 7; Luke viii. 28), and what light and interest it throws upon the καὶ ἰδὼν κ. τ. λ. of Mark ix. 20 in the case of the demoniac boy! Again, of what real importance is the simple πορευθεὶς both in 1 Peter iii. 19 and 22! How it hints at a literal and local descent in one case, and how it enables us to cite an Apostle as attesting the literal and local ascent in the other! When we combine the latter with the ἀνεφέρετο of Luke xxiv. 51 (a passage undoubtedly genuine), and pause to mark the tense, can we share in any of the modern difficulties that have been felt about the actual, and so to say material, nature of the heavenly mystery of the Lord's Ascension?

We pause, but only to pass onward by a very slight transition to a third class of passages in which important deductions may be made from details which an ordinary reader might think of the most trivial or accidental nature. Who, for instance, would take much notice of the order in which certain provinces are enumerated in 1 Peter i. 1? and yet, from the general direction the order involves (East to West), the locality of the writer has been surmised at, and an item supplied toward settling the geographical question in chap. v. 13 of the same Epistle. Who, again, would be likely to pause much on the fact that Samaria was placed in order before Galilee in Luke xvii. 11? and yet, unless we adopt a very unnatural explanation of the passage, the order may be considered as placing the verse in connection with John xi. 54, and as pointing to the interesting fact that the last journey of our Lord was a kind of farewell-circuit, which, beginning from Ephraim, extended through Samaria, Galilee, and Peræa, and terminated at Bethany and Jerusalem. Few perhaps would at first sight be inclined to pause long on the words ἐρχόμενος ἀπὸ ἀγροῦ used both by St. Mark (ch. xv. 21), and St. Luke (ch. xxiii. 26) in reference to Simon of Cyrene; and yet they supply some ground for drawing the inference that, in the earlier part of the day referred to, field-work had been done, and consequently that it was not Nisan 15, but Nisan 14, and that thus, even according to the Synoptical Evangelists, the Lord celebrated the Last Supper on the day preceding the legal Passover. Again, would not the term "*green* grass" (Mark vi. 39) seem to imply but little? and yet this specification of the graphic Evangelist exactly harmonizes with what we learn from another Evangelist (John vi. 4), viz., that the time was spring, and further renders the supposition that the rich plain at the north-eastern corner of the Lake of Gennesareth was the scene of the Feeding of the Five Thousand in every respect worthy of attention. Lastly, the agitated words of Mary Magdalene to St. Peter (John xx. 2) might be thought of very little use in helping to decide between conflicting views on the harmony of this portion of the narrative: yet from the plural *οἴδαμεν*, when compared with *οἶδα*, ver. 13, we seem justified in drawing the important inference that though St. John only specifies Mary Magdalene as having gone to the tomb, he was nevertheless perfectly well aware, that, even as she herself implies, there were others who went with her to do honour to the Holy Body.

Our four rules of interpretation have now at length been stated and illustrated. That they are important, and of considerable practical use, will perhaps have now been made plain by the examples which have been adduced. From these we shall probably have perceived that the rules have not only their positive but their negative uses; and that, while the first two rules are serviceable in tending to ensure precision and stimulate research, the second and third are no less useful in restraining prejudice, and checking that impatient and over-hasty method of reading the Scripture which will not pause to seek in the text for the associations that are really to be found there. Further, the rules proposed have apparently the merit of being simple and obvious. They involve no refinements, and may be expressed in very few words: all the four being, in fact, reducible to one general canon—*Interpret grammatically, historically, contextually, and minutely.*

But the real point of interest has yet to be discussed.

On carefully considering the nature and characteristics of the above rules, it must be plain to the thoughtful reader that, though useful and adequate exponents of the grammatical and historical method of interpreting Scripture, they are still rules that might be applied with nearly equal success to the interpretation of any other collection of ancient documents. There is nothing in any one of them that makes it especially a rule of interpreting *Scripture.* We have really to a certain extent been agreeing to interpret Scripture like any other book. It is true that we have advocated a greater punctiliousness than would be thought necessary even for interpreting Plato or Aristotle ; it is true that we have pleaded for a minuteness of attention to detail, which in the case of an ordinary Greek writer would be tiresome and pedantic ; still there is plainly no feature in any one of the rules that can fairly be considered as of such an unique character as we should expect to find in the rules for the interpretation of an unique book ; and, if our premises are right that Scripture is really unlike any other book in numerous points, we should certainly expect to find in numerous points that our present rules are insufficient and incomplete.

And so we find them.

There are at least three large classes of passages in which they fail in ascertaining for us the true mind of Scripture ; and these very failures, it will be observed, force upon us additional rules, gradually more and more of an unique character, till we find ourselves at last frankly accepting the yet lacking general rule of true Scriptural interpretation. But let us not anticipate. We have said there are at least three classes of passages for which the above rules are not sufficient. These may be defined roughly, as (1) passages of *general* difficulty, where the context gives us no means of deciding between two or more competing translations, of equal correctness in point of logic or grammar ; (2) passages of *doctrinal* difficulty, where either the tenor of the declaration is doubtful, or where opposing deductions have been made as to the doctrine actually conveyed ; (3) passages of what may be termed *theological* difficulty, i. e. where the fact specified or the principle referred to involves mysterious relations between things human and Divine which are at best very imperfectly known to us. In all these three cases, especially the two last, the rules we have discussed, though of the greatest use in clearing away preliminary difficulties, often leave the main difficulty untouched. Let us illustrate this by a few examples, and feel out by degrees for the further rule or rules that are still needed for our guidance.

(1.) Let us take for our first example a clause from a passage of general difficulty, and indisputably of great importance, the opening verses of St. Paul's Epistle to the Ephesians. In the third verse much turns on the exact meaning of the peculiar term ἐν τοῖς ἐπουρανίοις, and (to narrow the question by leaving unnoticed obviously untenable interpretations) on a decision of the question,—whether, with the Greek expositors, we are to give the words an ethical reference, or whether, with the Oriental versions, we are to conceive the words only to refer to locality. The context does not seem definitely to favour either view; and grammatical considerations, it is almost unnecessary to add, leave the matter equally undecided. In other words, our first and third rules, on which, in all cases of local difficulty, we almost wholly rely, here fail to guide us. How then are we to decide? If we turn to the best modern commentaries we shall find, and rightly find, that the local meaning is now very generally adopted, such seeming certainly to be the meaning in the other passages in the Epistle (ch. i. 20, ii. 6, iii. 10, vi. 12) where the formula occurs. In a word the *usus scribendi* of the author has decided the question. . . . The meaning of the difficult and similarly ambiguous expression στοιχεῖα τοῦ κόσμου (Gal. iv. 3) is usually decided, though conversely, on the same principle; a comparison of the passage with Col. ii. 8, 20 seeming to cause the arguments in favour of the ethical meaning (rudimentary religious teaching of a non-Christian character) decidedly to preponderate. . . Somewhat similar principles are used in deciding on the meaning of the doubtful παραθήκην (*Rec.* παρακαταθήκην) in 1 Tim. vi. 20 compared with 2 Tim. i. 12, 14. . . In a much more difficult passage to which we have already alluded, Col. ii. 15, a great part of the obscurity rests on the first clause, and especially on the meaning of the word ἀπεκδυσάμενος. In spite of the contextual argument that may be drawn from the meaning of the associated participle θριαμβεύσας, the translation of the Vulgate ("exspolians") and indeed of our own Authorized Version, is now commonly given up by careful scholars in favour of the more grammatically accurate, but certainly at first sight less intelligible "exuens se" of the Claromontane and Coptic Versions. What has led to this decision? To a certain extent grammatical precision, but mainly the undoubted use of the word by the Apostle a few verses later (Col. iii. 9) in the second of the two senses just specified.

But the examples above alluded to have had mainly to do with verbal difficulties. Exactly the same, however, might be shown in cases of difficulties in the sentiment conveyed. Of this let 1 Pet. iii. 19 and ch. iv. 6 be briefly specified as examples. They are sister-texts, and so clearly allude to a kindred mystery, that no interpreter of the one passage would fail to refer to the other and be guided by it, as supplying him with the most natural and indeed authoritative illustration. If, for example, he felt swayed by the local term πορευθεὶς in the first passage, he would probably find much difficulty in believing that the term νεκροῖς in the second passage was to be referred to the spiritually dead, those "dead in trespasses and sins" (Eph. ii. 1), rather than to the dead in the ordinary and physical meaning of the term. If one passage has a definite and local reference, so apparently has the other. The same may be said of the excessively difficult passages Col. i. 19 and ch. ii. 9, the latter of which supplies the only authoritative hint for the translation of the former.

Now to what do all these examples point but to this,—the admission that difficulties, even of a very serious nature, are often to be removed by attending to the *usus scribendi* of the author; or, in other words, the plain and serviceable rule emerges to view,—*Let the writer interpret himself.*

But it will certainly be said, this is exactly what is or ought to be done in the case of any other writer whose precise meaning we wished to ascertain. True;

but the difference of the subject-matter makes the two cases really very far from identical. In the one case the writer may be dealing with subjects in which the assumption of a regular and consistent way of expressing himself in reference to them may be deemed perfectly reasonable and natural. In the other case, the assumption really amounts to nearly as much as this,—the expression of a conviction, that in discussing subjects often transcending human faculties, and in communicating the mysteries of a revelation from God, the writer is consistent with himself. The rule above-mentioned, in the case of one of the New Testament writers, is really little less than an express recognition of a general and pervading inspiration,—an influence which, contrary to what might have been looked for in the case of a writer on subjects above man's natural powers, kept the writer always in harmony with himself, and his words always self-explanatory and consistent.

(2.) But, to pass onward, let us next observe what amplifications of the rule are suggested by examples of the second class of Scriptural difficulties. Let us begin with a passage of very great difficulty, principally of a doctrinal nature, and one in which interpreters have arrived at widely different results,—the description of the Man of Sin in 2 Thess. ii. 3 *seq.* Here no interpreter would probably fail to refer to the parallel supplied by Daniel (ch. xi. 36 *seq.*), on the one hand, and to the description of the characteristics of Antichrist as given by St. John in his first Epistle (ch. ii. 22, iv. 3 *seq.*), on the other. The expositor would in fact seek for his most trustworthy elucidation of the passage before him in two books of Scripture written by two authors, a Prophet and an Evangelist, between whose dates there was probably nearly as great an interval as 600 years. Does not this point to a tacit amplification of the preceding rule, and does it not, in effect, amount to this,—*Where possible, let Scripture interpret itself*, or, in other words, *Interpret according to the analogy of Scripture?*

If this be stated fairly and correctly, is it not clear

that the assumptions that were practically involved in the former rule, *Let the writer interpret himself*, become still more significant and suggestive? According to the obvious tenor of the latter rule, Scripture appears tacitly to be recognized as an organized and harmonious whole, all parts of which are so quickened by the same life and animated by the same Spirit, that no sentiment of any one of the Sacred Writers can ever receive a more convincing and trustworthy interpretation than that which is supplied by the sentiments or expressions of another. This, properly considered, practically amounts to an admission of the inspiration of Scripture of the most clear and decided kind.

But let us take yet one step further, and consider the interpretation of a clause in another passage of doctrinal difficulty which all will agree in deeming of the most profound importance. What is the true meaning of the words *πρωτότοκος πάσης κτίσεως* (Col. i. 15) in their reference to the Eternal Son? Here we have two interpretations, widely different, yet both grammatically tenable, and one (the second) considered merely with regard to grammar, perhaps even obvious and plausible. According to the one interpretation, our Lord would be represented as "begotten before every creature," and the reference would be to the eternal generation of Christ; according to the other, it would be "first-begotten of every creature," or, as in the Syriac, "of all creatures,"—prior to them in origin, yet a created being like themselves. Which view are we to take? Grammar is silent, the context difficult and not decisive (the following *ἐν ἀυτῷ* is probably not "*by* Him"), the reasoning deep and mysterious. The answer of every calm and attentive reader of Scripture will probably be promptly given,—"Undoubtedly the former." But why? "Because the whole tenor of Scripture is opposed to the latter view." But how can this tenor of Scripture be confidently stated? on what does the assertion rest? Is it the result of actual and rigorous investigation of the whole of Scripture, or mere reliance on the opinion of the safe side? "No, neither the one nor the other." Then on what is the adoption of the former of the two views really based? "On the teaching of the Creeds, as the authoritative expositions of the true tenor of Scripture." In other words, the example has at last led us to the full expression of the rule that has been gradually disclosing itself. Scripture itself has at length taught us, by the gentle leading of its own difficulties, the true and vital principle of all really Scriptural exegesis,—*Interpret according to the analogy of Faith.*

And this is the rule. This the rule—carped at, as it has been, by the sceptical, disregarded by the self-confident, violated by party bias, slighted by the disloyal, and derided by the profane—to which we have at last come, almost by an inductive process, and with the aid of which, in conjunction with preceding rules, we may even venture to draw near to the third class of difficulties,—the great and the deep things of God.

(3.) Into these, however, we cannot now even attempt to enter. Our limits wholly preclude us from discussing passages of which each would require not only a lengthened consideration of the context, but also the introduction of details which would be unsuitable in a general essay like the present. To show, however, what class of passages we are alluding to, we will pause simply to specify a few that now suggest themselves, and may partly justify the distinctions above laid down. In addition to 1 Pet. iii. 19 and others, above alluded to, which perhaps may seem to belong more exactly to the present class, let us specify Matt. xxvi. 29, xxvii. 52; Mark xiii. 32; Luke x. 18; John xxi. 22; Rom. viii. 19 *seq.*, 26, ix. 18 *seq.*; 1 Cor. iii. 13, vi. 3, xv. 28 *seq.*; 2 Cor. v. 2 *seq.*, xii. 2 *seq.*; Eph. i. 12, 23, ii. 2; Col. i. 19, 20, 24; 1 Thess. iv. 15 *seq.*; Heb. iv. 12, vi. 4; 2 Pet. ii. 4, iii. 10; Jude 6, 9; and, it is necessary to add, the greater part of the Book of Revelation.

On one of these passages, however, and on one only, let us make a passing comment, and that because the passage has been more than once alluded to as a corrective and counterpoise to what are termed high views of the Divinity of the Lord Jesus Christ. The passage is Mark xiii. 32, the words of which, whether considered in reference to the occasion or to the context, merit, indeed, some higher description than "simple and touching," and are, as they have always been deemed to be, among the most deep and solemn that have ever been uttered in the ears of man. Yet if we interpret them according to the analogy of Faith, and, let us not fail to add, according to the very implied limitations of the passage itself, we can feel no difficulty as to their true meaning. In the very silent logic of the associated terms, the *οὐδείς*, the *οἱ ἄγγελοι οἱ ἐν οὐρανῷ*, we feel a kind of implied circumscription, which seems to prepare us for the sense in which we are to understand the culminating *οὐδὲ ὁ υἱός*, "none in earth, none in heaven, nay not even the Son," in so far as He shares any element in common with either, in so far as He vouchsafes to assume finiteness and corporeity. What we instinctively surmise as we read the passage, the analogy of Scripture and Faith assures us of,—that when the Lord thus spake to His four chosen Apostles, He does virtually assure us that He was so truly man, that when He assumed that nature He assumed it with all its limitations, and that in that nature He vouchsafed to know not what as God He had known from everlasting. Why are we to be deterred from this ancient interpretation, why are we to obelize the words with Ambrose,* or regard them as a conventional statement with Augustine,† when they admit of an explanation so simple, and so consonant with all that we are told of Him who vouchsafed not only to be incarnate, but to increase in wisdom, and to be a veritable sharer in all the sinless imperfections of humanity? Is there really any greater difficulty in such a passage than in John xi. 33, 35, where we are told that those holy cheeks were still wet with human tears while the loud voice was crying, "Lazarus, come forth!"

13. This portion of our subject has thus at length come to its close. The four rules of interpreting Scrip-

* 'De Fide,' v. 16 (193). † 'De Genesi contr. Manich,' i. 22 (34).

ture have received the supplement they lacked. The canon which embraced them has now the addition necessary to make it applicable to those passages where the difficulties are of a doctrinal nature, and, further, even to those still deeper passages where the difficulties arise from the profound nature of the revelation, and from the allusions such passages may contain to mysteries beyond our full powers of comprehension. Scripture interpretation is now not merely to be grammatical, historical, contextual, and minute, but it is to be also—*according to the analogy of Faith.*

Against such a rule, we are well aware, many an argument will be urged, many an exception will be taken. We have been told, and we shall often be told again, that to interpret by the Nicene or the Athanasian Creed is not only to mar the simplicity of Scripture, by bringing it in contact with what is artificial and technical, but consciously to involve ourselves in a plain and patent anachronism.

To such mere assertions, for mere assertions they really are, it is not necessary, after what has been said, to return any formal answer. It may be enough to make the two following remarks, and with them this portion of the subject shall be concluded:—*First*, the charge of anachronism may be readily disposed of by observing that, in thus interpreting Scripture, we are really interpreting it by what, in a certain sense, is anterior to it, viz. the principles of that faith of which Scripture is itself the exponent. *Ante mare fluctus.* What right have we to assume that all the early Christian preaching was only the outpouring of "attachment to a recently departed friend and Lord"? With what justice can we say that the whole of Christianity was contained in the words, "Believe in the Lord Jesus Christ, and thou mayest be saved," when, even in the very earliest of an Apostle's letters, there seems satisfactory evidence (comp. 1 Thess. v. 1, 2 Thess. ii. 5) that deeper things were communicated orally to the earliest Christian converts than were afterwards committed to writing? Most justly, then, has it been observed that, when we thus appeal to the principles of the faith for our guidance in expounding Scriptural difficulty, we are interpreting, not by "the result of three or four centuries of controversy," but by appeals to fixed principles of Christian doctrine, the greater part of which were known, believed, and acted on in the very earliest age of the Gospel.* In succeeding centuries these fundamental truths may have been couched in terms of greater scientific exactness; the various controversies of the times may have caused the Church to put forth her doctrines in forms more technically accurate or more logically precise, but the substance was the same from the very first, and it is on that substance that our interpretation of Scripture is really based, it is to that essential truth of which the Church is a pillar, that we make our natural and reasonable appeal.

The *second* remark is this, that those who are much opposed to us in their estimate of the character and inspiration of Scripture, really in effect admit the principle we are contending for. To say nothing of the occurrence on their pages of such terms as "the analogy of Scripture," when the subject is the best mode of interpreting it, or of the silent but important admission that the principle which "enables us to apply the words of Christ and His Apostles" is neither more nor less than "the analogy of faith,"†—to pass over all these tacit and almost instinctive recognitions of the one great truth (1 Tim. iii. 15), from which all that has been said above comes by way of legitimate deduction, let us merely take the rule which others have laid down, and fairly consider whether the recommendation to "interpret Scripture from itself" is not in effect and substance plainly identical with much that has been already advocated in these pages. Such a rule, in the first place, involves the very important assumption which we have above alluded to, viz., that Scripture is consistent with itself, even when such consistency might be appealed

* See Moberly, Preface to 'Sermons on the Beatitudes,' p. lii. *seq.*, where this argument is put forward with great clearness and force.

† See 'Essays and Reviews,' p. 416.

to as a very evidence of its Divine origin; and in the second place, after every possible limitation—viz., that we are to understand it to mean interpreting "like by like,"—such a rule is still, and must remain, based on the recognition of the sound and proper principle that Scripture difficulty must be explained consistently with Scripture truth. Of this truth the Creeds, especially the two shorter, are not only compendious but authoritative abstracts, summarily vouched for by the keeper of our archives and the upholder of their integrity, the Catholic Church of Christ. The same authority might justify us in similarly applying much of her own history and traditions as illustrative of Holy Scripture, if even not deserving the title of an aid in its interpretation. It may be sufficient, however, to claim the Creeds as authoritative summaries of Scripture, and so authoritative guides in interpreting Scripture, being in fact themselves the epitome of that from which it has been properly conceded that Scripture ought to be illustrated and expounded.

§ 4.

14. The main department of our subject may now be considered as brought to its natural conclusion. Two portions, however, still remain which require of us a passing notice. They are, in fact, the two extremes between which the portion of the subject on which we have been recently engaged seems to lie midway; the one relating exclusively to the laws of the letter, the other to the principles of applying the spirit,—in a word, the Grammar of the Sacred Text, on the one hand, and the various practical applications of the fully-ascertained meaning of that Text on the other. A few words shall be said on each of these portions of our subject, but a few words only, there being by no means that amount of misconception and error in reference to either of these portions of the subject as to that which lies between them. Still a few comments may be profitably made on each.

Let us speak first of the application of Scripture, as

this seems most naturally to follow a discussion on the interpretation of it,—application, in fact, being nothing more than interpretation in its ultimate and most extended form.

The different forms which the application of Scripture may assume are obviously as many and as diversified as the aspects of Scripture itself. We have already seen that Scripture involves a system of prophecies and types; we have recognized, also, that it contains a wide range of double meanings even in simply historical passages; and, lastly, we have found it to be so pervaded by the Spirit of God, that not only in its sentiments, but sometimes even in its very words and expressions (see above, p. 468), it is found to involve a deep and a Divine significance. These three characteristics at once lead to three corresponding modes of application, on each of which, as being one of the three more edifying and practically useful modes of applying Scripture, a few comments shall be made.

I. The subject of Prophecy and Typology is, undoubtedly, one of difficulty, and in its practical bearings and expansions still more so. It is extremely difficult to lay down any rules, and yet it is very precarious to attempt such methods of applying Scripture without some external guidance. In the case of unfulfilled prophecy, especially, the temptation to indulge in unauthorized speculation is often excessive. Uneducated and undisciplined minds are completely carried away by it, and even the more devout and self-restrained frequently give themselves up to sad extravagances in this form of the application of God's Word. The result is, only too often, that better educated and more logical minds, in recoiling from what they justly deem unlicensed and preposterous, pass over too much into the other extreme, and deem Prophecy in every form as a subject far too doubtful and debateable ever to fall within the province of Scripture application. It is, we fear, by no means too much to say, that a great part of the present melancholy scepticism as to Messianic prophecy is due to the almost indignant reaction which has been brought about by the excesses of apocalyptic interpretation. The utmost caution, then, is justly called for. Nay, it perhaps would be well if unfulfilled prophecy were never to be applied to any other purposes than those of general encouragement and consolation. We may often be thus made to feel that we are in the midst of a providential dispensation, that though our eyes may be holden as to the relations of contemporaneous events to the future, whether of the Church or of the world, we may yet descry certain bold and broad outlines, certain tendencies and developments, which may make us wend our way onward, thoughtfully and circumspectly,—wayfarers who gaze with ever-deepening interest on the contour of the distant hills, even though we cannot clearly distinguish the clustered details of the nearer and separating plain. But though it may thus be wise only to notice unfulfilled prophecy in the broadest and most general way, it is far otherwise with applications or illustrations derived from what has either obviously received its fulfilment, or, like Deut. xxviii., is so plainly still receiving it, that doubt becomes unreasonable and impossible. In this last case, for instance, the mere existence of such a prophecy has been with reason appealed to as almost sufficient in itself to establish the inspiration of the whole associated Pentateuch. More particularly can every form of Messianic prophecy be dwelt upon by the conscientious interpreter. This, indeed, is the loftiest and most blessed application of prophecy, for purposes of edification, that man can make. Hereby, more especially, are we permitted to realize all the deep harmonies between the earlier and the later dispensation. In the light shed by Messianic prophecy, the two covenants seem no longer disunited, but one. The Old Testament as it "telleth of Christ that should come," blends insensibly into the New, that "telleth of Christ that is come," * until both become recognized

* Compare Hooker, 'Laws of Eccl. Polity,' 1. 14. 4, vol. i., p. 270 (ed. Keble).

as organically connected parts of one Divine whole. The Scripture is at length seen and felt to be what it truly is—one living Book; one, because pervaded by the holy presence of one ever-blessed Lord; living, because ever teaching of Him who Himself is the Life, and whose "Life is the light of men."

In the case of *types*, and all the varied forms of supposed typical relations between the Old and New Testaments, some greater latitude of application may perhaps be permitted. Much, probably, will have to be lost to that which must sometimes be the only guide—the "spiritual understanding" (Col. i. 9) of the expounder. Even in such cases, however, it will be found desirable to recognize some general fixed principles. Special rules it is never very easy to lay down; but perhaps it may be said that in tracing out types, the prudent expounder will do well to observe, or at any rate conform to, the general spirit of these two rules: *First*, not positively to assert the existence of typical relations between persons, places, or things, unless it should appear, either directly or by reasonable inference, that such relations are recognized in Scripture; *Secondly*, even in the case of apparently reasonable inferences from Scripture, not to press the typical allusion unless we have the consent of the best of the earlier expositors. The use and general bearing of each rule shall be briefly exemplified.

The first rule, it will be easily seen, will be especially useful in lopping away all those supposed typical meanings which, as we have already seen, some even of the soundest of the early interpreters were ever discovering even in the simplest incidents of the Old Testament. By this rule, for instance, the mystical or typical meaning assigned to Rahab's scarlet thread, or to Lot's two daughters, old as they may be, and belonging, as these two cases really do, to the sub-apostolic age, must still be regarded as at best only precarious fancies. By the same rule, too, many of the exaggerated attitudes of popular typology will become beneficially restrained. While we may enlarge with all confidence not only on such undoubted historical types as Adam (Rom. v. 14; 1 Cor. xv. 45), or Melchizedec (Heb. vii. 3) of one kind, and the Flood (1 Pet. iii. 21), or the Red Sea (1 Cor. x. 2) of another, but even on such clear instances as the rite of circumcision (Col. ii. 11), the paschal lamb (1 Cor. v. 7), the functions of the High-priest on the Day of Atonement, and other things alluded to by the author of the Epistle to the Hebrews, we may feel very suspended in our judgment as to such an ancient and, at first sight, plausible type as Egypt and the evil world. The acknowledged typical relations of Canaan and the Christian's heavenly home, and of the Red Sea and Baptism, might seem to throw back some probability on such a relation between the world which the Christian renounces and the place from which Israel was called; but such a type could never be insisted on: no argument could ever be built upon it, nor could it ever claim to be ranked really higher than an ancient and ingenious fancy. Nay, even such an almost self-evident type as Isaac, with all its startling coincidences of place and circumstances (Gen. xxii. 6; John xix. 17), can scarcely be regarded as *definitely* resting on the authority of Scripture (Heb. xi. 19 does not seem to prove it), but can only justly be regarded as an inference from its general tenor, though, on the other hand, no reasonable expounder in the world could fail to accept it as an example that rests on the instinctive and unanimous consent of the Church.

We thus are brought to our second rule, and can now see that what otherwise might have seemed superfluous cannot very readily be dispensed with. The united judgment of the earliest and soundest expositors is, we perceive, not wholly to be set aside; the tradition of the Church not to be rejected when the inference from Scripture might seem of a doubtful or suspended character. And if the rule be thus useful in its affirmative, undoubtedly it is so in its negative aspects, as serving to repress mere conjecture and ingenuity. To conclude with an instance of its negative use, we may allude to an ingenious attempt to connect the circumstances mentioned by all the four Evangelists in reference to our Lord and Barabbas, with the sortition in reference to the two goats (Lev. xvi. 5 *seq.*) on the Day of Atonement. At first there seems a strange persuasiveness in the suggested relations of type to antitype; nay, there might be thought to be some Scriptural basis in the similar comparisons that are indicated or hinted at (comp. ch. xiii. 11, 12) in the Epistle to the Hebrews. The opinion of the early writers here interposes a salutary caution. We find that the ceremonies connected with the scape-goat, and the somewhat similar ceremonies in the cleansing of the leper (Lev. xiv. 2 *seq.*) were almost unanimously referred *alone* to Christ,—to Christ, as both dying for us, and, by his Resurrection, living again for evermore. The circumstances of the case, it was justly argued, required a type which, to be complete, must necessarily be two-fold, and which, to be fully significant, must present two aspects, as it were, of the same antitypal mystery. If it be admitted that the scape-goat can, by inference, be deemed a Scriptural type of Christ, it is probable that we shall reject the ingenious parallel, and accept the view taken by the earlier expositors.

The substance of the preceding remarks is this,—not, by any means, that the typical relations between the Old and New Testaments are few and limited, for it is really probable that they are much more numerous and extensive even than they have been supposed to be, but simply that the number of examples of such relations that rest on an undoubted Scriptural basis is not large, and hence that caution is required in pressing as types what cannot actually be proved to be at all more than ingenious and plausible analogies. In a word, we may frequently and beneficially use typology by way of illustration, but it is not often that we can use it as the foundation of an argument.

II. If caution be required in dealing with types, still more so is it necessary in attempting to set forth second meanings in passages, historical or otherwise, which have not been authoritatively declared to involve them. It is not unreasonable to suppose that the passages which may have further and deeper meanings than appear on the surface are by no means of uncommon occurrence. In a meditative reading, even of a few chapters, we can scarcely fail to meet with passage after passage which we feel, almost instinctively, to be fraught with a significance much beyond that of the mere letter, but in the case of which we can never positively assert the existence of such a meaning, much less state what we deem it to be. In the New Testament, the passages which calm and reasonable expositors have adduced as involving second and deeper meanings are probably under ten, and out of these the more plausible,—the reference of the Parable of the Good Samaritan to our Lord, the reference of John vi. 35 to one Sacrament, and of John xix. 34 *seq.* to both; and, lastly, the significance of the position of the two thieves (Luke xxiii. 33),—are all so debatable that more perhaps can never be said than this, that they serve to render it presumable that there *are* many passages which may have second meanings; not, however, that they substantiate their existence. On such a subject then, no rule can be laid down; this only may be said, that he who reads Scripture under the persuasion that it often contains depths not yet sounded, and meanings not yet ascertained, will certainly read it with far greater spiritual profit to himself than he who believes he has fully arrived at the mind of Scripture when he has made out the mere outward meaning of the letter. The subject involves many curious details, such as the recurrence of certain numbers (of e. g. "forty" in several incidents both of the Old and of the New Testaments), and the trace of a supposed mystical economy of times and seasons;—but with these the wise and reverent interpreter will never overmuch busy himself. He may feel and know that God is a God of order, and not of confusion, and he may see much in details in which that order seems plainly to be traceable, but he will never seek to prove it by an appeal to facts that may probably have no such relations as those ascribed to them, or by urging principles which all graver thinkers would not hesitate to pronounce as illusory or undemonstrable.

III. The same caution must obviously be displayed in the *third* form of Scriptural application,—practical deductions from Scriptural statements. The very principle on which such a mode of applying Scripture is based, viz., that Scripture is divinely inspired, and that deductions may be safely made from what are thus, without metaphor, the very Oracles of God, alike indicates the necessity of such caution, and hints at its required amount. In all passages, doctrinal or otherwise, in which the meaning seems to be clear and unquestionable, deductions obviously may be made of such a kind as to assume almost the aspect of definite and authoritative revelations. In other passages, in which the difficulties are more of what we have termed a *theological* character, positive deductions will often be found to be not only precarious, but presumptuous. They may sometimes be permitted for private edification, being in fact a sort of expanded form of religious meditation, but can rarely or ever be safely pressed upon others, or be profitably drawn out into systematic developments.

To illustrate what we mean by an example: we may rightly and properly make some deductions of a definite character from such a passage as 1 Thess. iv. 15–17. There both the plain and distinct statements of the passage, and the certain fact that this was really a definite revelation for definite purposes of Christian comfort (ver. 13, 18), seem to warrant our drawing inferences and recognizing harmonies with other passages of Scripture which, however strange and mysterious they may appear, are yet to be considered certain and legitimate. We seem to have the fullest right for assuring ourselves that there will be a first resurrection (ver. 16 compared with Rev. xx. 5) in which the elect will alone participate, that the rising of the holy dead will precede the assumption of the holy living, and that the latter, after the similitude of the Lord's Ascension (Acts i. 9), robed round by upbearing clouds (ἐν νεφέλαις), perchance the mystic chambers of the last change (1 Cor. xv. 52), will leave earth, and rise to meet the Lord in the air. Such statements may seem revolting to the false and morbid spiritualism of our times, but they are statements which the gravest expounders of an earlier day (while traditions of the true meaning of such revelations might yet be lingering in the Church) have not shrunk from putting forward, and which may be justly regarded as calm, historical conclusions from a deep but historical passage.

The case is different with such a passage as Matt. xxvi. 29. Here we may perhaps allow ourselves, with all reverence, to express a humble opinion that the words *may* allude to some participations in the elements of a new and glorified creation, in which the Lord may vouchsafe to be united with His elect; but to say more than this, to draw any deductions as to the nature of the resurrection-body, would obviously be in the highest degree wild and hazardous. Equally rash would it be to draw any definite conclusions from such passages as Eph. iii. 9, 10, as to the limits of the knowledge of angels in reference to the mysteries of salvation (comp. 1 Peter i. 12), or of the *precise* part which these Blessed Spirits take in human affairs from such passages as Matt. xviii. 10, Heb. i. 14, or from the record of such special interpositions as those related in Acts v. 19, x. 3, xii. 7, al. Even in passages of a simpler nature, our real ignorance of the relations between the visible and invisible world may prevent our making any positive deductions from such passages as Luke iv. 39, or Mark iv. 39; though we can hardly fail gravely to meditate on the strange fact that in one case the seeming recognition of the disease as a hostile potency is certainly where we should have least expected it—in the record of a physician, and that in the other the warring elements were checked by personifying words, which (with every deduction for Oriental forms of speech, or whatever else may be used to dilute plain terms) it does seem somewhat hazardous to explain away as merely picturesque or rhetorical. Again, to take a last instance, we may feel that in the touching words at the close of Matt. xxvi. 38 (γρηγορεῖτε μετ' ἐμοῦ) some desire, on the part of the Saviour of the world, for the sympathy in the dread hour of His agony of those He loved, is actually though mysteriously disclosed. We may muse hereon in adoring wonder, and feel, perhaps still more freshly, the blessed comfort that flows from such words as Heb. iv. 15, but we forbear applying any such statements to the profound questions connected with the two Natures, and refuse to see in them anything more than silent but persuasive hints against the varied assumptions and speculations of Apollinarian error.

To gather up all,—if in each of the three cases on which we have dwelt we would apply Scripture with profit, let us learn, *first*, to use all types not Scripturally vouched for, as illustrations, and not as supplying arguments; *secondly*, to recognize the existence of second meanings, but, except in such cases as inspiration may have revealed them, not to be wise above what is written; and, *lastly*, to let our deductions ever be of a devotional rather than of a definitely doctrinal or historical aspect,—to accept them as often tending much to inward comfort and edification, but as rarely adding much to our knowledge of the deeper mysteries of Scripture, and never to be so applied without our incurring the heavy charge of great irreverence and presumption.

§ 5.

15. One portion of the subject now alone remains to be noticed. We have hitherto been concerned mainly with the general aspects and spirit of the Sacred Volume; but, as these must ever depend on just recognitions of the laws of the letter, we will make a few concluding comments on the language of Scripture, and on those grammatical principles by which it seems to be ruled and conditioned.

Our remarks, however, must be confined simply to the language of the New Testament. It is for others to speak of the language of the Old Testament, and to state how far our present knowledge of the letter of the original is capable of extension or improvement. Some of the remarks that have been already made, and perhaps some even of the comments that follow, may admit of partial applications to the Old Testament; but it is clear that the circumstances under which the two parts of the Sacred Volume appear before us, as regards language, are very different, and that but little of what is said in reference to the details of the one can be pertinently applied to the details of the other. Independently of all the recognized philological differences, we have, in the case of the Old Testament, a collection of writings which themselves constitute all that deserves the name of the literature of the language; while in the case of the New we have a small number of histories and letters which only form a very minute, and that too in some respects an exceptional, portion of the general literature of the language in which they are written. Still some broad principles may remain which may perhaps equally apply to the interpretation of the letter in both Testaments. It would certainly seem that, much as has of late been done for the study of the Hebrew language, especially in Germany, there is still room for a more scientific development of many of the laws by which that ancient language appears to be governed. There is even now, as a reference to any of the more recent commentaries on the books of the Old Testament will clearly show, less linguistic precision, less mastery of details, less recognition of those bye-laws which, in every language, but especially in the Semitic, so much regulate special interpretation, less, in a word, of scholarship, as distinguished from learning, than we might have expected from the corresponding advances in the Greek language. Nay, even in what falls more especially under the head of learning, study of the ancient Versions, much is still lacking. Our modern commentaries on books of the Old Testament are herein scarcely, if at all, more advanced than the current commentaries on the New Testament, though in some cases, especially in that of the Syriac, and perhaps also of parts of the Arabic Version,* more real benefit, from the affinities of language, is to be expected from their use in the Old Testament than in the New.

16. But, to pass to that with which we are more immediately concerned,—the language of the New Testament,—we may find it convenient first to make a few comments of a general nature relating to the language as viewed in connexion with earlier or contemporary Greek, and then in the second place to append a small list of selected comments on such details of syntax as may seem to require notice or illustration.

With regard to the *general* character of the Greek of the New Testament, the estimate commonly formed by modern writers on this subject appears perfectly correct, viz., that it is neither in every respect classically pure on the one hand, nor yet simply and essentially Hebraistic on the other, but that it has for its basis that "common" or "Hellenic dialect" which the conquests of Alexander and those who succeeded him spread over a great part of the East, and which, from involving a mixture of dialects, and especially of the Macedonian, has sometimes been designated simply by this last-mentioned name. It must not, however, be forgotten that this "common," "Hellenic," or "Macedonian dialect," though undoubtedly the foundation of the Greek of the New Testament, received at least *three* very important modifications when it became blessed by being the vehicle of the message of salvation to the world at large. In the first place, the writers of the New Testament, though undoubtedly possessing a very competent knowledge of the Greek language as used and spoken in their own times, must have often *thought* in their native Aramaic, and so unconsciously have im-

* It is perhaps right to observe that nearly all the other Versions of the Old Testament, except of course the Vulgate, are known to be, or with reason supposed to be, derived from the Septuagint. This, of course, greatly detracts from their value as exegetical aids in reading the original.

parted that Hebraistic tinge to their language which is undoubtedly to be traced in it. The observation is perfectly correct that the pure Hebraisms of the New Testament are not very numerous, and that they are more of a lexical than a grammatical character,* still it cannot be denied that semi-Hebraisms, or traces of this occasionally thinking in their own language while they were writing in another, are neither so few nor so faint as sometimes has been asserted by writers on this subject. No discriminating reader can fail to observe this, especially in the not uncommon tendency to co-ordination, where subordination would have seemed more conformable to the spirit of the language in which they were writing; in the striking predominance of the direct over the indirect or oblique form when the words or thoughts of another are referred to; in the partially redundant uses of pronouns, and even prepositions, and the corresponding and equally characteristic want of freedom in the uses of the conjunction; in the comparatively rare occurrence of the optative mood, and yet again in uses of the infinitive (especially in reference to purpose) even more varied than we find them in earlier ages of the language. All this cannot fail to strike the observant reader, and to remind him how much beyond the recurrence of simple and definite Hebraisms, like *πρόσωπον λαμβάνειν*, or *ζητεῖν ψυχήν*, the semi-Hebraisms or rather the Aramaic tinge of the New Testament must really be considered to extend.†

Another general difference between the language of the New Testament and the language of the ordinary Greek writers of the same or even an earlier period, is clearly to be explained by the fact that so much of the New Testament is marked, in respect of language, by what may be roughly termed *oral* characteristics. The Gospels had only assumed the form in which we find

* See Winer, 'Grammatik des Neutest. Sprach.' § 3, p. 26 (ed. 6).

† Winer very properly calls attention to the existence of two classes of Hebraisms in the New Testament: pure Hebraisms, and what he terms "imperfect" Hebraisms, or expressions, which, though not without some parallelism in earlier or later Greek, are probably to be referred simply to the influence of the mother tongue. See 'Grammatik,' § 3, p. 26 *seq.*

them, after some years, at least, of oral delivery. Probably the greater part of the Epistles, and certainly by far the greater part of those which came from St. Paul, were written down from dictation. Even in the book (the Acts) which more nearly approaches formal history than any of the others, the speeches are not only numerous, but to all appearance faithful recitals of words actually spoken. The oral element thus pervades the whole Sacred Volume, and, on the one hand, may justly be considered as contributing in a very great degree to that combined simplicity and force which is so observable in the narrative portions, and, on the other hand, is equally clearly to be seen and felt in the longer sentences, suspended structures, and relapses to a nominative which we so often meet with in the epistolary portion, especially in the writings of St. Paul. The whole subject is well worthy of attention. It has often been alluded to by writers on the language of the New Testament, but has never yet received that consideration and recognition which it seems most fully to deserve.

A third difference is to be observed in the use of words and terms, in what may be called a specially *Christian* sense. Words sufficiently familiar to the general reader of Greek, *e. g.*, *πίστις, πιστεύειν, σωτηρία, σάρξ, κ. τ. λ.*, reappear in the New Testament in perfectly new combinations, and are found to be invested with meanings completely distinctive and peculiar. Many of these may be traced to the Old Testament, while some others may have been applications in another language of expressions not unknown to the Rabbinical writings of the day; still, in a general and popular way of speaking, they may be considered to mark a specially Christian aspect of the language we are considering, and one which is not always sufficiently taken into account in comparisons of it with ordinary Greek. Long familiarity with these terms renders us less sensitive to this difference than we are to some others, but to an intelligent reader of Greek, in whose hands the New Testament was placed for the first time, this perhaps would seem the most striking point in which its language differed, not only from that of the classical authors, but even from that of the Hellenic writers who lived nearer to Christian times.

These three elements—a Hebraistic tone of thought, not only showing itself in isolated terms but in the connexion and dependence of clauses, the oral element, giving its character to whole groups of sentences, and the Christian element to words and expressions, all combine to place before us a form of the "common dialect" as unique as, even in a mere literary point of view, it is also interesting and instructive. But though so unique it is still neither to be exempted from the application of the ordinary laws of the Greek language, nor to be dealt with as if it had neither certainty nor accuracy. This last is one of the convenient assumptions of the time. Even grammar is thus made to bend to prejudice. What seems tolerably certain and agreed upon is at once dispensed with whenever the "verifying faculty" is thought to demand it. The plausible rule of interpreting Scripture like any other book gives place at once to protests against the scholasticism of philology, warnings against the danger of making words mean too much, and hints that scholarship may not unlikely lead us to impress a false system on words and constructions. Into all the forms of this really deceitful dealing with written words we will not here enter. They can only be dealt satisfactorily with in detail, and disproved by a just consideration of individual passages. We may, however, dispose of the danger supposed to come from overmuch scholarship by these two brief remarks:—First, that no one is to be esteemed really a good scholar in reference to the New Testament unless he is well acquainted with the minutiæ of Hellenic as well as of Attic Greek, and knows well when to recognize later usage (*e. g.* μὴ with participles, tendency to double compounds, &c.), and when (*e. g.* in tenses, conditional sentences, &c.) to apply with some rigour the rules of classical Greek. Secondly, let this undoubted fact never be forgotten,—

that the "common dialect," which we so justly recognize as the basis of the language of the New Testament, was really itself placed on the corner-stone of Attic prose, and that a good knowledge of Attic Greek is simply indispensable. All sound scholars are now alike agreed in recognizing two contrary principles in Hellenic Greek: on the one hand a tendency to assimilate provincialisms; on the other hand a tendency to recur to Attic usage, which passes at last often into a hypercritical affectation. Are we then to relax our study of a pure phase of language which thus implicitly is to be seen and recognized in the writings of the New Testament, and which, by being itself so capable of precise definition, is ever such a useful standard with which to compare supposed deviations or corruptions? This single remark may be appended by way of conclusion,—that if the Greek of the New Testament be carefully examined with reference to this standard (Attic Greek), it will be seen clearly enough, that the difference is very far from being so great as might have been expected, and that it is really more to be felt in what is lacking and limited, in the less free use of the particles of connexion, and the less facile combination of clauses, than in what is definitely solecistic and erroneous. A few instances of this latter kind of usage may undoubtedly be found, as for instance *ἵνα* with a present indicative (1 Cor. iv. 6, Gal. iv. 17*), but they are very rare, and, considering the various elements that enter into the language of the New Testament, even strikingly exceptional.

17. Let us close this portion of the subject, and illustrate in some measure what has been already said, by a short list of such systematic *details* as may perhaps be useful in their collected form to the student of the Greek Testament, and may not be wholly out of place even in a general essay like the present. We will endeavour to avoid all technicalities of language

* The attempt of Fritzche and others to explain this by supposing *ἵνα* an adverb, does not seem at all natural or plausible. See Winer, 'Grammatik,' § 41, p. 259.

or arrangement; but, for the sake of perspicuity, will adhere to the ordinary heads under which such observations are usually distributed.

(1.) The *article* claims the first place, and may be said still to require more careful study than it has ever yet received, especially in regard to its usage in those portions of the New Testament which are supposed to be of latest date. We are told, indeed, that such discussions have "already gone far beyond the line of utility," but we shall scarcely be moved by such comments, when a reference to the pages almost of any expositor shows how much uncertainty still prevails on this subject, and how common an error it is to press the force of the article when it is only present in consequence of the action of some general rule. Thus, for example, what the grammarians call the law of "correlation," or, to speak more simply, the general rule that if two substantives are in regimen, either both will have the article, or both be without it, is constantly and sometimes even absurdly violated. Words are often passed as peculiarly definite, which only assume the form of definiteness in consequence of the action of the general rule; and, again, deductions are made from their supposed indefiniteness when the presence of the defining article would be a simple solecism. The omission of the article, however, in the later Epistles is perhaps the point which at present most requires consideration; nay, even in the case of a writer where we should not have expected it, the Evangelist St. Luke, the oldest manuscripts, especially as supported by the new Codex Sinaiticus, disclose a far greater amount of probable omissions than we should at all have been likely, *à priori*, to expect. Careful consideration of these will probably lead to *some* modification of the existing rules connected with the use of the article in the New Testament. Meanwhile to group hastily together what we know, it may be remarked:—(*a*) That the words which assume the privilege of proper names and dispense with the article where it might have been expected, are very numerous in the New Testament. Very important examples of this may often be found in the uses of the words *Πνεῦμα* and *νόμος*, and doctrinal statements or deductions much modified by a recognition of what is now, in the case of both these words, a matter of simple demonstration. (*b*) That the article is often omitted after a preposition, but apparently subject to this sort of rough limitation, viz., that when it is the apparent desire of the writer to be peculiarly distinct and definite he rarely fails to insert it. Of this, 1 Tim. ii. 15 may perhaps be referred to as a pertinent example. The rule seems to be in such cases,—"Press the article when present, but do not press the absence of it when it happens to be absent." (*c*) The popularly known omission of the article after the verb substantive and verbs implying names or designations, is not always sufficiently remembered by the interpreter of the New Testament. (*d*) The amount and extent of the omissions of the article where the substantive practically coalesces with the clause which follows (*e. g.* Col. i. 8, *τὴν ὑμῶν ἀγάπην ἐν Πνεύματι*, or Eph. i. 15, *τὴν καθ' ὑμᾶς πίστιν ἐν τῷ Κυρίῳ Ἰησοῦ*) have not yet, perhaps, been fully recognized or agreed upon. Perhaps some rule similar to that alluded to in (*b*) may not be found in the sequel to be much exaggerated. (*e*) Lastly, several examples of what is called Granville Sharp's rule, or the inference from the presence of the article only before the first of two substantives connected with *κὰι* that they both refer to the same person or class, must be deemed very doubtful. The rule is sound in principle, but, in the case of proper names or quasi-proper names, cannot safely be pressed.

(2.) With regard to *substantives*, the points that seem most to need attention are the different connections and constructions of the genitive and, in a less degree, of the dative cases. The use of the former, especially when under the regimen of a preceding substantive, is peculiarly varied, and will require considerable tact on the part of the accurate interpreter. Without descending to very minute details, or attempting to discuss all the nine or ten divisions into which the various forms of the genitive may be separated, we may direct attention to the following selected exemplifications of the uses of this case as found in the New Testament:—(*a*) The use of the genitive as specifying something in apposition to, or identical with, the noun, by which it is governed, *e. g.*, 2 Cor. v. 5, *τὸν ἀῤῥαβῶνα τοῦ Πνεύματος*, Eph. vi. 14, *τὸν θώρακα τῆς δικαιοσύνης*; (*b*) a widely extended use to denote the ideas of origination (Rom. iv. 13, *δικαιοσύνη πίστεως*), and not unfrequently of definite agency (2 Thess. ii. 13, *ἁγιασμὸς Πνεύματος*); (*c*) a still more extended use in which very varied relations, both of time (Jude 6, *κρίσις μεγάλης ἡμέρας*) and of place, whether topographical (Matt. i. 11, *μετοικεσία Βαβυλῶνος*, *ib.* ch. x. 5, *ὁδὸς ἐθνῶν*) or general (Col. i. 20, *αἷμα τοῦ σταυροῦ*), are all simply and briefly expressed by this flexible case. If we add to these (*d*) a smaller class, in which ideas, so to speak, of ethical substance or contents appear to predominate (see Eph. i. 13, *τὸν λόγον τῆς ἀληθείας τό εὐαγγέλιον τῆς σωτηρίας ὑμῶν*, where both ideas appear in adjacent clauses); and lastly (*e*), the not uncommon use of the genitive to denote the prevailing character or quality (Luke xvi. 8, *οἰκονόμος τῆς ἀδικίας*),—a use which probably owes its frequency to the part which, in Aramaic, the dependent noun plays as a representative of the adjective,—we shall perhaps have enumerated all the more noticeable forms in which the dependent genitive appears in the New Testament. Attention to this case, especially in deeper and doctrinal passages, will often be found to yield very important practical results, and to suggest topics for application which popular writers, who commonly treat all this as mere scholastic pedantry, are completely unaware of.

The use of the dative is much varied, and may be disposed of in two or three sentences. If the essential idea of the case as that of limitation and circumscription (the where*at* case, just as the genitive is the where*from* case, and the accusative the where*to* case) be properly borne in mind, it is not probable that even in the less direct uses,—*e. g.*, in reference to ethical locality

(1 Cor. xiv. 20), rule and measure (Acts xv. 1), &c., any real difficulty will be felt. The only usage which seems to require any notice is one of occasional occurrence, where ideas of instrumentality or manner seem to merge into those of the imaginary place *where*, or the general circumstances *owing to which*, the action is supposed to have taken place. Thus St. Paul writes, in Gal. i. 22, that he was ἀγνοούμενος τῷ προσώπῳ to the Churches of Judea;—his countenance was not the instrument, but rather the imaginary scene of the display of the ἄγνοια. Again, he tells his converts at Rome that the Jews (under the image of the natural branches) τῇ ἀπιστίᾳ ἐξεκλάσθησαν (Rom. xi. 20; comp. ver. 30, 1 Cor. viii. 7) by which he would seem to refer, not to the actual instrument *by which*, but to the state of heart and feeling *owing to which* the judicial act was performed.

(3.) We may pass onward to *verbs*. Here, again, we can only make a few general comments, as anything like even a mere rudimentary outline of the more striking usages would far exceed our present limits. We may remark, however, *first*, that the usual rules of correct Greek are observed very persistently, in the moods, tenses, connection of dependent clauses, and even in the refinements of the conditional sentence. In this latter case, however, one important element will commonly be found lacking,—the optative mood. It occurs very rarely in such sentences (comp., however, 1 Pet. iii. 14, 17, Acts xxiv. 19), and, indeed, but seldom in the New Testament generally; its rarity of occurrence serving to remind the reader that he is now within the precints of what Lobeck somewhat quaintly terms "fatiscens Græcitas." A *second* general remark may be made on another sign of grammatical degeneracy, the use of the verb-substantive with participles, to mark with some distinctness, ideas of continuance or contemporaneity. This we find in nearly all the writings of the New Testament, and, perhaps, more frequently than elsewhere, in the writings of an author who we might have thought would have been least likely to have adopted it, the well-educated and practised St.

Luke. The cases, however, in which it occurs do not appear at all of a confused or promiscuous nature; but, as we have above suggested, whenever the Sacred Writer desired to be particularly definite in reference to time and its duration. A *third* general remark in reference to verbs (capable also of being extended to other parts of speech) is this,—that compound forms cannot *always* be safely pressed. There appears to have been a very marked tendency in later Greek to an increase in composition without in every case a corresponding increase of meaning, and from this the New Testament is not exempt. Caution, however, must be shown in applying this remark, as our knowledge of the exact meaning of compound verbs in the New Testament is still very limited. It is, indeed, much to be regretted that the German grammarian Winer never completed his treatise on this subject. The four or five parts of it that have been published are excellent specimens of a careful and scholarly analysis of a subject that requires much reading, and not a little tact and penetration.

If we allow ourselves to devote a few sentences to matters of detail, we may profitably direct attention to four points:—(*a*) an occasional use of the middle voice in the New Testament (Col. i. 6, *καρποφορούμενον,* and 1 Tim. i. 16, *ἐνδείξηται*, may perhaps be cited as examples) in which all tinge of a reflexive sense appears lost, and in which we seem to recognize the presence of that sort of "intensive" force which the best and latest grammarians* have assigned to this yet imperfectly-understood voice; (*b*) the use of the present tense, not, as we are too often told, "for the future," but with its usual proper force to mark what is abiding, fixed, and predetermined, especially in reference to the course of things as appointed by God (Col. iii. 6; Matt. xvii. 11; xxvi. 2, al.); (*c*) the somewhat expansive use of the future in the New Testament, and its partial assimilation of various shades of meaning of an imperative

* See Donaldson, 'Greek Grammar,' § 432. 2. *bb;* Krüger, 'Sprachlehre,' § 52. 8.

character, especially when in connexion with a negative (comp. Matt. vi. 5; Acts xiii. 10; Matt. v. 21; Rom. vii. 7; xiii. 9); lastly, (*d*) the uses of present and aoristic participles with a finite verb (especially in St. Luke and St. Paul) to mark the ideas of time, cause, manner, and concession (comp. Luke iv. 35; ix. 16; Col. 1. 3 *seq.*, al.). These uses, though not exhibiting quite the same amount of flexibility as in earlier Greek, are still sufficiently varied to call for a far greater amount of attention from the interpreter than they have yet received.

(4.) We have now remaining only two groups of words on which observation seems necessary, the *particles* and the *prepositions*. In regard to their uses we may notice a very clear and instructive difference, serving to remind us how sensibly the influence of the Aramaic element makes itself felt, both positively and negatively, in some parts of the syntax of the New Testament. In the *prepositions*, for instance, we observe a redundancy as well as variety of use, which, if we did not call to mind the characteristics of the mother-tongue of the writers, might seem particularly strange and perplexing. This desire to imitate the expressiveness (in this respect) of the Aramaic, combined, probably, with a certain loss of sensitiveness to the full force of cases, may account for the appearance of the prepositions ἀπὸ and ἐκ with verbs of "giving" (Luke xxiv. 42), "receiving" (Mark xii. 2), and even of "eating and drinking" (Matt. xv. 27; John iv. 14), where, to say the very least, they would be excessively unusual in classical Greek. The same may be said of the union of εἰς and πρὸς with a large class of verbs where a dative would have seemed much more consonant with the genius of the language. The variety again of the usage of individual prepositions is peculiarly striking, and still more so the studied accumulations of them in a single sentence, especially in St. Paul's Epistles (Rom. xi. 36; Col. i. 16, al.). These latter, though sometimes perhaps called forth and suggested by doctrinal distinctions (Eph. iv. 6), seem especially to indicate an ease and freedom that would have been looked for in vain in the ordinary Greek of the time. Equally well marked is the general correctness with which these varied usages are distinguished. If we except the tendency to over-use, which we have already observed, and a few combinations (e. g. of εἰς with some verbs of rest, ἐν with some verbs of motion, and the extended use of the latter preposition to forms and expressions where ὑπὸ or διὰ might have seemed more usual) which, though not without parallelism in earlier Greek, do certainly seem to reflect some tinges of incipient degeneracy,* or some reminiscences of the mother-tongue, there is really not only no prevailing incorrectness whatever in the use of the preposition in the New Testament, but very frequently a sharpness and precision (comp. Rom. xiii. 1) that reminds the student of the best days of the language. When, then, a recent writer on the interpretation of Scripture urges that in Gal. iv. 13, διὰ with the accusative is to be conceived as used for or equivalent in meaning to διὰ with the genitive, he not only shows himself a lax interpreter of the passage in question, but also shows a deficient knowledge of a general fact, — the accuracy of prepositional usage in the New Testament, which ought to have made such an assumption seem *à priori* in a very high degree improbable.

(5.) In strong contrast to this usage of prepositions stands that of the Greek *particles*. With the exception of *καί, οὖν, δέ, γάρ,* and perhaps also ὡς and *ἀλλά,* in the uses of which there is not only variety but sometimes well marked idiomatic force and character, there are not many other particles in the New Testament which are used with complete ease and freedom. There is a certain degree of monotony, a deficient amount of combination, and a want of flexibility in the use of the particles of the New Testament which stand in marked

* No trace whatever of that utter insensibility to the fundamental meaning of cases which led the Byzantine writers to confound, for example, μετὰ with a gen. and μετὰ with an accus., or to join ἀπὸ with an accus. or dat., σὺν with a gen., or κατὰ with a dative, is to be found anywhere in the New Testament.

antithesis to the ease and even redundancy which are to be observed in the use of the prepositions. Yet, as it was in the case of the latter, so is it with the particles; there is a prevailing accuracy in their usage, and a very general conformity to the laws of the language in its earlier and better state. There are some exceptional aspects, as for instance, the use of *μὴ* with participles when there is no tinge of a subjective negation intended (the rule indeed is, "Press *οὐ* when connected with a participle, but not *μή*"), the weakened force of *ἵνα*, and its occasional use to designate something lying, as it were, midway between purpose and result, the use of *ὅτι* to introduce another's words in their direct form, combinations like *καθώς* and juxta-positions like *ἆρ' οὖν*,—such there are, but all such childish statements as the use of one particle for another, and so forth, are to be dismissed, as they have long been dismissed by all better scholars, as very unprofitable delusions. It is, however, painful to observe how, in some quarters, such prejudices still hold their ground, and how even those who affect to lay down well-considered rules on Scripture interpretation, tell us that "it is an error to interpret every particle in the New Testament as if it were a link in the argument when it is often a mere excrescence of style." Such comments on supposed error are really themselves *very* erroneous; and the pages of any one of the better expositors of the day, who has attended to the sequence of thought in his author, would not only show them to be so, but would also make us feel very sensibly how completely subversive they are of all principles of faithful and consistent interpretation. The German commentaries of De Wette and Meyer are very good standing protests against such hasty and ill-considered comments. These writers, though in no way pledged to orthodoxy in matters of doctrine, have had far too great experience in the language of the New Testament to be heterodox in point of grammar. They never hesitate to bestow the greatest possible attention on all minutiæ, and exhibit in a very satisfactory way what striking results are to be obtained from a careful estimate of connecting particles, and how very near an approach can be made to the mind of the inspired writer by this mode of patient and philosophical investigation.

18. This last portion of our subject must now be brought to its close. We have left very many points untouched, on which comment might seem in some measure desirable, but our article has already exceeded its prescribed limits, and it now becomes necessary to transgress no further on the patience of our readers. Yet it seems impossible to part from those who have traversed with us the wide domain which belongs to such subjects as those we have considered, without a few words of valediction, and a few expressions of mingled anxiety and hope.

Those against whom our observations have been directed will probably not be affected by anything that we have urged. The tone of self-confidence which marks their writings; the unfairness, or, to use the mildest term, the slipperiness that pervades their arguments; the really cruel and thoughtless way in which they have allowed themselves to scatter doubt and uneasiness; their utter carelessness for the feeble, and the unstable, and the many who, with all their frailties and shortcomings, still deserve the name of "babes in Christ,"—all these many painful characteristics make us feel that as far as they are concerned we have written and have spoken in vain. There are others, however, with whom it may not be so. There are kindly eyes that may have fallen on these pages, which, though not seeing wholly as we see, may yet have been encouraged to gaze longer and more earnestly, and to wait gently and patiently for a glimpse of the fair landscape that lies beyond what now may seem to them only a cloud-land of eddying vapour and wandering storm. God in His everlasting mercy, for our dear Lord's sake, grant that it may be so! God grant that such may see and feel that these are no cunningly devised fables, no mere arguments put forward for love of controversy, no mere assumption of orthodox attitudes for the sake of self-interest (untrue and ignoble taunt of embittered opponents!), but a statement of earnest and serious convictions, which deepen with deepening reflection, to which every fleeting day bears its tribute of increasing assurance, which every prayer quickens, every blessing stimulates, every trial confirms. May they be moved to judge us thus kindly and fairly; and may our poor words be permitted in return to impart some comfort in anxieties, and to answer some of those doubts with which honest and good hearts are often permitted to be tried.

Lastly, may the great Father of love and mercy draw all who love His ever blessed Son, and who see in Him the propitiation for the sins of a whole guilty world, still nearer together. It may be, when all was well, we dealt hardly with each other, that we thought unkindly and spoke with bitterness. It may be even that we have acted in the same spirit, that we have helped to break up the household of faith into hostile camps, that we have smitten friends and brethren, and led those who would not use our shibboleths to the vale of slaughter and spared them not. But now the foe is on the frontier. If love is still cold, yet at least let danger reunite. Let us yield to instincts, if we care not yet for principles. Let us do only this, and it may be that even thus we may be allowed to see and feel that all was so ordered by a loving Father,—that danger was to bring about reunion, and reunion to rekindle love. And then at last, with linked hands and united hearts, may we again join in praising and blessing our common Lord, evermore adoring Him who round our weakness and divisions winds the encircling bond of His strength and love, "round our incompleteness His completeness, round our restlessness His rest."

THE END.

REVOLUTIONS IN ENGLISH HISTORY.

BY

ROBERT VAUGHAN, D.D.

VOL. I.

REVOLUTIONS OF RACE.

PRICE $2.

In this work, Dr. VAUGHAN, the Editor of the *British Quarterly Review*, intends to group together the leading facts of English History, so as to reveal at a glance the progress of the nation. It is a step towards the simplification of English History. By the term Revolutions, the author intends to denote the great phases of change, through which both the government and people of England have passed, during the historical period of their existence.

"A work of this kind," says *Blackwood's Magazine*, "cannot be superfluous, if it is worthily executed; and the honorable position which Dr. Vaughan has earned for himself in both theology and literature, gives us a guarantee that this will be the case. The specimen before us we have read with interest and improvement. We should particularize the ecclesiastical portion of the history as being executed with special care, and as remarkable for the spirit of justice and liberality he displays. To these pages we may honestly recommend the reader, as the fruit of steady and conscientious labor, directed by a liberal and enlightened spirit."

"This treatise," says the *London Athenæum*, "or rather narrative, is deeply and variously interesting. Written plainly, but with all the characteristics of independent thought and accomplished scholarship, it may be pronounced a masterly survey of English civilization from the remotest epoch to the commencement of the fifteenth century. We have found this volume in every way excellent. It is at once a narrative and a disquisition, learned, genial, critical, and also picturesque. The spirit of English history animates it throughout. Dr. Vaughan, by completing such a work will have done good service to literature."

The *Westminster Review*, the very highest critical authority upon English literature, said of this work, upon its original publication in England—"We can sincerely recommend Dr. Vaughan's Revolutions in English History as a thoughtful, interesting, scholarly presentment of the principal sociological vicissitudes of more than two thousand years of our British existence. Dr. Vaughan's composition is extremely lucid and nervous; not without a certain sedate ornamentation, but quite free from the misleading exaggerations of a seductive rhetoric.

18 CHRISTIAN CENTURIES.

BY

THE REV. JAMES WHITE,

AUTHOR OF A HISTORY OF FRANCE.

1 Vol. 12mo. Cloth. 538 pages. $1 25.

CONTENTS.

I. Cent.—The Bad Emperors.—II. The Good Emperors.—III. Anarchy and Confusion.—Growth of the Christian Church.—IV. The Removal to Constantinople.—Establishment of Christianity.—Apostasy of Julian.—Settlement of the Goths.—V. End of the Roman Empire.—Formation of Modern States.—Growth of Ecclesiastical Authority.—VI. Belisarius and Narses in Italy—Settlement of the Lombards.—Laws of Justinian.—Birth of Mohammed.—VII. Power of Rome supported by the Monks.—Conquests of the Mohammedans.—VIII. Temporal Power of the Popes.—The Empire of Charlemagne.—IX.—Dismemberment of Charlemagne's Empire.—Danish Invasion of England.—Weakness of France.—Reign of Alfred.—X. Darkness and Despair.—XI. The Commencement of Improvement.—Gregory the Seventh.—First Crusade.—XII. Elevation of Learning.—Power of the Church.—Thomas à Becket.—XIII. First Crusade against Heretics.—The Albigenses.—Magna Charta.—Edward I.—XIV. Abolition of the Order of Templars.—Rise of Modern Literature.—Schism of the Church.—XV. Decline of Feudalism.—Agincourt.—Joan of Arc.—The Printing Press.—Discovery of America.—XVI. The Reformation.—The Jesuits.—Policy of Elizabeth.—XVII. English Rebellion and Revolution.—Despotism of Louis the Fourteenth.—XVIII. India.—America.—France.—Index.

OPINIONS OF THE PRESS.

Mr. White possesses in a high degree the power of epitomizing—that faculty which enables him to distil the essence from a mass of facts, and to condense it in description; a battle, siege, or other remarkable event, which, without his skill, might occupy a chapter, is compressed within the compass of a page or two, and this without the sacrifice of any feature essential or significant.—CENTURY.

Mr. White has been very happy in touching upon the salient points in the history of each century in the Christian era, and yet has avoided making his work a mere bald analysis or chronological table.—PROV. JOURNAL.

In no single volume of English literature can so satisfying and clear an idea of the historical character of these eighteen centuries be obtained.—HOME JOURNAL.

In this volume we have THE BEST EPITOME OF CHRISTIAN HISTORY EXTANT. This is high praise, but at the same time JUST. The author's peculiar success is in making the great points and facts of history stand out in sharp relief. His style may be said to be STEREOSCOPIC, and the effect is exceedingly impressive.—PROVIDENCE PRESS.

www.ingramcontent.com/pod-product-compliance
Lightning Source LLC
LaVergne TN
LVHW021300110826
845150LV00003B/437

* 9 7 8 1 4 2 5 5 6 0 2 5 6 *